How to Restore Your MUSTANG 1964½-1973

Frank Bohanan

CarTech®

CarTech®

CarTech®, Inc.
838 Lake Street South
Forest Lake, MN 55025 USA
Phone: 651-277-1200 or 800-551-4754
Fax: 651-277-1203
www.cartechbooks.com

© 2010 by Frank Bohanan

All rights reserved. No part of this publication may be reproduced or utilized in any form or by any means, electronic or mechanical, including photocopying, recording, or by any information storage and retrieval system, without prior permission from the Publisher. All text, photographs, and artwork are the property of the Author unless otherwise noted or credited.

The information in this work is true and complete to the best of our knowledge. However, all information is presented without any guarantee on the part of the Author or Publisher, who also disclaim any liability incurred in connection with the use of the information and any implied warranties of merchantability or fitness for a particular purpose. Readers are responsible for taking suitable and appropriate safety measures when performing any of the operations or activities described in this work.

All trademarks, trade names, model names and numbers, and other product designations referred to herein are the property of their respective owners and are used solely for identification purposes. This work is a publication of CarTech, Inc., and has not been licensed, approved, sponsored, or endorsed by any other person or entity. The publisher is not associated with any product, service, or vendor mentioned in this book, and does not endorse the products or services of any vendor mentioned in this book.

Edit by Paul Johnson
Layout by Monica Seiberlich

ISBN 978-1-61325-412-7
Item No. SA165P

Library of Congress Cataloging-in-Publication Data

Bohanan, Frank.
  How to restore your Mustang, 1964 1/2-1973 / Frank Bohanan.
    p. cm.
  ISBN 978-1-932494-96-9
  1. Mustang automobile–Conservation and restoration. I. Title.

TL215.M8B64 2010
629.28'722–dc22

2009045917

Written, edited, and designed in the U.S.A.
Printed in U.S.A.

Title Page:
It's time to apply stripes over the freshly painted surface. Here we show how the "C" stripe for our car was laid out prior to the car being masked off. A stripe was painted on similar to the original factory stripe.

Back Cover Photos

Top Left:
In order to perform a rebuild, the engine and transmission are removed as a unit. While both do not have to come out together, the engine and transmission provide better balance as a single unit, so the removal process is less of a hassle.

Top Right:
A new inner fender is spot welded into place. As you go from weld to weld, remove any of the screws you used to hold the panel in place as you come to them. You need to get proper weld penetration through both panels and do not allow too much weld material to build up in the holes.

Middle Left:
You should wet sand between coats so the next coat provides better adherence. This approach can also be used to eliminate any runs, sags, and/or dust, etc., which may have contaminated the just-painted surface.

Middle Right:
A new seat cover is stretched over the rest of the foam/bun and around the sides. This may take some effort and patience. A heat gun can be used to soften the cover enough to help pull it over the foam/bun easily.

Bottom Left:
During the C4 transmission disassembly, the main shaft assembly is removed and installed/loaded from the top, hence the name. Be careful as you are lifting the assembly out, so the shaft surfaces and the gear teeth don't get nicked or scratched.

Bottom Right:
A far better way to trigger the ignition is with electronic modules, such as this Pertronix Ignitor II unit. It fits inside the distributor so it is relatively invisible, other than for the presence of two external wires instead of only one.

CONTENTS

Acknowledgments 4
Introduction 4

Chapter 1: Choose Your Mustang 6
   What Type of Restoration Do You Want? 6
   Who Will Do the Work? 7
   What Models and Drivetrain Options to Look For 9
   What to Avoid 11
   Matching the Numbers 13
   Where to Find Your Mustang 14

Chapter 2: Getting Started 16
   Initial Inspection, Evaluation and Creating a
     "Needs" List 17
   Planning and Organization 21
   Initial/Basic Disassembly 23
   Tools and Equipment 25
   Trim Removal and Repair 26
   Finding Replacement Parts 27
   Cataloging and Organizing Your Parts 28

Chapter 3: Body Makes Beautiful 30
   Minor/Surface Rust Repair 31
   Small Area Repair: Fabrication 35
   Large Area Repair: Panel Replacement 36
   Dent and Ding Repair 42

Chapter 4: Painting Your Mustang 44
   Decision Time: Paint It Yourself or Go to a
     Professional? 45
   Final Surface Preparation: Using Body Fillers 46
   Painting Basics 48

Chapter 5: Engine Rebuilding 56
   Disassembly and Evaluation 56
   Cylinder Block and Head Preparation 57
   Short Block Assembly 64
   Cylinder Head Installation 75
   Final Engine Assembly 75

Chapter 6: Rebuilding Transmissions 80
   Automatic Transmission Disassembly and
     Inspection 81
   Automatic Transmission Reassembly 87

   Torque Converter 93
   Clutch, Flywheel and Pressure Plate 93
   Manual Transmission Disassembly
     and Inspection 95
   Shift Linkage 105

Chapter 7: Drivetrain 109
   The Driveshaft 109
   Rebuilding the Rear Axle Assembly 111

Chapter 8: Brakes 122
   Initial Inspection and Evaluation 123
   Front Brakes: Installation 126
   Rear Brakes: Conversion and Installation 127

Chapter 9: Suspension 131
   Inspection and Evaluation 132
   Front Suspension 137
   Rear Suspension 143

Chapter 10: Electrical 150
   The Basics: Grounds, Connections and Shorts 150
   Some Common Trouble Areas 157
   Miscellaneous Accessories and Possible Upgrades ... 160

Chapter 11: Interior 162
   Initial Inspection and Evaluation 163
   Carpet Replacement 164
   Interior Trim Panel Refurbishment 168
   Rear Fold-Down-Seat Installation 170
   Inner Door Panel Replacement 172
   Miscellaneous Interior Refurbishment 174
   Seat Reupholstery 175

Chapter 12: Other Mechanicals 184
   Fuel System 184
   Exhaust System 184
   Cooling System 187
   Steering System 187
   Air-Conditioning System 189

Conclusion 191
Source Guide 192

ACKNOWLEDGMENTS

Writing a book is no small feat, and this book in particular was the culmination of 18 months of documenting an entire Mustang restoration project, performing research, and photographing all the crucial stages. There were many long days spent at Mustang Country (Lakewood, CA), and elsewhere, working on and photographing the car, and lots of seemingly endless nights banging away at the computer keyboard to get the text done. While actually writing a book may be an individual effort, it takes a team to make a book like this possible, and I'd like to thank everyone who helped me out along the way.

In particular, thanks to my good friend Miles Cook for buying and making the decision to restore his Mustang, which became the primary subject of this book. Without his cooperation and assistance, I would have had to find another suitable subject car for the project, and his 1968 Mustang GT equipped with a J-Code 302-ci V-8 and C-4 transmission is certainly a suitable subject. It's not a pedestrian six-cylinder Mustang coupe or an exotic Boss Mustang. Instead, his small-block V-8 Mustang and the multitude of Mustangs like it have been and continue to be a popular platform for daily-driver, weekend cruiser, and even show-car restorations. As such, it was the ideal candidate for this book. I'd also like to extend my thanks to Miles' brother Wayne Cook, who provided valuable assistance at various stages of the project.

Without Allan Cohn and the crew at Mustang Country, I wouldn't have been able to pull off this project. He and his crew provided shop space, expertise, parts, and his patience as the project progressed from one stage to the next. In addition, I thank Ron Bramlett of Mustangs Plus, Doug Nordin of Global West Suspension, Ray Currie of Currie Enterprises, Jim Larr of Orange Engine Rebuilding, Butch McKee of Big 4 Transmissions, Rick Schmidt of National Parts Depot, Pat Staton of Year One, and Jim Hairston of Pertronix Performance Products. All of these kind and generous industry leaders played an integral role in making this book a reality. In addition, other companies that also contributed parts and/or services to the project are listed in the Source Guide.

Finally, yet most importantly, I would like to thank my family for putting up with my long hours spent working alone in the office instead of being available for family functions and events, etc. Without their love and support I wouldn't have done it.

ABOUT THE AUTHOR

Frank Bohanan is an automotive consultant and journalist specializing in matters relating to vehicle technology, legislation/regulation, and the specialty automotive aftermarket. He has a mechanical engineering background with extensive experience in the areas of powertrain development, emissions testing, and vehicle electronics. Frank has worked for Ford Motor Company in both the engineering and product planning areas and has also gained additional expertise with high output engines while working at McLaren Engines and Chrysler Corporation. He continues to work closely with the automakers, government agencies/officials, specialty parts manufacturers and consumers. Frank's writing credits include columns regularly published in *Mustang & Fords, Mustang Enthusiast* and *SEMA News* magazines plus The Car Connection Internet site, as well as numerous freelance articles published in various nationally circulated magazines. When not writing, lobbying on behalf of vehicle enthusiasts or helping aftermarket companies develop and/or certify their products Frank is an avid motorsports fan and car collector who travels extensively to attend numerous events and, on occasion, even works at them with the broadcast crew for live television shows.

INTRODUCTION

Many restoration books have populated the bookstore shelves over the years. But in many cases, these books didn't explain how to perform actual restoration procedures for returning a car to its original factory condition. Rather, these books provided detailed information on factory original equipment, such as option codes, paint and interior codes, correct trim and emblems, engine and drivetrain options—and the list goes on and on. Some books provided exploded factory drawings of major components, but often these books lacked the real-world, hands-on information for actually performing the restoration procedures. That's where this book comes in. I won't get into exhaustive and monotonous detail on the correctness of air cleaner stickers and bumper bolts. Instead, I provide an unprecedented level of how-to information, and in fact, the book contains a plethora of step-by-step procedures for restoring key components.

This is a comprehensive guide for restoring a first-generation Mustang to near-original condition. But it's more than a simple restoration guide, it shows how to incorporate modern equipment, such as disc brakes, breakerless ignition, and much more, so the car's performance, usability, and safety are improved without detracting from the collector value. Unlike "restomod" books that dramatically alter the look and underpinnings of a vehicle, this book honors the original design of the Mustang.

How to Restore Your Mustang 1964½–1973 will help you determine the right vehicle for your taste and budget. It explains how to avoid mistakes in buying the vehicle, and how to solve common problems in a cost-effective way. Whenever possible, multiple options are presented. Beyond that, it shows you how to turn a Mustang into a beautiful, dependable, high-performance classic car. After all, this is a book for people who love to drive their cars, who love classic cars, and who don't want to have to choose between the two.

This guide covers the steps involved in a given process and then discusses various options to complete those steps. It often provides the most common procedures for a particular restoration job, but it cannot cover the virtually infinite number of build combinations for these vehicles and exhaustively cover every single minor procedure. The emphasis is, therefore, on thorough evaluation of the vehicle and detailing the challenges, tools, techniques, and products for a certain procedure. Sometimes the at-home restorer doesn't have the skills, resources, or equipment to perform a restoration procedure, and needs to contract a shop to perform certain services. In the final analysis, everyone can't be expert on every area of restoration. Certain jobs need to be properly contracted, organized, and managed, and this book offers guidance for that with an emphasis on budget and cost effectiveness.

Mechanically inclined restorers perform much of work themselves but often use other information sources, such as factory shop manuals and the internet for the model-specific information. Often, at-home restorers use professional shops for machining and other tasks when it is not practical to do the work themselves, but this book provides the guidance to help you manage these outsourced jobs so the desired results are attained. In addition, most owners often do not seek outside help for simple repairs and, thus, this book does not generally address service-type procedures for the repair of a daily driver. The emphasis is on good-quality vehicles that are not extremely rare or astronomically valuable. This book is about cars that will be driven more than shown.

I discourage selecting a vehicle in poor condition for a restoration project and I do not generally address high-end restorations for show car competition. Hence, this is not a simple repair manual intended to restore function to a daily driver, nor is it a guide for building a concours-correct vehicle that will rarely, if ever, be driven on the road. Instead, this book provides a practical "working man's" type of restoration at a moderate budget. As a result, the vehicle retains its original form/appearance defined by the vehicle manufacturer (Ford Motor Company), while function is enhanced when reasonable/necessary/desired (and not overtly in conflict with the desired appearance).

Other restoration books may focus on the history of the vehicle and restoration projects that duplicate that history in exacting detail to increase the chances of winning awards or to get a big sale price. This book seeks a more middle ground of building a special vehicle that honors the original design yet has been discreetly enhanced to improve both performance and dependability, such that frequent use is both more feasible and more enjoyable.

It's extremely satisfying to restore a Mustang to its original condition so everyone can appreciate its glory and you can enjoy the driving experience. I venture to say it's exhilarating, because few things in life can compare to revitalizing the condition of a classic pony car and preserving a piece of American automotive heritage. There's no doubt that restoring a Mustang comes with its fair share of challenges, and professional-caliber restoration results are not easy to come by. But the journey—as well as the destination—of your restoration should allow you to develop skills and have an experience many others will not match. The pride of a job well done is all the more rewarding when you have something you can drive regularly rather than just show rarely.

CHAPTER 1

CHOOSE YOUR MUSTANG

The process of restoring a car is much like most other things in life. You need to know where you are going and how to get there. Therefore you need to make a plan and stick to it as much as possible, to avoid extra expense and a less-than-satisfying result. Still, it's almost never possible to completely plan everything out to the last detail. The inevitable and unforeseeable events, that always accompany a project of such magnitude, make planning a challenge for even the most experienced restorer. Anybody who says otherwise is dreaming. No two cars are alike; no two projects are completely alike. Most of all, no two people are alike and what each person wants out of the restoration, and has the means to accomplish, is the single largest factor in determining its ultimate success. As the saying goes, any journey starts with a single step. When it comes to restoring a vehicle, the first step is to decide what you want to end up with.

What Type of Restoration Do You Want?

This is simultaneously a simple and a complex question. It starts with what you'd like to do, but continues on to what is reasonable to do for the condition of the vehicle, progresses on to what resources are available, and ends with what can actually be done under the circumstances. I get into all of these particulars in detail throughout the book, but first things first. What would you like to do? The answer to this question may not be simple either. There are different levels of restorations, which range from a relatively minor refreshing to a full-on concours level in which money is no object. I don't cover minor refreshing or a complete frame-up restoration but, rather, the middle range. This covers most restorations. For the sake of simplicity, I break things down into three classifications: daily driver, weekend cruiser, and show car.

A weekend-cruiser level of restoration is one where the car remains very driveable and is brought up to a relatively high level of refinement. The goal is a usable, good-performing vehicle that looks great yet still provides some flexibility for personal expression. Upgrading with factory parts is possible.

Daily Driver

This is the entry-level restoration. The vehicle will be used on a frequent basis and will have to be reliable and capable of transporting people and their belongings without concern for normal wear and tear, etc. At this level, the restoration is more of a refurbishment to the "nice car" level than it is an attempt to have an award winner. The goal is to take a car that's already in decent condition and make it look and run better on a relatively modest budget.

Weekend Cruiser

A car restored to this level is one that stands out from the crowd yet can run with it. It may have been sitting around for a long time. When all is said and done, a car at this level will have been thoroughly gone over and will look great for it. The emphasis will have been more on usability than accuracy, in terms of what is strictly "correct" for the car, production options, etc. Budgets vary from moderate to high.

Show Car

While not a 100-percent concours-correct situation, this type of restoration can get very close to it. This level is for a car that can be driven but rarely is. It's for cars that will most likely be trailered to a show that's more than a couple of hours away but will probably still be driven to local and regional shows. This level is for people who want to win awards at relatively big shows and/or who want to get a good price at a well-known auction. The budget level is high.

Choosing what level of restoration you want up front has a dramatic impact on the decisions that follow. The quality of parts used in a show car is inevitably higher and is also likely to be more true to how the car was originally produced. The weekend cruiser will probably feature factory upgrades—such as converting drum brakes to discs, using Ford parts—because I'm only discussing restoration, not modification. The daily driver probably sees the fewest hardware changes and may not even get a full repaint unless it really needs it. As you progress from daily driver to show car, professional restoration and a bigger budget is required. Every restoration project is different to some extent, but these general classifications will help you plan your project, forecast the required time, calculate the expense, and choose your vehicle.

Who Will Do the Work?

Deciding who will complete the various tasks involved in your restoration project really involves your answers to several other questions. These include, but are not limited to, the following:

- What needs to be done?
- What skill level do I have?
- What equipment do I have access to?
- Where is the work going to be done?
- How much time do I have?
- How much can I budget for the project?
- Do I plan to keep the car or sell it soon after the restoration?

Of course, there's also the matter of taking pride in having done some of the work yourself. Some people want to spend as much time as possible working on their car, so they can discuss, often in minute detail, how they did this or that to make sure it was done the way they wanted. Others have neither the interest nor the time to do this, but they do have the finances to make sure somebody else does it for them. Neither approach is better than the other—it's a matter of what works for you. Let's discuss each question briefly to provide some thoughts that should help you decide who does what.

The type of restoration you want to do and the condition of the car mainly determine the answer to the question of what needs to be done. The lower the level of the restoration, the less you have to do. The worse the condition of the vehicle, the more you have to do. To a large extent, a daily-driver restoration of a car in reasonably good shape can usually be done by the owner if he or she is so inclined and capable.

If it is a car that has not been properly maintained for 20 years, it typically needs a considerable amount of work to return it to its former glory and/or to become a show car regardless of the owner's abilities or inclinations. In many cases, owners tend to do a lot of work to their weekend cruisers because they tend to be mechanically inclined, and this

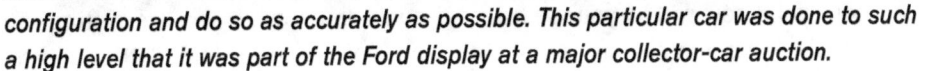

The goal of a show-car restoration, particularly for special models like this Shelby G.T. 500, is to return the vehicle to its "as built" configuration and do so as accurately as possible. This particular car was done to such a high level that it was part of the Ford display at a major collector-car auction.

CHAPTER 1

type of restoration is used to make a more personal statement.

A daily-driver restoration may involve little more than some parts swapping, a general cleanup, and some touching up of the paint and interior surfaces. The weekend-cruiser restoration likely involves a full repaint, lots of new parts and/or upgrades, and probably a partial rebuild of the engine and driveline, at a minimum. It may not involve a full "frame off" or rotisserie-level tear down, but it may involve welding in some replacement panels and the like. The show-car restoration requires the full tear down, a full rebuild of the engine and driveline, the use of many high-quality new/reproduction parts, and the complete refurbishment of original parts where appropriate. The preparation of the body before paint is extensive, and the paint will be virtually flawless in an original factory color. The interior, the metal trim pieces, and so forth are all show quality but not necessarily 100-percent original.

I get into much more detail on the specifics of what needs to be done for a given type of restoration later on. For now, you need to make an honest assessment of what you can do and what you feel comfortable doing. If you have little experience working on early Mustangs, then it's best to at least have someone more experienced show you what you need to know if you want to do some things yourself. For the daily-driver level, this is probably fine as long as you don't need to do any serious rebuilding or refinishing but just limit your activities to mainly replacing parts. If you have experience rebuilding an engine or a transmission, you should be able to restore these components for a weekend cruiser. The things you still likely have to rely on outside help for are machining work, metalworking, and most likely painting. Even if you're able to take the engine apart, for example, you still need a machine shop to perform various operations on the engine if you are rebuilding it. Likewise, you may be able to do some of the prep work prior to paint but you will most likely have to take the car somewhere to be painted.

The primary reason for this is equipment, or rather the lack thereof. The cost of some equipment that is needed in many restoration projects is simply too much for most people, especially if it won't be used that often. Add in the fact that such equipment almost always requires some special skill level to operate it, and you come to the conclusion that some tasks are best left to the experts. For many show-car restorations, even people who have some of this special equipment and knowledge still defer to someone else. They simply recognize that the restoration shop probably has even better equipment and people who are even more skilled at using it. There's definitely something to be said for experience, and it's not too hard to understand that somebody who uses better equipment on a daily basis, and does so for a living, almost always produces a better result than someone with lesser equipment, less experience, and who only uses their equipment infrequently. There's a lot of feel as well as knowledge involved in many restoration skills, which takes time to develop. If you don't have the right equipment, skill level, or time to do the job properly, then it's best to let the experts handle it.

You also need a proper workshop to do your restoration. At the daily-driver level, you may only be doing some parts swapping and minor freshening up, and you can probably get away with doing it in your garage or driveway. If you don't have everyday access to a garage, you may need to find one you can rent or see if someone you know will let you use theirs for a while. Regardless of what you might want to believe, you shouldn't work on your car outside unless it's a simple project that takes just a few hours. Besides probably not scoring any points with the neighbors (or the homeowners association) there are practical problems such as weather and the lack of utilities that make the task unwise even if you think it will only take a few hours. More often than most would like to admit, something unforeseen happens and the job takes longer than you thought. A bolt might break, a thread may strip, or you may lose a part down a drain—whatever. The point is you don't want to be stuck in a situation where the car has to be left outside because you can't drive it away when you thought you could. Do your work inside and if you know it's going to be a long-term project, make sure you have plenty of room around the car to store parts, tools, and equipment as well as to do work comfortably. If you don't have a good place to work on the car, you're better off letting someone else do it.

No matter how long you think your restoration will take, you're probably wrong. Inevitably some things break, you may not be able to find parts, some other unforeseen things come up, you may temporarily run out of money, or some combination of these and other things happen. If you have a restoration shop do the work, they too likely have similar problems, although probably not as often. And they likely have a backup plan in place for when such things do happen. Simply put, unless you know you will have enough time, skill, money, etc., to do a restoration project, you probably should not try to do it all yourself; it will most likely take longer than you think. If you are in no rush and you want to take your time because you enjoy doing it and you want to do it your way, then that's fine too. As long as you know what you are getting into and you *do* have the skill, resources, patience, and location, etc., to do it in such a way that you're happy with the outcome, then do as much as you can.

For most people, a restoration proves to be a series of ongoing partnerships. You do some of the work and you have others do the rest. Who does what depends on the aspects of the project that I've already discussed. There will be variables neither party can control, such as the availability of parts, the weather, and so on, but the key is to clearly define what each party is responsible for and then have everyone do their best to meet their commitments. When something unforeseen comes up, as always happens, everyone involved just needs to be flexible and adapt as necessary. You may want to think that doing everything by yourself makes you immune to such hiccups, but it doesn't. The key here is to be realistic and seek help when it is appropriate. You'll be happier when you're done because the result will be better.

Along with the time required, it's virtually impossible to precisely determine the ultimate cost of a restoration. If you do some of the work yourself, there is probably less of a monetary outlay, but it all comes down to what you can or will do and what your time is worth. With a show-level restoration, most people defer to a well-known and well-respected shop to do the work. These shops often produce a better result and it can enhance the car's reputation and/or its resale value. Unless you're the original owner of the car, when you begin stripping a car down, you almost always find a few things you didn't know about—some rust here, body filler there, whatever. Lifting the carpet or the trunk liner is often a real eye opener for many people. Media blasting reveals all. This can usually be worked around; it's just that it takes more time, skill, parts, and money to do it.

If you're doing a daily-driver or weekend-cruiser restoration, it's less of a problem than for a show car, where you pretty much want all repairs to be invisible. Invisibility costs a lot. If you're taking the car to a national show where it will be judged by experts or you want to sell it at a high-end auction, you can be sure the cost will be much higher than for the daily driver or weekend cruiser. And that's only for a 90- to 95-percent-perfect car. If you want to go for that last few percent because the car is a rare, so-called numbers matching car (more on that later in the book), then get ready to lay out some serious cash to get to that level.

If you're going for the show level or above, regardless of whether you intend to sell the car soon, your best bet is to work with a well-known restoration shop. They can do much of the work to the level that's needed and their involvement adds credibility to the restoration. Such credibility can add significantly to the perceived value of a show-level car.

What Models and Drivetrain Options to Look For

What vehicle you should look for depends primarily on what you like, what you want it to do for you, what you can afford (both to buy and to restore), and what is actually available on the market. Resale value may also be a consideration, of course, though I will not try to speculate on what the value of any given vehicle might be before or after it is restored. Our discussion is about restorations, not investment potential. All the factors should be considered, but the priority of each depends on the individual.

It's safe to say most of us would love to have a Boss 302 or a Boss 429, but few of us could probably afford one at current market price. From a restoration perspective, such a vehicle would also be at the high end of the expense scale because the available correct parts would be very, very expensive in most cases. It would be much too valuable to drive around very often and it would not be very practical, to say the least. But that's not to say you couldn't if you wanted to. It is a very subjective decision but, realistically, truly rare and valuable cars like these are show cars most of the time. A few may be used as weekend cruisers, but it's a safe bet even fewer such vehicles will ever be used as daily drivers. Still, it's nice to see any first-generation Mustang being driven rather than just parked somewhere.

The first general rule you can use when deciding what vehicle to buy might be: Buy what you like and can comfortably afford. Buy it, restore it, drive it, and enjoy it. Restore it to the level you are comfortable with. Don't buy something based mainly on its perceived resale value. The market is very fluid. True, some of the really rare special models will always be worth a lot, but whether you can make a profit after sinking a lot of money into a show-level restoration is another matter. While sale prices vary considerably, some trends are consistent for first-generation Mustangs. A coupe generally sells for less than a fastback or a convertible. A heavily modified vehicle or a racecar is generally not the best candidate for an original restoration. You almost always come out ahead if you pay a little more up front to get a car that's in better condition than if you buy a car with problems. Of course, there are exceptions to all of these rules, but they are generally accepted guidelines.

If you do find that authentic, numbers-matching Mach 1 in somebody's barn for only a few hundred dollars, you take it as long as it still rolls out in one piece. The parts alone are worth that much. But if you plan on doing any kind of serious restoration, you better accept the fact the bill will be high and you may not get it back if you ever decide to sell it. Try to buy what you like, and then drive it and enjoy it.

CHAPTER 1

Some other things to help you decide what to look for depend on how the vehicle will be used. If it will be a daily driver, you probably are better off with a small-block engine than a big-block, not only for fuel economy but also for reliability, lower cost of maintenance, and even drivability. Big-block cars are fine for the weekend cruiser and show cars, but they just aren't as practical to use on a regular basis if you have to deal with a long commute, traffic, and so on. They usually perform better in a straight line, but that isn't the only thing to consider.

A small-block car with an automatic transmission is easily the best combination to go with for frequent use. If you don't have to deal with traffic very often and you want some additional performance, then a manual transmission works too. If you decide to go with a big-block for a daily driver you're much better off with the automatic transmission for dealing with traffic and getting much the same acceleration as a manual. If you want to do smoky burnouts all the time or you like to emulate Parnelli Jones in the corners, you are probably better off with the stick.

For the weekend cruiser it's pretty much up to personal choice, with big-blocks probably being the preferred option since they do tend to get more attention. The show-car restoration will almost always retain the engine the car came with, unless the vehicle is being made into a clone of a rarer special/limited-edition model.

The rear axle is another aspect to consider. If you will be driving the car a lot or will take long trips, you should avoid a numerically high rear-end ratio to keep engine revs (and overall wear) down. If you have a limited-use big-block car, then the higher-number gears are fine and maybe even desirable for better acceleration. For the higher-output engine options, you want to make sure you have a stronger rear axle such as the 9-inch unit. If you have a relatively lower-powered engine, then a smaller axle like the 8-inch may be fine as long as you don't intend to abuse it too much. All of the axles can be modified internally to handle more power but that shouldn't be necessary when restoring back to factory specifications. In the case of a show car it may also be undesirable in terms of judging and the potential loss of perceived value.

The choice of differential type is also very important. An open differential is fine for a daily driver or weekend cruiser. However, as the power level rises and maximum rear wheel traction becomes more important, a limited-slip differential becomes necessary. A fully locking differential can be problematic in a car that's driven regularly in terms of noise, tire wear, and how it behaves in poor weather. If you are willing to put up with such things and/or you won't be driving the car so much, then it's not as big an issue. If you will be driving the car a lot, you want something you can live with that will last. For the show-car restoration, this discussion is again more or less moot—you just keep what the car came with.

You are also, of course, limited by what is actually available. If you want a 1964½ fastback, sorry, they didn't make any. Likewise, if you love Highland Green as a paint color, you'll be looking for a 1968 model year because it's the only year that color was offered. Sure, you can paint your car any color you like, but the cost goes up if you really want to do it right. And in the case of a show car, the value may actually go down if you don't keep the original colors. Changing the color of the interior is less controversial, but it can also be a detriment in some cases. The tradeoff between keeping a rare but unappealing color versus changing to a more popular color scheme comes down to your personal preference, the cost of converting, and the potential effect on resale value, if that matters. Every situation is different so you won't find any firm rules here but, in general, you usually can't go wrong if you keep it original or just go with what you prefer if you don't intend to sell it.

Finally, choosing your car may involve popularity and rarity. While what you may like is completely subjective, there are some popularly held opinions that do seem to form a loose consensus. For example, if you like the coupe body style, then many people would say the 1967 and 1968 coupes are the best looking. The convertibles of

Two of the most popular and desirable body styles for first-generation Mustangs are the 1965/1966 and 1969/1970 fastback models. These styles consistently command a higher market price than the same-year coupe models; often the convertibles as well. It's best to buy a more popular style if that's what suits your taste.

those years also seem to be among the most popular, though the 1964½ to 1966 models are right there with them. The 1969 and 1970 models tend to be best known for the "Sportsroof" body style. The question of whether you prefer the four-headlight front end of the 1969 models or the two headlights of the 1970 models is one where there is much less of a clear winner. Ditto for taillight styles (those on the 1969 stick out and those of the 1970 are recessed). For some people it comes down to really liking the side vent on the rear quarter panel that was only available in 1969. There is no clear winner here. Many would argue the 1965–1966 fastbacks are as nice or nicer, but even the 1967–1968 fastbacks have their fans. It really becomes strictly a matter of personal taste. The models listed above are generally considered among the most popular of the first generation but not everyone agrees on this.

The 1971–1973 models are generally not as popular and hold less collector value than the earlier models. The 1971–1973s were larger and heavier, and emission control laws reduced the number of engine options and power levels that were available. They were easier to fit a big-block into, unlike the 1964½ to 1966 cars that, for example, did not offer such an option. Even the 1967 and 1968 cars were a tight fit with the 390-engine option. Clearly, the most popular big-block cars were the 1969 and 1970 models, although the small-block Boss 302s were (and still are) very high on many people's list of desirable vehicles. If perceived popularity matters to you, you may want to take these things into consideration. If you plan to restore the car and hold on to it indefinitely, then it's a matter of what you like and can afford.

A daily driver also needs to be practical and user friendly. A show car is almost always restored to its original, as-built condition. A weekend cruiser is a balance between personal preference, the desire to make an impression, and what is feasible. You should look for what works for you on the levels already discussed. The only other consideration may be that of the vehicle's rarity.

Truly rare models such as the Boss models and any of the special factory race cars and so forth are a part of history. These vehicles are most valuable when they are either very mildly restored (more or less left as is), or they are so-called "survivor cars" in good shape, or they are fully restored back to their original condition. There are plenty of higher-volume, less-collectible cars that can be modified. A car can only be born once, and relatively few of the rare models were produced. In order to keep their original flavor, many owners refuse to modify them or over-restore them. Keeping the truly rare vehicles in their original configuration allows them to be enjoyed by those who didn't experience them when they were new and helps provide information about how these cars were really built. They truly are museum pieces, yet they are best enjoyed when they're being driven.

What to Avoid

Several precautions have already been mentioned but there are a few more to discuss. One is: Do not buy a wreck. If a car is in really, really poor condition it is almost always not worth the trouble.

The 1971–1973 model-year Mustangs are regarded by some as less desirable than the earlier cars due to the fact they were larger and heavier, and they had reduced performance due to emission-control laws. On the plus side, it is easier to fit a big block into one and they often don't cost as much.

Extremely rare race cars such as these are most valuable when left close to the condition they were raced in. Their unique "battle scars" give insight to their history. They should only be repaired, if necessary, in a way that retains this history. Such vehicles should not be over-restored.

CHAPTER 1

Even if the car is a rare one-off vehicle that you think will make you rich, it probably won't. You may just end up buying the VIN number and little else. If the car does have all of the original numbers-matching parts and it is a car of special/historic value, it still is a gamble if the cost of restoring it to a show-car level will be more than what it might bring at resale. Sure, you may get lucky at some famous auction but the odds are definitely against you. You would be depending on at least two people with big bucks (already a small group) becoming emotionally attached to your car (even smaller group) and bidding the price up. You are free to speculate, but the bills to restore the car to the highest level are very tangible.

The bottom line is: Don't make the restoration any more expensive than it needs to be. A car in better shape always costs less to restore, and it will be worth more when it's done. If you do decide to invest in a rare or valuable model, be sure you're getting what you think you're getting (more about this at the end of this chapter). Secure as much valid documentation about the car as possible, in order to prove its alleged pedigree.

As when buying any car, do a thorough evaluation of the car's condition before you buy it to make sure you don't find any surprises later. This is not only a matter of getting what you pay for and not being cheated, it can make the difference in deciding if the car is worth restoring. This is a greater concern with a show car and/or one of the more rare vehicles, but even a daily driver can have issues that prohibit putting any more money into it. If you're buying from a known and trusted source and the car is well documented, this should not be a concern. When you buy from a stranger, be sure to get some references about the seller and also check out the car's history in whatever way you can—talk to previous owners, check DMV records, talk to people in car clubs with similar cars, etc. The higher the car's profile, the easier this will be.

You also want to avoid any car that has a salvage title or has otherwise been heavily damaged. It may look as though the car has been fully repaired, but chances are it was not. Floodwater can get into places that are unreachable unless you completely take the car apart—a reason for salvage. Similarly, a fire or major collision also does damage that may not be seen but certainly can affect functionality and drivability. This damage provides unneeded surprises and lowered car value. What may seem like a low-price bargain usually costs more in the end. You get what you pay for; buy a better-quality vehicle.

I've already stated it's best to avoid a heavily modified vehicle, but this deserves some clarification. If a vehicle has been heavily modified, it has probably been driven hard. That's not good for a daily driver or a weekend cruiser because you can't be sure of its reliability. Having been driven hard is less of an issue for a show car because you're going to be rebuilding and/or replacing most things anyway. With a show car you are more concerned about the extra expense of having to undo body modifications, such as removing wheel tubs for large tires and so forth. Modified and/or raced cars usually have welded-in roll bars or cages, heavily modified

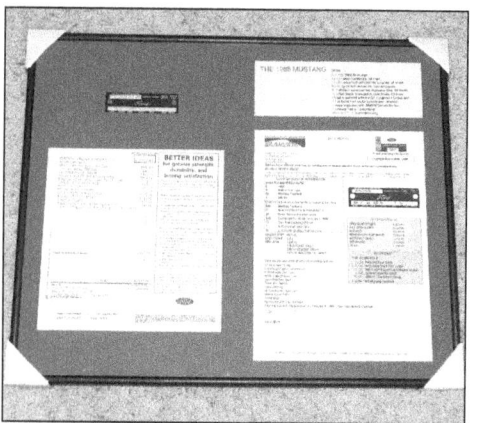

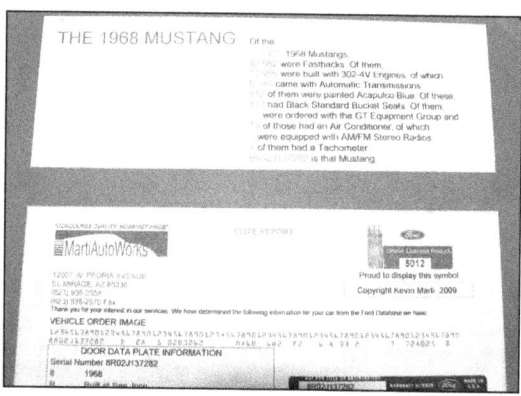

For owners and prospective buyers of 1967-and-later Mustangs, a Marti report is often an invaluable resource for determining the authenticity of a vehicle. Shown here is the top of the line Elite Report, which comes framed and includes a replica of the door date tag, the decoding information, and a replica of the factory window sticker. It also contains optional equipment information, when it was built, when it was ordered, where it was sold, and many other unique bits of information. An Elite Report typically takes 4 to 6 months to receive, while the less-inclusive Basic and Deluxe Reports take less time and also cost less.

In general, the rarer a vehicle is, the more it is worth, particularly when it was originally equipped with many of the desirable options. Here, we see how our 1968 Fastback is a true "1 of 1" vehicle, based on the fact that it had a unique combination of options when it was ordered/sold. Of these, the combination of the factory AM/FM radio along with the factory tachometer and air conditioning are primarily responsible for its unique production status. These were rare yet desirable options, which when combined with our car's color choices and powertrain options make it both a highly desirable and very drivable vehicle.

suspensions and drivetrains, and so forth, all of which have to be removed to create a show car. You would avoid considerable time, effort, and expense if you buy a mainly stock or fairly original car. Even a weekend cruiser or a daily driver would have to have most if not all of such modifications removed because they are generally not feasible for practical street use. Again, added expense and complication.

And no matter how good the repair process is, the car still is never really as good or will be worth as much as if the modifications were never done. You can find replacement panels, floorpans, and so forth pretty easily for a first-generation Mustang, but they are rarely identical to the factory parts (for reasons I explain in Chapter 3). If your goal is primarily restoration, avoid cars that were heavily modified, raced, or abused. However, if the car was one of those rare factory racecars, that's another story. If the modifications were simply bolt-ons, then that's okay if they can be removed and replaced with the factory parts and you can verify the car has not been beat up too much. A complete, professional-grade restoration is a complex and time-consuming process, so it's best to start with a car that does not require a lot of repair work before the restoration is started. In the end, it most likely would not be worth as much anyway, no matter how well the restoration is done.

Finally, if resale value is very important to you, you should try to buy one of the more popular body styles and/or color combinations. People tend to buy what they like and off-beat colors appeal to fewer people. If it happens to be a rare color like Grabber Blue, the rarity and the nostalgia may add value to it. That's especially true with the rarer higher-performance models. The loud color is a match for the loud car. On a more mainstream vehicle such colors are somewhat out of place, just as a relatively low-key color like gold or bronze would be on a performance model. The color intensity should match the car, and you should recognize that some colors just don't appeal to very many people no matter what car they're on. A rare, performance model might still get a good price with an odd color, but it almost always brings a better price with a more popular color. A rare color is not automatically worth more. Low-volume figures for a particular color usually just mean the color was as unpopular in its day as it probably is now.

Likewise, the combination of the interior color and that of the exterior should be a good match. Black on black, black on white, red on black, and so forth are some of the more popular combinations. Bright or light-color interiors are less appealing to many people. A light-blue interior in a blue car works fine, as does a red interior in a white car, but these still may not generate as much interest as the more popular combinations. If you like a particular color combination and/or you want to make a bold statement, none of this matters much if you are going to keep the car. For a show-car level restoration, you almost always restore the car back to its original colors. However, you should consider the resale value of the car. You probably should look for one of the more popular color combinations and avoid the more obscure color choices that not only draw attention from fewer potential buyers, but are also harder to find matching parts.

Matching the Numbers

When you purchase a first-generation Mustang you have all of the concerns you have with the purchase of any car in terms of its condition, etc. However, since there may be the additional aspects of collectability and/or its potential impact on resale value, there is another

When trying to establish the true identity/history of a vehicle, the VIN is the place to start. Because the VIN can have such a significant impact on the value of the vehicle, it must be verified to the best of your ability. If you are contemplating the purchase of an especially rare and valuable vehicle, consider having a professional both verify the VIN and perform a thorough appraisal of the vehicle before you buy it.

Vehicles tend to be worth more if they have their original parts. Many of the major parts such as the engine block, transmission, etc. got marked at the factory with at least some portion of the VIN to show what vehicle they were installed in. Here we see how the engine block of our 1968 was stamped with a series of numbers that match up with our vehicle's VIN. Similar markings were also present on various other components; plus these agree with the documentation we had so we were pretty sure we had the original parts. Be aware, however, that stamped numbers such as these can be fraudulent if the block has been machined. A non-original part could have had its numbers removed and the part could then be re-stamped with a number that would match the VIN and thus increase the value of the car. Look for any signs of this, such as machining marks or an incorrect stamp/font.

matter to consider. This is the concept of "matching numbers." Basically, this has to do with the fact that an original vehicle with all of its original major parts (engine, transmission, rear axle, etc.) is worth more, all else being equal, than the same specification/condition car where the parts have been replaced. When you purchase a vehicle you logically pay a premium for such a car, just as you expect a similar premium at the time of sale. Here are a few tips to make sure you get what you are paying for.

When you examine a vehicle prior to purchase there are two basic things you need to know: what it really is, and what it was when it was "born"/manufactured. I won't get into all of the normal checks you make when you buy a car as far as making sure it is in good running condition, has no hidden damage, etc., but the point is to do your homework as far as what's on the car being consistent with what's supposed to be on it. There are numerous guides available to provide you with very specific descriptions of what came standard and what was optional for a given model. You need to make sure the parts on the car were correct for the car in terms of having been offered on the model it is supposed to be. Ultimately, this all traces back to the VIN (Vehicle Identification Number).

The VIN tells you, to at least some extent, what model the car is supposed to be—the parts that can be on it from the standpoint of originality. Locate the VIN and make sure it has not been changed. You do this by checking for agreement at all of the various VIN locations, and to the extent possible, verify the correct VIN (or portion thereof) is also present on those components that have VIN-based markings, such as the engine block, for example.

Owners of 1967-and-later Mustangs have an additional resource available to them in the form of a Marti Report. Once you have established the VIN is valid for the vehicle you can obtain a report from Marti Auto Works that tells you everything from when and where the car was both built and sold, to what specific options were on the car at the time and how many other cars like it were produced. There are multiple levels of Marti reports, ranging from as little about $20 for the "Basic" report to upwards of $200 for the "Elite" report, which even includes a reproduction of the driver's-side door date plate professionally mounted, along with the other documents in a nice frame.

With 1964½ to 1966 Mustangs, you have to do your own homework as far as decoding the VIN to determine what the car should have and could have on it based on when it was built. In any case, the point is to verify the VIN and the documentation available for the car so you know you have what you are supposed to have and can determine a fair price for it.

Where to Find Your Mustang

There's no shortage of sources for classic Mustangs. I'll try to point you toward the best places to look for a Mustang that will undergo a particular type of restoration. I'll also give some tips on where you might get a better deal with fewer problems.

If you're planning to do a daily-driver restoration, there really isn't any difference from looking for a regular car except for the fact that you want an older Mustang. Probably the best place to start looking is with Mustang and Ford car clubs. You'll likely find what you're looking for, plus you can get references about both the car and the seller. Many clubs have classified ads in their newsletter and on their website, plus they often conduct open "Buy, Sell, or Trade" sessions at meetings. If you can't find the specific car you want, club members often know of other cars for sale or volunteer to check around for you. Car shows are another good source, though For Sale signs are not often allowed. You can walk around and see all types of vehicles to help you decide what you want and can learn more about them by talking to their owners and others. If you see something you like, you can check with the owner to see if it's available.

Local newspapers are not as good a source for finding an early Mustang as they used to be. Their classified sections are getting smaller and have few classic car ads. You're usually better off looking in weekly car-buying publications, such as *Autoswapper* and *Autotrader*. There may be a few ads in the regular editions, but you want the special "old car" or similar edition if they publish one. A good online alternative is Craigslist.org. You may not find a large selection of what you want but at least you can search very specifically and save time. Prices on Craigslist can be very good and the chances of finding something special, while slim, are probably as good as it gets.

Other online sources, such as Autotrader.com, Cars.com, and eBay.com, are also very good places to shop, especially if you want something specific and you don't mind traveling to pick it up. You see more dealer ads but you are less likely to get a great deal or an undiscovered gem because these venues are very closely watched and most people posting ads tend to know auto values. A final place to look for a daily driver is local dealer auctions and even government or bank auctions. These are very hit or miss; you don't see many older Mustangs, but it can happen if you get lucky. Get a list of what's going up for bid before you go, to see if there's anything you might want. You should use a similar approach with used-car dealers that specialize in collectible/classic vehicles. Call and talk to someone who can give you accurate info about the car before you go there.

For a weekend cruiser or a show car, you can use all of the same sources; you just have to adjust your criteria for what may be acceptable. For the former, you can be more flexible in terms of the condition of the car so long as you're willing to do a more involved restoration and are able to handle the expense. Again, it's always best to start with a car that's in better shape, but take a bigger chance on something you just have to have. A show car ideally starts with the best possible car, to keep what is already a large expense from getting any larger.

All of the previous sources are good places to look, plus you can add the classified sections of national magazines and their websites. The larger collector-car auctions are also a possibility for these types of restorations, although most of the cars there have already been restored. Avoid the higher-price vehicles that go across the block at popular time slots on Friday night and Saturday. Focus on the days before and after these popular time slots, when better deals can be had. You can be sure the sellers know what they have, so there is less chance of making a bad purchase as long as you verify things completely. With a no-reserve-type auction, you may even get lucky if there's no interest in the car from anyone else. Commissions tend to be pretty high at these auctions, so you have to weigh the costs you pay for the higher-quality car.

Another option is to essentially start from scratch with a complete, new body shell from a company called Dynacorn. At the time this book was being written, the only Mustang models available were 1967 and 1968 fastbacks. You still have to find a lot of other parts, many of which are also made by Dynacorn, but at least you have the benefit of knowing there are no issues with rust and wear. There are also some claimed advantages about the type of steel used, manufacturing methods, etc. You still have to fit many parts to the car due to production tolerances, as you would likely also have to do in a restoration with a Ford-produced Mustang. The price is significant (about $16,000 for the complete body shell with shipping), and you have to register the vehicle differently since it does not come with a VIN.

You would be essentially building a kit car that happens to be more or less functionally and visually identical to a 1967 or 1968 Mustang fastback. This would be possible, if not always practical, to do for a daily driver or a weekend cruiser. It would most likely not be appropriate for a show car, at least not one trying to be passed off as an authentic Mustang. If you prefer to use as many new parts as possible, this may be the way to go. While some may consider this more an assembly of parts (like the states that require you register it as a "specially constructed vehicle" or kit car), the actual process of turning the body shell into a drivable car is basically the same as for a regular restoration. The exception to this is if there's more time making things fit and less time repairing flaws in the body. If you're mainly concerned about the look and function of the final vehicle and don't really care about authenticity and resale value, then this option may be one worth considering.

Most of the cars at larger collector-car auctions have already been restored and thus command relatively high prices, especially when sales commissions are considered. There can still be some good deals to be had during the non-peak selling periods on cars that haven't yet been restored.

One option for restoring certain vehicles is to start with a brand-new body shell from Dynacorn. You won't have to worry about rust, etc., but you will have to register the car differently since it never had a VIN. The cost isn't low but it's reasonable for many. The blue car started out like the shell above it.

CHAPTER 2

GETTING STARTED

In Chapter 1, I provided some advice on how to better define the type of restoration project you intend to pursue and what type of vehicle might be best suited for it. I also gave some tips on where to look for a vehicle and things to avoid. And I covered some resources you can use to help ensure you're getting what you are paying for—that the vehicle is what the seller says it is. Assuming you now have a better idea of what you want to do and have a vehicle to restore, let's get into the actual process of what you need to do to begin the restoration project.

The first thing to do is to evaluate the overall condition of the vehicle and identify the areas that require restoration. You've already done this to some extent by now, but it needs to be done again with a different emphasis and in greater detail. You may have noticed some things to address when you were looking the car over before you bought it. Now that you have the car in your possession, you can thoroughly inspect it and come up with a comprehensive list of tasks. This will not be the final list because you will surely find other components and areas to restore as you take the vehicle apart. I cover some of these more specific evaluations in subsequent chapters, as is appropriate. For now, I want to explore some of the bigger items to incorporate into your overall planning for the project.

The type of project you're planning, and the time and funds that can be allocated to it, dictate how the project is structured. Someone with a daily driver may just do things on an as-needed basis and/or when the funds become available, thus requiring little or no real planning. This mainly involves the removal and replacement of components only and does not require disassembly of the whole vehicle. Painting, if done, is on an individual panel basis, at most. The owner of a show car may want to complete the project in a linear fashion but may not be very concerned about how long it takes or the final cost. Such a project inevitably involves a complete disassembly of the vehicle, which most likely ends up on a rotisserie. The vehicle is

This vehicle is the primary subject of this book. It was stored for more than 20 years, yet it was still in good running condition after it was given some very minimal attention (flush out the cooling system, oil change, new gas, etc.). The body is solid with only a few dings and dents, and no need for any significant panel replacements. The glass is all original and intact. The interior is in fantastic condition, and the car is close to original, except for some headers and a few other minor changes. The history of the car was well documented. We decided to undertake a weekend-cruiser project because it was such a great canvas to work with, and we wanted to drive it a lot without any age or performance limitations.

GETTING STARTED

completely stripped down to bare metal and then fully prepped and painted to a very high standard.

The restoration project of a weekend cruiser shown in this book falls between these two extremes. It's done in a more focused fashion than the pay-as-you-go, daily-driver situation, but it is also done on a schedule more sensitive to time and finances than a typical show-car project. I provide much useful information that applies to those situations as well, but our focus will be on a restoration project that should take several months to a year to complete. Also, it generally tends to have lower overall project expense.

Here is a typical scenario for a moderate weekend-cruiser-type project: We found a very good vehicle that would not require major surgery (as I recommended in Chapter 1). The car needed some cosmetic touching up and some parts replaced, but many of the original parts were reused with only a minor amount of refurbishment. This helped keeps costs down and, in many cases, also saves time.

We repainted the car, but not fully because we didn't take out the dash, headliner, or windows. They were all in exceptionally good shape, so we saw no need to replace them.

We removed all of the trim and exterior panels (fenders, doors, hood trunk, etc.) to be repaired and repainted as necessary. But the car was never completely disassembled and stripped to just the bare metal. It didn't need to be. We did repair a couple of rusted panels, but the amount of bodywork was minimal. We stripped all of the exterior panels down to bare metal for the bodywork, but it wasn't necessary for the interior, so we left it as is.

The underbody and engine bay needed only minimal prep before they were painted and/or undercoated. We did, however, have to replace an inner fender panel and do some metal work on the trunk lid prior to painting. The repair work done in these two areas used the same basic process as you would use to replace floorpans, quarter panels, and so forth.

Later in the book I show the actual processes for these and most of the work we did. For now I'll just discuss how we planned out what needed to be done and how we went about organizing it. There are some very good ways to reduce the overall time and expense of a project if you plan accordingly and execute the plan in a logical fashion. There will

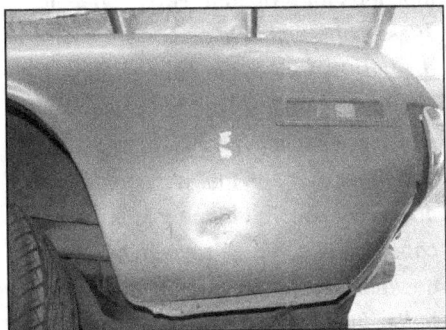

When looking your car over and developing a restoration plan, cover all of the things you noticed when you bought the car and then some. If you've owned the car for a while already, you may finally be getting to those things you've wanted to address for some time. This dent and other areas needing repair are pretty obvious. The bad news is it has this dent, as well as several others, but the good news is the panel is very solid with no rust. The bodywork required to fix it is not very challenging, so there really is no need to make any special plans for it. Depending on personal preference, budget, and the advice and/or skill of who's doing the bodywork, you need to decide what type of repair you want to do and plan accordingly. The most common approach for a dent such as this is to flatten the metal as much as possible so as to use as little filler as possible. (I get into the specifics of this type of bodywork in Chapter 3.)

always be some unexpected issues, but these are all much easier to deal with if you have a plan in place and have already made contact with appropriate people and organizations.

Initial Inspection, Evaluation and Creating a "Needs" List

The type of project you have in mind determines the extent of your initial inspection and evaluation, as does the condition of the vehicle. If the vehicle is in good shape or you're taking the pay-as-you-go approach, you may be less exhaustive. If you're restoring a show car, you need to do a full-blown inspection. In our case, we had a good car and were doing a moderate project, so we limited our initial inspection to seeing if there were any major surprises. We wanted to make sure we could get parts and arrange

This type of repair involves bringing the metal back as much as possible to its original shape before applying filler and painting. Unlike the prior photo, where the metal could easily be hit from behind to reshape it, this repair may require pulling the metal as well. You can also see we needed to get a new reflector frame because it's seldom practical to try to repair plastic pieces. It's also apparent the bumper is bent and needs to be straightened or replaced. These are the kinds of decisions that need to be made early; it could take a lot of time to find a suitable bumper or line up a proper repair. We ultimately decided to just get a new bumper.

for any needed services (more on these later). We also knew we'd be doing more extensive evaluations of individual systems as we got to them.

In a minor refreshening for a daily driver, you primarily identify parts to be replaced. This assumes there are no major problems with rust or failed components. At most, a panel or two may need to be repainted but, in general, there is minimal or no painting done at this level—just a thorough reconditioning of the original painted finishes. Carpets can be replaced, seats can be reupholstered, trim panels and moldings

This photo reveals several areas that need attention. First, the rusted areas on the trunk lid need to be removed and repaired with new metal. The previous owner also installed an alarm that had the key switch in the rear panel. We didn't want to keep this, so we also need to patch the hole that will be left. Although the tail lamp lenses look reusable, the metal trim rings are too corroded/pitted for us to repair. For a survivor car or a show car, this may be feasible and require a lengthy process. We used new, readily available (yet high-quality) reproduction pieces on our car.

The front of the car was also in pretty good shape though we needed some new moldings for around the grille opening. These soft aluminum pieces are easily dented. The grille is in good enough shape for a daily driver, but closer inspection revealed considerable pitting and other damage that we wouldn't want on a nicer car. The bumper is in similar condition. It could be reused, but we decided we wanted something that looked better than this if it were just reconditioned. Rechroming is cost prohibitive and not available, or even possible, in many states because of environmental laws, so a replacement bumper was used. Again, unless you need the original, a replacement makes more sense.

Looking in the trunk and other enclosed areas that allow you to see behind the exterior panels can be very informative. Signs of previous repair work and evidence of damage not readily apparent from the outside generally show up here. When you find hidden damage after the restoration has started, you need to adjust your plans to fix these areas. We didn't find any unexpected bodywork. If you're doing a strictly original restoration, you want the appropriate trunk mat and other items our car no longer had. For most first-generation Mustangs, such items are easy to find, but they can be problematic for rarer cars.

The engine compartment was somewhat weathered. Many of the parts—hood hinges, water bottle, export brace, engine brackets, and throttle linkage—could be reconditioned, repainted, and reused. New decals and a surprising number of basic underhood parts are still easy to find. After we took the engine out, we'd have the opportunity to refurbish the entire underhood area. You might not do this with a daily driver but you surely would with a show car. We preferred to go with something a little more polished and functional.

The shock tower's condition is one of the critical areas to inspect on any early Mustang, especially the 1964½ to 1966 models. These are prone to cracking, which can cause serious problems for the suspension, steering, and braking systems. Cars that have been raced or otherwise run hard are most susceptible to cracking and stress damage. Cars from colder climates where road salt is used often have these issues. (I show how this can be fixed in Chapter 9.)

GETTING STARTED

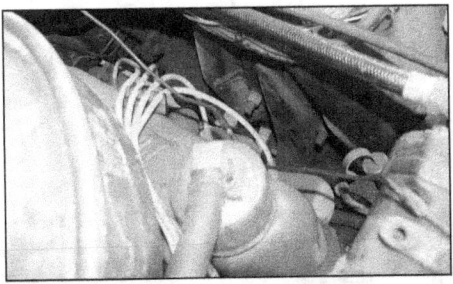

The rest of the engine compartment was in solid shape. The heater and air conditioner are common rust areas, but we had none at the firewall. We needed a new air-conditioning condenser that mounts in front of the radiator; the original wasn't usable. This was not easy to replace because few suppliers actually have them in stock. We had to wait several weeks for ours.

More subtle things, such as this door window molding, are easier to miss. It has clearly become damaged beyond any repair due to time, sunlight, etc. Many of these items get noticed when you are prepping the car for paint. If you take the time to look for them earlier, you can get the new parts sooner to install when the car is done being painted. Parts like this are fine to put on the car right away because they don't interfere with other parts that go on later. We didn't change the glass, so there was no risk of this for us.

can be replaced, but there is no significant bodywork. Worn or damaged mechanical parts can be replaced—up to a rebuild of the engine, transmission, and/or rear axle. All of this can be done piecemeal, for the most part, as time and budget allow.

The next level, or a moderate level of restoration, exceeds minor freshening and all major areas are repaired so the car can be fully prepped and repainted. It's basically a matter of trying to keep the look consistent. You don't want to have a nice new paint job and dinged-up trim or moldings, for example. With the overall project done to a higher level, the restoration level for the daily-driver minor refreshening is not acceptable. More parts are replaced and refurbished to make them look better. The cost is

The wheels and tires would also be usable for a daily driver, but we will be making some changes. We repainted the wheels, including the GT logo on the center caps. We handled it ourselves and thus didn't need to make any arrangements with others. But we plan to keep the colors factory correct. It doesn't have to be perfect, but we want it close. Restoration specialists, such as the Eastwood Company, stock paints that will work for us. We also considered new trim rings, but there was a question of cost effectiveness. If only one had been dinged, we probably would have bought a full set to keep them looking consistent. Thus, the question became, "Is the worst of the bunch acceptable or not?" We decided to keep the originals and just polish them all; none of them were really that bad.

The interior, in general, was in pretty decent shape, but a few things obviously needed work. We knew we would need new armrests, for example, because the original ones were too far gone. Likewise, new seat covers and new carpets, but we actually could have kept the door panels if we wanted to; they were that good. Items such as the lower door molding would just need some TLC; a good thing because these can be very pricey. Other than new sill plates and a couple of lenses for the gauges, there was not much to worry about. If you needed to recondition the original dash pad, for example, you would definitely have to allow enough time for it. A replacement is much cheaper and more easily obtained, but it can also be much harder to source a perfect match for the true factory look.

CHAPTER 2

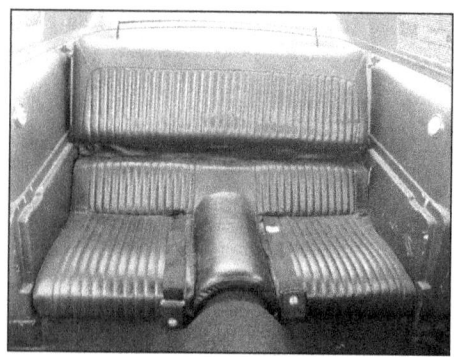

The rear seats were in fantastic shape. We would not have needed to do anything to them if we weren't replacing the seat covers up front. Again, we were facing the issue of the new and old looking different, so we put new seat covers on the rear as well. Another reason was the high quality and very authentic appearance of the covers from Distinctive Industries. If the reproduction covers weren't such a good match to the originals, we might have kept the rear seat original. While the texture and fit could be made to match, the colors wouldn't match due to the effects of many years of aging. Some might suggest dyeing both the new front and original rear seats to match, but we didn't feel it was worth the risk, especially since the reproductions looked so good. The new covers should last longer also.

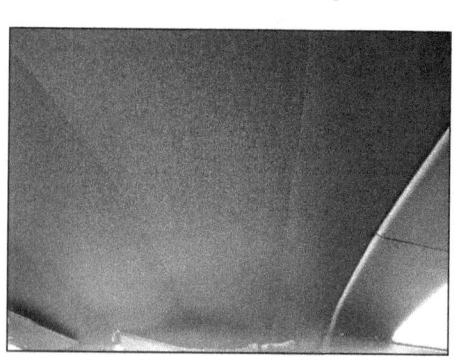

The headliner in the car was perfect, so we kept it. This saved time and expense, plus it also allowed us to feel better about our decision to stick with the original glass. This is a classic example of the interdependence of certain parts. Keeping both the headliner and the glass eliminated the need to buy replacements that would not likely match the look of the originals as much as some other parts do (the factory markings on the glass will really be special, as will the texture of the headliner). The only potential down side is that we didn't get to see the underside of the roof to check for any problems, but we didn't worry about it because the rest of the car's consistently good condition.

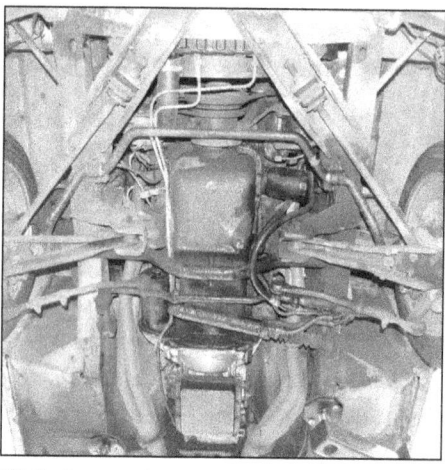

While I cover the evaluation of the undercar areas and systems in individual chapters, it is still necessary to get a preliminary idea of the extent of the work. When we got our car up in the air, we discovered the steering system and the exhaust would need some repair. The oil leak would automatically be taken care of when we rebuilt the engine. The headers that came with the car would not be reused because they were in poor condition and we wanted a stock appearance. We used freer-flowing "K" manifolds, which were a challenge in terms of availability and compatibility of parts. Luckily, we planned and researched early, so we had the parts on hand when we needed to ensure everything fit. The steering parts were difficult to find because they were commonly not in stock. We could have tried to rebuild the originals; that may be the answer for some. We decided on new parts mainly to reduce cost and maximize durability, but it ended up costing us some time when the parts proved to be difficult to obtain.

The rear section of the car looks as good as the rest. The gas tank was in exceptional condition on the outside, but we still gave it a good internal inspection. This tank was useable, but replacements are easy to find. We disregarded exhaust; we knew it would be replaced, as would the majority of the brakes and suspension (more on those in Chapter 8 and Chapter 9, respectively). The rear axle didn't show any signs of undue stress, and was therefore a good candidate for rebuilding. From a parts perspective we knew we'd need all of the little parts like hangers, clamps, and so forth, but these weren't a problem in our case. For those building a rarer vehicle, even these common parts can be difficult to locate if the highest levels of authenticity are necessary for the project.

higher and the project more time-consuming. There still is no requirement the work be done in a continuous fashion but the body prep and paint work, the biggest part of this type of restoration, inevitably is done this way. Rebuilding the engine, refurbishing the interior, and other areas can be done whenever. But it's best to get some work out of the way first to avoid damage to the new paint.

This is the key difference between the minor refreshing and the moderate level of restoration: scheduling and coordination of the work. This needs to be done to save time and money and to avoid having to redo some things. You also need to consider the availability of

GETTING STARTED

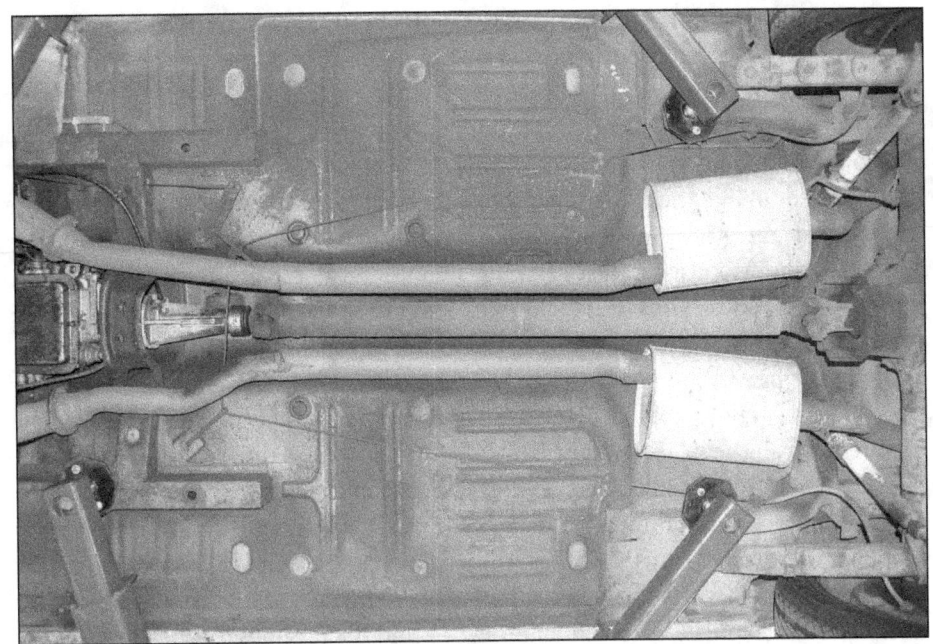

The floors on this car were as solid as you'd ever see. This was a real relief because we didn't need to do any extensive surgery to repair rust. All of the body plugs were in place and original fasteners and other parts were there. This confirmation is part of closely documenting how things went together and for keeping the parts together as they came off the car. I briefly discuss that later in this chapter. We already knew we'd need a new exhaust system, but it was interesting to see what the previous owner had done in hope of making a bit more power and, perhaps, also having a more aggressive exhaust note.

parts and/or shop services. Because some work is more elaborate, you need to schedule work with shops and source parts to keep the project moving. Last, the moderate-level weekend-cruiser restoration is meant for a car that will be driven *and* shown off, so you also need to allow some time to work out any bugs that may occur in fit, drivability, whatever. The daily-driver car won't be shown off as much and the level of change at any given time is generally less, thus minimizing potential problems. Similarly, the show car generally changes very little from the stock configuration, but isn't intended for much driving—factors which inherently minimize the potential for problems.

The show-car build goes well beyond the moderate level. Consequently, the vehicle has to be completely disassembled, stripped, and prepped prior to a very high level of restoration. All parts are evaluated against the highest standards of authenticity, finish, and function. What's good for the other build levels often isn't good enough for a show car because it's not perfect or authentic enough. Many parts that are taken off of a show car can still be used for other restoration projects with less restrictive criteria. The show car generally has the original parts refurbished to the highest standard or uses the best available reproduction parts (more on that in a bit). All seals, weather stripping, seat covers, door/trim panels, and other soft/wearable parts are generally replaced unless you are going for maximum authenticity and/or are building a survivor car and keeping the original patina (surface aging). For a show car, every part is examined for originality and is held to a higher standard than the other restoration levels. Functionality is secondary to aesthetics and authenticity. Time and cost are also lesser concerns.

Planning and Organization

After you've completed a thorough inspection, you should have a feel for what you want and need to do to meet the goal for your project type. If you're doing a daily driver/pay-as-you-go kind of restoration, there really isn't much planning involved. You take each task on a case-by-case basis and get to them as time and budget allow. These are usually weekend projects, which do not involve significant disassembly of the vehicle. Generally, you need few special tools or trips to a shop to leave it there for specific services. You can either buy any needed specialty tools for specific work or you can usually just rent them from retailers like Autozone. You still need to purchase parts in advance and arrange to have a place to do the work. You should always allow for the unexpected and perform the work indoors because you need to keep your parts, tools, and vehicle clean and protected. An enclosed garage that can be heated or cooled is best to protect the vehicle and make working on it more comfortable. It also is more secure because you can lock it and leave it. Just about any job can benefit from being performed in an enclosed garage or under a canopy, etc. If you have a vehicle you consider worth restoring you should plan to work on it inside.

I cover sourcing parts later in this chapter, but one issue to address up front is scheduling any services to be performed. Some jobs such as wheel alignment usually mean you just bring the car to the shop and wait your turn. If you can schedule an appointment, you are better off. One caveat: Some shops are very busy

CHAPTER 2

and difficult to get your car into, especially those doing the best work. This is particularly true for high-end restorations. You don't just show up at one of those shops and expect to be able to leave your car and wait for a call and a bill.

A show-car restoration at a high-end shop is a commitment not only in terms of finances and time but also on the part of both the shop and the owner to get it done right. Almost any decision about time and money spent can affect project outcome and quality. The good news is the shop will probably help considerably with the overall planning and organization in a high-end show-car project—they get paid for it and have a reputation to preserve. With such a restoration, you can generally have as much or as little involvement as you desire with the project.

Most Mustang projects are pretty straightforward because there's an established recipe or criteria, so there are fewer compromises to make. Because the shop effectively becomes your prime subcontractor, they handle many of the tasks involved. They can deal with specialty shops for jobs, such as chrome plating, engine building, etc., if they don't have these in-house capabilities. They can help you find parts and information specific to the vehicle. If you've got the time and the money, you can't beat just dropping the car off at a reputable, high-end restoration shop and letting them get the job done right for you.

But that's not why you're reading this book. If you want to create a high-end show car, use this book to help keep the high-end shop on target. If you're doing a daily driver, use this book to supplement the factory service manual, so that your vehicle performs beyond factory level. Those benefiting most are those building the weekend cruiser, where you are the prime contractor and source out what you can't or don't want to do. You'll also benefit from the following tips on how to structure the project and choose providers of parts and services.

Usually, bodywork and paint takes the longest time in any restoration project. This should be the thing you try to get started on ASAP. Whether you're doing a full rotisserie job or just stripping down the exterior while leaving some parts in place, the sooner you can get the body to the paint shop, the better.

The best way to approach this is to first remove all the major exterior panels like the hood, trunk, and fenders, so they will be out of harm's way while you remove the larger items. Neither the doors nor the glass have to come off at this time, but you need to remove the trim items and moldings.

In a show-car project, you likely will take the car down to the bare shell in one step because it is almost certainly going onto a rotisserie for further work. In our weekend-cruiser-style project we did not take out the glass because it was in excellent shape with no leaks. Why risk breaking the glass if there is no problem? (We were especially concerned about the rear glass because it had the factory center stripe and would not be easy, or cheap, to replace if something went wrong.) We decided to leave the doors on for the time being so the interior wouldn't get dirty while the car was hauled to the body shop on a flatbed truck. We left the doors and windows closed to prevent wind and dirt from damaging the headliner we decided to keep.

Every project comprises these same basic elements and follows a similar plan. The steps may differ. For example, some are added or deleted to achieve a certain level of performance, function, finish/appearance, authenticity, and final overall quality. All projects start with a general evaluation of the vehicle to define what needs to be done to reach the goal. Some parts and services are identified after this initial inspection; others become obvious later, throughout the project.

To the extent you can get the parts you need, it seldom hurts to get them ASAP; you never know when they may be hard to find, on backorder, etc. It's the same thing with services from outside shops. Start talking to the body shop, engine shop, transmission shop, etc., as soon as you decide to use them. This may help to schedule the project and find parts (they may have some and/or have sources you didn't know about), and they can also serve as a reality check for what you want to do. You can't overvalue the resource of a good shops, so talk to friends, club members, whomever, to find them. Shops featured in magazine articles are worth considering as well because they have proven they can meet a relatively high standard of work under a deadline.

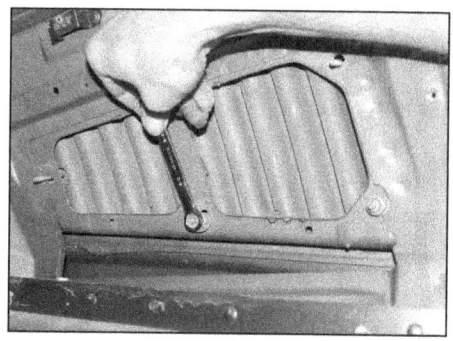

It's important to note how things came apart and where unique parts came from. The venting system is a perfect example because it's somewhat of a special Mustang feature. Note that there are five cup-like spacers that go between the retaining nut and the body panel. These pieces are unique to the car both in appearance and function. Basically, they help compensate for production variations and the natural curvature of the body. You won't see parts like these used in many other places. The key is to record their location (with a photo, if possible) and then keep such items together in a properly labeled bag.

GETTING STARTED

When planning and organizing your restoration project, keep the proper sequence of events in mind and schedule outside work earlier rather than later. For our project, we made sure we sent the components that needed rebuilding to their respective shops ASAP. We then focused on taking off whatever else we needed to remove, so we could get the body to the paint shop. While the body was being taken care of, we reconditioned the parts that needed some attention and acquired new parts for the things we decided to change. Leaving the glass, headliner, and dash in the car saved some time and cost, but it also meant we had to be extra careful to not damage these items while we painted and worked in the interior.

We stuck to our plan and had a rebuilt engine, rebuilt transmission, rebuilt rear axle, new suspension, new brakes, and reconditioned interior parts ready to go when we got the car back from the paint shop. Other than a few parts that were backordered, we were all set.

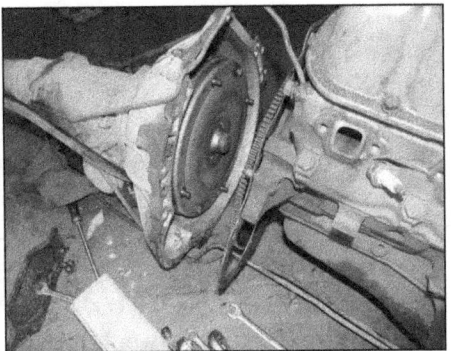

Out of the car, the engine and transmission can be separated to go to their respective shops for rebuilds. Record the condition of small items, such as fasteners and brackets, before removing and storing them. Generally, you want to remove as much as possible before sending larger parts away so they're cleaned and safely in your possession. The shops also prefer this. Just be sure you don't remove anything needed by the shop for attachment, testing, or any other reason. The torque converter, for example, does not need to go to the transmission shop unless you want them to work on it too. There isn't much you can do to a converter and you're usually better off sending the transmission without it, in most cases.

Initial/Basic Disassembly

Rebuilding the engine, transmission, and rear axle should take less time than doing the bodywork and paint, so you should get to work on these items after the hood, radiator, and other adjacent parts have been removed to prevent damage. This is where scheduling issues become more critical. The time it takes to complete various services vary, so the goal is to complete tasks in the proper

Larger items, such as the radiator, are fairly easy to identify and keep track of, so the main goal is to prevent damage while they are being stored. The fins on the radiator are a good example of something that must be protected. Like most parts, a radiator can benefit from a good cleaning and repainting. However, special consideration must be given to the type of paint used; common enamel paint can reduce the heat-transfer efficiency of the radiator. Special radiator paint is available, from companies such as Eastwood, which not only gives the radiator a nice appearance but also helps ensure maximum heat-transfer capability.

After removing any parts that might get in the way or be damaged in the process, the engine and transmission can be removed as a unit. It's not mandatory that both come out together, but the engine and tranny provide better balance as an entire assembly, so the removal process is easier. You can tilt the engine and tranny to different angles as they are lifted. Use the largest fasteners possible to hold the chain's attachment tabs on the engine, and make sure you have enough thread engagement for all studs or bolts. Try to attach to the strongest points and materials (iron versus aluminum, for example) whenever possible. Lift slowly.

CHAPTER 2

It requires great care and often special tools to remove small parts like this emblem. The wide blade of this tool spreads the prying force so you reduce the chance of breaking it. Still, take care to not damage the part or the surface under it. Even though we'll repaint the vehicle, there is no reason to create extra finish repair work. Small parts like these are usually easy to source, so it's not too bad if you break one; but it's nice to reuse the original parts if possible. This one only needs a little cleaning and paint, if the pitting comes off after being rubbed with steel wool. If not, we use a new set.

sequence and minimize holdups, the potential for damage, or having to redo things. It's logical to start those tasks and have the finished parts ready for reinstallation after the body is done. You can also take care of the interior panels, seats, brakes, suspension, etc.

We found it useful to leave the suspension and brakes on the car while it was being painted, so it would make it easier to move the car around. We knew we'd replace most of the parts anyway, so we didn't need to take the original parts off the car to recondition them. If you need to do so in your case, it's best to do that after the car gets to the body shop, while the bodywork is being done.

The refurbished and/or new parts can be put back on the car before it goes to the paint both, if necessary, but this is not generally required. The paint shop should have a dolly setup to put under the car to move it around. But if you need to roll it around on the suspension, be sure to mask off the parts you'll be using so they don't get covered with overspray in the paint booth. We used a dummy rear axle and the stock front setup because we would be putting in all new components for the suspension and brakes. The axle was rebuilt while the car was being painted, and we simply reinstalled the newly rebuilt axle after the car left the body shop.

If you are doing a show-car level of restoration for which everything comes off the car, you should refurbish the original parts while the body and paintwork is being done. That way everything is ready when the car goes back together. If you leave some parts on the car during paint (as we did), have them masked off and be sure you have decided how to handle blend lines and so forth. If you're repainting the car the same original color, this is less of an issue than if you're changing colors. In the latter case, you need to decide where to make the color

Special tools are mandatory in some cases, as in removing this delicate molding. Special tools can make easy work of removing sealant, clips, and retaining pins. Trying to do this with a screwdriver or other generic tool would almost surely damage the molding and maybe even other parts. Even with the right tool(s), taking these moldings off requires an amount of finesse that only comes with experience. The moldings on our car were in absolutely pristine condition, so we let the experts handle this job. In our case, no replacement would look as good as the original parts.

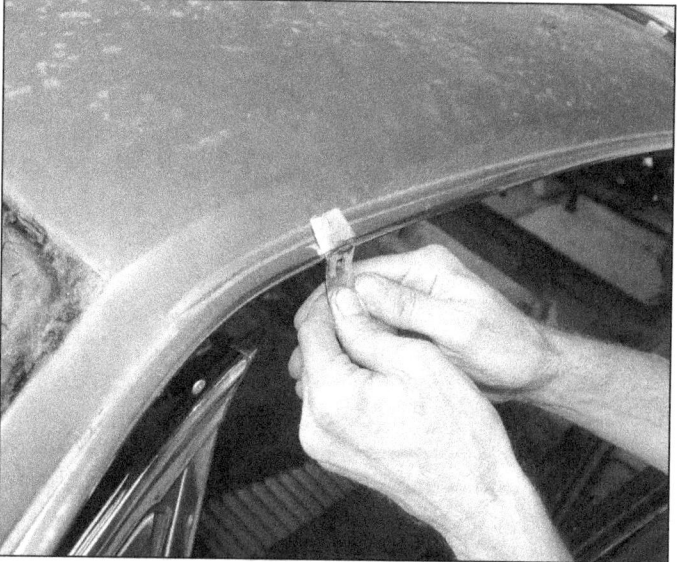

While there are plenty of special tools that can be bought or borrowed, there are others that can be easily made. Here, a simple can opener and some masking tape are combined to make a tool that greatly simplifies removing moldings and other trim items with minimal damage. Finesse is required here, but the point is that you don't always have to buy special tools.

GETTING STARTED

switch in places like door jambs and the trunk area. If you're going to be covering areas with trim or custom panels, this is also where you prevent problems.

These are issues to consider up front rather than after the painting starts. Since we did a re-spray of the original color and only left the dash, glass, and headliner in, we were spared any really tough decisions. The door moldings, sill plates, and similarity of the old and new paint colors made things much easier. Perhaps our biggest problem was the underhood area where we used a different coating for the engine bay than for the lower portion of the car. (In Chapter 4, I discuss how we handled the merge line.)

Tools and Equipment

Regardless of what level of restoration you undertake, you will surely need a pretty good assortment of tools. Of course, you need the usual wrenches, ratchets, screwdrivers, etc. How many other tools you need depends on how much of the work you intend to do yourself. It's safe to say you will at least need a decent floor jack and some good jack stands. Don't try to save pennies on these; the stamped-steel types generally aren't the wisest or safest choice. Spend a little more and get something you know is strong enough to last. You also need a few good drain pans for things like oil, coolant, brake fluid, etc., as well as containers to dispose of what you accumulate. Don't assume any old plastic container will work; some may not be strong enough and you'll soon have one heck of a mess. Metal or compatible plastics are the only way to go.

When it comes to removing trim, moldings, and so forth, you usually need special tools to do the job with the least chance of damaging the components. These special tools can generally be purchased at auto parts stores or places such as Sears and Walmart, in many cases. Tool retailers, such as Harbor Freight, also carry some of the more popular items. Some can be made out of other tools or from scratch, if you have the expertise and a model to follow. In general, these special tools are not terribly expensive and are well worth having if you plan to do more restoration work.

If you only need something for a short time, you can also borrow many special tools from auto parts stores and their tool loaner programs. You generally just leave a deposit, which you get back when you return the tool. The selection isn't complete, of course, and you won't find the less-expensive ones available, but you can surely find things like a brake service set at most stores that have such a program.

A good torque wrench is one tool you should definitely invest in. At a minimum, purchase a 3/8-inch drive with a range up to about 250 ft-lbs or so. A click style is more convenient, but a dial type can often be more accurate. You need something that's going to stay accurate because an inaccurate reading can be a safety problem and/or cause very expensive damage if it's in the powertrain, suspension, or brake areas. Buy a better model of a good brand, as your budget allows. One usage note: Always set it back to zero before you store it and check the calibration as needed to maintain acceptable accuracy.

In addition to common hand tools, it's useful to have access to grinding wheels, hydraulic presses, impact wrenches, transmission jacks, and engines hoists, etc., depending on how much you plan to do yourself. Some of these are worth always having around and some are not worth the expense, if you only plan on using them for one or two projects. You also need space to store everything, which may or may not be an issue. You may be able to disassemble an engine hoist, so it will technically fit in a closet, but your significant other may not be too thrilled with the idea.

Beyond needing a compressor and air lines for pneumatic tools, you may also need 220v and/or high-current circuits for some equipment. If you don't have it, then don't consider such equipment unless you plan to do more of such work in the future. The lure of a temperature-controlled, well-equipped garage is irresistible for most people who plan to work on their car(s) very often, so you may find yourself using your restoration project to justify some upgrades around the garage as well.

The simple rule is to first buy what you'll use the most often and then upgrade as your needs and your skill level changes. You may find you need to make a purchase to finish something you've started, either because what you were using broke or couldn't handle the job. That's why it usually pays to spend a little more to get some extra capability even if you may not have an immediate need for it. And it's always good to have extras of some tools for when your buddies are available to help you, or in case something breaks during use.

If you want to do as much of the work as possible and have the expertise, you also need welding equipment, special bodywork tools, and so forth. The necessary welding equipment can range from simple arc welders and flux-core MIG all the way to professional-type TIG. Similarly, bodywork tools can range from handheld dollies to plasma cutters. These can be fairly expensive and require considerable knowledge to use properly. If you have that knowledge, you probably already have the right equipment. If not, but can buy the equipment, it's still not usually a good idea to learn as you go on a restoration project. If you do decide you want to take such an approach, it's

CHAPTER 2

A very simple, yet effective means of reconditioning chrome-plated parts is to gently rub them with 0000-grade steel wool and a small amount of chrome polish. This usually removes virtually all of the minor pitting and corrosion that can form on chrome-plated parts. More serious damage requires either stripping and rechroming or buying a new part. With ever-tightening environmental laws, it's difficult to find a shop that does chrome plating. Then, after you find one, you probably want to be sitting down when you get the quote for the work. Usually, this is only feasible for a high-dollar show car that needs to retain as many original parts as possible.

best to practice your welding, bodywork, and other skills on other vehicles before your restoration project. The potential for causing very expensive damage to either the car or yourself can be significant.

If you have any doubts about what you're doing, you should probably farm the work out to an experienced and trusted shop that has the necessary equipment and expertise. This is almost always the case when it comes to rebuilding engines, transmissions, and the like. Throughout the book, I show some of the special tools and techniques such shops can provide. For now, it's only necessary to identify any special tools you need using the factory service manual and/or advice from others who've done similar work before. Also identify the various sources from which you can purchase or borrow tools should you have an unexpected need for one.

Trim Removal and Repair

Always remove trim, moldings, and similar parts before more serious disassembly begins. This is mainly to protect these pieces from potential damage. Special tools really are mandatory in most cases to avoid damage to the parts while removing them. They are a relatively small investment, well worth it for any level of project.

Most of the trim, moldings, emblems, logos, and lettering on first-generation Mustangs are held on with various forms of clips, nuts, and other fasteners. In most cases, they were not intended to be removed at all, so they weren't attached with more normal nuts and bolts. They also tend to be relatively undisturbed and unprotected other than by, perhaps, a coating of wax. If the car has not been garaged or otherwise protected from the elements, there is probably some corrosion. The potential for other damage (impacts, scratches, etc.) is always present, too. It is a rare case when all of the original moldings and so forth can be reused. We were, thankfully, very lucky in this regard with our car.

Those doing a show-car restoration or building a survivor car usually keep the original parts, if at all possible. This is much more likely for a survivor car. While reproduction parts may be available for many or most of these items, they often do not match the originals perfectly. This can be due to a number of factors. The tooling used to create the reproductions may not precisely match the features of the factory tooling. Even when so-called original factory tooling is used to make the parts, there can still be a problem if the tooling is too worn. Ford replaced tooling on a regular basis during production. It is usually too expensive for an aftermarket company. Thus, there can still be differences if the tooling is worn beyond Ford's specifications.

Differences in materials can also cause matching problems. Differences in alloys, plating processes, and other manufacturing variations from original factory to aftermarket parts can make the parts look, fit, and/or perform differently. Chrome-plated steel or aluminum may be substituted for stainless steel, for example. Specifications and processes for chrome plating may differ.

The point is that there truly is no substitute for most original parts. Higher-quality reproductions will do the best job of replicating the factory parts and, in some cases, match them to the point where only an expert can tell the difference. For a show car where authenticity matters, this is what you want to go with. For a weekend cruiser or a daily driver, you may not be able to justify the extra expense of this level.

Instead, you may just want to recondition what you have. If you find extensive impact damage or corrosion, there's usually no point in trying to save the original parts. However, if there is just some moderate scratching or pitting and/or some relatively small dents, etc., these can probably be fixed. A lot depends on the material—stainless steel is very forgiving, aluminum less so, chrome-plated steel or pot metal the least so.

In general, deal with any damage or dents first. Then, with the part back in proper form, the surface finish can be addressed. Stainless steel and aluminum can usually be rubbed with 0000-grade steel wool to remove most imperfections, and can then be polished to achieve the desired finish. This does not apply,

When looking for replacement parts, many factors come into play. Proper fit and function are common goals regardless of the type of restoration. However, aesthetics plays a key role in weekend-cruiser and show-car builds. Both require a high-quality appearance, but the show car must also strictly adhere to the original factory look. The correct material choice, the proper colors and textures, etc., make a huge difference in preserving the original look of the vehicle. To get such quality and accuracy, you can expect to pay significantly more than for a lower-quality part. This original part can be reused after some minor cleaning—that's the best way to go if you can.

Another example of how some replacement parts are better than others is in the construction of the part. This factory grille is assembled with rivets holding the parts together. Many reproductions, even high-quality parts, often use a nut-and-bolt arrangement instead of rivets. This is much less costly to manufacture and, for most people, is fine for function and appearance because the fasteners are not easily visible. On a show car, such a difference can prove to be quite significant.

Some of the more obscure and very special parts like vapor barriers, backing mats, etc., which are unique for each individual vehicle, are often harder to source than other parts. These parts are usually replaced because the originals have deteriorated or were damaged when removed. There is virtually nothing that can be done to preserve or recondition such parts; replacement is the most common option. In very rare cases, the originals may be used as templates to create a new set but, again, this is only feasible in extreme situations, as with a show car.

however, if the finish is relatively dull. There are ways to restore such a finish, but these are best left to professionals. Mildly pitted chrome finishes can also be rubbed with 0000-grade steel wool and usually require no further attention. Significantly pitted chrome-plated parts often require stripping and rechroming. This is very expensive and cannot be done everywhere due to local laws. Also, the base material may not survive the process, depending on its condition.

The good news is that reproduction chrome parts generally look better than other material finishes. Chrome also makes it easier to paint recesses and other colored features. You can apply paint, let it set up, and then carefully remove it from only the chrome. There's often no need for any masking.

Smaller items, such as emblems, letters, logos, etc., are usually made from either plastic or pot metal and are easier to replace than to recondition/repair. Modern molding technologies can actually yield very accurate reproductions, so lack of availability and/or cost would be the main reasons for trying to reuse the original parts. This furthers the point made earlier about consistency of appearance. If you replace one letter in a string, you'll probably end up replacing all of them because the new and old items will not look the same.

Similarly, you don't want nice new trim and old/worn lettering or logos, etc. One of the best reasons for replacing these items is they tend to become loose over time, and there really is no good way of securing them to the car. The material wears, corrodes, or breaks off and the fasteners don't have enough material to hold onto anymore. The parts become loose, rattle, and can allow water to accumulate where you don't want it

to. Unless you're doing a survivor vehicle or can't get new replacement parts, you are generally better off replacing most of the small bits that attach to body panels than you are trying to make them look or fit better. Reconditioning those you must reuse requires extra care in ensuring the compatibility of any coatings, paints, etc., as well as choosing a repair method that prevents damage. If it's a complex and/or delicate component, let a professional do the job. Otherwise, consult those who have successfully done such work for the best techniques.

Finding Replacement Parts

Remember: When it comes to parts, you get what you pay for. Perhaps the first questions to ask when shopping for a part is, "What do I really need," and/or "What can I afford?"

If you're building a daily driver and/or don't have much of a budget, perhaps functionality is your primary concern. You don't mind if the part looks and feels a little different, so long as it does the job. You can probably save some money and time looking for your parts in this case, but you shouldn't expect the same overall quality or authentic look of a better-quality part. You need to ensure the part at least meets certain standards for performance, durability, and feasibility. Avoid poorly made (usually imported) parts that have a low price but aren't made well enough to fit properly, work well enough, or last very long. Any retailer may sell such products, so make sure there is good return policy wherever you buy. Of course, it helps to deal with more established sources no matter what type of car you're building. When you're trying to keep costs low, however, you're more likely to buy something online or from a private party, thus potentially increasing the chances of getting an inferior part.

If you buy online you should only buy from shops and/or individuals with a good return policy and, to the extent they are available, good customer reviews and feedback scores. It helps to know people who have bought from a particular seller and were satisfied with the parts. You can also go onto forums and see what others have to say about a given seller; you will likely also find more sources for the parts you need. The classifieds section of many forums is a great place to find parts, as are the websites and publications of local car clubs. Craigslist.org and eBay.com are well-known sources for buying used items on the Internet, but Mustang owners also need to look at sites such as corral.net, stangnet.com, allfordmustangs.com, and vintage-mustang.com. (A larger list is provided in the Source Guide on page 192.) These types of online and/or local sources are generally the best places to start your search if you're looking for something common and want to keep costs low.

Depending on the item you're looking for, you may even be able to simply go to your local auto parts store. Many standard replacement parts are still available even though these cars are 40 or so years old. Also, don't forget salvage yards either. While their quality varies, they offer some good potential, especially if they cater to specific vehicles such as Mustangs.

If you're building a weekend cruiser or show car and are less concerned with cost than with quality, availability, and/or authenticity, you also want look at businesses specializing in restoration parts in general and Mustangs in particular. The largest and perhaps most widely known are companies such as Mustangs Plus, National Parts Depot (NPD), and Year One. They have Mustang-specific catalogs, sometimes even organized by generation, plus they tend to stock very large assortments of replacement parts and some aftermarket parts.

You can also go onto the Internet and find Ford- or Mustang-specific salvage yards, such as Mustang Village in San Bernadino, California. In some cases, you can also go to the websites of parts suppliers, such as Scott Drake Enterprises, Tony D. Branda Performance, Inc., or Distinctive Industries (Specialty Division), either to buy parts directly or to get the name of an authorized distributor. They can tell you what's right for your car or, if authenticity is not a priority, what other options may be better.

Because we're not restoring a show car or survivor car, authentic parts are not a requirement. For our weekend cruiser, we had a readily available supply of original and reproduction parts; therefore it was unusual that an unavailable part held up our project.

There are plenty of sources, but things like price, quality level, and customer service vary considerably among them. It's a definite benefit to build relationships with qualified craftsman and concentrate most of your business on a smaller number of shops. They tend to take extra time to help you find what you need, often even if they don't have it. If you always go to the source with the lowest price, your total cost will probably end up higher. Sure, you can go online to find great prices, but you won't always get a quality part and you won't be getting the added value of an experienced group of people who can provide you with invaluable information and assistance throughout the course of your build. Besides, one of the best parts of being involved in a restoration project is the people you meet and the relationships you make before and after it's done.

Cataloging and Organizing Your Parts

As you are taking the vehicle apart and/or acquiring new parts to be installed, it is extremely helpful if you keep track of everything as you go. Sure, you can tell a left front fender from a right front fender, but what about the hundreds of little parts attached to the bigger pieces? It's very difficult to remember how fasteners go back together. Even if a screw or bolt looks the same when it's installed, there may be a difference in length that is more important than you might think. Some bolts go through water passages, may need seals, have a special thread, etc. Some screws need to be different lengths on the same part for specific reasons. The point is, there's no way most people can remember all of this unless they do this type of work on a regular basis.

Rather than try to remember all the specifics, there are better ways to make

GETTING STARTED

sure the right parts go back in the right places. One simple way is to take a lot of digital photos during disassembly. With inexpensive digital cameras and camera phones readily available, there is no limit to how may photos you can take, other than time and the amount of memory you feel like paying for. Showing how a part looks before it comes apart and then showing related fasteners is one way to make sure you don't lose track of things.

After you save the photos, you need to store the parts until you need them again. Large parts are not so much of a problem, but you should try to keep related parts together in a secure area. Protect the parts after they've been removed, so they don't get damaged from being walked into, spilled on, hit with overspray, becoming too hot or too cold, getting wet, whatever. Parts can be wrapped, bagged, and/or labeled. Smaller parts, like fasteners, emblems, etc., are best kept in labeled Ziploc-type bags. Put the bags in a small box near the parts the fasteners they go with. Organize everything into logical groups that you'll remember, such as steering, suspension, and brakes. You can subdivide into front, rear, left, right, driver side, passenger side, etc., as you see fit.

The bottom line is that more information is better than less, so long as it makes sense to you. Having a separate shelf, drawer, or section of floor for the different vehicle sections is best, as long as you can ensure the parts are safe and undisturbed.

A final note: Sometimes it's best to not disassemble things too far or, if you have to, to partially reassemble them before you store them for further reassembly. Obviously, components like the engine, transmission, and differential are mostly assembled before they go back into the car. This is most true with parts that require unique assembly process and/or when you will be reusing the cleaned-up original parts. An example is the seat belt fastening bolts. There is a certain trick to putting this seemingly simple assembly back together before it can be put into the car. This extra care in the beginning can save time and frustration later.

Whatever degree of disassembly you undertake with however many parts (new or reused), you must be able to find them come reassembly time. Everything is smoother if you organize what you have into a reasonable number of logical groups and keep a log of what is where. A simple inventory with some additional details goes a long way to ensure you have what you need when you need it.

If you really want to get fancy, restoration project management software is available. These programs help you keep track of all your parts and gauge the overall progress of the whole restoration against specific timelines and projections. Such software can even provide some generic milestones that are common to most restorations, in a flow path structure. You still have to plug in the estimated times (or use generic estimates), but the structure can be beneficial, especially for a novice. Even the most experienced restoration shops use such project management software. Whether you use software or you just draw up a plan and try to stick to it as best you can, the key is to anticipate what you need to do, do as much as you can as soon as you can without causing complications later, and leave enough flexibility to be able to make adjustments for the unexpected issues that arise.

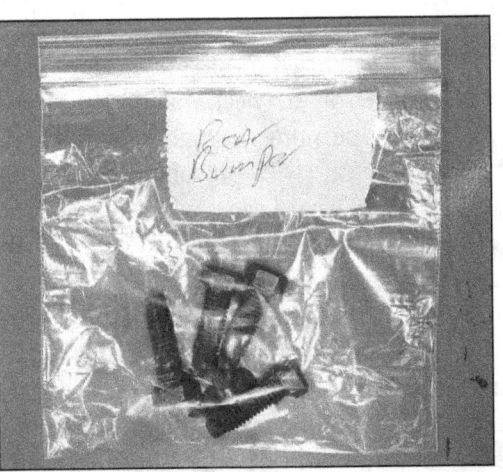

Keeping your parts organized saves time and ensures a higher-quality build. Fasteners particularly need to be cataloged and organized in a very logical fashion. One of the best ways is to use Ziploc-type plastic bags—write on them directly if they have a label or use masking tape as shown. These bags keep the parts clean, dry, and visible. Keep the bags of fasteners for a given group of components in a nearby box.

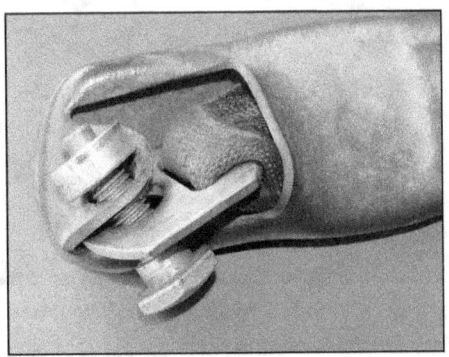

Oftentimes, it's best to keep certain parts, including fasteners, partially assembled to help remember how things go together. Here, a seat belt attachment bolt and spacer are kept with the belt for reassembly. Proper assembly order means proper function of the parts. Getting the belt through the rubber sleeve requires a little talent to avoid damage. And to tighten the bolts, you must first pull a length of the belt through the sleeve to provide clearance for the wrench. The metal tab of the belt pivots on the shoulder of the bolt, and there is just enough clearance for the tab and sleeve to turn freely.

CHAPTER 3

BODY MAKES BEAUTIFUL

The quality of the bodywork is a telltale sign of the quality of the restoration. Regardless of what level of restoration you undertake, you want to achieve professional results. The body needs to resemble the original bodywork, and be free of rust, dents, and damage for years of faithful service. Beyond components such as moldings and glass that can be replaced or refurbished, the condition of the body and paint has the greatest impact on the car's appearance. (Because these are substantial aspects of restoration, I devote a separate chapter to each of these topics.)

This underhood area has been stripped of all old paint, so it can be primed and then repainted with the proper finish. Depending on how the rest of body will be finished, the area can either be media blasted or chemically stripped. Restorers tend to media blast or chemically strip daily-driver project cars. A chemical strip offers lower cost and convenient cleanup. Media blasting is often the preferred method for weekend cruisers and show cars because they tend to be more fully disassembled and are not as time constrained. The chemical strippers require a little more care to make sure all residue is removed (usually by wiping everything off with lacquer thinner or another suitable solvent), but it's easier to do in a tight garage.

In this chapter, I address some basic repairs, such as fixing dents and rust, and installing panels. While there is naturally some overlap with Chapter 4 on paint when it comes to things like using body filler, I have kept this chapter focused on just the body, rather than on its subsequently coatings.

Most enthusiasts who attempt such repairs either already have some experience doing them or are being guided by someone who does. So I must be perfectly clear: Bodywork is not for the inexperienced. It requires certain types of expertise and specialized equipment that most people don't have. I've tried to highlight some of the steps that need to be taken to get the best results for a daily-driver or a weekend-cruiser project. Those pursuing the higher standards of a show car will probably have to go beyond what I can cover here. Such projects are almost always done at the professional level.

Regardless of your project level, this chapter will help ensure the work is done properly and the repairs last a long time, with minimal fear of future problems. I cover some of the more common approaches to repairing rust, small imperfections (dents, for example), smaller more-complex areas, and larger more-simply-shaped areas. These procedures should translate to most areas of the vehicle, even though I show specific parts.

First, I cover the basic steps in removing rust from a solid part or panel prior to sealing and/or priming in preparation for paint. This common process can be applied to virtually any part of the car with minor adaptations for a particular situation.

Then I cover three types of repairs—small area, large area, and dents/dings—and the work required to repair or refurbish each one, so it can be sealed and/or eventually primed for paint. These basically involve the repair of severe mechanical damage, as opposed to simply the repair of the surface of the metal. The goal of each is to repair the severe damage by removing, replacing, and/or reshaping the damaged metal. The repairs are then sealed and prepared as with surface rust repair. (Subsequent filling, smoothing, priming, and painting will be covered in Chapter 4.)

Minor/Surface Rust Repair

The cardinal rule when repairing rust damage is to not just treat the symptom (the rust) but to also treat the disease (whatever caused the rust). This seems simple enough, but it can take considerable detective work to figure out how moisture got to the affected area. The bottom line is there is no point in making a repair that you only have to make again because you didn't eliminate the cause of the rust problem. (In this section, I only cover what to do after you've identified and fixed the cause.)

One of the first things to determine is why you are getting rid of the rust. Is it mostly for aesthetics or is there a more functional aspect to it? Many large, heavy/thick underbody parts normally develop a thin coating of rust that goes unaddressed because it has no real functional effect, in most cases. True, given enough time and additional moisture, any rust problem can eventually eat away at enough metal to cause a functional problem. Realistically, however, some parts of the frame, crossmembers, and suspension normally have a certain amount of rust that is tolerated. It's not a serious concern because it doesn't detract from the car's value or functionality unless it becomes excessive. On a daily driver, you probably won't address this. On a weekend cruiser, you want to clean this to your level of personal preference. On a show car, this has to go for sure, and the fix must be done at the highest possible level.

Rust in thinner steel parts, such as body panels and so forth, is almost always a problem because these areas tend to be more visible and, if they are structural to any degree, there is less reserve strength to keep the part from failing when it rusts. These parts also tend to allow water and/or dirt to get into areas where it is not wanted (interior, trunk, etc.). Many early Mustang owners had to deal with water coming into the footwell area because of rust in the cowl vent and around the windshield. Water on your feet and a wet carpet (which can lead to rusted-out floorpans) is a higher priority than rust on the rear axle housing, especially for a daily driver.

Rust is never good, but the point is it may not automatically be bad enough to require the time and expense to repair it in every case. If the only benefit will be aesthetic, you may just want to simply treat it and paint over it.

If you're trying to make a heavy part look better, such as a rear axle or control arm, you just need to remove the loose rust before applying your choice of coating(s). This can be done with a wire brush, by grinding, by media blasting, or even by chemical conversion in some instances. The key is that the texture of the surface is not a real priority in such instances; some pitting or surface roughness is considered acceptable. If you want

Some rust on larger, less-aesthetic parts, such as suspension components or frame rails, is acceptable in many cases. Those who want a more pleasing appearance, however, typically put either a rust conversion and/or rust sealing compound over this surface rust to prevent it from progressing and to make it look better. This look may be fine for a daily driver or a survivor vehicle that needs its original patina, but this would not be tolerated on a show car or weekend cruiser.

a smooth-as-glass finish, that's a whole different story. I won't cover that process because it involves expensive finishing, such as powdercoating.

For our project car, we're dealing mainly with thicker, primarily undercar parts, where you first simply remove as much of the rust you can by physical and/or chemical means. There are numerous rust-removing solutions commercially marketed. Some are simply brushed on and left for a period of time before wiping off; some require immersion; and some actually remain on the part and chemically convert the rust into a protective coating that can be further sealed, primed, and/or painted. This approach can be used on virtually any rusted area that has not rusted through completely or has become severely pitted, including body panels.

Using The Eastwood Company line of products as an example, first wire brush, media blast, or otherwise remove the loose rust from the part. Then use either their Rust Dissolver or Rust Converter to chemically remove or convert the remaining rust. Which way you go depends on a number of factors. When dealing with a heavily functional, yet less-visible part, often the rust converter is the best choice for simply sealing the surface prior to painting. In the case of a thinner and more visible part, use the rust dissolver to remove as much rust as possible, to get down to bare metal.

Either approach works well; it's often a choice based on budget or time. The rust converter approach is quicker and cheaper (in most cases) but will not provide as good a foundation for other treatment or repairs as the bare metal. If you intend to weld the metal, for example, you would use the rust dissolver approach and then use a suitable pre-cleaner such as lacquer thinner or Eastwood's PRE to remove any residue. A smoother surface simply requires more steps and preparation.

After you've either converted or dissolved the rust, it's wise to seal the painted parts and bare metal surfaces against further rust. In either case, use Eastwood Rust Encapsulator or a similar product. This step provides extra insurance against future rust because it does a better job of sealing the surface than standard primers, which are mainly intended to provide a better surface for the topcoats to stick to. Sealing is not their primary purpose. When applied over the converted surface, you actually get a double benefit because both the converted surface and the Rust Encapsulator have sealing capabilities.

You also have the potential to effect a color change since the converted surface is always black, while the Rust Encapsulator is available in black, red, and silver formulations. Another benefit of Eastwood's Rust Encapsulator is that it provides some degree of surface smoothing by filling small pinholes and similar irregularities. It can also be used either under or over body fillers; so if you want a smoother surface, you can use filler to get the smoothness you want and then seal both the metal and the filler.

Standard primers as well as lacquer, enamel, or polyurethane paints can be applied over the "encapsulated" surface (see Chapter 4 for more detail). Note, however, that it is also possible to simply use a sandable filler/primer over the encapsulated surface to provide an extra degree of surface smoothing capability, without having to resort to the use of body filler. In many cases, minor scratches and pitting can be successfully hidden due to the buildup qualities of the Eastwood Rust Encapsulator and/or the use of a sandable primer.

After you have the surface sealed and smoothed to the degree you desire, it can then be finished in any number of ways. For undercar and underhood areas, your most likely choice is to use a combination of coatings such as Eastwood's Extreme Chassis Black and their Under Hood Black. There's also Eastwood's special, professionally oriented 2K Ceramic Chassis Black two-part coating that must be applied with a spray gun (the Extreme product is also available in aerosol spray can). Both Chassis Black formulations are available in either gloss or satin finishes, while the

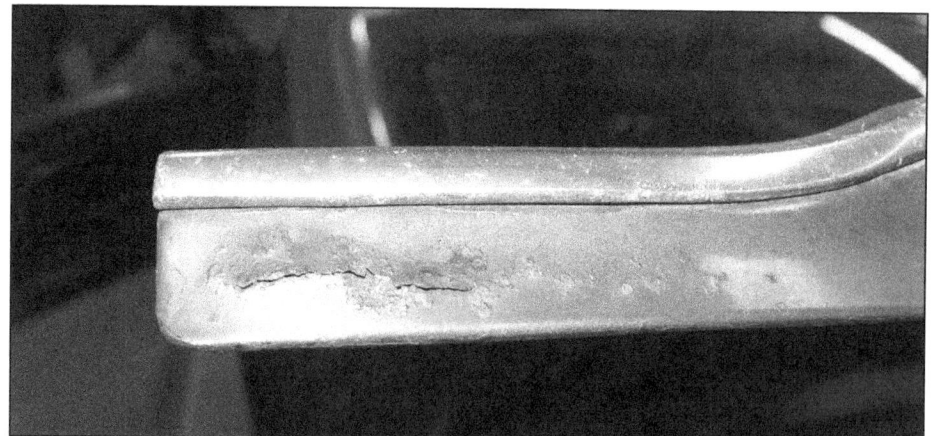

We had rust damage at both ends of the deck lid that required repair. We suspect the water got in from the holes used to mount the molding. The water just seeped under the fasteners and got between the inner and outer metal pieces. It accumulated over time to cause rust from the inside out. When we repair these areas, we seal the fastener holes better to prevent this from happening again. While not an especially complicated repair, it serves to show the generic process.

Under Hood product only comes in a 10- to 20-percent semi-gloss finish that's correct for most radiator supports, inner fender panels, hood brackets, etc. The latter is available as both an aerosol spray or in one-quart cans. Eastwood claims these products outperform other automotive paints in terms of durability, resistance to chips, scratches, UV rays, and corrosion while also being resistant to most automotive chemicals. They also offer varying degrees of surface filling capability and are formulated to more easily allow multiple coats with fast drying times and to provide a superior finish.

Rust repair areas that will be finished in the same color as the rest of the body

Trunk Lid Repair

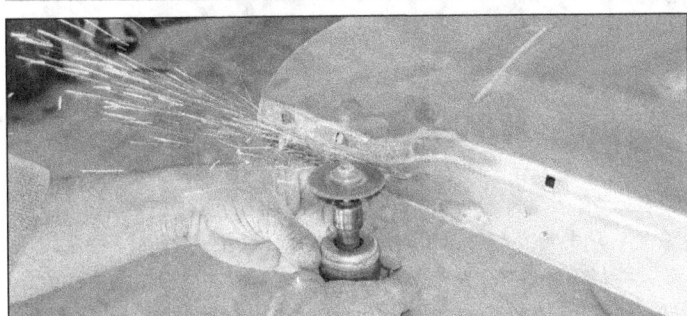

1 The repair process begins by cutting away the outer metal skin, so we can remove the rust that has formed inside. In this case, it's a thin section with the other metal close by. Many times you need to remove metal from around a cavity, such as the base of the door jamb, to get to the rust inside. This type of problem is very common when drain holes get plugged. We used a pneumatic cutoff wheel to carefully break through the outer skin without damaging the opposite side. In larger areas, such as floorpans, you can also remove the metal with plasma cutters, saws, etc.

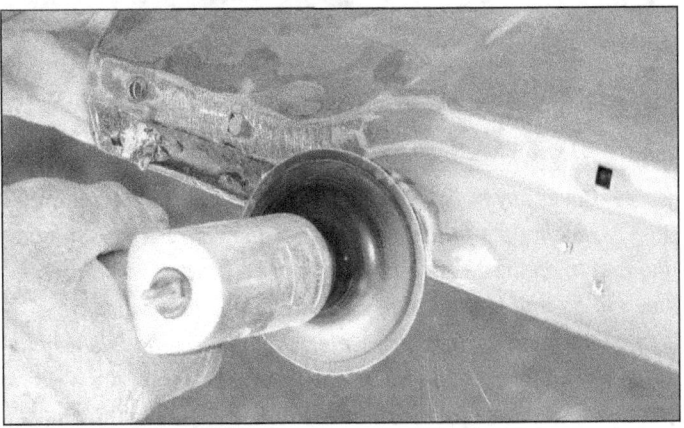

2 After the outer metal skin has been removed, grind down any rough spots, so the patch panel you install sits more flush. You also want to get down to the bare metal to get a better welding surface. In this shot, you can also see the gap between the inner and outer skins in the left fastener hole. We believe this is how the water got inside to cause the rust. We'll be sure to seal this properly later.

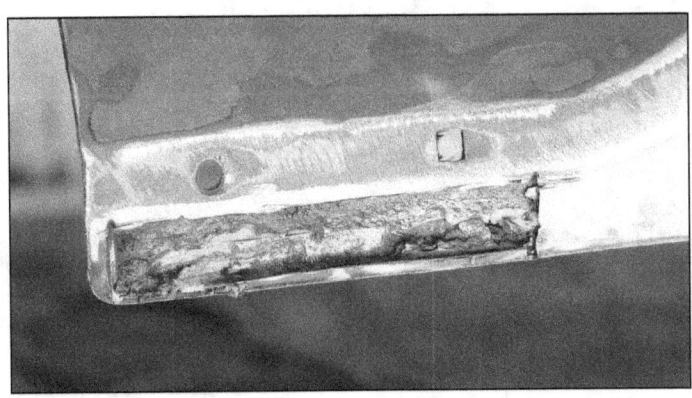

3 As you can see, we removed the majority of the loose rust, but we left some inside to prevent the metal from becoming too thin and to help support the patch we weld on. If the metal feels too weak after you have removed the loose rust, you may have to replace the other side as well. The presence of the rust is not the concern; it's the strength of the underlying metal. Even though this doesn't look that great, it actually was pretty solid and would be even more so afterward.

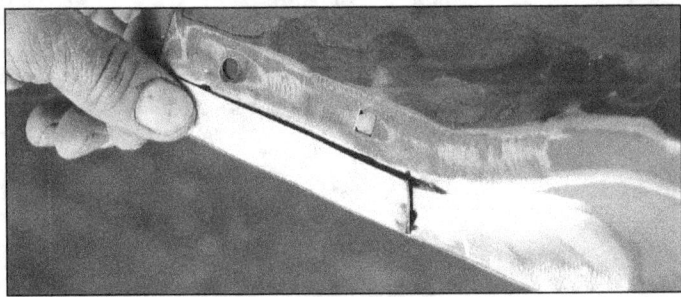

4 We cut a metal patch piece and then test fitted it to the opening. You can see we did a pretty decent job when cutting it. Accurately measure the opening and use tin snips to cut a piece of similar metal. Match the gauge/thickness and material specification as closely as possible and leave a relatively small gap between the patch and the area you're fixing. The patch piece should be as clean as possible and free of any coatings that would interfere with (or be damaged by) welding. Unfortunately, there usually isn't a good way to protect the back of such patches unless you have access to the backside after they've been welded.

Trunk Lid Repair CONTINUED

5 Cover any noticeable rust with a suitable sealer before welding the patch piece. Use a rust converter to change the rust to an inert substance that can be painted. We didn't need to do that in this case; the fact that the rust would be sealed from the air (and any water, should some find its way to it) was what we were after. Do not get any sealer on the weld joint, but otherwise apply it liberally to any areas that still have rust or are likely places for rust to form. A small brush usually works best in tight areas such as this.

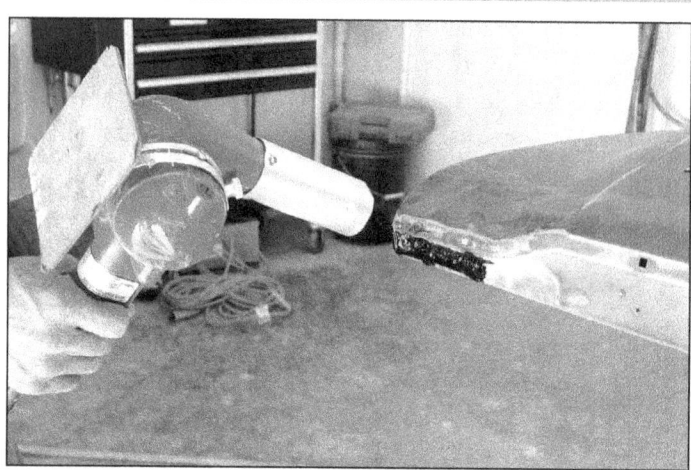

6 The heat from welding helps dry/cure the rust sealer. However, we preferred to use a heat gun to dry the rust sealer, so it didn't seep into the joint while we were welding. After applying heat, we removed any residue on the weld line prior to setting the patch piece in place. Welding such thin metal is its own challenge. It's more complicated when it has been weakened by rust. Make sure you weld all around the patch for maximum strength.

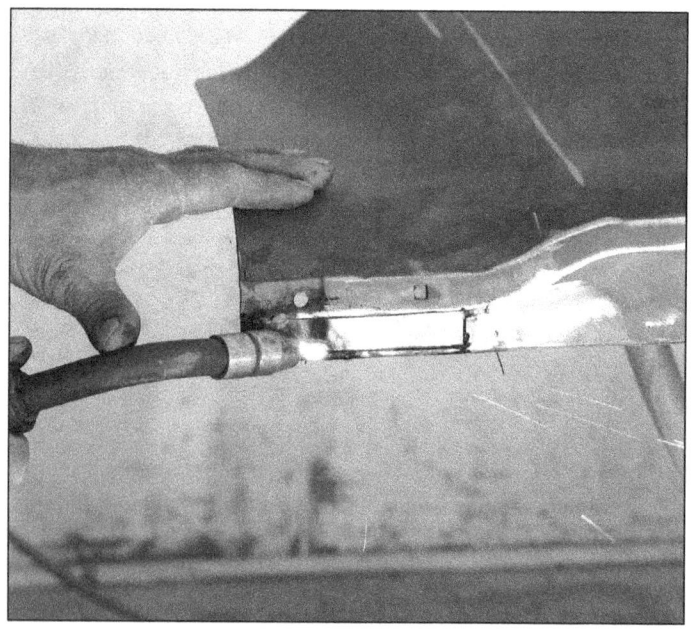

7 You generally want to tack weld the patch piece down in a few places before you do the final welding. This helps prevent shifting or distortion, and deters some heat from being transferred to the adjacent metal. When welding on relatively thin sections such as this, it is usually best to go in short bursts to prevent overheating the area. Use heat sinks and/or special gels that stop heat transfer, if necessary.

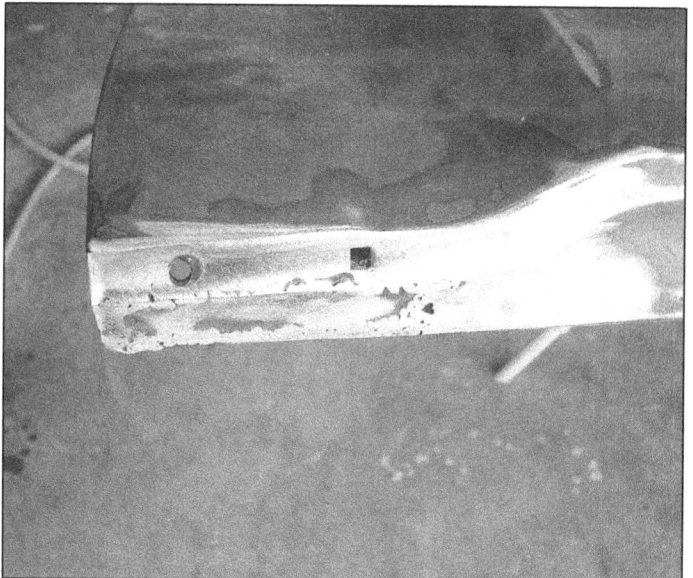

8 After welding, the surface should be ground down as smooth as possible to minimize filler use. Ideally, you would be able to grind the area and leave a smooth, bare-metal surface so you don't see the weld lines. We were not able to fully support the patch piece from behind, so it sunk into the cavity we cut. This resulted in the weld lines being above the surface of the patch to a greater extent than we'd have liked. Not a big problem, but it will need more body filler.

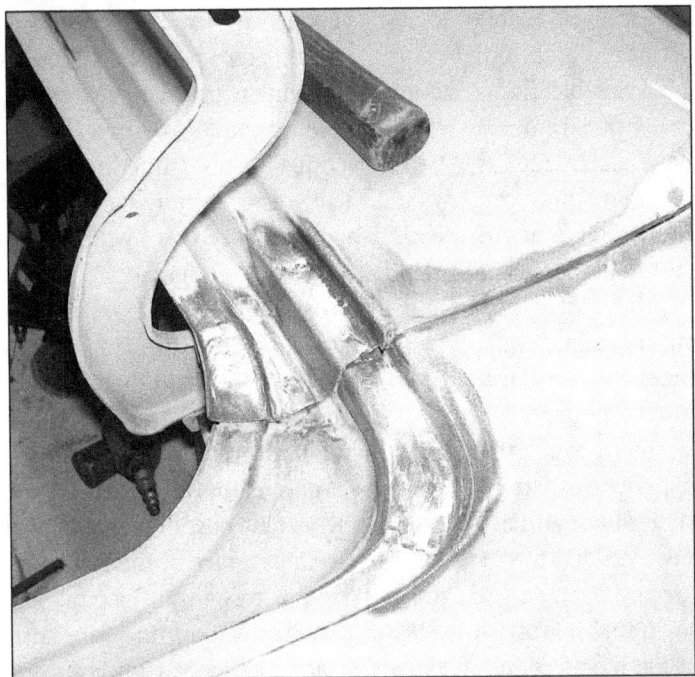

9 Here is another car that shows how complicated this type of small area fabrication can get. The pieces of metal patch had to be very specifically shaped to blend in with the surrounding metal. Some filling needs to be done here, more filling would have been needed if so much extra care was not taken in shaping the patch pieces. In the case of a show car like this one, the decision to make the repair completely smooth or not usually depends on how the area looked from the factory. You wouldn't want to make it look too smooth; it needs to look authentic rather than perfect.

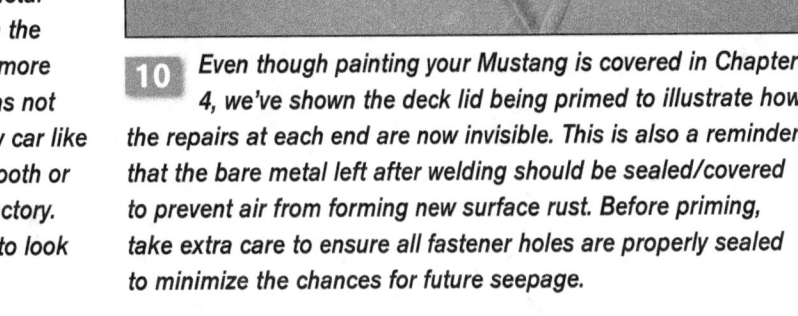

10 Even though painting your Mustang is covered in Chapter 4, we've shown the deck lid being primed to illustrate how the repairs at each end are now invisible. This is also a reminder that the bare metal left after welding should be sealed/covered to prevent air from forming new surface rust. Before priming, take extra care to ensure all fastener holes are properly sealed to minimize the chances for future seepage.

are treated the same as the rest of the body. The beauty of the repair process just outlined is that it simply removes and/or converts the rust you do not want, leaving behind a surface that accepts the same filler, primer, and paint you use on the rest of the vehicle. Of course you need to make sure you let the repaired area(s) dry/cure long enough before you apply the subsequent layers, but you need to properly prep the surface in any event. The ultimate goal is to not only remove/repair rust but also to do so in a totally invisible fashion so there is no trace of the work after the car is finished. This process restores a rusted surface so it can match adjacent, undamaged areas and thereby blend in more seamlessly with them.

Small Area Repair: Fabrication

The first category of metal repair is when repairs are to be done in a relatively small area and/or when relatively complex shapes are involved. Often, this is a more severely damaged area of the vehicle where the underlying metal is not solid. This usually requires a significant amount of skill in metalworking and fabrication. Typical instances where this comes into play are the channels around the front or rear window glass, the channel around the trunk opening, the lower edges of the doors, and areas where several panels meet. These are a few of many, many possible examples, yet they tend to have the common characteristic of being places where water collects under normal circumstances. The cowl vent/heater box area and clogged drainage passages can create yet other lists of possibilities.

Wherever this type of damage occurs, it generally involves fabrication of a relatively complicated metal patch to replace the damaged section that must be removed. We were fortunate with our 1968 to not have such problems in the most common areas mentioned, so I show this type of repair being made to the edge of the deck lid. This didn't require quite as much special fabrication of metal pieces, but the concept is the same regardless of where the work is done. Similarly blending in the patch pieces and sealing, priming, and painting them is also identical in process. The key is to restore the base metal integrity while blending with and retaining the shape of the adjacent metal. After that is done, the whole area can be treated as if it were undamaged and can be finished in normal fashion.

Large Area Repair: Panel Replacement

Often, this category of repair is at a more severely damaged area of the vehicle where the underlying metal is not solid. Over the years, many products have been developed to help resolve common problems. In body repair, there are many patch panels available for repairing rusted, damaged areas. All of the usual suspects are available: floorpans, trunk floors, quarter panels, doors skins, etc. These make such repairs much easier to complete and they can also help improve the overall result if you stick with quality parts. As I described in Chapter 2, there are different levels of quality out there, and some of the greatest differences are in replacement parts and body panels. Our 1968 only needed one replacement panel: the inner fender panel where the battery mounts. Battery acid had totally destroyed this part so we needed to cut it out and put in a new one.

Experience has shown that it is often best to see if you can get at least a couple patch panels from difference sources and compare them before you decide which one to use. If you do a lot of business with a particular shop, and they carry more than one manufacturer's products, this can happen. A good shop wants satisfied customers and realizes different customers have different needs and expectations. A customer with a daily driver may be willing to accept a less-expensive part with lower quality and authenticity than would the owner of a show car. We went with a higher-quality item, which more closely matched the original factory part and even cost even less.

The actual process of cutting out the old panel is more involved than it might first appear. We not only need to preserve the structural integrity of the vehicle, but we also want to retain the factory look to the greatest extent possible. This applies most to the appearance of the welds. We did not have access to an electric spot welder at the body shop (they are fairly expensive and not very common) and couldn't perfectly duplicate the look of the original factory spot welds. Those building show cars that are to be judged may need to find a shop with such

Inner Fender Repair

1 *This was what was left of the battery tray in our car. It was the only area in the car that had substantial corrosion. Many years ago, before the days of maintenance-free batteries, battery acid had accumulated on the tray. Over time, it ate its way through the metal of the tray and the inner fender panel. This is a lot less likely with modern batteries that do not require filling with water and are essentially sealed units if they are kept upright. Many batteries (gel cells and AGM-types, for example) can actually be mounted in any position, since they have no fluid.*

2 *This wheel-well side view shows the extensive battery acid damage to the bodywork. If it had deteriorated much more, the battery would be free to move around because nothing would be left to hold it in place. Fortunately, there are replacement panels available for this that greatly simply repairing this area.*

equipment, but for the purposes of our weekend-cruiser project or a daily-driver car, the process we used turned out to be more than acceptable.

It basically involved first removing the majority of the original panel by cutting around its periphery with a cutoff wheel and/or a reciprocating saw. The bulk of the panel was removed, leaving only thin strips containing the original spot welds. Then we ground down the spot welds individually and removed what remained of the factory panel with an air chisel. This included the small area left on the radiator support.

After the factory panel has been taken off, the next step is to prepare the area for the new panel. This involves grinding off any unwanted welds, paint, or other things that might interfere with welding. You may also need to flatten the sheetmetal with a hammer and dolly or similar tools to restore the adjacent panels to their correct shape if they became distorted by this work. The new panel also needs to have any paint or other coating material removed from the areas where it will be welded. It must also be checked for flatness and proper shape and corrected if necessary.

Then drill holes around the periphery of the part at roughly the same positions as where the factory spot welds were. You can use the original part as a guide but these do not have to be precisely in the same spot. You should have at least the same number of holes as there were spot welds. These are the spots where you manually weld on the new panel. Of course, if your shop does have a spot welder, you can skip this step and simply spot weld the panel on. In either case, you also need to drill a few small pilot holes for sheetmetal screws, which will be used to hold the panel in place while it is being welded. These should be spaced somewhat evenly around the part and not be in areas that are too obvious even though they will be filled in with weld and ground down after the panel is in place. Then weld the panel in place and grind down the welds to look like spot welds (or leave as is, if spot welded).

After the panel has been welded in place, take care of any other holes that need to be drilled. The replacement panels don't always have all the required holes, other clearance slots, etc., pre-drilled, so you may have to do this, as we did on our car. You can also take out the locating screws and fill in the holes with weld before grinding them flat. These may also require some filler or sandable primer to better disguise them if they remain too obvious after grinding.

When you are sure you will not be making any more holes or welds you should at least apply a layer of primer over any exposed metal to prevent surface rust from forming. Whether or not you finish the repair in terms of painting depends on where the panel is. If it will be painted body color then it should be painted with the rest of the body. In our case, we simply waited

3 The replacement we used is a close match to the factory piece. The new piece has the metal that the original part is missing. The first things you notice are the extra holes on the new part. These maximize the interchangeability of the part (a single part fits multiple cars) and also help better duplicate the crash behavior of the part. At least most of the holes are the right shape, even if there are extras. The original also has fewer stretch lines on the flat areas.

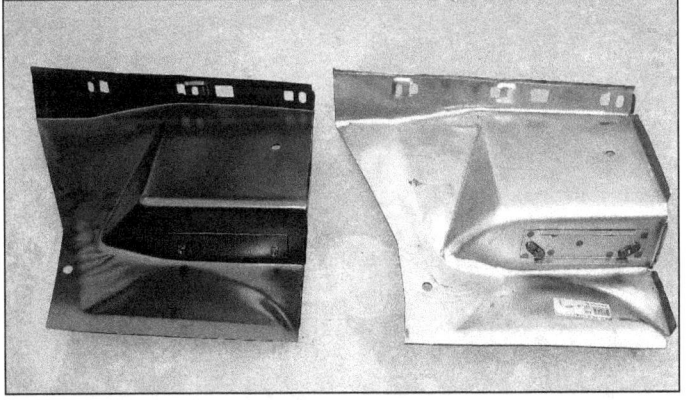

4 A comparison of the higher-quality part we used (on the left) with a similar, lower-quality part (right) reveals several differences. The most obvious is that our part was covered in "e-coat" to prevent rust; the other part was bare metal. You can also see the difference in the type of fasteners used for the bolts that hold the battery tray in place. Our part used a simpler method. It also had sharper creases and corners, in general. This indicates the other part was made on dies that are more worn out.

Inner Fender Repair CONTINUED

5 Our part had much cleaner flanges than the lower-quality part. Notice how the other part is more wrinkled and distorted; this certainly wouldn't have helped with installation. We would have had to take extra time to flatten these areas down for welding and to make them fit properly. You can also see the part still has machine oil residue on it. This was used in the die to prevent galling, but means we would have had to clean the part before using it or the welds and/or paint might not hold.

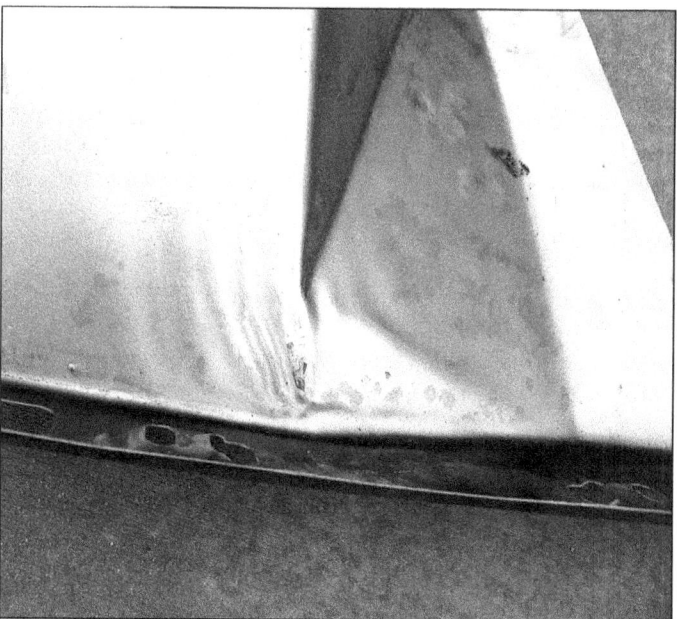

6 This shot also shows how poorly made the other part is. There are several places where the metal has been distorted similar to what you see here, and you can also better see the residue left on the metal and the inconsistencies in the finish. What's ironic is that this part actually would have ended up costing more than the better part we used.

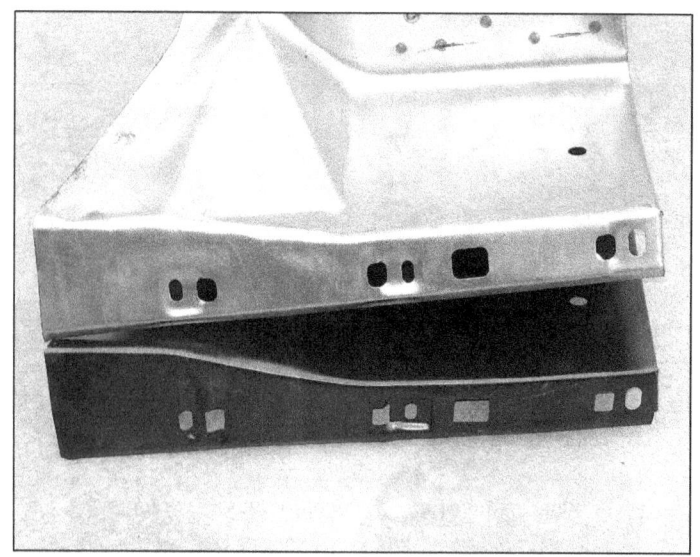

7 A comparison of the holes shows some pretty significant differences as well. The lower part has more-squared-off holes like the factory part; the holes in the upper part are more rounded. The depressions for the clips that hold the retaining nuts are also creased more sharply in the better piece. Again, the lower-quality part has more-rounded edges, which indicates the manufacturing dies were wearing out.

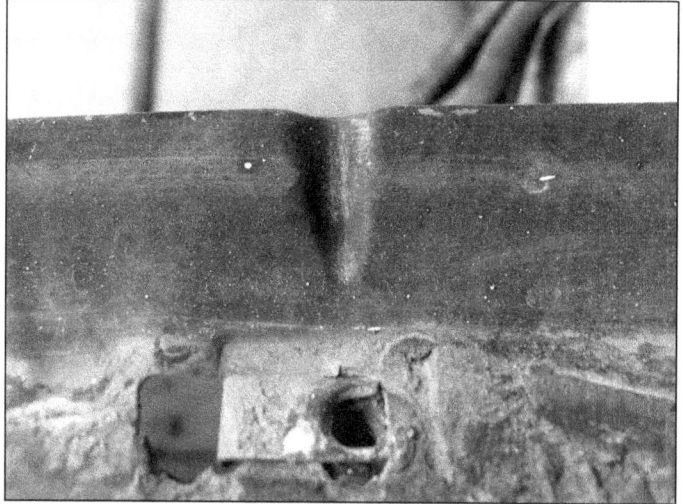

8 Indentations, such as these, were present in the original factory panel but not in either replacement panel. These are strategically placed to serve a very specific purpose: They cause the fender to crush/crumple in a very specific way in a crash. Basically, they help the car absorb the energy of a crash and better protect the occupants. They also prove authenticity because it's rare that replacement panel manufacturers incur the cost to include them.

9 Use a cutoff wheel and/or reciprocating saw to cut the original panel. The cuts must be made so enough material remains to securely weld the new part. Usually, leaving about an inch or so from the edge in all areas ensures you don't take off too much metal. Do not cut the underlying panel or the original welds. The new panel is welded over the adjacent factory panels, just as the original was. Remove the old panel that's being replaced without damaging these others, if possible.

10 The original panel is removed when it has been cut all the way around its periphery. You will recognize how interdependent the various body panels are when a piece like this is taken out. The radiator support panel is now mostly unsupported along its side and is free to move around with surprisingly little pressure. Be careful not to bend it by mistake.

11 This is another view showing how the cuts were made so they did not go into the underlying panels attached to the removed piece. Only the panel that was being replaced was cut. You can see the shock tower panel edge in front of what's left of the panel we took out. You can also see we purposely left material behind the frame rail and radiator support.

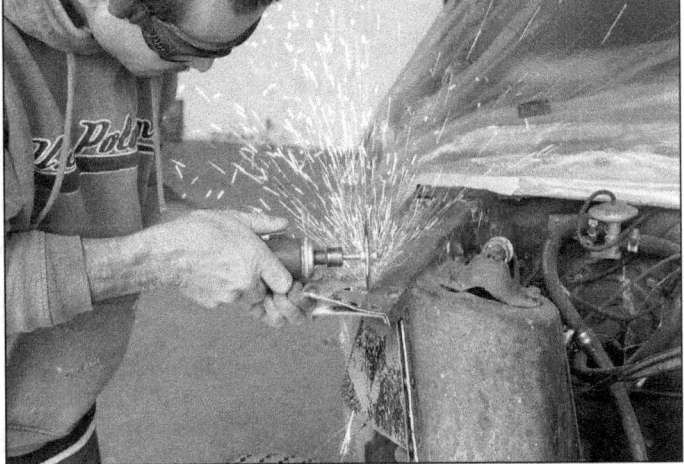

12 The remaining part of the original panel that overlaps at the top is the place to start grinding out the original spot welds. Remove just enough metal to pry off the remnant of the original panel, as shown. It was important to not damage the panel underneath because we will weld the replacement panel to it. You can use special drill bits that are essentially flat-faced to remove the weld without taking away too much of the lower panel. There are different sizes available to match different spot welds. Use your preferred method, but in any case the goal is to remove only the welds.

Inner Fender Repair CONTINUED

13 Spot welds applied along the remainder of the original panel were ground down with an impact chisel, to ease removal of the old panel. Place the point of the chisel directly in line with where the spot weld was and also tilt it at an angle to minimize distortion of the panel that remains in place. It's very important that the underlying panel does not get torn or otherwise damaged. When the residue of the original panel is being removed, break the spot welds only.

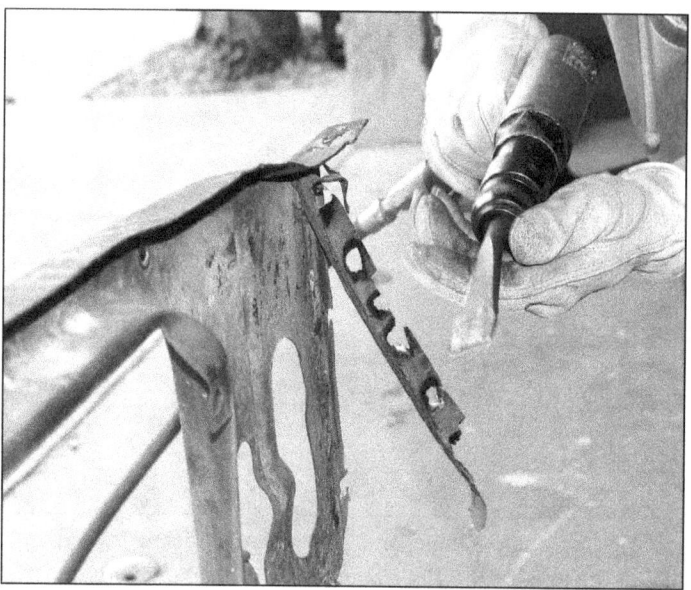

14 Use the same process at the radiator support, but it will take a little extra care because it isn't as secure and moves around. When working with a panel that no longer is adequately supported, brace it from behind or at least have someone else help you hold it while you grind away the welds and/or use the impact chisel to remove what's left from the panel to be replaced. Some minor damage is inevitable.

15 With the remains of the panel completely removed, you can grind away any excess residue. Make sure the surfaces you are welding are flat and clean. Also verify that there are no bumps, which will prevent the replacement panel from fitting properly. A sanding disc similar to that shown is likely the best way to go.

16 To restore the shape of the metal on the car for welding, you may need to use a hammer and dolly. The dolly is held behind the metal to be shaped while the hammer blows are applied from the front. Use a flat-faced hammer when trying to smooth a straight surface. There are many different types of hammers and dollies to suit different needs.

BODY MAKES BEAUTIFUL

17 Drill the holes for the new panel near the original spot welds. You don't need to be precisely over the old spot welds because you are making new welds with a different technique, so you want to make it look as similar as possible. You also need to grind off any coating in the area around each hole to ensure the best possible weld. Set the replacement panel in place and secure it with a few sheetmetal screws to hold it steady. Make sure everything is properly lined up first.

18 Make a weld at each hole to simulate a spot weld. After all the welds have been laid down, grind each one flush with the panel. Don't worry about minor pinholes or other visual defects as long as they have no functional effect. As long as the weld penetration was sufficient there should be plenty of strength to hold everything together. While this approach may not perfectly replicate the look of a spot weld, it does a pretty decent job for a lot less cost. The main thing is that the welds are strong.

19 Often replacement panels do not include all of the holes on an original panel. Therefore, you may have to drill holes in the replacement panel to match the original. Again, this is mainly a matter of parts interchangeability. The panel is used for multiple applications and defaults to not having holes where some might be needed for certain vehicles. To prevent rust from occurring at these drilled holes, make sure you seal the bare metal edges.

20 Properly lining up the replacement panel on the frame or mounting brackets is critical. Therefore, make sure the panels are also properly located. We ensured that the radiator support was properly located on the new panel before we welded the two together. If you fail to properly align these components, fenders and other parts can be difficult if not impossible to install later on. This is especially true with parts and panels that locate critical items.

until we painted the underhood area and also applied the undercoating to the wheelhouse side.

Some areas can also benefit from the application of additional sealants or compounds intended to keep moisture from accumulating. Be wary of products that may clog drainage holes or passages and also be sure that any bare metal is covered with at least a sealer. Pay particular attention to where two panels meet; the mating line can often act as a path for water to wick to other areas. Even when a fastener helps clamp the two panels together, their bare edges should still be sealed somehow. A dab of the Rust Encapsulator or some other form of sealant can go a long way toward preventing rust from starting underneath a fastener joint or deep in some unseen recess behind a panel. The key is to ensure you have a continuous barrier between any bare metal and the air.

Dent and Ding Repair

Although the repair of dents and dings is more similar to repair of minor/surface rust, I saved it for the end of the chapter because it is the proper lead-in to Chapter 4 on paint.

With a dent or ding you have a solid foundation to work with, as was the case with minor/surface rust. The difference is that instead of being concerned about the removal of rust or corrosion, you're more concerned about being able to restore the area to the correct shape and finish. It's more a matter of correcting a physical/dimensional problem than it is of correcting a chemical/material problem. The bottom line is that you have to move metal back into a very specific shape. The goal is to get the metal close enough to the final desired shape so that you can then use as little body filler as possible to finish the job before painting. In cases where the damage is too great, that may not be possible, you may end up having to replace the panel if it's too badly distorted or torn. For the most part, the repair is a matter of access and finesse. You need the correct access to be able to properly manipulate the metal back into shape, and the finesse to get it as close as possible to the final form.

It really helps if you have access to both sides of a panel that needs to be repaired. You can apply pressure with various tools to push the panel back to the desired shape. Tools such as special hammers, dollies, spoons, etc., can help return

Inner Fender Repair CONTINUED

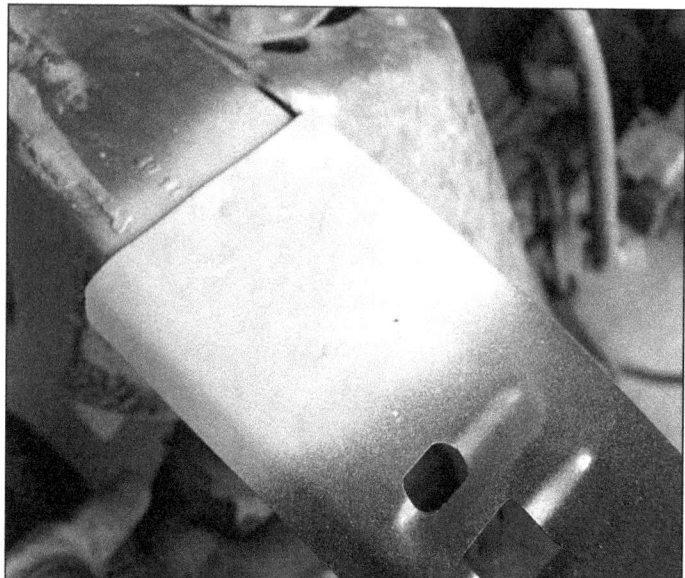

21 *After all welds have been made, coat all exposed bare-metal surfaces with primer or another suitable sealer to prevent surface rust. Primer helps to highlight the appearance of the welds. You could also grind the weld smooth and use a sandable primer to make them virtually disappear. This would not be authentic looking, of course, but some may prefer a more uniform and smooth appearance for certain projects or situations.*

Here is the replacement panel installed solidly in place prior to priming and painting. All of the welds have been ground down and made flush. All screws have been removed and their holes welded, if necessary. We will clean the whole underhood area later so, at this point, we just sealed any areas that required it and then applied a coat of primer.

the metal to the shape you want. There is a degree of skill involved, however, to cold work the metal back into shape. It's not just a matter of banging on it until it looks better. Good body people can get a better result in less time with less effort due to their knowledge of specific techniques to make the metal behave the way they want. If you are not aware of these techniques, read up on them or get some advice from someone who's done the type of repair work you want to try.

Bodywork is one of the areas where it usually pays to have a pro do the job if you haven't tried to do it before. It usually ends up saving time and expense. This is especially true if you don't have access to both sides of the damaged area; you would likely have to use a stud welder and puller or a similar type of equipment to pull the metal from the front rather than being able to push it from behind. This takes even more skill and special equipment because the studs must be applied very carefully to hold the metal and they must also be carefully pulled using a slide hammer. After the pulling has been completed, the studs must be ground off and the area where they were attached must be smoothed. It's an extra, but necessary, step.

Repairing dents and dings is mainly a matter of carefully manipulating the damaged metal back to the desired shape so that it can then be filled and sanded as little as possible prior to being primed and otherwise prepped for painting. Here, less truly is more in terms of getting the desired shape with minimal effort and use of body filler and or other buildup. (Proper application of body filler and other steps involved in preparation for painting are shown in Chapter 4.)

Apply pressure from behind to repair a dent like this. It can be done with specially shaped hammers and/or dollies, which are used to work the metal back to the desired shape. If easy access is impossible, so-called dentless repair tools can be inserted though holes made in adjacent panels. These are then carefully pushed against the damaged area and turned to change the shape back to what it was. This process can yield amazingly good results. But remember, this is a skill acquired by professional body shop workers with years of practice. Therefore, you should have realistic expectations for your results. The only real downside is the need to make, and then seal, the access holes after the repair has been made. In some cases, there may be no need to use body filler or paint.

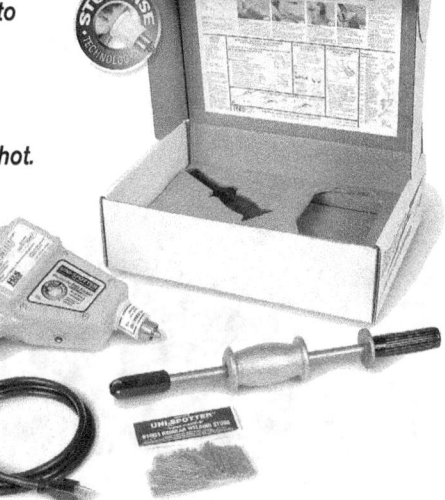

This is one example of a stud welding kit, which was manufactured by H&S Auto Shot. The operation and use is surprisingly simple. You basically load the stud into the gun and then press the gun against where you want the stud. Press the trigger and the stud is welded. Of course, there must be proper preparation of the surface and there is a certain knack to making sure the studs take hold, but it's pretty easy to figure out. The slide hammer grips the stud, and the weight on the slide hammer is moved rapidly to apply force to the stud. It's best to use a larger number of stud/points and lower force levels than it is to pull everything out with a few blows. This approach can greatly reduce the amount of body filler required.

CHAPTER 4

PAINTING YOUR MUSTANG

While a rusted-out area or a large dent is easier to see from a distance, the final steps of the paint process are just as important when you get up close. The validity of that depends on the level of restoration project you are undertaking. All of the procedures are relatively time-intensive. While taking more time may not always give you better results, not taking enough time to do steps carefully and correctly produces poor results.

The requirements and the expected quality level for a daily-driver vehicle are much different than the criteria used to evaluate a show car. On a show car, this is probably the area where the largest portion of the restoration budget is spent. A top-quality paint job simply takes lots of time. I'll highlight what's involved in painting your Mustang, but I cannot delve into the minute details of every step or discuss some of the more exotic processes that may come into play on the higher end of the scale. Again, our focus is on a weekend-cruiser project with a near- but not-quite-show-quality appearance. I touch on a few things that can make a good paint job better but can't get into the sky-is-the-limit types of things needed for a national show winner or a high-end auction.

Perhaps the best reason to have a professional paint your car, instead of doing it yourself, is that the pro has a pretty decent paint booth like this one. It controls temperature, humidity, and overspray, while keeping contaminants away from your freshly painted surface. Few can duplicate these advantages in a garage or similar home-based setting. The skill of experienced technicians and their premium-quality equipment and materials are rarely duplicated in a non-professional setting. You pay more up front for a professional paint job, but you likely end up saving money in the long run and have a far greater chance of getting the high-quality result you're looking for.

Decision Time: Paint It Yourself or Go to a Professional?

Paint and bodywork are as much an art as a science. And many people are not artistically inclined. Sure, the actual processes of preparing the surface and applying the paint can be relatively straightforward, but knowing what to do and being able to do it well are two different things. It's a matter of feel as much as it is one of knowledge. You can read the can of body filler or paint and understand what it says, but that doesn't mean things will turn out well, especially if you're working under challenging conditions. Doing any restoration or repair work requires a clean and spacious area that is at least partially isolated from the elements.

Painting adds even more requirements in terms of temperature, humidity, and freedom from dust. You also have to worry about overspray, noise, odors, etc., disturbing any close neighbors. Unless you are doing a relatively small job on a small area of a daily driver, you probably should have a professional do the job and use the information provided here to help decide what level you want to take the job to. Many have tried to save a few bucks by doing a paint job themselves, and found they ended up spending more when they had to take it to a paint shop to fix the mess they made. There surely are enthusiasts who have a proper location and the skill to do a decent job themselves, but these few are clearly a minority even if they have the necessary equipment to do professional level of work. The risks are pretty high.

It may be feasible for you to repair a small dent, ding, or rusty area on a daily driver. But you need to have the tools and skills to perform a professional-grade job, or the results will be of lesser quality. You will likely perform a spray-can-based paint job, and this can save some money if you are able to make the affected area blend in well and look the way you want it to. If you have a decent assortment of sanding/filing tools or products and perhaps even an air compressor and a spray gun, then so much the better. Still, it comes down to ability and feel to make the best of whatever you have. If you need to weld in a panel, then the expertise and equipment required takes another leap.

Still, many people can fix a small area if they take the time to practice and acquire the skill/feel necessary to make the end product look good enough. But it's pretty hard to make such a repair blend in well with the rest of the paint in the adjacent areas, especially if the car is older and the paint has faded a bit. Similarly, matching the exact appearance of a metallic, pearl, candy, or other special paints is also an issue no matter who is doing the work. If you're limited to spray cans or a pre-mixed paint then your options are few. You won't be able to custom mix the paint to be a closer match to what's on your car now. You may only be able to match what the original factory color was and, if you're lucky, the appearance of the flake or pearl.

I don't recommend doing paint work yourself unless you have prior experience and a certain degree of skill/feel and knowledge; have a proper place to do it; have at least some of the necessary equipment; and are only working on a relatively small, solid (not rusted-through) area on a (hopefully) solid-color car that hasn't faded too much. Oh, and you better set some additional time aside, especially if you have to take things apart. The bottom line is professionals should handle substantial paintwork or spraying the entire car. For the at-home mechanic, unless you have semi-professional skills and the right equipment, it usually isn't worth the risk. Going to a professional paint shop costs more up front, but less than paying them to fix a botched job. They can discuss and give advice on the best way to go for your particular project.

A good paint shop has a relatively new spray booth that controls the temperature well, contains dust and overspray, and possibly even has other features to reduce drying time and provide a better finish. You won't be putting one of these in your garage. Likewise, a good paint shop has a computerized paint mixing system that allows paint to be custom mixed to better match the rest of the car or a specific color of your choice. Batch-to-batch variability is greatly reduced, thus ensuring a more uniform appearance on your vehicle. Systems such as these rely on precise weighing of individual paint pigments, as opposed to the potentially random purchase of different paint lots at the retail level. Last, the spray guns, tools, chemicals, materials, and equipment in general are of a higher grade than all but the best-heeled consumers would be able to match, even if they knew how to use it all properly. A good paint shop has workers with superior talent who are able to get it right the first time (most of the time).

In the vast majority of cases where a large area or the whole car is to be painted, it simply makes more sense to take the car to a well-known and well-respected paint shop rather than do the work yourself. Even on a daily-driver or weekend-cruiser project, where there is an element of keeping costs more moderate, this generally is the best solution. On a high-end show car, you want to find the best shop that you can afford because the value of the vehicle, in terms of judging and/or resale, will be significantly affected by the quality of the paintwork. When you are going for the highest level of quality you need the skill, knowledge, and equipment of a good shop.

CHAPTER 4

Final Surface Preparation: Using Body Fillers

In Chapter 3, I discussed how to repair rusted and damaged body panels prior to their final surface preparation and painting. The goal was to restore a solid, relatively smooth surface to work with. High-build/sandable primers and other coatings or sealers sometimes provide the necessary level of smoothness required prior to painting, but this is generally the case for less visible areas, such as under the car or underhood. Larger areas such as main body panels, the hood, trunk lid, etc., generally need additional finishing. This requires using body filler to mask any remaining surface irregularities and to achieve the final desired shape of the panel.

There are different types of body fillers for different stages of the process, but I will discuss only the regular filler used to cover the damaged area and the glazing/spot putty skim coat that is used to fill in smaller imperfections like pinholes. I will only deal with two-part so-called plastic body fillers that are mixed just prior to application. (I will not get into more exotic fillers such as lead, which require heating with a torch. The skill required with these techniques and materials is beyond what most shops are capable of; their use is gradually becoming a lost art.)

While some may say the use of lead and similar technologies provides a superior result, this has become less true as the technology of conventional fillers has improved. When you consider the potential toxicity of working with lead, plus the additional safety considerations and equipment involved, there generally isn't a compelling argument to use it for anything but authenticity. That's not likely to be a concern with first-generation Mustangs.

After the underlying material (metal or otherwise) is as close to the final shape

Body Filler Application

1 Before applying body filler, metal in the damaged area needs to be worked as close to its final shape as possible. As noted in Chapter 3, there are many different of tools that can apply pressure from behind the panel and bring it close to the final shape. If it's possible to access the panel and area from behind, there are also things like stud welders, slide hammers, picks, and so forth to pull the area into shape from the front side.

2 After the metal has been worked into the final desired shape, it must be ground or sanded to abrade the surface and then cleaned to remove any dust or other residue. This helps ensure proper adhesion of the filler to the metal body panels. The paint on the adjacent metal should be "feathered" to provide a gradual transition between the areas. Make sure the area is fully dry before proceeding.

3 The body filler must first be mixed to activate the hardening process. When mixed, you have limited time to apply the filler, so you need to work fast. All layers should be relatively thin, but the first layer should also be applied with firm pressure to push the filler into the surface irregularities. The filler should be applied in overlapping layers with smooth, constant strokes. Apply as little filler as possible to cover the damaged area and fill in all irregularities. Applying too much is a waste of time and material because you just have to remove it anyway.

PAINTING YOUR MUSTANG

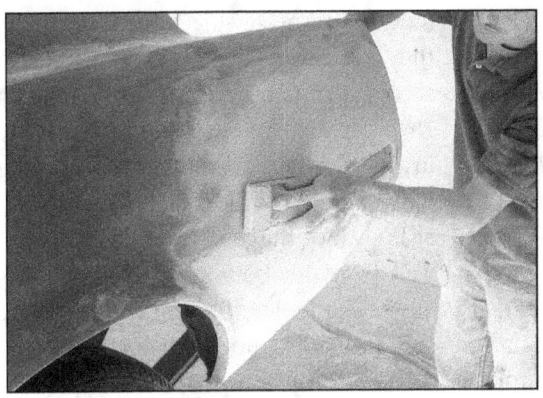

4 *After allowing the filler to fully dry/harden (usually about 15 to 20 minutes, depending on conditions), it can be sanded to shape using a series of progressively finer-grit abrasive sheets. The initial sanding should remove material quickly, but not too much. In the latter stages, you should achieve the desired final shape and surface smoothness, and all visible scratches from the sanding should virtually disappear. A thin coat of special glazing/spot putty is used as a top layer before priming.*

5 *Those with some experience and a feel for doing bodywork can often use a handheld sander to make removal of the filler easier and quicker. Take great care to not remove too much material; this equipment can easily remove too much. In that case, reapply filler and repeat the sanding step more carefully.*

6 *After sanding is complete and the necessary amount of filler has been removed, the area often looks stratified from the removed layers of paint and filler. These different-colored layers should all be relatively thin and smooth. You shouldn't feel any edges, scratches, or other imperfections. The surface should also be free from any waviness or other localized unevenness.*

body filler on a suitable pallet. When mixed, you must work fast because the filler begins to harden as soon as the components meet. Use a putty spreader to apply the first layer of the filler to the area being worked on. Use firm pressure for the initial layer to help force the filler into the surface. Make all layers thin and don't use any more filler than is necessary; you'll only have to sand it off later.

Drying time is about 20 minutes or so, depending upon temperature, humidity, and the specific mixture of the filler. Make sure the filler is fully hard and dry.

Choose a sanding block that's suitable for the size and shape of the area being repaired and attach a 40-grit abrasive sheet. Sand the area to a rough approximation of the final shape. With care you can also use a handheld rotary sander at this stage, again using 40-grit for the disc. You are simply trying to remove material quickly; you do not want to remove too much or you'll have a low spot, which will require more filler. Just take it slow and remove only enough filler to yield the shape you want; you want it just a bit larger than the final shape.

Change the sanding sheet/disc to 80-grit to take the area down to the final shape and to remove the deepest surface scratches. You want the surface to be smooth and level, with a gradual transition to the surrounding areas (a feathered edge).

Next, change the abrasive sheet to 180-grit and lightly sand to remove visible scratches and to provide a smooth transition to the surrounding painted areas. At this point, you should be working with a hand-held sanding block only and should make sure there is minimal filler thickness at the edges of the repair area. You do not want filler on top of the surrounding paint if you can help it; you want the filler and the paint to be level.

as possible, clean it before applying any type of body filler. First wash the area with soapy water, and then thoroughly dry it with lint-free towels and/or compressed air. Next wipe down the area with a suitable solvent remover to eliminate any unwanted residue, such as oily films, adhesives, etc., Then sand the area with a relatively rough (40–80 grit) abrasive to provide a better surface for the filler to adhere to.

You should remove all paint within 1 or 2 inches of the damaged area to be filled. Then mix the components of the

Mix and apply a thin layer of a suitable glazing/spot putty over the entire repair area, making sure to overlap onto the adjacent painted areas. Allow this skim coat to fully dry (about 15 minutes) and then use a 180-grit sheet on the sanding block to sand the area until it is level. It is critical to keep the block flat to the surface and apply only very light pressure, to avoid removing too much material.

Repeat this step, using a 320-grit sheet to remove any remaining visible scratches. Finer-grit sheets can be used as well, but there really isn't much point beyond 400-grit or so because you want a somewhat rough surface for the primer to grip. The main objective is to remove scratches and make it smooth.

After the areas to be filled have been sanded smooth to their final shapes, a coat of primer is usually applied. This not only seals any exposed metal from the atmosphere, and prevents new surface rust, but it also helps reveal any flaws that were missed. Many defects won't be obvious until the whole car is covered in primer; the patchwork of body filler and paint tends to mask things somewhat.

There are multiple types of primer, ranging from epoxy-based primers to those formulated for multiple layers to mask small imperfections. The type to use depends on the situation and is one of those things that an experienced shop can provide guidance on. In general, you want to minimize the total thickness of the primer and paint coats, within reason. Up to a point, a good primer can lessen the amount of sanding needed, but a thick application of primer should never be used as a way to mask poor surface preparation.

Each coat of primer should be sanded (blocked) before the next coat or any topcoat is applied. This is where the real difference is made in the final appearance. Blocking is a very time-consuming process because you're establishing the final surface/shape for painting. The cost of your paint job is almost always directly related to the amount of blocking. A daily driver will have minimal blocking, but a show car often has considerable blocking to be nearly perfect. A weekend cruiser like ours can often approach the show-car level but usually stops short of it. The difference is the show-car paint job means spending a lot of time to remove the smallest flaws, whereas the weekend-cruiser project accepts that there is a point of diminishing returns (and increasing costs). From a couple of feet away, nobody will know the difference.

For a show car that will be judged or that is to be sold at a national auction, even this level is not high enough. Only the best will do and the cost of getting there can be significantly higher than for a weekend-cruiser project, in most cases. In either case, a common approach is to apply a color coat to door jambs, hood, and deck lid openings, etc., before final blocking to help make a smoother visual transition around these areas and to prevent excessive build up of paint. While these areas are only visible on occasion, and they generally are only repaired if there was substantial damage, it is still beneficial to paint them early to facilitate masking off the main areas.

Another aspect of the blocking process is that parts that need to line up with the main body panels should be installed prior to the blocking process. This primarily applies to doors where there are character lines that run from the door panel to the quarter panel, etc. Make sure that when you are blocking everything the lines are true to each other, even across different panels and components. This is not as critical with the deck lid or the hood; they have enough adjustability built in to compensate for most misalignment.

Fenders and other exterior panels, however, should be installed prior to blocking to make sure things line up. If they need to be removed again to gain access to certain areas for paint, you can always realign things after painting. You just need to ensure you get the blocking right so it is possible for things to line up again. All of the main exterior panels, as well as smaller bolt-on parts, should ideally be painted during the same painting session to minimize color variation. Again, a shop should have a large paint booth, and this should have enough room for the car and more parts at the same time. The shop should also have a computerized paint mixing system for matching paint to any car.

A pro painter applies the primer and paint consistently yet still knows how to make minor adjustments to compensate for any problems that may arise. Even something as seemingly simple as masking the car off before applying the color coats can involve some special tricks. Pro painters can improve the appearance of the final product by more fully hiding blend lines and minimizing the potential for overspray.

Painting Basics

I cannot get into the specific details of how any particular car should be painted because that depends far too much on the condition of the car, budget, location, equipment available, materials used, skill of the painter, and desired result. These, again, are the main things to consider when choosing a shop to do the paint and/or body work for you. The shop will work with you to decide the details of how the car gets painted. I'll share some of the information from our project to hopefully inform your discussion with the shop and lead to a better result.

Our task was relatively easy because we did not completely strip

Spray Priming and Painting Parts

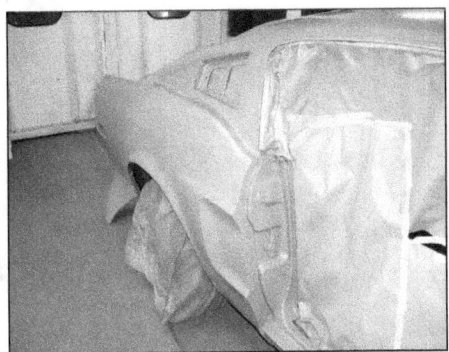

1 After the primer is applied, the fruits of your labor should become more obvious. The primer coats help mask any minor imperfections (pinholes, scratches, etc.) that may have remained, and also help reveal where additional sanding is needed to get the desired final shape. This is part of the blocking process for final surface prep.

2 Smaller, bolt-on parts that will also be painted body color must be similarly prepared. While there should be considerably less need for any repair/filling, there may still be a need to use some of the spot putty to hide minor imperfections. The same process of gradually sanding down the material that's applied is used before the part is wiped/blown clean.

3 The bolt-on components are also primed before painting. There's no reason to use more than a coat or two because the primer should not be built up to any degree. Metal parts should be primed and/or sealed all over to prevent rust. Areas that are visible next to body color panels need to be painted body color as well. However, these parts are painted off the car for better coverage of the part and better access to the necessary areas of the car body. Try to use the same paint batch for painting adjacent pieces for a better match.

4 Here, we see where our trunk lid repair has been filled in to hide the imperfections left from our metal repair. Smaller areas are treated essentially the same as larger ones, except that properly positioning of the sanding block is more difficult. If the pressure is not evenly applied to the block, it often creates uneven surfaces. Slower, flat strokes are necessary for flat, even surfaces.

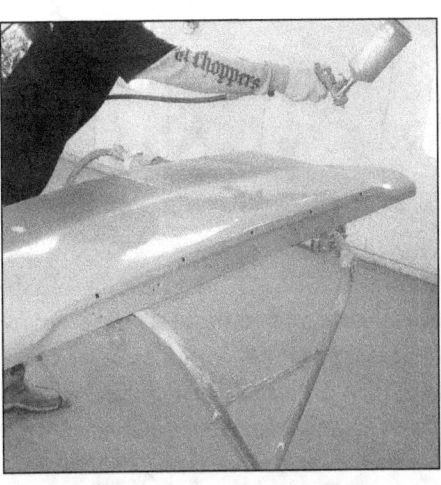

5 Larger panels, such as trunk lid, hood, and doors, are generally removed from the car and prepped, due to issues of access and ease. The same sanding and priming procedures apply, although the backside of these pieces are usually also painted body color. Thus, these parts require more care than some of the smaller parts.

6 Proper prep is important for badges or emblems because the fasteners pass through the panel from the outside and are exposed to the elements. These holes must be adequately sealed to prevent water from entering the panel and rust forming between the inner and outer skins. We repaired this deck lid on both corners due to this problem and don't want the problem to recur. We applied sealer internally. Another way to help ensure this is to make sure you use an appropriate sealer before applying the primer coats. Only the hole on the right required this; the hole on the left is only internal.

Sanding and Painting the Body

1 A color coat is commonly applied to the door jambs and other openings on the body (hood, trunk, etc.). These areas are not as visible and will not be blocked due to their more complex shapes. It is also preferable they have color applied to help with subsequent masking and blending as the larger, more visible areas get blocked and painted.

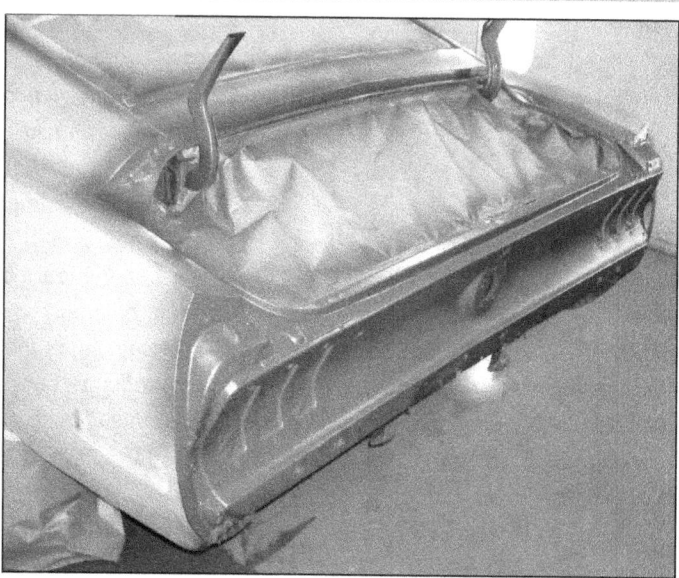

2 This trunk lid opening area shows how some areas get sprayed with color because it's difficult to block their more complex shapes. In this area, many of the blend lines are covered by the installation of other components such as the fender ends caps, the trunk seal, etc. The larger, visible area can be hand-sanded to remove any minor imperfections between coats.

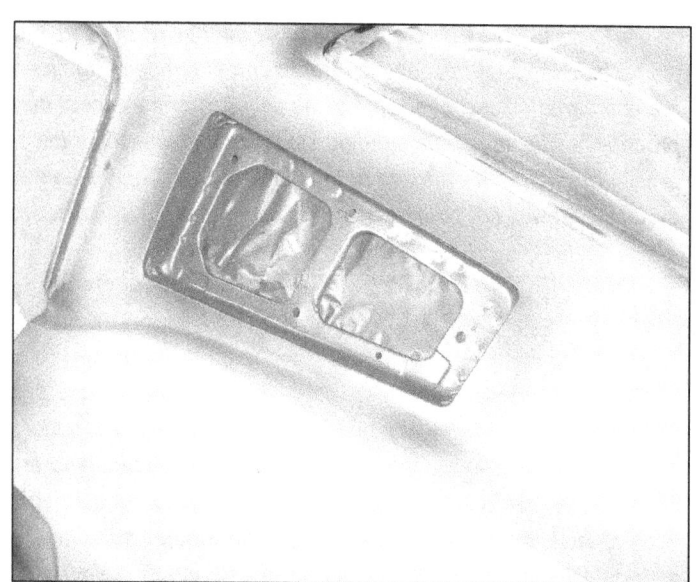

3 Some areas, such as these quarter panel vents, require greater care when masking to prevent overspray from getting into the interior or other unwanted areas. This area will be almost completely hidden when the car is reassembled, but applying color now ensures the edges of the opening are fully covered and blend well with all of the surrounding areas.

4 After the selective application of color to certain areas, inspect the main sections that will receive color for any remaining imperfections. These are usually just pinholes that developed as the primer dried, scratches from the sanding, runs/sags that were removed, or areas that simply didn't properly blend in with the rest of the panel. Use small amounts of glazing/spot putty to fix these.

PAINTING YOUR MUSTANG

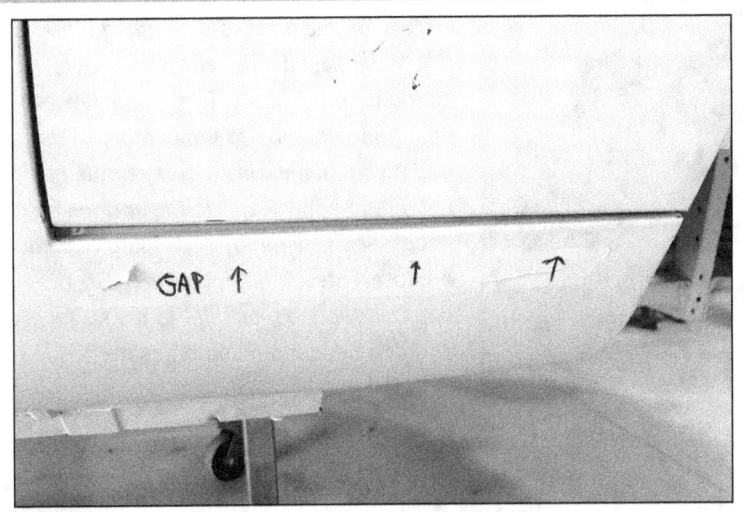

5 The vehicle must now be re-masked for painting. This involves partially covering areas that have already been color sprayed. Some surface areas need to show to make a more gradual, less-visible transition to the main panels. The edges of the tape generally lie on areas that are completely covered when other components and/or weather stripping are installed. The vehicle must also be masked to prevent overspray.

6 Prior to the blocking process, the doors and any other panels/parts that have to blend in with the feature lines on the side of the car are usually installed. The best possible alignment between the adjacent parts is maintained. This is generally not necessary with the hood, deck lid, and fenders if they have sufficient adjustment capability and only have a straight-line gap to consider. Mounting the doors also helps reduce the amount of masking needed to prevent unwanted intrusion of overspray. Before painting, adjust the door gaps to avoid damaging the final finish. Also this provides a better visual reference for comparison while blocking.

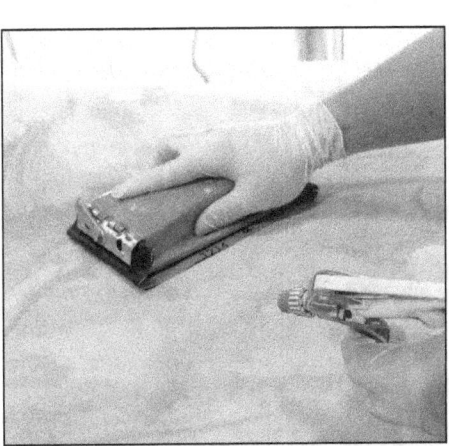

7 The main blocking/sanding process can now be completed. Sand blocks and other equipment are used to carefully sand larger sections to get the smoothest, straightest surface possible. The key is to go slow, use smooth strokes and to keep the sanding device flat on the surface. Additional coats of primer are often applied to build up some areas as needed. All sanding is done wet to help improve the surface finish and prevent loading up abrasive sheets. While some of the work can also be done by hand (no blocks), the need to maintain the straightest lines possible generally forces the use of special tools.

our car to bare metal and we repainted the car in the original factory color. If you are going to completely strip the car, you have total freedom to get the result you want. You can fix any flaws, choose any color, etc., and be assured of great results as long as the work is done properly. If you paint over an existing paint job, however, you inherit whatever flaws it had and need to make sure none of these will cause future problems.

Beyond repairing body panels and parts, you need to ensure the surface you paint over is sound enough to be covered and that any new substance (filler, primer, paint) will stick to it.

First remove any loose paint, and then thoroughly sand the entire surface/car to be painted with the appropriate grit to rough up the surface and remove minor imperfections. Again, the goal is to have a smooth surface with no imperfections. Next, prime the car after it has been sanded and/or repaired with filler. Finally, consider a different approach to priming (different primer, more coats, etc.) if you will be painting over a different color or type of paint. Again, the shop should know what to do, but you should ask them how they plan to do it, especially if you're changing the paint type or color. In any event, after the surface is smooth and clean you are ready to paint.

Some vehicles may require additional procedures for stripes or graphics. Of course, there are stick-on vinyl products, but I recommend you choose high-quality graphics for superior durability and appearance. If you prefer a paint-on design, the vehicle is masked off and the special feature is painted over the base color. Depending on the look you want, you may or may not put on the design before you completely finish the base paint job. Typically, you apply the base coat(s), dry it, and bake it in the paint

Sanding and Painting the Body CONTINUED

8 For most areas, a sanding block is sufficient. The abrasive sheets clamp onto the block. This one is flexible enough to conform to the contour of the underlying panel. Use a spray bottle or sponge to apply water to the surface as necessary. This removes sanding residue and prevents loading up of the abrasive paper. Keep the block flat to the surface and don't use too much pressure.

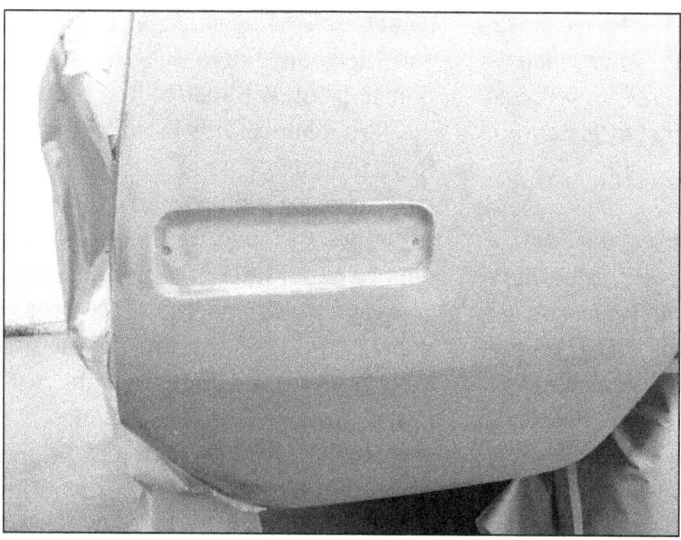

9 For completely flat areas, it is often better to use a rigid block instead of a flexible one. This generally ensures a better result, but you must be more careful; use light strokes. The block is very lightly held with only fingertip pressure. A simple piece of rounded-off metal bar stock is sufficient.

10 After the blocking is complete, the surface should be completely smooth and free of any imperfections. This is where the greatest cost of a paint job lies, in the amount of time spent to reach a given level of perfection. Blocking is generally the most time-consuming and skill-intensive part of the paint process. And finish quality equals cost. A show-car build takes things to a much higher level than other projects.

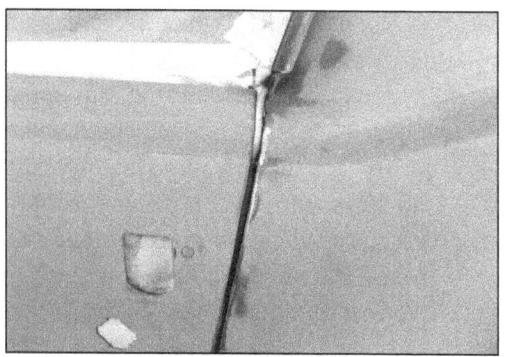

11 This foam sealing tape can be used to fill gaps and seal off areas from paint. This prevents additional overspray and provides a smoother transition of the painted areas. It must be pushed back from the edge of the panel, ideally to a point where any spray that does makes it into the gap won't be too obvious.

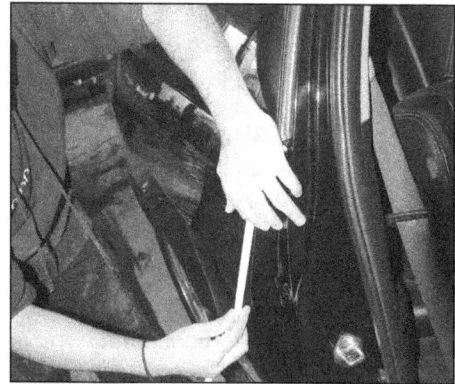

12 The foam tape is available in multiple thicknesses and is simply pressed on. The tape can be very easily manipulated to follow the contours of a panel or part. Take care when closing the door or other parts over the tape, but it doesn't usually move after proper application. It simply is pulled off later.

13 As the color and clear coats are applied, you see the benefits of the extra time spent blocking and masking properly. You should paint all of the major, most-visible areas during the same paint session with the same paint batches so the color tone is consistent. The fenders, hood, deck lid, and so forth should be painted with a single fill of the paint gun, if possible. There should be no obvious problems with transitions between areas that already were color coated. There should be no significant surface imperfections remaining. For our project, the transitions were smooth with minimal imperfections. But keep in mind, there is always the possibility of paint runs, sags, dust/dirt, but this is a matter of experience and skill as much as equipment and booth facility. A properly controlled environment, such as shown here, minimizes the potential for pain process issues.

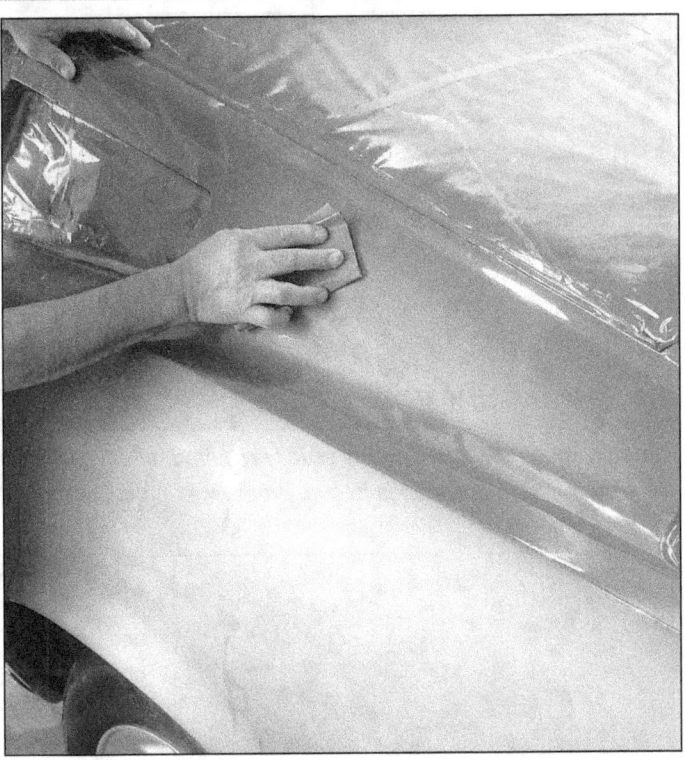

14 Between coats of paint, you might want to wet-sand the previous coat to provide a better adhesion for the subsequent layer. This approach can also be used to eliminate any runs, sags, and/or dust, etc., which may have contaminated the painted surface. Different shops have different approaches for applying the color coats; it also varies depending on the paint being used and the type of project. Whether or not to apply a clear coat and/or stripes also factors in the equation. In any case, it is critical to allow enough time between coats.

booth (probably can't do that in your garage) to cure the paint. A clear coat over the base color may require additional steps, depending on the specific formulations used and whether or not any additional pigment (pearls, etc.) are to be added to the clear coat.

All of these factors determine when the stripes/graphics are applied. For example, a graphic or stripe with a flat finish should be applied to the car after the clear coat because many tape stripes and hood graphics came from the factory in a flat-black finish. Often, things like spoilers and window louvers did as well. You wouldn't want to put a clear coat over something that's supposed to have a flat finish. Similarly, you may not want to put a clear coat over a finish with stripes if you are going to add pigment. These are all personal choices to some extent, but they do affect both the overall appearance of the vehicle and the judging for authenticity.

Generally, if no stripes or graphics are applied, the base coat is polished by lightly wet sanding with 1500- or 2000-grit sandpaper before the appropriate polishing compound and wax is applied. If the car is clear coated, polishing takes place after the clear coat has been dried/baked. Painted-on stripes normally go between the base coat and the clear coat. Stick-on stripes/graphics normally go over the clear coat or base coat after either has been polished. At least one coat of a premium wax should be used to seal in everything after the necessary drying/curing and any stick-on stripes or graphics have been applied.

After the car has been painted and waxed, protect any vulnerable areas with painter's tape to prevent any damage to the newly painted surface as other parts are reinstalled.

CHAPTER 4

Polishing the Paint and Applying Stripes

1 Begin the polishing process after the final color or clear coat layer has been applied and the vehicle has been baked to cure the paint. This involves first sanding the cured paint with an extremely fine (1500- to 2000-grit) abrasive before it is polished with the appropriate compound. A combination of hand work and using a variable speed electric buffer is usually required. In any event, the paint must be fully dry/cured before this step is begun. Proper waxing is the final step.

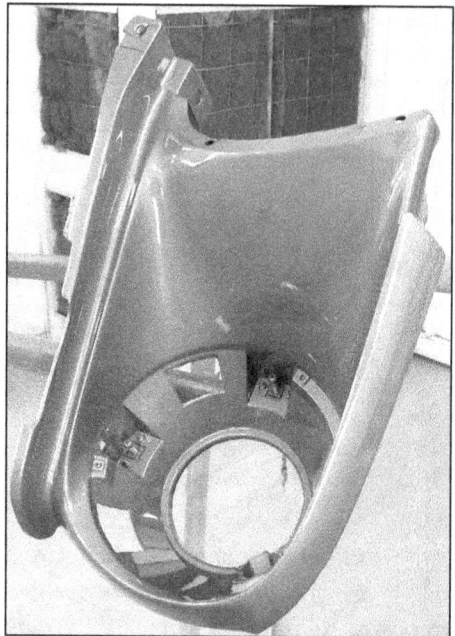

2 Smaller components are handled in a similar manner, although fewer color coats and less sanding/polishing are required. The best possible color match, along with minimized if not eliminated visual flaws, is the key. It's especially important that the edges of parts such as these, which are next to other parts/panels, get fully/properly painted to provide the best transition.

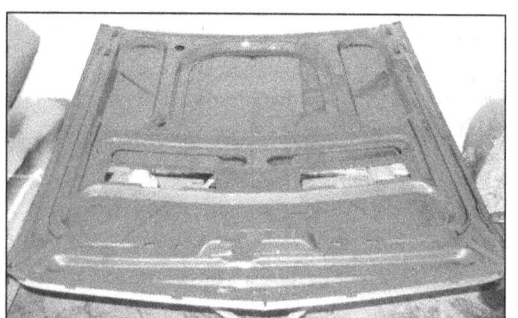

3 On larger panels such as the hood and trunk lid, where the underside will also be body color, one side must dry before the other side can be painted. With computerized paint mixing, color consistency is not a concern. However, the top/visible side should be painted along with the other exterior panels using the same paint batch whenever possible. The underside should be painted after the top side. There will be some difference in any case because the underside will not likely be sanded as much, nor will it likely receive as many color coats as the exterior surfaces. Masking should not be needed.

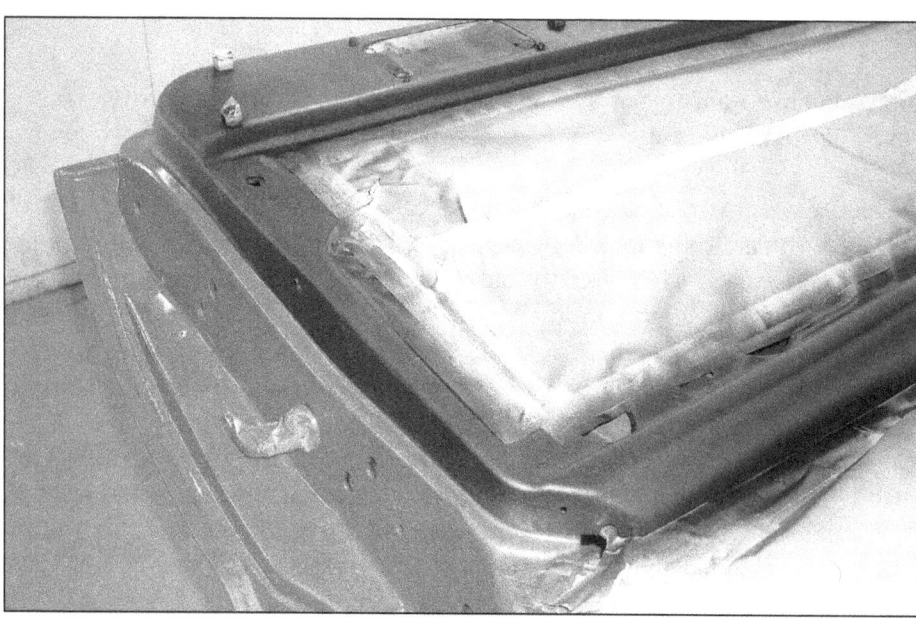

4 Sometimes there is a need to mask off the exterior surfaces to allow painting a different color on a nearby area. This case of the door surfaces is a good example. First apply color to the exterior surfaces with the color brought around to the other side as is needed. After these body-colored areas have been dried/cured, they can be masked off and the additional color(s) can be applied. Proper paint application and positioning of the masking tape is crucial to ensure a sharp transition line and no potential overspray.

PAINTING YOUR MUSTANG

5 Similarly, a sound-deadening or corrosion-resistant coating can be used on the back of a body-color panel. Many of the exterior body panels, such as the valance panel shown here, will have a coating applied as protection and to help seal out the elements. In this instance, you should apply the exterior color coat before the rear coating because the coating produces an uneven surface that's less conducive to proper masking.

6 There are several options for applying stripes or graphics over the newly painted surface. Here we show how the "C" stripe for our car was laid out prior to the car being masked off. We used a painted-on stripe like the original, so it had to go on top of the body color but underneath the clear coat. Notice how the paint has been left wet-sanded to provide better adhesion for the stripe.

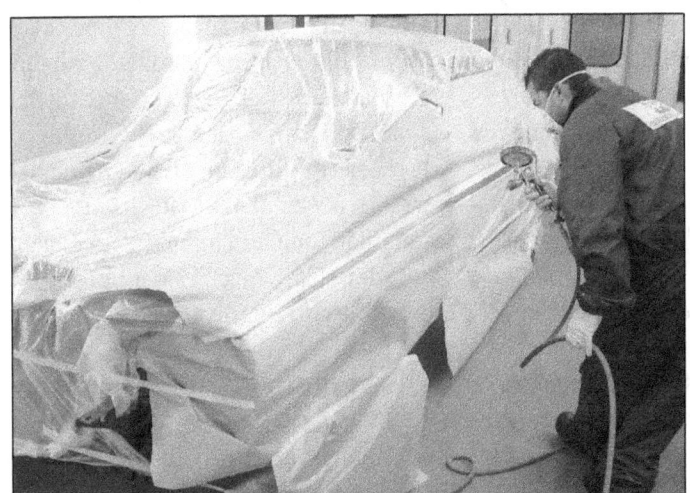

7 The entire vehicle was masked off prior to the stripes being painted on. Because the stripes are a different color, it's crucial to completely cover the vehicle. Even in a well-ventilated booth like this one, it is possible for stray particles to ruin your day. The normal sanding/polishing process would likely remove any of the lighter paint that might settle in an unwanted area, but it is better to avoid such things if possible. Although the stripes were just additional paint layers they clearly would not blend in.

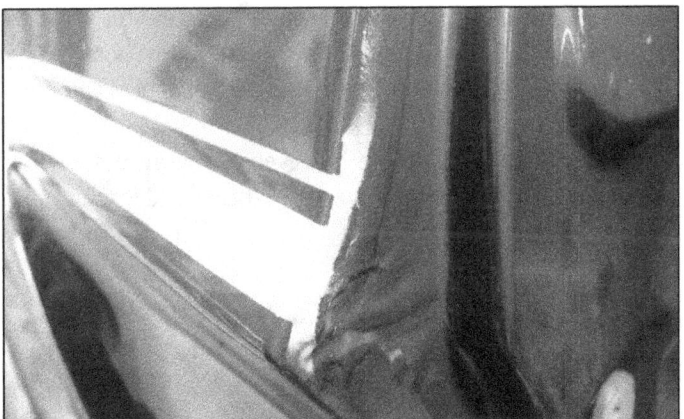

8 We still had a problem with the masking tape lifting off the irregular surface of the doorjamb despite the care we took when masking the car before spraying paint for the stripes. Depending on when such a problem is discovered, it may be possible to remove the excess paint from the stripe with thinner on a rag and some carefully rubbing. This can work if the underlying paint has already been baked and cured. Otherwise, the portions of the paint stripe that are kept can be masked off before the excess is lightly sanded off and the area is touched up with body color paint. In areas such as this, it is easier to blend in the fix.

CHAPTER 5

ENGINE REBUILDING

Of the various tasks involved in restoring a vehicle, the engine rebuild requires perhaps the greatest precision and expertise. Measurements are frequently made in thousandths of an inch, and the need for parts to be properly tightened with a torque wrench is critical. Failure to adhere to these and other requirements can quickly become very costly. A poorly built engine does not make the power or have the reliability it could have. At best, it performs poorly and wears out prematurely. At worst it fails, sometimes catastrophically, soon after it is fired up. Furthermore, even a properly built engine still needs to be broken in properly.

Much of the engine work shown here will, by necessity, be farmed out to a machine shop or other professional(s) who have the needed equipment and knowledge. By showing the steps involved in some detail, this book should help ensure that the work is done right. Similarly, whether you assemble the engine yourself or have it done for you, I will point out some common aspects, procedures, and concerns that need to be considered to avoid possible problems due to unique differences among similar engines.

There are so many different engines with many changes by option code, model year, build date, etc., that it simply is not be feasible to cover them all here. Instead, I go through the main steps involved in rebuilding an engine for a weekend-cruiser type of vehicle. I include procedures that go beyond a simple rebuild for repair purposes, but I don't get to the level of a full-on performance/racing blueprinting job. When appropriate, we use updated components, which improve performance and reliability while still maintaining a basically factory appearance. (A prime example of this is using a roller hydraulic camshaft rather than the standard flat-tappet hydraulic cam.) The result of these selective upgrades is an engine that is more powerful than stock. Also, it is smoother, quieter, more fuel efficient, and should last longer under normal (for an enthusiast), non-competitive use.

Disassembly and Evaluation

You need to closely inspect and evaluate the engine to determine depth and scope of the rebuild. Regardless of whether or not you intend to do everything from the get-go, you still need to ascertain the condition of the existing parts. Then you can figure out which parts need to be replaced or rebuilt. The process of taking the engine apart is also very useful for getting a feel for what the engine may have been through and how

After the 302 J-code V-8 was removed from the car, we thoroughly inspected it to assess its condition. Our car had been sitting for a very long time, so the engine was a bit dirtier than most, yet it still didn't have any really bad leaks. The engine was rated at 230 bhp and was running well with no signs of smoke in the exhaust and no unusual noises. The inside of the intake manifold looked pretty clean, so that further indicated a low likelihood of gasket problems, excessive blowby, or carburetor issues.

well it may (or may not) have been cared for. Such clues can definitely influence your plans. For example, after seeing the corrosion on the thermostat housing, we were hoping the timing cover was not corroded because it's a more difficult (and expensive) part to replace. Such corrosion usually occurs due to changes in the chemistry and the acidity of the coolant mixture. If one part is affected, it's logical to assume other parts made of the same or a similar material (aluminum, in this case) would be affected as well. Fortunately, the coolant passages in the timing cover showed virtually no signs of corrosion, so we'll reuse it. Signs of abuse and/or neglect clearly may influence you to investigate even further to make sure a problem does not exist. I cover a few such areas on which to spend some extra time to help identify possible issues.

We restored a 1968 Mustang GT, and this particular car is equipped with a J-code 302 V-8 and 4-barrel carburetor.

Cylinder Block and Head Preparation

Based on our evaluation of the project car's engine condition and the intended use of the vehicle, we determined it was best to do a complete rebuild of the engine. This was based primarily on the fact that our engine had been fitted with relatively cheap pistons when it was previously rebuilt, and because it didn't have hardened exhaust valveseats.

The former meant the cylinder bores would be too big to properly fit the superior pistons we intended to use because there would be more clearance between the new pistons and the bores. Likewise, the lack of hardened seats would mean premature wear and valve recession after our rebuild unless we resorted to using some kind of fuel additive, which we did not want to have to do. Our rebuild, therefore, includes re-boring and honing the block as well as equalizing the deck heights and making sure they are parallel to the centerline of the crankshaft.

We didn't do a full racing-style blueprint job since the power level and intended use don't really justify it; the benefits aren't worth the extra cost. We also cleaned up the cylinder heads to ensure their deck surfaces are flat and the ports are properly matched, etc. Installing hardened valveseats, however, is the most critical operation for the heads in terms of longevity.

Once you've determined the scope of your engine rebuilding project, round up the needed parts before you begin. In our case, things were made a bit easier by virtue of the camshaft being offered as a kit along with the timing chain, springs, retainers, locks, and so forth. We also rounded up the pistons, valves, a new high-performance oil pump, and the many seals, bearings, etc. We went with high-quality components, not the lower-cost imported ones, because we want the best performance with the least risk of any problems over the long term. Sticking with name brands, such as Competition Cams, Sealed Power, Clevite, Melling, etc. may cost a little more up front, but it is a wise investment. If you install newer technology as we did with our roller hydraulic cam, you can also build an engine that is better than new because it has been put together with more precision and it has features that enhance its overall performance and efficiency. A worthy goal.

Engine Disassembly and Inspection

1 *Removing the valve covers revealed there were relatively few deposits inside the engine. Considering how long the engine sat and the fact that the time of the last oil change was unknown, it could have been much worse. The valvetrain was solid, with no excessive lash or play. You can see that the exhaust port second from the right is a bit darker than the other three. Therefore, we'll check the valveguide (to see if it's loose) and the color of the piston crown. If the piston for this cylinder is also darker than the rest, it could mean anything from a problem with the rings to something as simple as poor air/fuel distribution in the intake manifold. When one cylinder is substantially different from the others, you need to determine the cause because it's an indication that something is wrong.*

Engine Disassembly and Inspection CONTINUED

2 Removing the intake manifold and the cylinder heads was very enlightening. We discovered the engine had already been rebuilt because the pistons were obviously not factory items. Also the pistons were marked as being .030-inch oversize, thus indicating the block had already been re-bored at least once. The engine was rebuilt maybe 10,000 to 20,000 miles before the car was parked because there was no ridge or step at the top of the cylinder bore from wear. Similarly, there was still faint evidence of the machining marks left by the honing process. There is less material in the block now so our rebuild will be its last. We will be able to go to a .040-inch overbore, but no further without the cylinder walls getting too thin. Going to .040 inch over could be marginal if you wanted to make much more than 350 hp. We also checked the fit of the lifters in their bores and found them to be fine. While it's possible to repair loose lifter bores with sleeves and so forth, it's better to not have to. Because we're installing a roller cam, it's a critical item to check out.

3 Removing the oil pan proved to be similarly interesting. Silicone/RTV fragments on the oil pickup screen and, when we took off the valve covers, a lack of carbon deposits provided further evidence of a prior rebuild. Rocking each connecting rod back and forth revealed a fairly tight rod end play, which is another indication of a freshly rebuilt engine. Crankshaft end play was similarly minimal, as determined by wedging a screwdriver blade between one of the main bearing caps and an adjacent crankshaft counterweight and then moving the crankshaft to evaluate the amount of play. You need to alternate from one side of the main cap to the other. Next the rods, pistons, and then the crank can be removed.

4 The piston skirts revealed a fairly normal wear pattern for the type of pistons (cast) that were used in the prior rebuild. Such pistons can run with a relatively tight clearance to the cylinder wall, which is an advantage for improved sealing and wear. Higher-performance engines were often equipped with forged pistons because of their greater strength, causing a need to run more clearance. Many modern pistons are hypereutectic– stronger than cast but retaining a tight clearance. New pistons have innovations in manufacturing and design that that spread the forces over a greater area of the skirt, thus reducing the localized stress (and wear) in a given area. You can see how the wear on this piston is concentrated toward the center of the skirt, near the oil ring area. The hypereutectic pistons we use spread the load more evenly.

ENGINE REBUILDING

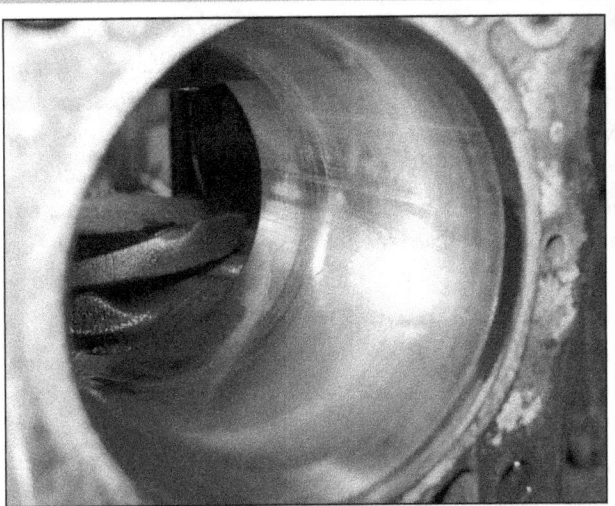

5 Cylinder wear was pretty minimal. There was no ridge/step at the top of the cylinders, just the normal discoloration that comes from the residue of unburned fuel above the top ring. The wear marks on the cylinders matched the wear pattern on the piston skirts, as expected. There was a very faint residual pattern from the previous rebuild, which indicated we might have the option of just doing a cleanup hone instead of re-boring and re-honing. After checking the bore dimensions with the appropriate equipment, however, we decided to go ahead with the re-bore to .040-inch over. The clearance that would have resulted with just a cleanup of the existing .030-inch bore would have been on the high side of the allowable range. We wanted to go with the better pistons anyway, so we decided the extra cost and effort of going to .040 inch over was well worth it for the improved performance, efficiency, and durability it would provide over the longer term.

6 The crankshaft journals also showed a very favorable wear scenario. There were no significant scratches, scoring, or other signs of unusual wear. Since we are not building a race motor, we should be able to get away with just a mild polishing of the journals. Had we wanted to build a higher-performance engine, we would consider special machining of the journal edges, oil holes, etc., to reduce stress concentration and/or increase the oil supply to the bearings. These measures are not needed for our application and in some cases could actually be counterproductive to a regularly driven street vehicle. We plan on running relatively close bearing clearances to get maximum life and smoothness from our engine. We won't need the extra bearing clearance normally provided for engines that will be raced or extensively driven under heavy load.

7 Further examination of the crankshaft revealed that it was an undersized unit; the main and the rod journals were .010 inch undersize. This was apparently done to remove surface imperfections. Special equipment is used to grind the crankshaft journals to the desired final size, usually in increments of .010 inch or less. While you benefit from removing any scratches, do not remove too much material. This weakens the crank to some degree by making the journals smaller but, more importantly, you reduce the hardened surface layer. In our case, the .010-inch reduction isn't enough to cause such problems, but a smaller crankshaft and/or a higher power level could be sufficient cause for concern, such that it may be advisable to replace the crankshaft rather than to risk a catastrophic failure under load. A crank with .010-inch-smaller journals is definitely a better option than one with any imperfections that could act as stress concentrators. For most rebuilds, it's okay to use one.

Engine Disassembly and Inspection CONTINUED

8 The cylinder heads showed no signs of trauma, but they did reveal a few items of interest. First, while not extreme by any means, there were some signs of mild valve recession, but this was expected because there were no hardened valveseats or valveseat inserts. This engine was rebuilt when leaded gasoline was still readily available, so there was no need to use hardened seats or inserts. The use of tetraethyl lead in gasoline has since been banned, thus creating a problem for older vehicles because lead lubricated the valveseats. When we rebuild these cylinder heads, we will install hardened valveseats to eliminate the problem. There was also evidence of somewhat leaky valveguides. The presence of oil in some cylinders, primarily around the edges of the valves, indicated some of the valveguides and valveseals were allowing oil from the upper head to run down the valvestem onto the head of the valve. A small amount of such oil is normal and acceptable; too much not only reduces performance and efficiency while increasing pollution, but it can also result in carbon deposits on the head of the valve. This also helps explain the different exhaust port coloration we observed earlier. Our engine had a couple of cylinders with above-average leakage, but it wasn't to the point where deposits had formed or it noticeably affected how well the engine operated. If allowed to persist, performance would deteriorate. We'll replacing the valvestem seals when we recondition the cylinder heads, so this shouldn't be a concern.

9 Pay attention to the water passages at the top of each cylinder. These areas are more likely to show signs of cracking or indicate if there was a problem with a head gasket. The proximity of the hole to the cylinder, and the distance from the head bolts, make this the most likely spot for trouble that might result from detonation or knock, causing high-pressure spikes in the cylinders. Our engine looked fine and showed no signs of such trouble. You can also see that two adjacent steam holes were plugged at the factory. These are left open on some applications if there might be a concern over the formation of air/steam pockets and/or if there is a need to increase coolant flow between the block and the heads. If these holes are plugged in your engine, you should probably leave them that way unless you plan to make a lot more power. If you do open them up you need to ensure the heads and the head gasket are compatible and the passage holes line up. Our heads did not and we're not upping the power by much anyway, so there was no point in our case.

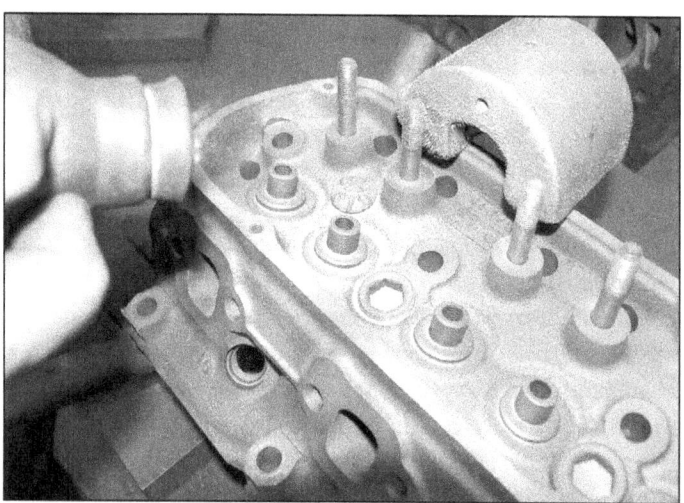

10 After the stock, iron cylinder heads have been cleaned, they need to be further checked for defects like cracks. A strong magnet and some iron powder, as shown, can be used to do this. Simply attach the magnet to various points on the head and then discharge some of the iron powder in the immediate area of any suspected crack. If there is a crack, the iron powder lines up around it instead of in a uniform layer. Also, a Magnaflux kit, which contains a special crack-detecting dye, is helpful for detecting cracks in castings. Most cracks are clearly visible to the eye, but sometimes this may not be the case so using a method such as this can help prevent putting a lot of wasted work into a part that must be repaired or maybe even tossed. The point is to make sure your parts are in the condition they need to be for your intended use. Our cylinders heads were fine.

ENGINE REBUILDING

Engine Machining

1 The dual valvesprings that we chose required us to make some changes to the heads. Note: The cast step around the valveguide was required for OEM-type single springs but it impedes the dual springs, so it was eliminated. To get the proper installed height, we took some material off the heads as shown. This ensures we do not bind the springs at full lift, and it also helps keep the spring pressure within the desired range of about 125 to 130 pounds on the seat. We also needed to cut the valveguides to make sure the retainers wouldn't hit them at full lift. The cam we chose is a fairly high-lift design, so between this fact and the different design of the retainers we needed to provide some extra clearance. And to use a different type of valvestem seal, we also needed to reduce the outer diameter of the valveguide bosses so the new seals would fit properly. The factory seal seating surface can be off-center relative to the valve by as much as .030 inch. The cutting tool we used pilots off the valveguide itself to make sure the seal is as concentric to the valve as possible. It even chamfers the top outer edge, so you can install the seal without tearing it.

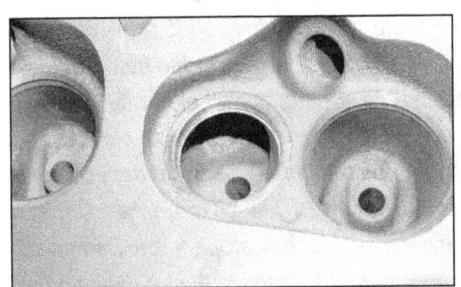

2 This photo shows one of the unfinished valveseat inserts in place. The cylinder head is machined to accept the insert and then it's pressed into place. The material lasts much longer than the cast iron of the cylinder head itself, especially when there is no tetraethyl lead in the gasoline to act as a lubricant. After all of the inserts have been installed, the valveseats are machined with a three-angle valve job to provide improved flow and longer life. Racers often use a radiused valveseat technique to get better flow, but they do so at the expense of shorter life and higher cost. The three-angle method provides better flow than the stock machining method, yet it still allows for enough surface area where the valve and the insert meet to have acceptable wear characteristics. We also clean up the bowl area to remove casting flaws and the step in the flow path, which resulted from the machining needed for the seat inserts.

3 The cylinder blocks that came out of the factories in the late 1960s and early 1970s were not the most precise examples of mass production machining. Many engines do not have flat deck surfaces or lie perfectly parallel to the crankshaft centerline. In fact, certain engine families were known to "droop" in one direction or another where the deck height actually varied from front to back on each side, usually in the same direction on both sides. With a cast-iron, closed-deck block like ours, the deck surface is usually fairly straight, but you need to check anyway. Before you go any further, make sure the deck surface on both sides (or just the one, if you have an inline 6-cylinder) is parallel to the centerline of the crankshaft/main bearing bore so that the deck height is equal front to back and side to side. If you are lucky, the amount of material you'll have to remove from the second deck will be less than that of the first, making it easy to even the deck heights. If not, you'll have to go back and take more off the first deck.

Engine Machining CONTINUED

4 The cylinder heads get the same treatment as the deck of the block, so the head surfaces are parallel and flat. This is especially critical to ensuring the compression ratio for each cylinder is as close to equal as possible. Iron heads are stock on virtually all first-generation Mustangs and are less prone to warping than aluminum heads. However, iron heads can warp pretty quickly if the engine overheats. Remove as little material as possible when truing up the heads so the compression ratio, stock pushrod length, and other components are not significantly affected. Generally, this is not a concern because relatively little material is removed. As with the block, material removal should be equalized for the heads; you may have to cut the first head twice for this.

5 We decided to bore the block out further to .040-inch over, rather than hone the cylinders and try to keep it at the current size. We overbored it to get the best possible fit with the new pistons and rings. While we did not use a deck plate during either this or the honing operation, the high nickel content of most of these older blocks makes them plenty strong and helps minimize unwanted deflection. For our power level, this degree of attention will be more than sufficient. Taking extra time to be sure the block is properly secured and aligned in the fixture will make a bigger difference than a deck plate would in a situation like ours. If, however, you are building a higher-output engine and/or have the budget to go the extra step, there is some benefit to using the deck plate during the boring and the honing operations. Generally, this work will be farmed out to a machine shop anyway, so it's best to discuss it with the shop owner to see if a deck plate is necessary or cost effective for your case.

6 The honing process is crucial to achieving a proper ring seal. The choice of stones used, the speeds (vertical and rotational), and even the fluid used all combine to determine the final finish on the cylinder walls. While each engine's needs are somewhat different, you generally need a uniform cross-hatch pattern of the correct surface roughness. The type of rings and pistons as well as the intended use of the engine determines the required crosshatch pattern. There are far too many possibilities to make specific recommendations here, but a good engine builder will be able to determine what's needed by evaluating the engine and the rebuilding goals. The choices made for a higher-output engine will be different than those we made, and a deck plate should be used during the honing operation for such engines. Our piston/ring/honing choices give us a much better sealing engine with significantly less blowby and longer engine life than ever would have been possible back in the day. We may not be going for that last pony, but we'll still do a lot better than when this engine was first produced.

ENGINE REBUILDING

7 For optimal cylinder bore finish, the best approach is to remove small amounts of material with each hone pass and then keep checking the bore diameter with a bore gauge, as shown here. This will prevent too much material from being removed, thus creating excessive clearance to the piston. It also allows for closer monitoring of the honing process so any problems, such as a cracked or broken stone, can be spotted immediately. In turn, this reduces the chance for any damage to the bore. It's worth the extra time and effort to avoid problems and get a superior bore. It's also a good idea to run a small brush or ball hone through each lifter bore to clean them up and prepare the surface so it holds more oil than the stock surface finish. This will help the lifters rotate sooner after the engine starts (in the case of a flat tappet camshaft), thus minimizing wear.

Engine Assembly

1 After the block has been fully machined and cleaned up, it can then be painted ("Ford blue," in our case) and readied for assembly. Use proper engine paint made specifically to handle the higher temperatures and harsh environment (fluids and debris) of an engine bay. The engine will never be easier to paint than it is right now. Using a cheap paint will only cost more in terms of appearance and rust later on. Note how, as a first step, we also used brass freeze plugs instead of plated steel versions because the brass won't rust. It also tends to be a bit softer, so it provides a superior seal. We still used a small amount of sealant on the block sealing face before we drove the plugs in, just to be sure. At this point, the block should be fully wiped down and blown off with compressed air to remove any dust and dirt that might still be present. You want the engine to be as clean as possible when it goes together because a small bit of dirt in the wrong place can cause big problems and even failure. You don't need a cleanroom environment, but it definitely does pay to be careful. This also helps prevent leaks, misaligned parts, and excessive wear later on.

2 Installing the cam bearings is normally the next step when working with a bare block that's just been reassembled. On a relatively standard engine, the choice of cam bearings is pretty straightforward; just stick with a quality replacement set and you'll be fine. If you plan on putting in a special cam and/or higher-rate valvesprings, you should consider other options, such as high-performance materials and/or alternative designs, but that's not necessary in most cases. You need to use the correct tools and be extra careful to not damage either the bearing surface or the edges of the bearing shells. If there is a need to line up any oiling holes in the bearing shell with holes in the block, then this should be done very carefully before installation. It should also be checked afterward to ensure the holes or other features line up. Each shell should be gently tapped in using a seal driver, in order, until it is centered and square to the bore it sits in. A little overhang of the bearing shell relative to the block's chamfer is not a problem. Too much might indicate you've got the wrong bearings and you should verify the part number. The bearing shells should fit tightly and not be free enough to rotate. There must be no scratches or other damage to the bearing shells or the bearing surface.

Engine Assembly CONTINUED

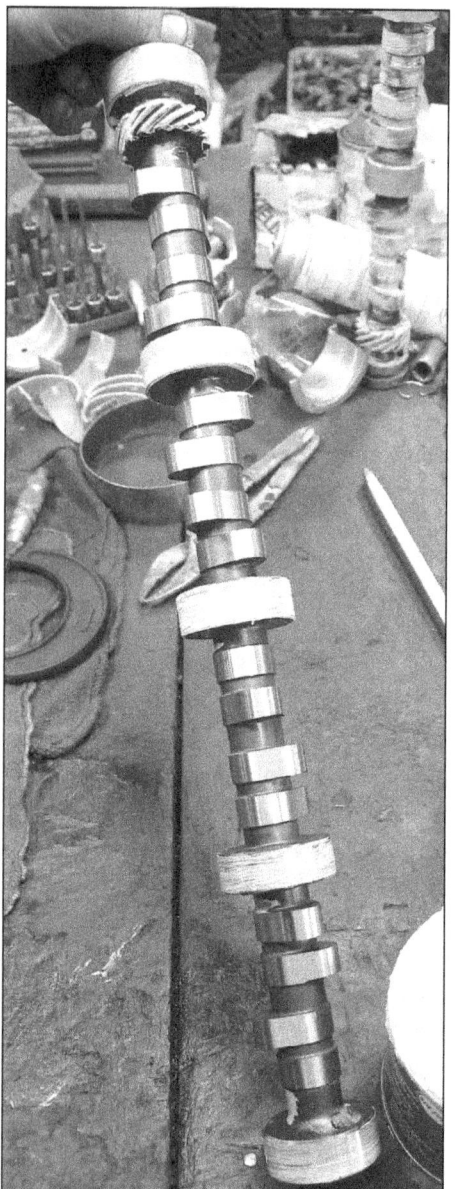

3 The first use for our special assembly lube is on the cam bearing surfaces and the distributor drive gear. Only a thin coat needs to be applied. We did not put any lube on the cam lobes themselves because we are using a hydraulic roller cam in this engine, and you want the rollers to start turning as soon as the engine is started. A little oil on the lifter rollers and pre-oiling the engine via spinning the engine without starting it will take care of this. If we were using a flat-tappet cam, however, it would be absolutely critical to ensure the cam lobes and the lifter faces were coated with the correct assembly lube (as is normally supplied with the cam). For a little extra insurance, you can also lightly smear some of the assembly lube on the bearing shells in the block.

4 The main bearing shells are pretty simple to install because they just slide into place with a slight snap. Make sure you put the thrust bearing in the right place (usually the middle or number-3 main web, as shown here), and you put the correct shells in the block, versus in the main caps. Here, the shell half that goes into the block is grooved and has a slot to allow oil from the block to reach the crank. The other half of the shell that sits against the main cap may or may not be grooved as well. Just make sure you put the shells in their correct positions and that they fit properly. Ensure there's no dirt between the shells and the block or main caps and then line up the tabs before pressing in the shells. They should fit fairly snug but should still be able to be lifted out easily. There should be no bearing material above the surface of the block, but there will normally be a bit extra on the main caps to ensure proper "crush."

Short Block Assembly

The short block is the foundation of the engine; it is also where the most care must be taken during assembly. Both accuracy and precision are mandatory when it comes to tightening fasteners. Too little torque and a fastener can come loose. Too much torque and a part can seize or bind. The consequences of either can be excessive wear and/or poor performance, at a minimum. In a worst-case scenario, you can have a catastrophic engine failure.

I can't go into the specifics of how to assemble a specific engine, but I highly recommend that the engine builder take the time to review and closely follow the recommended factory procedure in the service manual. I do provide some guidelines to supplement the factory procedures and point out a few areas where you can improve on traditional procedures by using newer technology.

ENGINE REBUILDING

5 The crankshaft in our engine had already been ground .010-inch undersize on both the main and the rod journals, so it was in pretty good shape. It only needed a minor polishing to be ready to go back into the engine. We also took the time to smooth out and open up the oiling holes a bit, but we didn't get into things like radiusing the fillet area for more strength. Those are things you might do in a highly stressed race motor, but they would just be a waste of money in our case. Similarly, we decided not to do a fine balance on our engine because it wouldn't be turning high RPM. We are also using all direct-replacement parts (granted, of superior quality) in the rotating assembly. Manufacturing technology has improved so much that the tolerances on higher-quality parts are close enough that they often compare with what you would get by doing a race-level blueprinting job when these engines were first built. That is no longer necessary for normal high-performance use. The higher-quality parts like ours are good enough for most cases. Our main concerns are that the journals are smooth and are of the proper diameter, which we've already verified. We'll also check rod side clearance and crank end play later on.

6 One area where we can make some real improvements over the original components found in first-generation Mustangs is materials technology. Case in point is the rear main seal. These engines were generally equipped with rope-style seals from the factory. They were not the most reliable or durable sealing method even when they were installed right. Let the engine sit for too long, and you could really have a leaker. Nowadays, we use elastometric seals, which work much better and last longer. They're also a lot easier to install properly because they basically just push in. Still, they need to be checked for a good seal. After applying our break-in lube to the main bearings and the crank journals, we pressed the correct rear main seal half into the block (make sure the seal is facing the right way, with the lip pointing toward the front of the engine) and gave it a light coat of our assembly lube. After lightly placing the crank in the block and rotating it, we noted there was a fine, uniform line of lube all the way around the rear main sealing surface. This indicates we're getting the contact we need for a good seal. Any lube around the seal end should be removed.

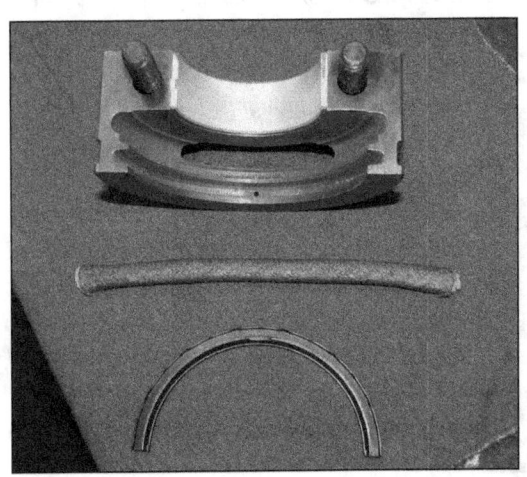

A comparison shows why a modern elastometric is superior to the older rope seal. The rope seal often must be trimmed to the correct length and even then the ends are not ideal for creating a seal. The rope seal also must be pinned in place (note the hole for a pin in the rear main cap) while the newer seal is inherently resistant to movement. The newer seal has a fine, single line contact with the crankshaft where the contact pattern of the old seal is both wider and less uniform. The rope seal is more prone to damage during installation and over time if the engine is not run, while the newer seal should be fine if the proper oil is used and is changed regularly. Elastometric seals can harden over a long period of time, but there are high-mileage oils with special additives to help prevent that and even soften the seals somewhat. There are no such options with rope seals. Once they begin to fail/leak, they usually and rapidly continue to only get worse.

Everybody, it seems, has recommendations for break-in lubes. Manufacturers of the camshaft, lifters, and other valvetrain components are probably the most vocal about this. And for good reason: Their parts will probably be the first to go if you get it wrong. This is especially true if a flat-tappet camshaft is used. Since we're using a roller hydraulic cam, this is less a matter of instant failure than it is one of trying to ensure the longest component life and best performance.

Note that our engine builder (Orange Engine Rebuilding) prefers to use a mixture of multipurpose white lithium grease and Lucas Heavy Duty Oil stabilizer for many areas of the engine that must be pre-lubed in some fashion.

Engine Assembly CONTINUED

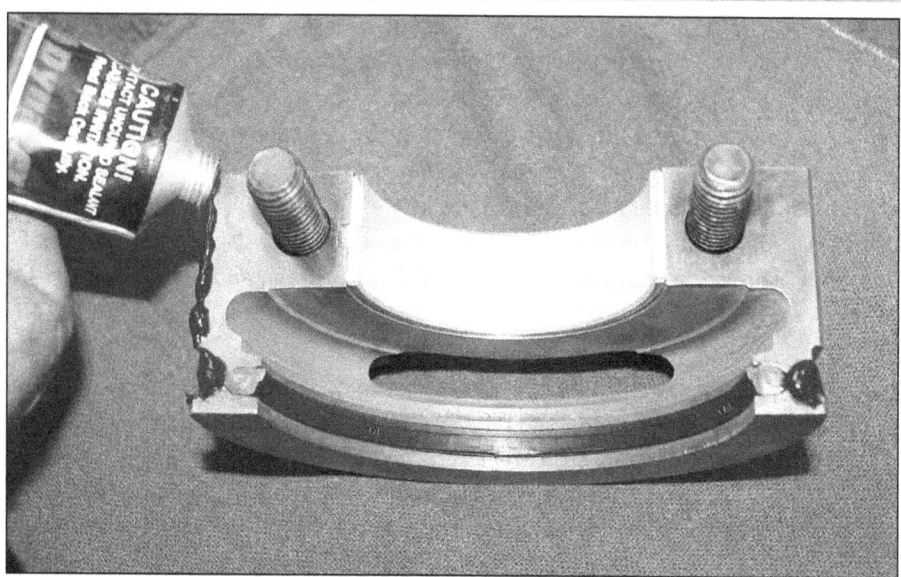

7 Even though the newer-style seal is a vast improvement over the older rope seal, you still need to take some steps to prevent leaks from other potential paths around the seal. Here, we apply some RTV silicone sealant to the edges of the main cap to minimize the potential for leaks. Note how the sealer is applied right up to the rear main seal itself. A relatively fine bead is all that is needed. Too much RTV will only result in it getting squeezed out and making a mess. In a worst-case scenario, some of this excess RTV could find its way to the oil pump pickup or to another area where it could potentially lead to engine damage. Use enough, but no extra.

8 With the rear cap in place, wipe off the RTV to prevent any future problems. More RTV is used later when the oil pan gasket goes on, but it's best to remove this excess before it hardens. Ideally, the engine assembly will be done in such a way that sealants and adhesives won't be allowed to cure before the engine is fully assembled. This helps in the event you have to redo something and makes sure the seal is not broken inadvertently. For example, even though we haven't torqued down the rear main cap, it is essentially in its final position so the necessary seal has been created. Tightening the main cap bolts will only improve the seal. If the cap was not pressed fully down, however, the RTV could begin to cure and might not provide as good a seal. When a sealer or adhesive is applied, it's best to fully tighten the associated parts as soon as is possible for the best seal.

Engine Assembly CONTINUED

9 Our engine only has 2-bolt main caps, so the torque sequence is pretty simple: just start in the middle and work outward. Some recommend alternating from side to side (3-2-4-1-5 sequence) but doing each side (3-2-1-4-5) should be fine in most cases as well. If you have a high-performance engine with 4-bolt mains, you may want to be a bit more careful in this regard, even to the point of tightening the bolts in multiple steps as well as in a special sequence. The key is to use a good, properly calibrated torque wrench, the proper torque(s) and the proper sequence, if any is required, as is specified in the factory service manual. When you're done, turn the crank by hand to make sure it rotates easily and smoothly. If it doesn't, remove the main caps to find the cause of the problem. You need to do a final check to verify the crankshaft end play. This usually should fall into a range of .004 to .006 inch and is checked with either a feeler gauge at the thrust washer face, or preferably, with a dial indicator on the rear face of the crank. Simply push/pull the crank back and forth to find the amount of play.

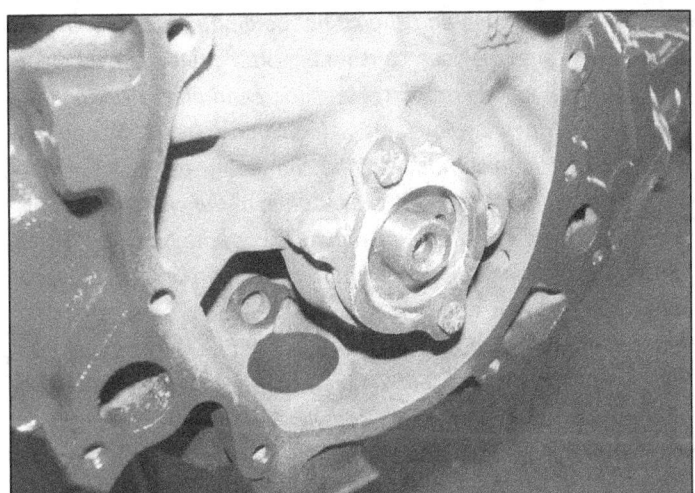

A thrust plate, such as that shown here, determines the location of the camshaft in the engine. The thickness of the thrust plate, the dimensions of the cam gear, and the engine block dictate the cam's position and the amount of end play. There were multiple versions of these parts depending on the specific engine, so it's critical you get the right parts match to avoid problems. Failure to do so can result in unwanted noise, premature wear, loss of performance, or even the complete failure of components. Verify that you have the right parts and check camshaft end play.

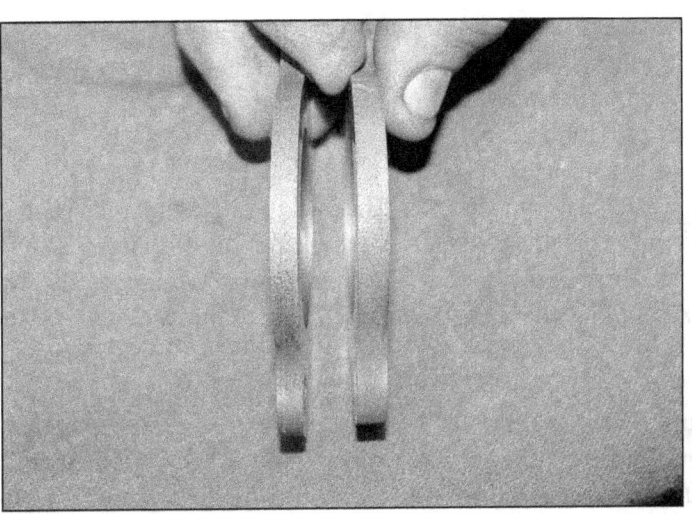

Here is a comparison of a couple of thrust plates to illustrate the difference. The earlier plate on the left is clearly not as thick as the later plate on the right. Some variations even included washers for the cam gear. There are even additional variations regarding oiling provisions and so forth. All of these factors must be properly reconciled to ensure the engine works right and stays trouble free. Be especially careful of so-called replacement parts that are advertised for a wide range of vehicle applications. These non-specific or universal-fit parts could be much more trouble than they are worth. Don't try to save a few dollars with such parts because they could end up costing you much more later. Make sure you use the right combination of parts for your specific engine even if it does cost a bit more.

Engine Assembly CONTINUED

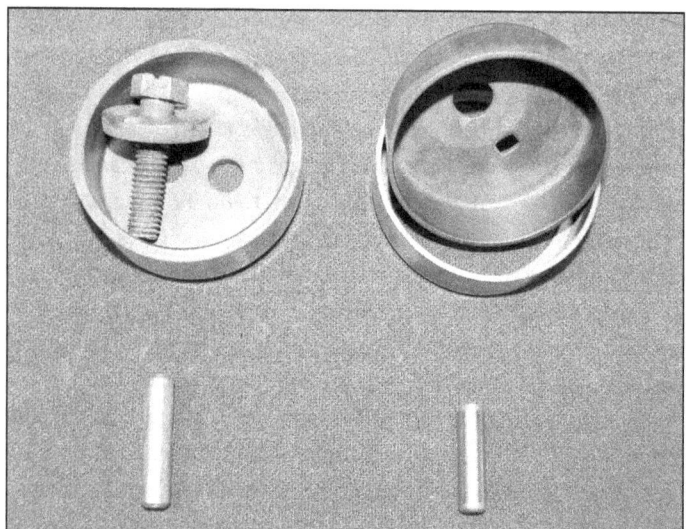

The fuel pump eccentrics can also have multiple variations, as shown here. The single-piece variety with the longer rod is generally regarded as the superior performer, and it will fit in most applications as long as all of the correct parts are used in combination. Since these parts are not visible, original-engine authenticity is not a concern, use the better parts. Be sure to use the correct retaining bolt and also apply the correct type and amount of thread locker to the threads. Of course, if you wish to convert to an electric fuel pump, you can eliminate the eccentric altogether as long as a suitable bolt and/or washer are used in place of the stock parts. But installing an electric fuel pump certainly strays away from an original restoration. You can also omit the plunger/rod and simply cover the fuel pump mounting hole on the side of the timing cover with an appropriate block-off plate and gasket.

10 Checking camshaft end play is a critical step in any engine rebuild and should not be omitted. A small amount of excessive end play can cause a big problem, and insufficient end play can be catastrophic. Measuring end play is pretty easy and straightforward. Mount a dial indicator to the block and put the indicator tip in contact with the cam gear while pointed in a direction that is parallel to the centerline of the camshaft, similar to what is shown. Push the camshaft toward the block until it stops and the dial indicator is set to zero. Then pull the camshaft away from the block and read the dial indicator to measure the amount the camshaft had moved. You want as little movement as possible; no more than 0.002 inch. With new parts you should be right around .001 inch or less, ideally. The factory manual may allow slightly more but as little as possible is best in terms of avoiding noise, wear, and heat. Make sure the camshaft spins freely by itself and there is no rubbing or binding with the block or thrust plate.

They have found this unique combination to be superior to oil alone or even to most assembly lubes. While not suitable for all situations, it is more tacky than many assembly lubes, and thus stays put and does not seep out over time. This ensures the engine is still protected if sits for a while before its first run.

One area for particular care is the installation of the camshaft. I already touched on some of the things to look out for based on whether the cam is a flat-tappet cam or a roller cam, but I also need to address camshaft end play. Too little end play is pretty easy to figure out because the camshaft will be tough to turn (or won't turn at all) after you get everything buttoned up. Too much end play, however, is less obvious. The consequences of too much end play can be anything from unwanted engine noise and loss of performance to (in an extreme case) a broken timing chain or other part failure.

Part of the confusion comes from the fact that Ford used different thickness thrust plates on different engines. It's very easy (and also somewhat common) to get them mixed up. Following are some generic guidelines to help ensure you use the right parts and have the correct camshaft end play in your engine.

The assembly of the rotating components is easy to accomplish in a relatively simple rebuild, such as ours, yet there are still benefits to paying attention to the details. For example, while we won't take the time to gap each piston ring by hand as you would do in a race engine, properly aligning the ring end gaps is advantageous. Similarly, it's always necessary

ENGINE REBUILDING

11 If you find too much end play, you will need to either machine the surface of the cam gear where it contacts the cam (as shown here) or, if your engine uses that setup, use a thinner washer. It is absolutely critical that any machining is done in a way in which the cut is perfectly flat and square; any material removal must be done in a uniform manner. One method is to mill the surface. Another is to carefully and lightly press the gear against a moving flat belt sander to remove a small amount of material at a time until the desired end play is achieved. To avoid having to get another cam gear, it is best to work remove material from the cam gear mounting face in very small steps. Remember, the mounting face is what will actually contact the camshaft. There is a separate thrust face (the lower step in the photo) that actually contacts the thrust plate.

12 With the proper end play established, the cam gear, crank gear, and timing chain can be installed. Since we're only building a mild-performance engine, we opted to install the engine "straight up" in terms of camshaft timing. This means we aligned the dots on the cam gear and the crank gear as shown. This should correspond to a more-or-less zero-degree setting, where the camshaft is neither advanced nor retarded in timing. In a high-performance or racing engine, there may be some advantage to "degreeing-in" the cam with a specific amount of advance or retard. This is done by using either offset crankshaft keys, offset cam bushings, or a cam gear that has been specifically cut with multiple keyways to allow for multiple mounting positions to accomplish this. CarTech offers several other books that explain degreeing a camshaft, engine blueprinting, and much more. Please refer to one of these if you are building a higher-output engine where degreeing the camshaft might prove to be more beneficial.

13 If you have not done so already, after the block was bored and honed, wipe down each cylinder with a lint-free cloth that's been moistened with lacquer thinner, brake cleaner, or a similar non-aqueous fluid that leaves no residue. After removing any dirt and/or dust, use another lint-free cloth to wipe the cylinders down a second time after the cylinders have been lightly sprayed with WD-40 or a similar silicone-type lubricant. This protects the surface until the engine is run and helps the rings seat a bit faster than just using clean oil. When using forged pistons and/or older-technology rings, however, it may be preferable to wipe the cylinder down with oil because it will provide a bit more cushioning with a larger piston-to-bore clearance. It really comes down to the piston material and the ring technology. Oil is the more universal choice, while silicone spray can offer some benefits with newer-technology components.

Engine Assembly CONTINUED

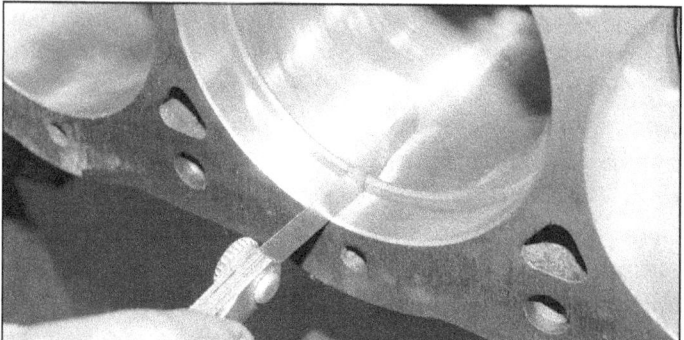

14 In a higher-performance or race engine, hand fit and check the gap of each piston ring to a specific cylinder. Since we used standard size replacement parts, we randomly checked one of each of the different ring types (top, second, oil) to make sure they were the right ones for our engine. While the exact ring gap depends on a lot of different factors, you generally want to see about .004 inch of gap for each 1 inch of bore diameter. All of our rings were within the correct gap range for our engine. Oil rings normally don't need to be checked for gap clearance, but you should first verify that they are the correct parts and make sure at least one set fits the bore before you install them on the pistons. This also the time to test fit the rings (at least one of each) in their piston grooves as well. Be sure to check for side fit and back clearance. With standard parts like ours there is rarely a problem. Such things can be an issue with higher-output engines where non-factory parts are often used.

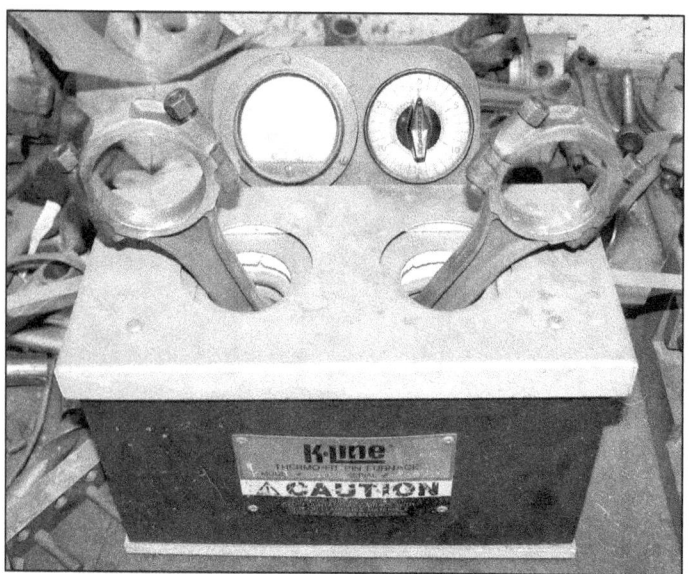

Race engines and higher-performance street engines (including some original equipment by Ford) tend to use full floating piston pins, which are retained by some form of clip arrangement on the piston. More-conventional engines use piston pins with an interference fit to the connecting rod, so the pin cannot move from side to side. Normally, the pin is pressed into the small end of the connecting rod while the piston straddles it, and as a result, the pin bores are all in alignment. This pressing operation tends to produce some distortion of the small end of the rod and some wear to the rod and the pin. A preferable method is to instead heat the small end of the rod using special equipment made for the purpose (shown). The bore in the small end of the rod will expand due to the heat, allowing the pin to easily slide into the piston and rod without resorting to high pressure. This reduces potential distortion and wear, and also results in more consistency for the pin's location within each piston and connecting rod.

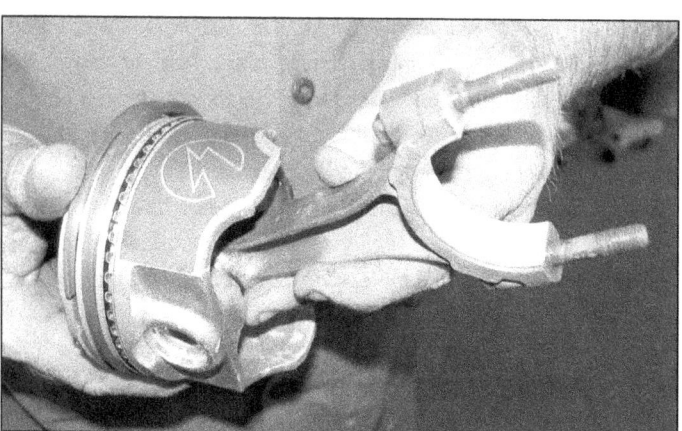

We will assemble each piston and connecting rods as shown. But there are certain guidelines that must be followed, which are detailed in the next two photos. Since direct-replacement pistons, such as these, generally have a slightly offset pin bore to reduce noise, it is critical that they be assembled with the "thrust face" pointing in the right direction. A directional mark on the piston crown must face a certain way. Similarly, the connecting rods also have a directional aspect to their installation. The correct combination of factors must be satisfied as the pistons are assembled onto the connecting rods, or there could be problems with wear, noise, or worse. You don't have to contend with these issues when rebuilding higher-performance engines with full floating pins because their bores are not offset, thus making each assembly similar and non-directional. Regardless of how your particular components must be assembled, be sure to apply a small amount of clean oil to each pin bore of each piston so that the oil has the chance to seep evenly between the pin and the piston (and the rod, if fully floating) before initial startup.

ENGINE REBUILDING

15 Our pistons had offset pin bores, so they must be installed with the mark facing toward the front of the engine. Most production and slightly modified street engines will have pistons that are directional like these. Some factory high-performance engines and most race or higher-performance engines will use pistons that do not have a pin bore/thrust face orientation. They may still be directional if special cuts are made to the top of the piston to clear the valves. Note also how the rings are marked with dots that must face upward. The rings are designed to twist in a certain way and seal properly as they move with the piston in the bore. Most piston rings are directional regardless of their intended use, so be sure to verify correct positioning.

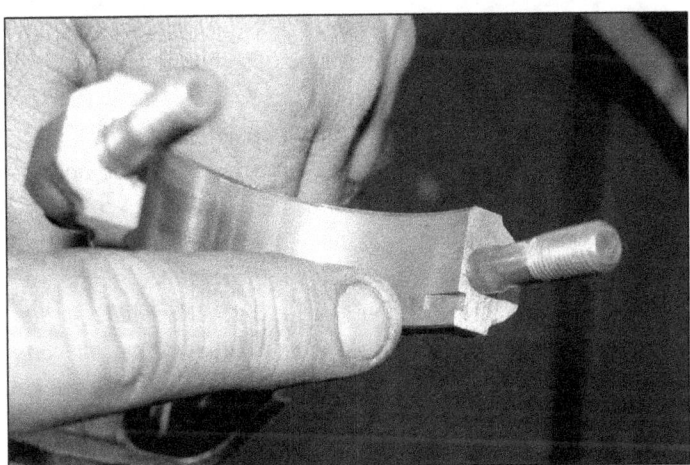

16 The connecting rods can also be installed in one of two ways. The preferred way is to have the locating tab for the rod bearing shell facing up (toward the camshaft) rather than down (toward the oil pan) if the engine is upright. Basically, you want the notch in the rod to be above the crank journal rather than beneath it. As with the directionality of the pistons, the potential benefit in doing this is based on how the components are loaded when the engine is running. With a production-type rod and piston combination, such as this, this can add an extra measure of insurance over the life of the engine. Higher-performance and race engines generally use forged rod designs so this is not a consideration.

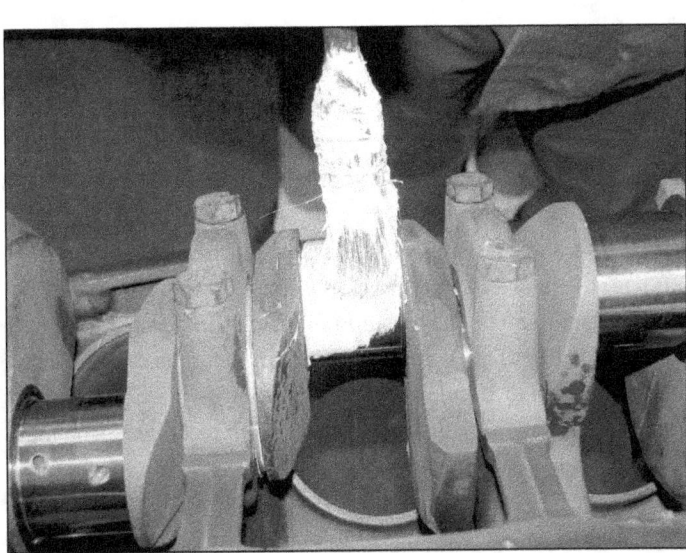

17 Prior to assembling the rod/piston pairs into the engine, each crank throw should be liberally and evenly coated with assembly lube. This is also the time to assemble the rings onto the pistons (if you have not already done so) and slide protective plastic boots (or some type of rubber or plastic hose) over the threads of the rod bolts to help avoid scratching the crank journals as you tap the piston/rod assemblies into each bore. This is also a good time to verify you have the right connecting rod bearings for your application and you've installed them correctly in the rod and the rod cap.

Engine Assembly *CONTINUED*

18 When installing the piston/rod assemblies, it pays to use a good ring compressor. Use either the squeeze-type (shown here) or the single-piece, tapered style; they both work fine if they are correct for the engine. The former is more flexible in that it can be used on more than one type of engine, while the latter is generally more efficient if you regularly build engines with the same bore size. Regardless of the style of ring compressor used, it is very important that you properly orient the ring gaps when each piston/rod assembly is installed. First, rub some clean oil or spray some WD-40/silicone on each ring and rotate it around to ensure even coverage on all sides of each ring before aligning the end gaps. The gaps of the compression rings should be 180 degrees apart to help reduce blowby. Positioning the end gaps over opposing pin bosses is a common approach. Relative to the oil ring, the position of the end gaps for the upper and lower rails (in a conventional three-piece oil ring) is less critical; they only need to be at least an inch or so apart. The oil ring gaps are commonly positioned toward the top, spaced evenly between the pin bosses at about 45 degrees from the vertical centerline of the piston. With the rings properly lubed and positioned, the assemblies can be carefully inserted into each bore.

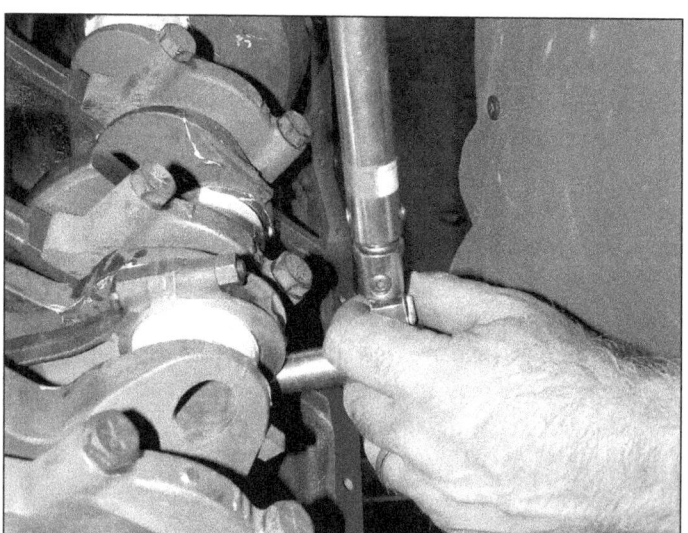

19 Take care to ensure the rod bolts don't contact the crank journals when each piston/rod assembly is pushed down the bore and the rings have cleared the deck surface. If you put a piece of rubber hose on each rod bolt as recommended, just guide each hose around the journal, thus taking the rod bolt with it. With the rod seated on the journal, the hose pieces can be removed and the rod cap (with the bearing shell already on it) and nuts can be installed. Torque the rod cap nuts (or bolts, as the case may be) to the proper torque as specified either in the factory service manual or by the manufacturer of the connecting rod/bolt. The torque figures for these different situations can vary widely but a good figure for many stock connecting rod bolts is about 30 ft-lbs. They can be tightened in one step.

20 After all of the pistons and rods have been installed, it is time to check each pair for side play. Do this with a feeler gauge inserted between the rod pair and/or between the rod and the crank face to determine the air gap between the parts. Too much clearance can result in excessive oil pressure loss and/or engine failure in extreme situations. Too little clearance can cause the engine to seize up due to insufficient lubrication between the rods and/or the crank. Each rod should slide freely on the crank and should also rotate freely with the crank as the latter is turned. Verify the side play for each rod pair is within the proper range per the service manual or by the rod manufacturer.

ENGINE REBUILDING

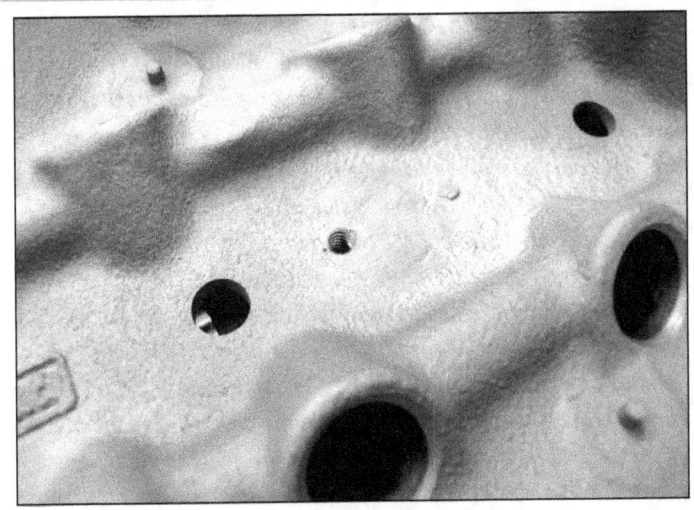

21 Converting to a roller hydraulic camshaft basically involves drilling two holes in the valley area of the engine to mount the "spider" (retention plate) that holds the lifter pairs properly in place. It does so by applying pressure to cross bars that connect them and keep them from rotating. Installing the spider involves using the spider itself as a template to determine where to drill the two holes. These holes generally line up with two cast bosses that are already in the valley area. The key is to make sure the "arms" of the spider are properly located between the lifter pairs and the holes are not drilled too deep. While it is necessary for a flat tappet/lifter to spin, it would be instantly disastrous for a roller lifter to do so. Hence the need for the cross bars and the spider to hold them and prevent rotation.

The finished installation is elegant in its simplicity. The spider retaining plate sits virtually flush with the floor of the valley area while its eight arms reach out to the center of the cross bars between the lifter pairs. Note that we applied some clean oil to the roller tips of the lifters before we dropped them in place. We also rubbed some Lucas Oil Stabilizer on the lifter bores beforehand. A similarly thick assembly lube would also serve for initial start-up lubrication. After the lifters are in the bores and the cross bars have been installed, it's also a good idea to pour a small amount of this over where the lifters and the crossbars touch. Try to avoid getting it on the pushrod seat of the lifter.

to torque components to the correct specifications and make sure the pistons are oriented properly.

I don't show every step involved in putting the entire rotating assembly (pistons, connecting rods, etc.) together, but I touch on a few of the highlights to provide guidelines either you or the shop building your engine for you should follow. These are meant to complement the information in the factory service manual, not replace it, for a particular engine. Some of the higher-performance factory engines in particular require unique procedures in this area. If you have chosen to go with non-factory parts in a higher-performance build, follow the recommendations of the component manufacturer(s) and or your engine builder if someone is doing the work for you. You can also find more specific information about blueprinting particular Ford engines in other CarTech/S-A Design books.

Our goal in restoring this car was to upgrade components and performance when and where it didn't negatively affect the value of the car. Therefore, we've upgraded several internal engine components, such as the camshaft and the oil pump, to improve daily drivability, usability, and reliability. Earlier in the chapter, I discussed the benefits of converting to a roller hydraulic camshaft over the stock flat-tappet-style camshaft, so I won't repeat the information here. I do note, however, that the conversion is surprisingly easy. Our Competition Cams camshaft kit includes all of the necessary components and installation information for the conversion.

Engine Assembly CONTINUED

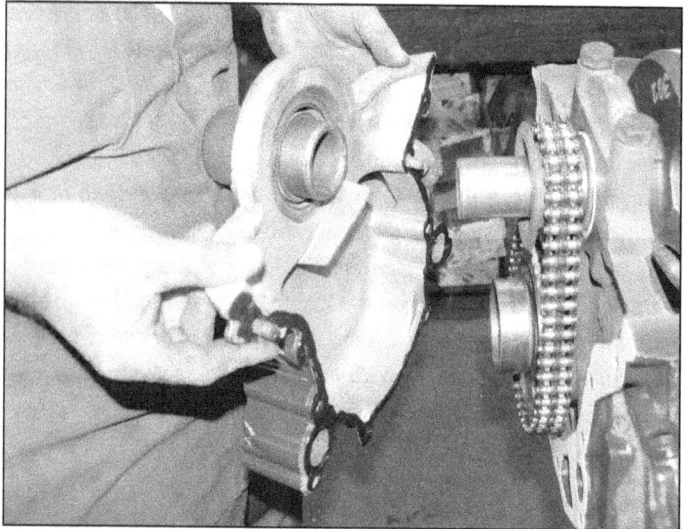

22 Assembling the remainder of the short block involves one primary goal: to minimize the potential for fluid leaks. The timing cover area is a common source for these. We've affixed the timing cover gasket to the block with the yellow 3M adhesive, a popular choice. This holds the gasket in place and provides an excellent seal as well. Leave the side of the gasket facing the timing cover bare and apply a generous amount of RTV to the gasket surface of the timing cover, as shown. Be sure to go fully around each water passage and bolt hole and remove any excess. There should be a thin, even layer, rather than a thick bead. Note the use of a crank spacer from a 390 engine inserted into the timing cover to act as a pilot to locate the cover. Install the metal splash shield onto the crankshaft (with the step facing the crank gear). Also pour some assembly lube on the crank gear and most of the timing chain before you finally put the timing cover on.

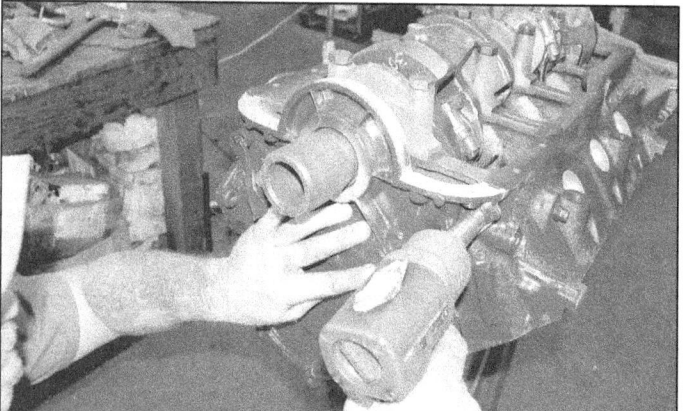

23 Correct placement of the timing cover is critical to avoiding leaks, especially around the crankshaft seal itself. Since there are no locating dowels on our engine, we've used the crankshaft spacer from a 390 engine to act as a pilot to center the timing cover. Carefully slide the spacer over the crank and push the timing cover toward the engine while allowing the spacer to guide the cover. Also put one of the lower bolts (near the oil pan rail) into the cover and let it act as a guide as well. Remember, with all of that RTV on the back of the cover, you want to be as close as possible when the cover finally contacts the gasket. Don't fight the centering effect of the spacer; let it be the primary guide. After the cover has made contact with the gasket, hold it in place while you partially tighten the first bolt. Install the other lower bolt, again only partially tight. Gradually install the remaining bolts in an evenly spaced order and slowly tighten all of the bolts to their final torque. Doing this slowly and evenly helps prevent the cover from moving away from the ideal location as determined by the spacer. This really helps minimize potential leaks.

24 Install the oil pump and pickup tube next. Be sure to use some RTV (just a thin layer) on both sides of the gaskets between the pump and the block, as well as between the pump and the pickup. Make sure you put some thread locking compound on the bolts that attach the oil pump to the engine and the pickup to the pump. Verify there is also play in how the oil pump drive shaft fits, that there is no binding. Prime the pump a bit by pouring some assembly lube into the pump and turning the shaft a few times to get it spread around the inside. Use a thicker fluid like assembly lube, Lucas Oil Stabilizer, or STP because these won't run out if the engine sits for a while before it is fully primed and run. Different engines may have slightly different components, but the concept is the same. Verify that the pickup is parallel to the bottom of the oil pan and also ensure the clearance of 1/8 to 1/4 inch between the pickup and the pan looks like it will be acceptable (remember to consider the thickness of the oil pan gasket(s). If adjustments need to be made, this is the time to make them.

ENGINE REBUILDING

25 Opinions differ on which type of oil pan gasket to use. Some argue that single-piece rubber gaskets are best regardless of the situation. Others argue the traditional multi-piece cork gaskets are best with a stamped-steel (versus a modern, cast-aluminum) pan. Either way, proper installation is the key. We used the old-style gasket to ensure we'd have the proper clearance to the oil pan pickup (rubber gaskets can be thicker). As with the timing cover, we used 3M yellow adhesive on the side of the gasket that touches the block. We also added some RTV at areas near the gasket that are more prone to leakage, such as at the main cap webs. We put a thicker bead on the timing cover and rear main cap sealing surfaces with a little extra at the joint near the gaskets. We put a thinner bead of RTV on the oil-pan sealing surfaces that contact the gasket and the rear main seal housing. Much of this RTV squeezes out when the oil pan is put on, so don't make the bead too thick or you could get RTV bits in the oil pickup.

26 First, place the dowel sleeves in the lower corner bolt-hole recesses, and then put on the head gaskets. These are usually directional and have a specific top/front mark, which ensures all of the holes line up correctly. Most engines use a relatively conventional gasket like ours, but some applications may require more specialized gaskets that have certain requirements for the surface finish of the block and heads and/or the need to cut grooves for O-rings. Our gasket only requires that the head and block surfaces are clean and free of any imperfections. Both were just machined and are true. If the gasket covers any holes in the block or heads, verify that's correct for your engine. Sometimes head gaskets are made to fit a number of different engines and details such as these can be overlooked. Recheck the part number in such cases.

For the oil pump we went with a higher-volume version for proper protection at higher power levels. The greater volume also helps a little with cooling because the greater oil flow removes more heat, especially from areas like the valvetrain that are not directly adjacent to the water jackets in the block. We didn't need a high-pressure oil pump because the engine wouldn't be running above normal RPM; higher pressure takes more horsepower to make as well.

Cylinder Head Installation

The cylinder heads can be installed after the main assembly of the short block has been completed. While I cannot show every step in detail, I do cover a few tips that involve common practices, whether you're building a daily driver, weekend cruiser, or show car. Always go by the factory service manual if you use stock and/or direct-replacement parts. If you use aftermarket parts in a higher-performance engine, you may need to follow the recommendation of the part manufacturers. This is especially critical with things like hydraulic lifter preload or valve lash (in the case of a solid-lifter camshaft).

Final Engine Assembly

Our engine build is not complete just yet; we want to install some of the remaining parts, such as the fuel pump, after the engine has been installed in the car. This minimizes the potential for damage to the parts or the car. The smaller the engine package and the fewer parts protruding from it, the easier the engine is to install into the car. If it's too difficult to install a part after the engine is in, it goes on the engine beforehand. Something like the fuel pump, which is fairly easy to install in the car, can be left off until the engine is in.

Engine Assembly CONTINUED

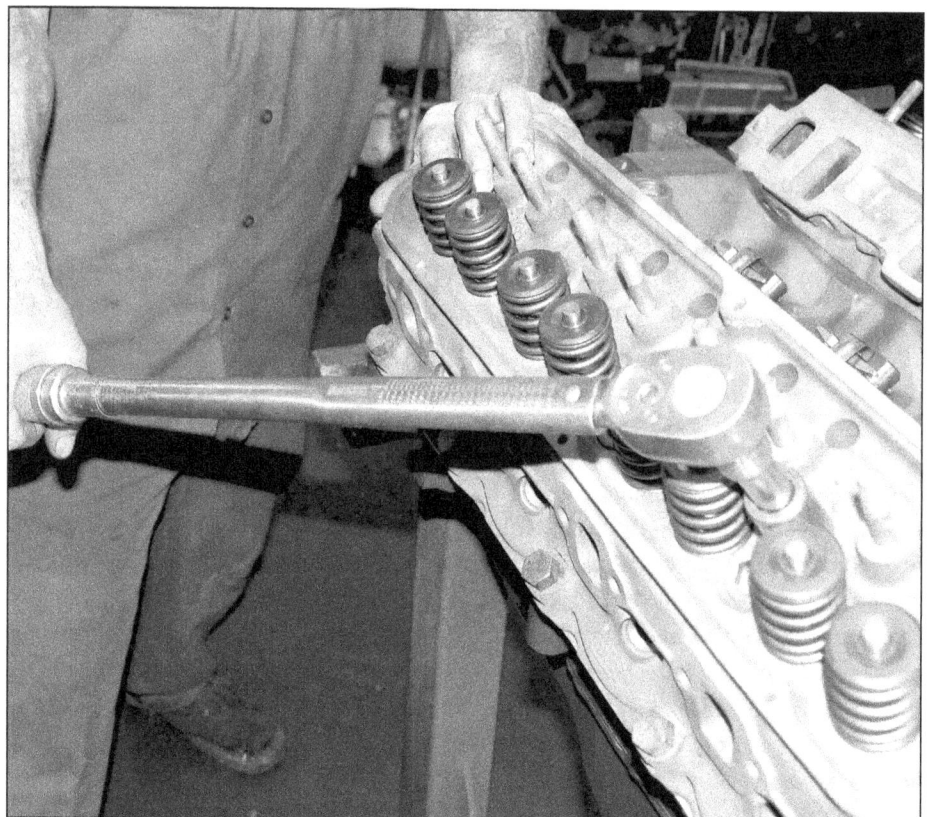

27 With the gasket in place, install and torque down the cylinder heads. Assemble the cylinder heads by installing the valves (rub assembly lube over the valvestems), valveguide seals, valvesprings, retainers, and valvelocks as specified either by the service manual or the manufacturer of the components. Be sure to verify the installed height and the spring pressures are within the applicable specifications for each valve. Place each head on the block and then partially tighten the longer center bolts first and then partially tighten the shorter outer bolts. Also spray each bolt's threads with some silicone (WD-40 or similar) to help prevent corrosion over time. Don't use thread lockers. After all the bolts have been snugged down at least once, you can then use the tightening method and torque specs for your particular engine. You should reference a factory service manual or info from the cylinder head gasket (or cylinder head) manufacturer. Generally an X-type pattern is used to tighten the bolts, starting in the center of the head and working outward. The longer bolts are often torqued to about 80 ft-lbs or so; the shorter bolts may sometimes be torqued less. It depends on the specific engine and components used so be sure to use the right data. While not always necessary, it is still a good idea to get to the final torque in at least two or three evenly spaced steps. For this procedure, you go through the full bolt pattern with the proper tightening sequence each time. It takes longer, but it provides extra insurance that the head gaskets will seal better.

28 There are two key elements to the proper assembly of the valvetrain: proper lubrication and proper adjustment. Due to the significantly higher point loading of the valvetrain components, normal assembly lubes don't prevent potential damage and wear at initial startup. Special lubes, usually some form of molybdenum disulfide compound, are required. Apply this at each end of each pushrod, at the top of each valve, and underneath each rocker arm pivot ball (or other load-bearing point of the rocker arm if you're using something different from the stock style). This substance is very tacky, so you don't need to use much; it will stay in place. Install each pushrod, rocker arm, rocker pivot ball, and lock nut in order and only tighten the lock nut until there are just a couple of threads of the rocker stud showing above it. Tightening the lock nuts all the way until snug could damage the lifters during the adjustment.

ENGINE REBUILDING

29 Next, adjust the lifter preload (or valve lash with solid lifters). A trick way to do this is to turn the crankshaft in the direction of normal rotation until the exhaust lifter of one of the cylinders just begins to move up. Watch the lifter, not the valve itself or the rocker arm. Adjust the intake valve of the same cylinder by tightening the rocker arm lock nut until there is zero lash. You reach zero valve lash by spinning the pushrod with your fingers and noting the first increase in resistance. Then tighten the intake lock nut more (usually another 1/2 to 3/4 turn or so) per either the factory service manual or the setting recommended by the lifter's manufacturer. With a solid-lifter camshaft, you instead insert feeler gauges between the rocker tip and the valve and adjust the rocker lock nut to the desired clearance. After adjusting the intake valve, rotate the crankshaft until the same intake valve opens and then closes about half way. Then adjust the exhaust valve of the same cylinder in the same manner. After adjusting the valves for the first cylinder, rotate the crankshaft again in the normal direction and adjust the valves for another cylinder. Repeat the process until all of the valves have been adjusted. If you have not already done so, install the cylinder head freeze plugs in the same manner as with the engine block; use RTV on the sealing surface and gently tap the plugs in place. Brass plugs are still preferred.

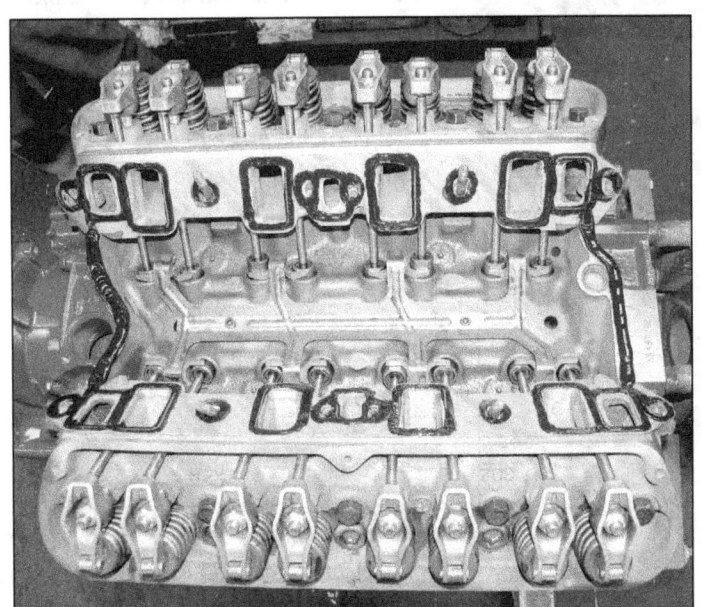

30 Our engine is now ready for final assembly. Before the engine is closed up, we pour some assembly lube over the lifters, rocker arm pivots, and rocker arm tips, for initial startup lubrication. Don't overdo it; just apply enough to coat the contact areas of the parts evenly and fully. Spray with silicone and install the four short mounting studs into the heads (if used) and then apply a thin bead of 3M yellow adhesive around each opening of each head. Install the intake gaskets and then apply a thin layer of RTV around each gasket opening. Spread it into a relatively thin, flat layer. Note how the intake ports have been opened slightly to better match the intake gaskets. (This same operation was performed on the intake manifold to improve engine performance.) For the end seals, use a thicker sealing bead. Opinions differ on the best way to prevent leaks from the ends of the valley area, plus the specific engine design and types of seals available also come into play. For our engine, we didn't use end seals at all and instead relied on RTV alone for a seal. This eliminates a number of extra joints and potential leak paths, especially when the RTV contacts the RTV already on the head gasket to create a continuous seal, as we have done. Modern RTV sealers are robust enough for this purpose and provide a strong, durable seal in a normal engine. Higher-output engines and/or blown engines with high levels of blowby may be able to breach this type of seal, but these are not our focus. You need to use the right amount of RTV because any extra could squeeze out into the engine and it could clog the oil pump pickup or other such area. Surface preparation is, of course, also critical. Be sure to wipe the metal sealing surfaces of the block and the intake manifold with brake cleaner, lacquer thinner, or a similar cleaner that leaves no residual film. Surfaces must be free of any contaminants or chemical residue before you apply the RTV.

Engine Assembly CONTINUED

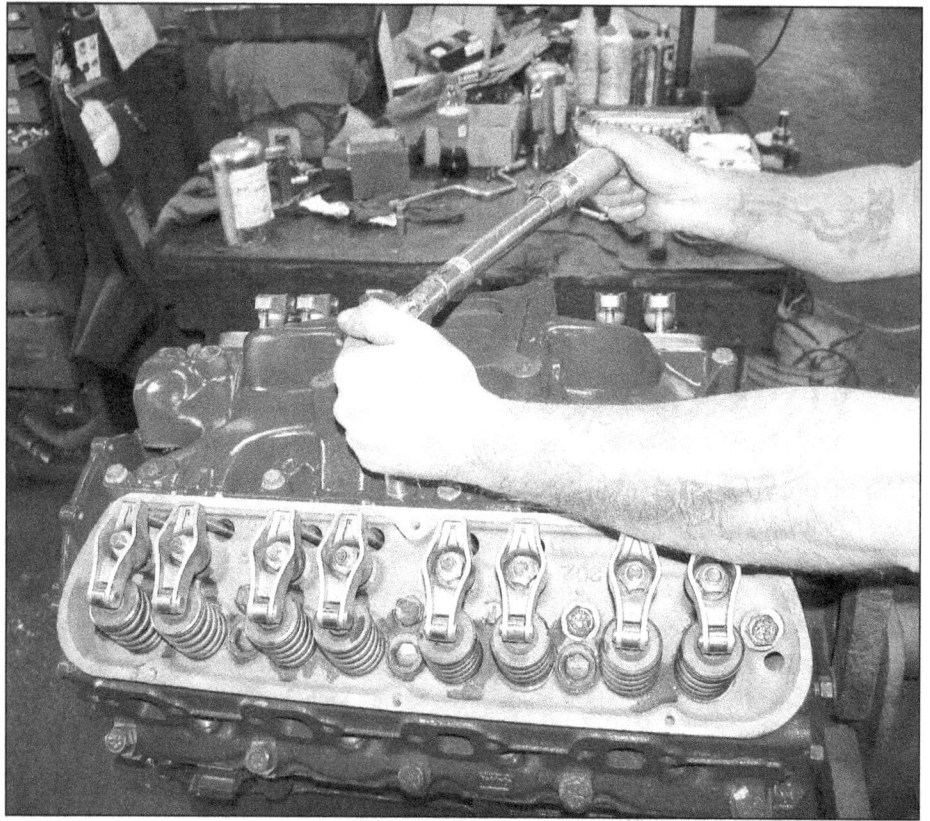

31 The intake manifold can then be lowered over the four short locating studs. Watch the RTV at the end seals to make sure too much has not been applied and is squeezing out. Install all the bolts and nuts (after spraying with WD-40 or silicone) until they are just hand tight. Tighten the four center bolts first using an X pattern. The correct torque is usually only about 18 to 20 ft-lbs, so only one pass will be needed. After the four center bolts have been tightened, you can just tighten the rest from the center out on each side. Don't overtighten these fasteners! Use the correct torque spec for your engine based on the factory manual, reliable source, or in special cases, per the manufacturer of the intake manifold or cylinder head. Overtorquing risks stripping threads and/or breaking fasteners. Besides, you may reduce the effectiveness of the gaskets and create either vacuum or coolant leaks due to the intake manifold warping and/or distortion.

32 Install the valve cover gaskets using the same procedure we've used elsewhere: 3M yellow adhesive on one side of the gasket (in this case the side that touches the valve cover) and RTV on the other side. Again, use a thin layer of sealer/adhesive in a manner that encircles all bolt hole openings. Some would argue, as was the case with the oil pan, that silicone rubber gaskets are superior to cork gaskets. Our rationale remains: While that may be the case with a thicker (cast/billet-aluminum or flanged-steel) valve cover, our engine builder prefers to use the cork gaskets when thin, steel factory-style covers are used. We wanted to keep the original "POWER BY FORD" logo covers, so we used the older cork gaskets. They shouldn't leak when installed properly and 3M adhesive and RTV sealant are used.

With the valve covers and intake manifold on, the engine can be given a final coat of paint to touch up any areas that were missed (bolt heads) and to hide the various sealers to present a cleaner appearance.

ENGINE REBUILDING

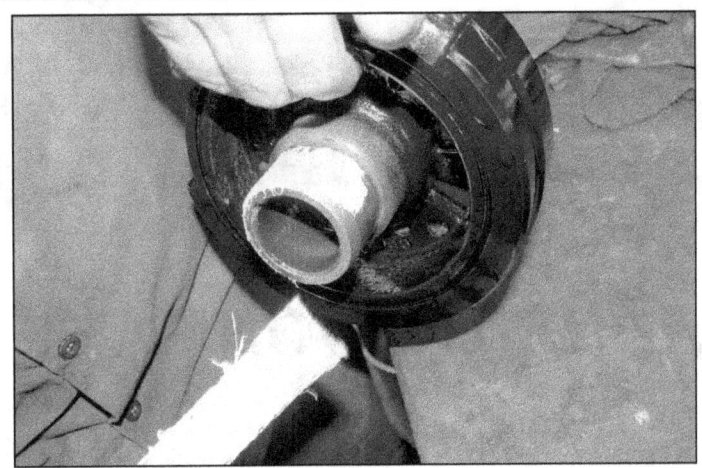

33 The harmonic balancer was painted and installed. We made sure we applied some of our assembly lube mix to the surface that contacts the timing cover seal, plus we also rubbed a thin layer of RTV on the inside surface that contacts the crankshaft. Likewise, we also put a layer of RTV underneath the washer for the large bolt that holds on the balancer to further help prevent oil leaks. The compression fit balancer is best installed using either a special tool made for the purpose or a block of wood placed across it to distribute the impact force from the blows of a 5-pound-or-so sledge hammer. With the balancer fully on, apply thread locker to its retaining bolt and then torque it down to the proper figure. The crankshaft pulley can be bolted to it. Apply a small amount of thread locker to the retaining bolts.

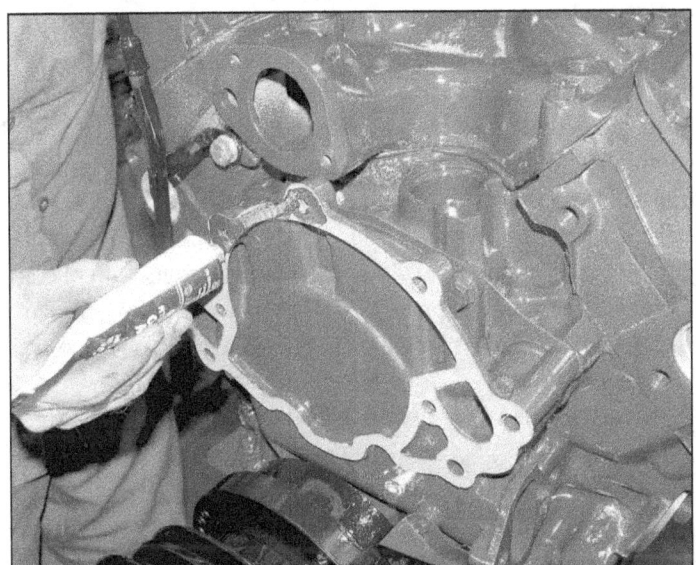

34 If desired, the oil dipstick can now be installed. Use a small amount of RTV on the end of the dipstick that gets inserted into the engine block to help prevent leaks. The water pump is the last major component to be installed. The gasket for it gets the same treatment: 3M yellow adhesive on one side, RTV on the other, and all openings encircled by both. We don't install all the water pump bolts at this time because some are used to mount other components that won't go on until the engine is in the car. Some of the water pump bolts go into coolant passages, and thus may create a leak if they are not torqued down correctly. Applying a small amount of RTV under the heads of such bolts can also help prevent leaks. We upgraded to an Edelbrock water pump because it provides greater water flow and more even distribution than a stock pump. The Edelbrock pump also uses superior materials and design features, so it should not only perform better but last longer and not be as likely to leak.

The finished engine assembly is a thing of beauty. We left the freeze plugs and water pump natural color to provide a bit of contrast to the blue engine color. We will not be putting the engine into the car immediately, so we mask off all of the various openings with tape, as we have begun to do with the intake manifold, to keep dirt out. We have intentionally left off a number of components, such as the exhaust manifolds, to make installing the engine into the car easier and to protect the paint. These can easily be installed after the engine is in the car. Others such as the thermostat housing and some of the hose fittings were left off because we have not obtained them yet. In the final chapter where we reassemble the vehicle we will cover these and many of the other finished and/or new parts best left for later installation.

CHAPTER 6

REBUILDING TRANSMISSIONS

Ford offered several different transmission types for the first-generation Mustangs, ranging from simple 3-speed manuals to beefy C6 automatics. The transmission choice was determined by engine size, trim level, production date, and of course the box on the order sheet that the buyer checked. I can't cover every possible variation (that's what factory service manuals are for), but I can give you some overall instructions to consider should you decide to service, rebuild, and/or upgrade your transmission yourself. Most of what you see here applies to any type of restoration project, though there may be some situations where those seeking complete authenticity may want to do things differently.

A good transmission repair shop should know what is correct for your particular vehicle if it is relatively unmodified. If you decide to farm the work out, most of my recommendations are also questions you can ask a shop to help ensure they do a good, thorough job. I highlight some known problem areas and steps to reduce the risk of trouble. I don't get into things like installing a late-model overdrive transmission because that is beyond the scope of this book.

Various manufacturers offer complete kits to make the swap fairly straightforward; as a result such conversions are more common. This can be a very beneficial enhancement for a weekend cruiser, if the economics work out. It reduces wear on the engine, improves fuel mileage, and also likely improves performance. Had we been building more of a so-called restomod, we'd likely have gone this route.

One of the first things to know when working on transmissions, especially automatics, is that cleanliness is mandatory. A little bit of dirt in the wrong place can cause all kinds of shifting issues, even on a manual transmission. Likewise, using improper tools or excessive force can come back to haunt you in many ways, from sticking shift levers to outright component failure. For the most part, not too many special tools are needed to rebuild a transmission; but when they are, it's best to use them or find an acceptable alternative.

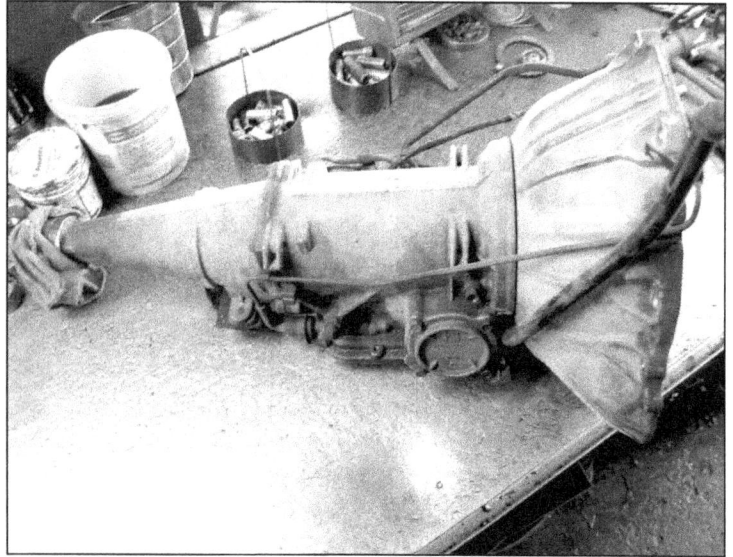

Our C4 transmission had only some minor seepage, which was expected because it was not used for 26 years. The tailshaft seal and the input shaft seal were also in good shape and not showing and signs of leakage or worn ushings/ bearings that could have caused it. There were no signs of damage or abuse. The bellhousing was removed first, followed by the dipstick/tube and the vacuum modulator hard line. The modulator can also be taken off now because it's always a good idea to replace this part in a rebuild. Do not lose the metal rod that extends into the transmission as you take the modulator off.

HOW TO RESTORE YOUR MUSTANG 1964½–1973

Automatic Transmission Disassembly and Inspection

You can save you quite a bit of money, if not time, by doing it yourself. You also have the satisfaction of knowing you did the job yourself and it was done properly. I provide some information you'd find in a factory manual and also some additional information to help ensure the best possible results on your rebuild. I show separate rebuilds for a manual (Toploader) and an automatic (C4) transmission. These will be specific to the transmissions we're working on, but many of the steps and much of the information can be used with other applications.

Automatic Transmission Disassembly and Inspection

Taking apart any automatic transmission requires considerable care, not only to avoid damaging components but also to avoid losing any of the small bits that tend to fly all over the place if you're not careful. Many things are under spring pressure and can shoot out suddenly and cause injury. Study the service manual diagrams to see where the springs are and take the appropriate safety precautions. Also many surfaces must be kept smooth and free of scratches to provide a proper seal, so take extra care removing O-rings, gaskets, and seals.

One of the most common problems with older automatics is that seals and O-rings harden over time and become brittle. This causes morning sickness, where the tranny has problems until it warms up and the seals begin to work better. Sometimes you can minimize this effect with special additives, but a rebuild ultimately is required. After you've decided to go that route, it's best to simply replace certain items preemptively to ensure you don't have problems later.

Transmission rebuild kits are usually not very expensive and they include all

Automatic Transmission Disassembly

1 Our C4 is a 1968 model, so we have the side vent tube setup shown here. Remove the tube carefully if it's stuck in the transmission housing, to ensure it will still seal properly when it's put back in. It won't seal or if it's bent or scratched. The bolt for the mounting bracket (one of the four for the piston housing) and the similar one on the opposite side of the tranny can be removed now as well. This provides the first real look into two of the many internal pressurized fluid paths of the tranny. The disassembly of these covers is a prime example of where a spring is applying pressure to them, so their bolts must be removed carefully.

2 The small amount of sediment present in the fluid is not a problem, especially since the color of the fluid is fine and there was no burned odor. The friction materials wear, and the smaller particles will not always be caught by the filter, if they even get that far. The bores in the cover shown at left and in the main housing are of greater significance and showed no signs of abnormal wear or damage. The seals on the piston were also fine. These often harden over time and cause problems, especially when the transmission is not up to temperature. They are replaced anyway as a matter of course during the rebuild. Not shown is the pilot shaft that locates the piston. These rarely have any problems, but if they do show signs of excessive wear or damage, they can be replaced, as is evident from the retaining clip seen on the piston.

3 Before removing the neutral safety switch, you first must remove the downshift control cable. Make a note of how it was positioned. Use the shift lever to make sure the transmission is in the neutral position and then insert a pin/nail into the alignment hole to keep the switch internals properly lined up for reinstallation. Remove the switch by simply undoing the two mounting bolts. The shift lever assembly is removed later. Note the location of one of the band adjustment bolts to the left of the switch assembly.

the gaskets, seals, and O-rings, etc., you need, as well as other components like springs. Springs may look good but may have relaxed over time, thus affecting their function. You can also step up to special performance-oriented rebuild kits, which provide faster, firmer shifts, and which may also upgrade the various friction materials to handle higher power levels. These are available for most automatic transmissions used in early Mustangs.

Regardless of the level of service you choose for your transmission, it is critical you keep everything as clean as possible when you put it back together. C4 transmissions, for example, are known to have problems with the governor sticking if dirt gets into it. Clean off the exterior of the tranny before disassembly to help prevent loose dirt from getting inside. After you open it up, you will surely find some areas where particles of worn friction material, etc., have accumulated. This is normal, up to a point. If the filter is virtually clogged with dirt and/or the bottom of the pan has a thick layer of so-called mud, you can reasonably expect to find more problems as you disassemble the rest of the tranny. Be prepared to do more than just replace parts in such a situation. Ideally, you see little accumulation of worn material, and you can simply replace the friction materials, seals, O-rings, etc., without replacing major components.

I show the main steps involved in taking an automatic transmission apart, in this case the C4 that came with our 1968 J-code GT, so it can be inspected and evaluated to determine what needs to be done. I only hit some high points and thus recommend you use the factory service manual for the detailed step-by-step procedure.

Our tranny was in really good shape, so I also won't show any major problems being resolved or any modifications. I only show the highlights of a straight factory rebuild, but I include some extra information on special things to consider that are not covered by the factory service manual. A very experienced transmission shop (Big 4 Transmissions in Paramount, California) rebuilt our transmission. This is the type of shop you should use if you decide to farm the job out.

The factory manual can only help so much, and diagrams are not always as clear as they need to be. There were numerous production variations, so it's not always possible to find the correct information for your specific transmission. If you are doing the work yourself, be sure to document how everything came apart—photographing the transmission at each critical step is very important, if not essential. You also need to properly tag and bag parts as you go, so all the components are clearly identified and organized should you find you are unsure of how to put something back together.

Since ours was a basic rebuild, I concentrate mainly on replacing worn friction materials, seals, O-rings, gaskets, and the like. I do, however, point out things to look for regarding the major components, which may indicate the need for more extensive repairs and/or the replacement of those parts. If you get to that point, and it's more than simply replacing a part, you may be better off having the work done professionally. When it's just a replacement, there is still a need for a certain amount of expertise. Components may have subtle differences or require specific installation procedures that may not be readily apparent. Something as simple as installing a bushing without properly lining up a slot or putting a gear in upside down can cause big problems.

Automatic Transmission Disassembly CONTINUED

4 Removing the pan confirmed our initial assessment. There was minimal accumulation of sediment in the pan or on the filter, and the inside of the transmission looked fairly clean. There were no signs of debris, broken parts, evidence of abuse, or burned fluid—all good signs. The valve body can come out next, but first it should be noted what type of valve body it is and where the different-size fasteners go. The shape of the "port" just above the filter is one clue to remember, as is the type and color of the spring that's visible below it. The bolts holding the valve body and filter are different sizes; make a note of how or where the various-size bolts go.

5 If the pump housing had an O-ring on the sealing face, there would also have been an extra hole in the housing between the two machined surfaces shown. Our car is a 1968, so we have neither the O-ring nor the hole. The minor dirt buildup seen here is typical and of no concern.

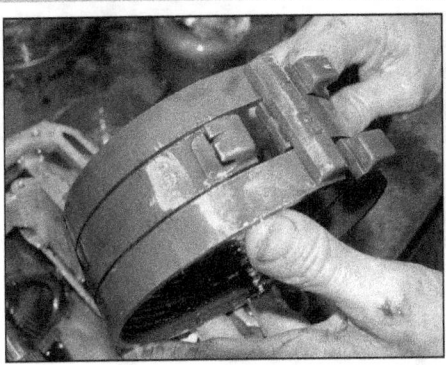

6 Original factory bands were generally cast, like the one shown here. This could cause problems with the lugs that contact the adjusters breaking off under certain conditions. Replacement bands are now often made of steel straps instead, thus eliminating this issue. In either case, the bands should generally be replaced during a rebuild because they all have some wear. If the friction material shows any signs of extreme or uneven wear, then find the cause and resolve the problem before using the tranny again. In many cases, this is a matter of an improper adjustment leading to slippage and wear.

7 With the front drum assemblies out of the way, inspect the rear components and the forward part of the output shaft. There shouldn't be any missing rollers or springs missing in the clutch and there shouldn't be any scratches or grooves on the shaft. The rollers and springs should always be replaced when the tranny is being rebuilt, as should the thrust washer underneath this sprag assembly.

8 The governor support housing on the rear of the main case should always be removed and inspected for any signs of excess wear or damage on the inner bore. Ours still had the cross-hatch pattern from the factory hone. The "stripes" are from the sealing rings on the output shaft and are normal as long as they are not too deep. You should be able to run your finger nail across them without even feeling them. This housing just gets a little time in the parts washer before it is dried and ready to be put back on.

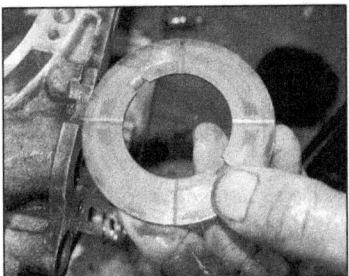

9 While it isn't always mandatory that you replace thrust washers, such as this one, it generally is a good idea because they aren't expensive. The main reason for not doing so is either that the particular one you need isn't readily available or that the replacement doesn't fit as well as the original. If it's best to reuse an original thrust washer, you must verify it's within specification and then lightly rub out any minor scratches with fine emery cloth. Any significant scratches, grooves, or embedded dirt means replacement. Make sure any washers used are clean and lubed with a thicker assembly-type lube, rather than just transmission fluid or oil, when you reassemble them into the transmission.

10 Replace the bushing and the seal in the tailshaft housing because it tends to be one of the more likely sites for trouble. A loose bushing causes the seal to wear unevenly (and thus leak), and can also cause a very noticeable driveline vibration. Both are relatively easy to replace; most rebuild kits include them. Make sure the notches in the bushing face to the rear (toward the driveshaft) and line up with at least one of the passages in the housing. The seal should only be driven in with evenly applied pressure via the correct seal installer, socket, or similar. Apply some RTV or a similar sealer to the seal before it's driven in further to prevent leaks.

Automatic Transmission Disassembly CONTINUED

11 Check several items in the planetary gear housing before using it again. First, check the condition of the thrust bearing. If it is available, it is best to replace it. Otherwise, it can be cleaned and lightly polished to clear up any minor imperfections. The planetary housing itself needs to be checked for any excessive wear at any of the rubbing surfaces, plus each gear needs to be closely examined for imperfections. The play of each gear in the lateral and radial directions must be measured to ensure they are within spec. While these parts generally do not exhibit problems, many are still possible and can have major consequences if they are not resolved before reassembly.

The friction plates are replaced as a matter of course when the transmission is rebuilt. These looked exceptionally good, but they still did show some wear. The replacements had more material, plus it was of a newer, superior specification. Never mix friction plates; only replace and use them as a matched set from the same manufacturer. The spacer plates or "steels" as they are sometimes called generally don't need replacing unless they are excessively worn or damaged. They can normally be lightly buffed with emery cloth or a ScotchBrite disc to remove any minor flaws. Be sure to fully wipe and lubricate them prior to installation.

12 The drums and their internal components rarely need replacement, but it is still advisable to replace the springs simply as a precaution. The inner bushings are getting harder to source in some cases, and thus may force the reuse of the original part if it is not worn or damaged. If you can find one, it's much less expensive that having one custom made. A special fixture is often used to compress the springs while the retaining clip is removed. Carefully avoid sending parts flying when removing the retaining ring; use the tool very slowly. Generally, the drums will simply be cleaned and reused if they are okay.

13 In some cases, there will be an O-ring or other type of seal inside the drum. These must always be replaced. Use a pick or similar tool to carefully remove the item as to not scratch or otherwise damage the sealing surfaces or the retaining groove. Note that while it appears there is wear on the inner walls of the drum, these are actually just surface rub/polish marks that are not deep enough to be of any concern.

14 We examined our transmission's pump housing/stator surfaces and found no signs of excess wear or damage that would prevent its reuse. This is a good indicator that the bushings they contact are also probably in good shape. If these machined surfaces had deeper grooves, scratches, or pitting, we would have repaired or replaced it. The sealing rings are also in good shape and don't even need to be replaced except as a precaution. The whole assembly can just be put in the parts washer for a rinse and then it can be wiped and dried until it's ready to go back in. However, that's assuming we don't find any other issues. While it is okay to lightly buff these surfaces with emery cloth or a fine abrasive pad, be careful to not damage the sealing rings either directly or due to residue getting down into their grooves. Unless the imperfections are more than just very superficial (similar to what is shown) it's probably best to not use any abrasive material to try to smooth things.

REBUILDING TRANSMISSIONS

15 When taking the pump assembly apart, it is important to note several subtle aspects of how parts fit together. One of the more critical things is that the inner gear has a beveled edge on the bore that must face the housing when the parts are reassembled. Each gear should also be inspected for any imperfections or other signs that there may be a problem with the contact pattern. If excessive dirt and/or debris were in the fluid, we would surely have seen the effects of it here because the pump gears would have pits or other problems. Our tranny had no signs of any surface imperfections on the gears or on the sliding surfaces of the housing/stator. Even the front shaft seal looked good enough to reuse but this is also one of those items you should just automatically replace.

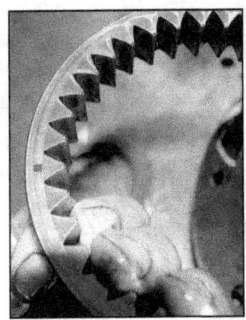

16 The outer pump gear is often directional. One side of the gear may be marked with a dot as shown. When reassembling the pump/stator assembly, this side of the gear must face the inside of the housing (same direction as the bevel on the inner gear). All of the same criteria for the inner gear apply to the outer gear. Therefore, the gear and where it makes contact with the housing must be free of damage or marring. Fortunately, these gears and the pump assembly in general rarely exhibit any problems unless they have been exposed to dirt or debris. If the filter is clean, these will usually be fine too.

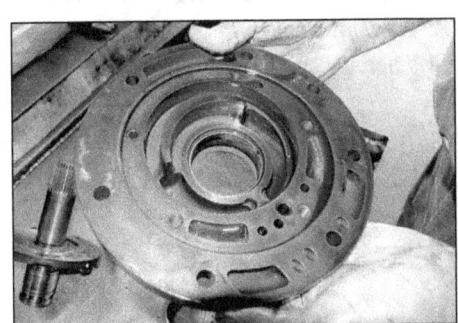

17 The pump/stator housing surfaces that contact the gears must also be inspected to ensure they are not excessively worn, pitted, or otherwise damaged. In addition to replacing the seal as indicated previously, the bushing must always be replaced as well. In the case of a C4 transmission like ours, you should use a C6 bushing because it is slightly larger and will provide more support. Whichever bushing you use, however, be sure to install it so the hole on the edge is away from the seal and so it lines up with the left (furthest, counterclockwise) machined hole in the housing. As you can see, that is not the case here. When we put in the new bushing, we will make sure it properly lines up with the hole.

18 Special tools, such as this fixture, can facilitate the removal of the drum assemblies. It compresses the spring-loaded plate and holds it down so the retaining clip can be removed. The fixture has a ratchet mechanism and is adjustable for various size components. With the retaining clip removed, the lever must be slowly lifted to relieve pressure so the springs don't fly all over. Trying to do this without the proper tools can damage the components and some of the smaller parts can be easily lost.

19 Disassembly of the drums varies with the drum you're working on, as well as the transmission you're dealing with. For example, 1969 and earlier transmissions will often use multiple smaller springs for the drum shown, while 1970 and later models are more likely to have a single coil spring. As has been the case this far, the O-ring and friction plates should automatically get replaced, but the steels may be reused provided they are not worn or damaged. While it's okay to lightly buff these steels with an emery cloth or pad (only if necessary to remove slight flaws) before reinstalling them it is not generally advisable to do so with components made of aluminum due to the potential for damage.

Automatic Transmission Disassembly CONTINUED

20 The outer surfaces of the drums must be inspected as well because the friction bands make contact with surfaces in some cases. Make sure there is no excess wear or damage. It's also advisable to check any splines or gear teeth to ensure the same holds true for these. The splines on this part show some slight wear, but it's little more than a mild, surface scuffing. Had they been deeper, it could mean replacement.

21 When disassembling the valve body, it is especially important to be aware of the possibility that small parts (check balls, for example) can come out as the parts are separated. The best approach is to remove the necessary bolts and then flip the assembly over so that the smaller casting (on the right) is on the bottom when the parts are split. This will keep the check balls in place rather than allow them to fall out. Note the location of each check ball because this varies by application. And there may be differences in the check balls themselves, so the balls need to be matched to their specific locations as well. Some sediment in the fluid passages is normal and will usually come off in the parts washer.

22 One of the distinctions of the various valve bodies you may come across is the configuration of the linkage for the manual control valve. The 1969-and-earlier versions like the one shown here have the detents on the valve body itself. The 1970-and-later versions tend to have the detents on the case. This affects the assembly procedure to the extent the linkage must be properly lined up when they are reassembled. The factory service manual should have the proper procedure for your particular application.

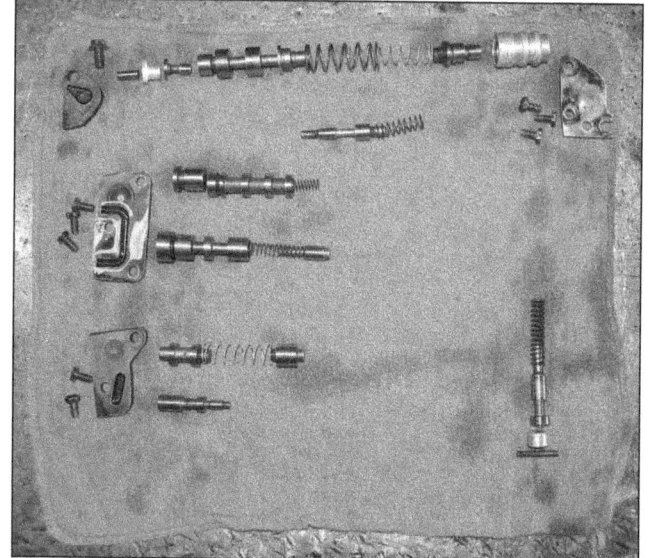

When disassembling the valve body, it's most important to recognize that parts are under spring pressure. Virtually all of the small valves, plungers, etc. will fly out of the valve body and possibly get lost or damaged, unless you prevent it. It's extremely critical that you note each part's location; improper assembly almost always has very negative consequences. If any of the parts are a bit sticky as they come out, then the plunger and/or the bore should be lightly buffed with an emery cloth or pad to remove any imperfections. Any residual abrasive material must be fully flushed out before reassembly. Most rebuild kits will also include replacement springs. High-performance rebuild kits may provide different color springs with different pressure levels to change the shift characteristics. Pay particular attention to the condition of the aluminum components; they are more prone to wear and/or pitting.

Automatic Transmission Reassembly

All parts should be cleaned and, if necessary, properly lubricated prior to assembly and/or installation. Different types of lubricants are required in different instances. In some cases I deviate from the service manual, based on information gleaned from those with many years of successful rebuilding experience, because a superior procedure has been developed. There have been significant advances in materials and lubricants since these vehicles were first built and the factory service manuals published. Even without upgrading to a high-performance rebuild kit, there have been changes that require things be done differently.

Even though parts are direct replacements for the original factory items, there may be design or material changes. Several of the items in our rebuild kit, including the friction bands, were designed significantly different from the original factory parts. Functionally, they are as good, or usually even better, but may require a different installation process.

Automatic Transmission Assembly

A typical rebuild kit includes gaskets, seals, O-rings, new friction materials, check balls, and even new sealing nuts for the band adjustment bolts. There may be extra parts if the kit covers multiple applications, so don't get upset if there are leftovers. Just be sure you use the correct items for your specific application. Materials technology has improved quite a bit since first-generation Mustangs were new. These new materials provide better sealing for the transmission to reduce the likelihood of leaks, and these often increase the service life after a rebuild. Although not shown here, we also replaced some of the hard parts such as springs, the vacuum modulator, and even one of the friction bands. Some rebuild kits include more than others, most items are available individually as well.

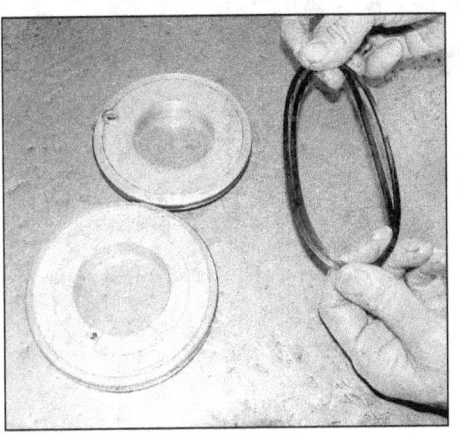

1 When trying to determine which seal or O-ring goes on a particular part, it is best to first separate the new pieces by seal type (square seal versus O-ring, for example) and then stretch them in pairs to get the relative lengths of each. Start with the largest component of each type and install the seals with the appropriate lubricant after first ensuring the sealing groove is clean. While most elastometric seals are not directional (and O-rings never are) check to make sure that is the case before installing it. There can be special features on the seal that may require a particular orientation. Seals that are molded onto a metal or plastic housing generally need to be installed in a specific manner. Always use the proper type of seal installer and lube.

2 Most of the spacer plates (or steels) are non-directional, but some must be installed in a specific manner. If there is a bevel, such as that shown, here then it must face into the clutch assembly, toward the friction discs. This is usually necessary to clear the retaining clip that holds the whole assembly together. All of the friction discs and spacer plates must be lubricated with transmission fluid prior final assembly. This swells them slightly, so we need to make sure there is sufficient clearance between them after everything is assembled. For high-pressure items, such as thrust washers, assembly grease should be used. Sleeve bushings and roller bearings generally also benefit from a dab of grease in certain locations. A thin film is best, and the components should also be rotated without any load to ensure the grease gets spread evenly.

Automatic Transmission Assembly CONTINUED

3 The inner planetary gear set is an example of where multiple lubricant types should be used. The thrust washer needs to be greased while the gears themselves should only be lubricated either with transmission fluid or lightweight oil. Be sure to not only lubricate the thrust washer itself but the surface it will contact as well. In this photo, both the thrust washer in the drum assembly and the tip of the planetary housing are greased. Note how dabs of grease were used to hold the larger thrust washer onto the planetary housing, so it didn't fall off when the planetary housing was turned upside down and installed into the drum assembly. Lube the splines also.

4 The shift lever seal must always be replaced when rebuilding a transmission. It is simply pried out and replaced while the shift lever assembly is out of the housing. Do not simply tap it in with a hammer. Use the back of a socket or seal installer with a flat face that applies pressure evenly. The valve body must be removed to get the shift lever out, so this is definitely the time to do it. The new seal must be lubricated before the shift lever is reinserted. Proper installation of this seal will minimize the chances for one of the most common leaks. This seal has a particularly tough job because it is more exposed to contamination than most of the other seals on the transmission, plus the shaft only rotates through a partial arc.

5 Reassembling the servos is not very complex, but a few tips apply. Be sure to lubricate the sealing surface and the shaft with a light film of oil. There shouldn't be too much play between the shaft and its bore, but it needs to slide freely. Be very careful when pushing the piston down into the housing, so you don't tear the edge of the seal. A thin film of RTV on the cover gasket can also help prevent leaks. It is also best to tighten the cover down slowly and evenly in several steps to prevent warping and leaks. Start with the bolts that hold the vent tube bracket and then go diagonally across in a star pattern to the final torque.

6 After both servos have been installed, check their operation by applying an air source to the appropriate ports in the housing. Just a quick burst of air should be enough to verify the shaft isn't sticking and there are no leaks. Be sure to not use too much air pressure or else damage can result. Here, you can also see the rear case bushing. If this is in good shape, it's probably best to reuse it because these can be hard to source in the proper size. If there are any minor imperfections that need to be removed, lightly rub with a fine emery cloth or pad.

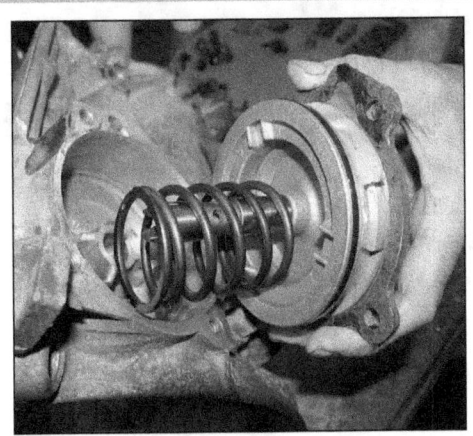

7 Some front servos have a sealing ring, rather than a square-edged seal on the piston. The same basic instructions apply for making sure the shaft and sealing surfaces are lubed with oil. However, you also need to properly align the cover so the gasket properly seals a port. It cannot simply be installed in any orientation. Hold the gasket onto the housing with RTV or grease and tighten the bolts slowly/evenly. Some servo covers are also stamped with a letter to designate the firmness of the spring: "H" is normal; "R" is firm. Ours was "H."

8 When installing the rear sprag, it may be necessary to move it around a bit to ensure it seats fully. The springs can sometimes stick together and/or contact the sprag, thus causing improper action. Therefore, these need to be greased applied to the necessary surfaces and check to make sure the sprag freely rotates clockwise. It should lock if you try to turn it counterclockwise. Also check the movement of the linkage going back into the case to ensure it doesn't stick. Lubricate as needed.

9 When installing the governor support housing, make sure the two tubes fully engage their respective ports in the main housing, but also that the bore of the housing is centered as well as it can be over the sprag assembly. To the extent possible due to the tolerances of the retaining bolts, move the housing around as the bolts are being tightened to provide the best concentricity. This will provide the best alignment of the tailshaft with minimal friction and potential for wear. After you've bolted this housing in, make sure the top surface and inner bores are wiped clean.

10 When assembling the new rollers and wave springs into the rear sprag assembly, it may be necessary to occasionally rotate the inner race to ensure the springs seat fully. While grease should be used as lubrication between the thrust washer and the race, only oil or transmission fluid should be used between the race and the rollers. It's best to squirt some at each roller after all the pieces have been assembled. Turn the race to spread it.

As the transmission is assembled, verify operation or functionality. This could mean anything from simply moving a lever or shaft to make sure nothing is binding, to using air pressure to ensure proper function of a servo. This helps ensure components are operating as intended so you do not have to tear the transmission apart again in order to fix something. Even though the fluid will not be at pressure, many functions can still be checked, at least in a basic sense. It's also a good idea to move things so lubricants put on during assembly are evenly distributed before the transmission is operated under load. This can help prevent problems on first use.

The final stages of assembly include not only the installation of major parts but also various adjustments beyond those already mentioned. The factory service manual is the best place to find out what particular adjustments apply in your case. I've provided a few reminders and also briefly described some of the remaining steps.

Automatic Transmission Assembly CONTINUED

11 Before installing any of the bands, soak them in some transmission fluid for a short while. This ensures the friction material has absorbed enough prior to first operation. Check the reverse band, shown here, one last time for excess wear at the points where the adjuster tips contact the band. A small amount of polishing is fine, but any grooving or cracking means for replacement. Before installing the rear drum, its outer surface should also be lightly sanded with fine emery cloth or a ScotchBrite-type pad to remove any imperfections and create a smoother, more even surface for the band to grip. There's no adjustment.

12 After proper inspection and installing new sealing rings, the tailshaft can be inserted into the governor housing and through the sprag and reverse drum. This will help line everything up for when we stack on the rest of the drums. Do not bolt the governor on yet. This is a good time, however, to put on the new band-adjustment sealing nuts and start the band adjustment bolts in their holes. Do not turn them in too far at this point; just thread them in far enough to not fall out.

13 Slide the entire planetary gear and forward drum stack onto the forward part of the tailshaft. All internal parts should be lubricated as needed beforehand. Be sure that the retaining clips are fully seated. Before the drum assemblies are installed, visually check to ensure all retaining clips have been fully seated into their grooves. Failure to do so can result in binding and/or failure. The rear planetary carrier is especially susceptible to this issue. Loosely install the forward band, but only tighten the adjusting nuts enough to hold the band and its related parts together. We will adjust the band later. Our replacement band was a steel strap style instead of the cast design of the original part (similar to the reverse band shown previously). This design is less prone to failure because the steel strap does not crack as easily as the casting does.

14 After verifying the input shaft is clean and free of any wear or damage, it can be inserted into the drum stack so its splines engage at the rear. The input shafts up to 1969 were the same at both ends, so it doesn't matter which way the shafts go in. The 1970-and-later shafts have a different length spline, so you have to make sure you put the correct end in first. Use an alignment bolt to hold the front pump housing gasket in place; a little RTV on the back of the gasket helps, but you still need the alignment bolt to locate the pump. The pump should have been pre-lubricated and have a new front seal and new sealing rings. Use oil to lubricate the sealing rings and grease to lubricate the bushings for the input shaft and the torque converter coupling. If you have a seal on the pump housing, rub some oil on it too and be careful pushing the pump into the main housing so as to not tear it.

REBUILDING TRANSMISSIONS

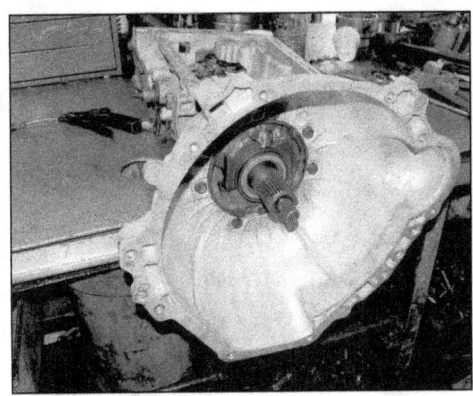

15 The bell housing can now be installed. The bellhousing bolts also hold the front pump assembly onto the main housing and keep it from rotating, so these bolts are longer while the shorter bolts are for the tailshaft housing. The inner/input shaft transmits the engine power to the rest of the transmission. The outer splined shaft does not turn, so it just supports the torque converter. The seal is necessary because the torque converter coupling passes through the seal and drives the inner gear to drive the pump. A little bit of oil should be rubbed on the front seal and the torque converter coupling when they are assembled together. The converter will have to be rotated until it can be pushed all the way in because the coupling drives the gear via a flat relief that mates with a similar key on the inner gear. This ensures whenever the engine is turning the pump in the tranny is also working to build pressure.

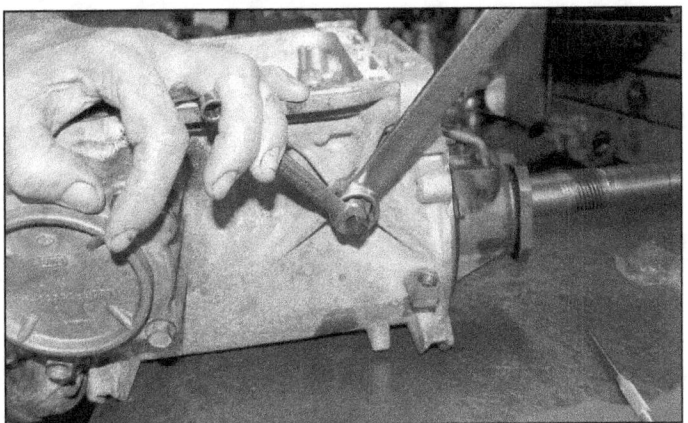

16 The factory manual details the procedure for adjusting the band(s) in your particular transmission. Generally, you turn the adjusting bolt a specific amount until you feel tension. Then you adjust it from there to the final setting. Always use new sealing bolts with a small amount of RTV applied around the seal itself as extra insurance against leaks. This is easily the most critical adjustment you will make when rebuilding the transmission, so be extra careful to get it right. An improper adjustment will cause all kinds of problems, from excessive wear to complete transmission failure. It's also a lot better to do it now than in the car.

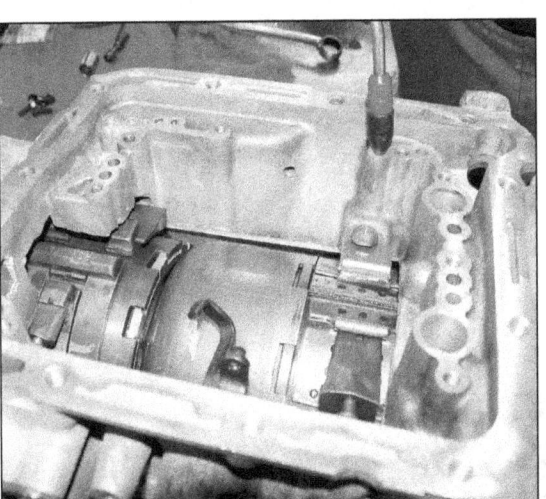

17 Use air pressure to blow out the appropriate port for the front servo to ensure the band functions properly when the whole assembly is assembled. You can clearly see the difference in design here between the steel-strap-type band and the original-style cast band. Beyond the advantages previously mentioned, the steel strap design will apply more even pressure and thus be smoother and wear more evenly, assuming it is properly adjusted. Squirt a small amount of transmission fluid on both bands and at the gaps on the planetary gear and drum cases to ensure some lubrication at initial startup.

18 Install this small screen filter in the governor support housing. The governor assembly is especially sensitive to any dirt or debris in the fluid, and this helps catch any that may be headed toward it. Blow out the passages with an air nozzle to try to dislodge any dirt. Then clean it in a parts washer or with a suitable spray, dry it, and install it. Replace it if it's damaged in any way. Make sure the mounting surface for the governor is clean and smooth before you install it. (These machining marks, seen here, are fine.) Torque the retaining bolts evenly and slowly, preferably in a star-shaped pattern.

Automatic Transmission Assembly CONTINUED

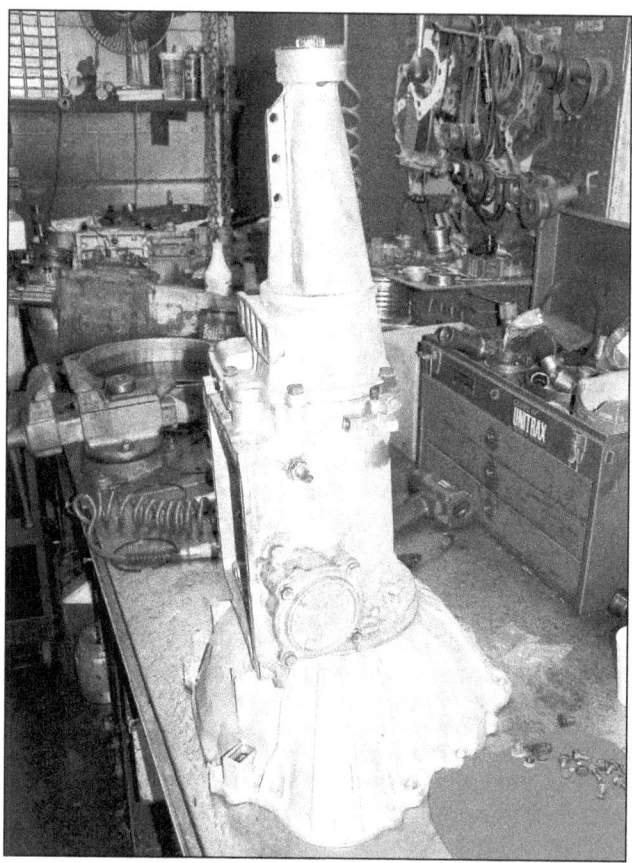

19 After having a new seal installed and putting a little RTV on its gasket, the tailshaft housing can go on along with some of the smaller items such as the vacuum modulator (don't forget the steel rod!) and the fittings for the transmission oil cooler lines. Depending on how you plan to install the tranny, you can also install its mount. Sometimes, it makes more sense to wait until the transmission has been lowered into the car before you put the mount on, to avoid it contacting anything and to have more room.

20 Use light pressure with a mild abrasive pad to clean up the separator plate for the valve body. This helps it seal better and removes any minor imperfections. Do this after you make any needed modifications (like drilling extra holes), should they be required with your rebuild/high-performance upgrade shift kit. Make sure you wipe off any residue and otherwise keep the plate as clean as possible.

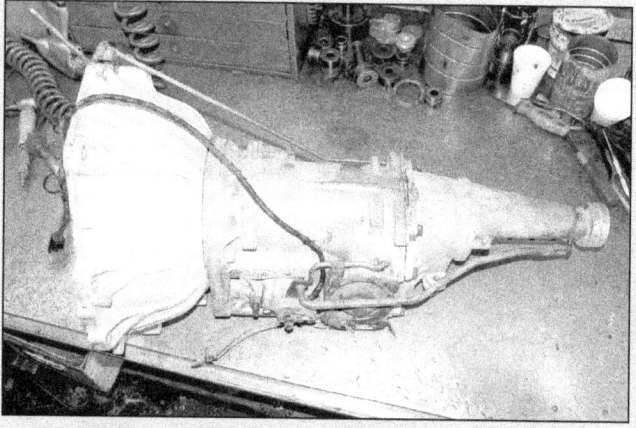

21 Reassemble the valve body with the filter. Be sure to put all check balls back in the proper locations in the valve body and check to make sure all plungers move freely and do not stick. Do not use any type of sealer on the valve body gaskets. You need to make sure everything is clean and dry when it goes back together. Do not overtorque the bolts because it could warp the valve body or crush the gasket and cause leaks. Put the shift lever in the proper position (usually straight up for Mustangs), so the valve body can be lowered over it and line up the manual control valve with it correctly. A thin film of RTV on the pan gasket can help avoid leaks but use as little as possible; you don't want bits of RTV squeezing into the transmission/filter.

The finished transmission now has the neutral safety switch, the downshift control cable, the vacuum modulator hard line, and the shift linkage added to complete it. We'll add the mount and dipstick/tube after we lower it into the car. Don't fill it until it's fully installed and be sure to use the correct type of fluid. If you've made any modifications, you should add additional cooling and/or use a compatible high-performance fluid just to be safe.

Torque Converter

The torque converter is commonly flushed, cleaned up, and reinstalled unless there is reason to believe it has a problem. There are numerous tests described in the service manual for diagnosing a suspected problem. If, however, the car drove fine before it was taken apart and there are no outward signs of damage on the torque converter (leaks, cracks, dents, heat damage, etc.), it is reasonable to assume it will be fine as long as there were no problems with the transmission either. If, however, the tranny fluid was dark/dirty and/or had a burnt odor, it is best to verify the function of the converter before you put it back in.

If you verify there is a problem with the converter, it is best to simply replace it. There really is no cost-effective means for most people to make repairs. In most cases a direct replacement will suffice. However, heavy-duty and/or high-performance/higher-stall speed versions are also available for various applications. Spending a little extra for a stronger, more durable construction is wise, especially if engine output has been increased and/or the car will be driven more aggressively.

Going with a much higher stall speed, however, is generally not a good choice for a street-driven car because it compromises both drivability and durability for a relatively minor and primarily straight-line performance gain. In many cases, using a significantly higher stall-speed converter also requires supplemental cooling for the transmission, thus raising cost, vehicle weight, and complexity. Generally, a street-driven daily driver or weekend cruiser type of vehicle should have a stall speed (at most) only slightly above stock in a converter that has been upgraded to handle the output of the engine.

The stock torque converter can usually be reused unless it is leaking or damaged. For the type of restoration and for the vehicles we are covering in this book, a stock converter, or a heavy-duty unit with a stall speed close to that of the stock part, is often the best choice for performance, drivability, and economy. Higher-stall-speed converters are really only meant for drag racing applications, but you should upgrade your converter to a heavy-duty unit if the engine power has been increased to any significant degree. If you are reusing the converter, flush it out completely and fill it with new, clean fluid before it is installed. Whatever converter you install, apply a light coat of oil to the coupling that goes into the transmission to lubricate the pump seal. Also use the correct bolts to mount both the flex plate and the torque converter because there can be clearance problems with the bolt heads.

Clutch, Flywheel and Pressure Plate

In a car equipped with a manual transmission, the clutch, flywheel, and pressure plate perform a similar function to that of a torque converter in a car equipped with an automatic transmission. The driver controls the action of the clutch while the torque converter is more or less passive. When restoring/rebuilding a manual-tranny vehicle, you need to determine the requirements based on the level of restoration—original, budget, or higher performance.

The clutch system is pretty simple, overall. The flywheel is generally reused as is unless there has been damage in the form of overheating and/or surface cracking. This can, up to a point, be repaired by precision grinding the flywheel surface. The pressure plate may also require the same treatment if it is similarly damaged. If the flywheel or pressure plate is repaired with grinding, they typically need to be rebalanced because material has been removed and this may throw off the balance and cause vibrations. The clutch disc can be reused if it has enough friction material left. If you are getting

If you decide to upgrade your flywheel, you can stay with a heavier but stronger unit like what came with the vehicle, or you can change to a lighter-weight aluminum flywheel, such as the one shown here. The lower weight improves acceleration and performance, but it may also require greater skill to prevent engine stalling when accelerating from a stop. The replaceable steel wear ring eliminates concerns over premature wear with aluminum alone, as does the hardened starter gear ring. Since the flywheel is not readily visible, this upgrade could be used in virtually any restoration project, but realistically it would probably only be a consideration for the performance-oriented weekend cruiser. There would be little if any benefit for the daily driver or the show car with authenticity as a priority.

too close to the metal rivets that hold the friction material on, it's time to get a new disc. There is no repair process for these. The restoration of the clutch linkage is pretty much a matter of replacing any worn bushings, cleaning and lubricating the parts that will be put back into the vehicle, and making the proper clutch pedal adjustment. The throwout bearing and pilot bushing in the crankshaft are usually replaced automatically.

All of these items can be changed to better suit the intended purpose of your vehicle. The flywheel can be switched to a lighter aluminum version to provide better performance and allow the engine to rev faster. A replaceable steel insert provides a more durable surface, so wear is not an issue. However, the reduced rotational inertia can reduce the flywheel effect and make it more difficult to smoothly pull away from a stop in some cases. The pressure plate can be made lighter for much the same reasons, but it also can have its clamping force increased to reduce the likelihood of the clutch slipping with a higher-output engine.

The downside of this is often a higher pedal pressure, but this does not always have to be the case. The clutch disc can be made in any number of ways, with any number of friction materials to reduce slippage and better handle abusive driving. For first-generation Mustangs, it is best to use a clutch disc with a sprung hub to reduce driveline shock as well as a "marcel" layer between the friction faces to also help improve both drivability and durability. The choice of friction material(s) largely depends on application, but aggressive ceramic or sintered metallic materials are generally not as easy to live with on the street and should thus be avoided. Hybrid discs with an organic lining on one side and a ceramic or metallic lining on the other can be suitable for higher-output cars.

Regardless of what type of flywheel you may choose, replace the pilot bearing or bushing in the end of the crankshaft. Most early Mustangs have a bushing that is simply pried out and replaced with a new one. These bushings are not particularly strong and must be driven in carefully with either a special tool for the purpose or a flat plate-style seal installer. The conversion to a roller bearing does have advantages in terms of both precision and durability, but these are generally not cost effective unless they are available as a direct-fit conversion for a particular vehicle.

If you upgrade over the standard clutch components for higher-performance applications, there are many options. This combination includes a lighter weight pressure plate that also has increased clamping force to reduce potential clutch slippage, while also reducing rotational inertia to improve performance. The clutch disc may appear to be too radical for a street car but it is actually quite acceptable for a weekend cruiser because the clutch engages smoothly and the discs wear well. The disc has both a sprung hub and a marcel layer to provide smooth engagement under normal driving conditions, yet it has a special friction material on the flywheel side of the disc (showing) to provide greater durability and performance in aggressive driving situations. The friction material on the other side is a more-common organic type that has also been enhanced to provide better performance.

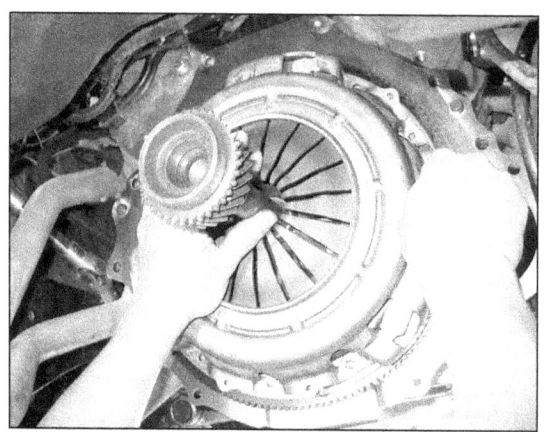

Whether installing an upgraded clutch or simply reinstalling a stock-style assembly, it is critical the clutch disc be properly aligned as the pressure plate bolts are tightened. Special tools are available for this, but an old transmission input shaft works just as well. With the disc centered, slowly and evenly tighten the pressure plate bolts to prevent the pressure plate cover from warping. Take the time to do this correctly; it will pay big dividends. Tighten each bolt a few turns at a time after you feel initial resistance and skip around in a star pattern, rather than moving to the adjacent bolt. All of the bolts need to be tightened and the pressure plate cover needs to make full contact with the flywheel. Next, each bolt needs to be tightened to its correct torque specification, again using a star pattern.

One very interesting enhancement for first-generation Mustangs is the elimination of the stock clutch linkage in favor of a system that uses hydraulic actuation. The alternative has several advantages such as providing more smooth and precise operation of the clutch, lower maintenance, lower weight, the potential for lower pedal pressures, and the elimination of clearance problems with the exhaust system and steering gear. There are conversion kits available for most early Mustangs (the one shown here is on a 1965 equipped with a late-model transmission). All of the stock clutch linkage is eliminated in favor of two hydraulic cylinders and some hose. Other than the unique mounting brackets for a particular application, there really is nothing more to it because it uses the stock clutch fork. The cost isn't high and the benefits are there, even for a daily driver.

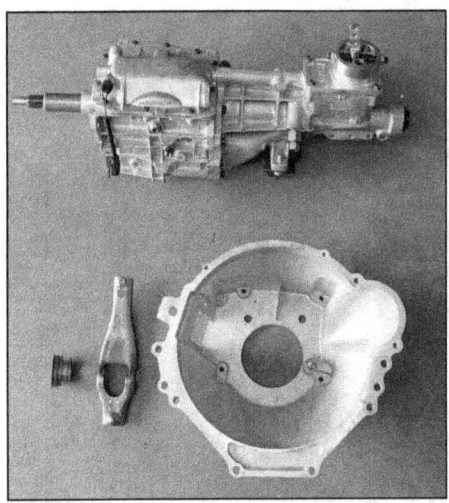

Those wishing to really make their weekend cruiser more enjoyable may want to consider installing a late-model overdrive transmission in place of the original transmission. Several companies offer complete kits that make this a pretty simple process. In cases where a T5 transmission from a later-model Mustang (similar to that shown) is used, the main adaptations are a new transmission crossmember, a new bellhousing, an adapter for the speedometer cable, a longer shift lever, and (sometimes) a different length driveshaft. These transmissions not only are capable of handling plenty of power, but they reduce the engine RPM on the highway by 30 percent or more, thus reducing wear, noise, and fuel consumption. Performance is also improved due to the extra gear and the wider total-ratio spread it allows. The kit shown also has a shorter-throw shifter from B&M Racing, and it is far more precise than the original unit. Special shift levers provide quick and positive shifting, and the shift knob shows the correct 5-speed pattern on the knob. While not a small investment, the ability to cruise at much lower RPM (with less engine wear) on the highway and use less fuel while doing it helps pay back that investment over time.

Most restorations simply involve repair-oriented procedures that are well covered by the factory manual and are easily accomplished at home or at a local machine shop. I chose to provide a few examples of some alternatives to a straight repair/rebuild that might make sense in a weekend cruiser. They could also be used in a daily driver, but they may not be necessary or cost effective unless the engine has been modified. For the most part, these would not be applicable to a show car in which retaining authenticity is a priority. Most of these alternatives are installed with the same procedures as factory parts, but they simply provide cost-effective enhancements.

Manual Transmission Disassembly and Inspection

One of the main advantages of a manual transmission over an automatic transmission, beyond the more-involved driving experience, is that they are very simple to use, fix, and rebuild. There generally are very few things you can do to make them better other than make them stronger if you intend to race them.

For street-driven vehicles, there may be a few minor material changes to improve strength and/or durability, but many if not most of the procedures are similar to factory service procedures. As a result, I won't show every step for rebuilding a typical manual tranny. I highlight important areas that need to be given some extra attention when rebuilding such a tranny, in this case the Toploader that was available for our 1968 GT. I show some of the major steps involved in taking this transmission apart and putting it back together again. We again relied on Big 4 Transmissions of Paramount, California, to share some of their expertise with working on this type of transmission. This helped me address some issues that aren't normally covered in the shop manual, but which have become commonplace over the years.

Rebuilding a transmission like this requires considerable expertise and some

CHAPTER 6

Manual Transmission Disassembly

1 One of the most useful tools needed when rebuilding a manual transmission is a pencil magnet, such as this one. It is invaluable when retrieving small springs, detent pins, and the like from small passages where oil and/or dirt conspire to keep them stuck out of reach. As you remove these small parts, make a note of where they came from, so they go back in the right place.

2 Many of the larger external parts of the transmission can be removed at the beginning of the process. These will include the shift linkage, the tranny mount, the top cover, and the input bearing collar, as is shown here. Inspect it for excessive wear or damage on the surface where the throwout bearing slides. Remove minor scratches with emery cloth, but any significant flaws mean replacement of the part. The shaft seal on the inside of the collar will be replaced; these have a tendency to harden with time and can thus develop a leak.

3 During the disassembly of a manual transmission, many small parts, such as detent pins and so on, need to be removed for access to other parts. There are also situations in which parts such as shafts need to be oriented to a certain position before they can be removed. The factory service manual generally describes these procedures in detail. However, the general rule is that if a part seems to be difficult to remove, don't force it. Look for of any pins or retaining rings that may have to come out before it can be removed. Also try rotating the part to different positions to see if that solves the problem. Lots of force should not be needed to remove the vast majority of components (except for bearings).

4 Look for any signs of wear or surface damage when removing the various support shafts. While it is rare, pitting or galling has occurred under some circumstances. Minor imperfections can be removed with a fine emery cloth or pad, and the parts can then be rinsed in the parts washer to remove any residue. Reversing the retaining pins is a good thing to do when reinstalling these shafts because the opposite sides of the pins are less worn and provide a more secure fit.

REBUILDING TRANSMISSIONS

5 The shift forks are one of the main components to examine for signs of wear. This usually occurs at the tips where the forks contact the sliding collars over the synchros. A small amount of polishing is fine, but any excessive wear can cause problems with incomplete engagement and/or the transmission coming out of gear. Also look for any cracks or excess wear in the bore for the shaft, but these are fairly rare unless the transmission was abused.

6 The sliding collars must also be examined for any signs of excess wear on the outer surface where the shift forks make contact and on the inner teeth as well. These generally are reused with only a trip to the parts washer needed before they're reinstalled in the same place.

7 The main shaft assembly gets removed and installed/loaded from the top, hence the name. Be careful lifting the assembly out, so the shaft surfaces and the gear teeth don't get nicked or scratched. These components are petty stout, but if one of the gear edges scrapes the shaft, damage can occur. When disassembling the main shaft, look for any galling on the shaft or on the inside of the gears. You want everything to be nice and smooth and free of flaws.

8 The main case normally will have some degree of sludge in it just because of the type of gear oil that was used. The main indicator of potential problems is how much material is on the magnetic plug, seen to the left of the reverse gear assembly. If there are a lot of metal filings on this plug, then you can be sure you're in for an unpleasant surprise in the near future. Larger particles are especially problematic because they can be an indicator of chipped gear teeth or a broken retention or detent pin. Any significant accumulation of material on the magnetic plug should be taken seriously to the point of making sure the source of the material is positively determined.

Manual Transmission Disassembly CONTINUED

9 There are generally two different sizes for the synchro "dogs": the shorter ones are for the 3/4 synchro, while the longer ones go with the 1/2 synchro. These normally do not exhibit much wear but are usually replaced anyway as precautions against wear and fatigue. The spring clips that these contact, however, generally do show signs of wear at the points where they touch. The dogs have a tendency to wear grooves in the clips, and thus the clips are always replaced in a rebuild. While not often, these clips have been known to wear through and break.

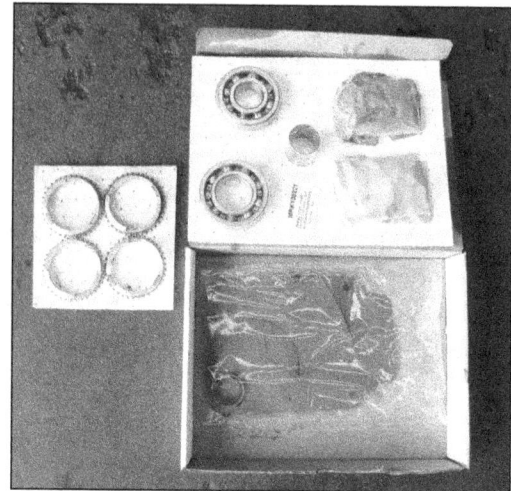

10 A rebuild kit for a manual transmission includes the usual assortment of gaskets, seals, and bushings, but it should also include new bearings/rollers, synchro rings, plus the various spring clips, retaining clips, and other small parts. While the bearings do not need to be packed with grease, they should be pre-lubricated with gear oil after they are lightly blown off with air.

Manual Transmission Assembly

1 Trial fit the new synchro rings on each of their respective gears after the gears have been cleaned. They should turn freely without any sticking. Compare the teeth on the new synchros to those of the gears because they should look fairly similar. If the gear teeth are too rounded, it may be necessary to replace the gear. Make one last inspection of the large gear teeth to ensure there is no pitting or other problem and then liberally apply assembly grease to the rear of the synchros and set the gears aside for reassembly.

2 The cluster shaft gears must also be inspected for pitting or other damage to ensure they can be reused. Bearing surfaces must be smooth as well. After the shaft has been cleaned, it can be assembled with new rollers. Use assembly grease to hold them in place and then place the correct shim on top of the rollers, again using grease to hold it in place for assembly.

Manual Transmission Assembly CONTINUED

3 Also verify the condition of the internal splines of the synchro collars to ensure that there is no excess wear or any imperfections, which may cause stickiness. The edges of each spline should be sharp, as should the points at each end. Any pitting or shipping is generally reason for replacement. The dog rests in the depression of each spline, so each must have a good edge and not be excessively rounded. These can be cleaned with a nylon or brass wire brush and they are non-directional.

4 After the main components of the synchro assemblies have all been cleaned and inspected for damage, they can also be reassembled with new dogs and clips in preparation for reassembly. Be sure to use the correct length dogs for each synchro and also verify the spring clips are properly positioned. There's no need for prelubrication of these components; they'll be oiled later.

5 The main shaft should only need to be cleaned before the components are reassembled on to it. The primary thing to look out for is any damage to the bearing surfaces. They should be smooth and free of pitting, scratches, and so on. Take care when sliding other components over these surfaces to make sure no dirt gets caught in between the parts and causes a problem. If you will hold the shaft assembly in a vise as shown here, be sure to use a protective sleeve around the shaft to prevent any damage.

special tools. It is not a task for the casual mechanic or someone with a daily driver, unless they were trying to lower the cost of a rebuild by doing it themselves. A show-car owner would also be less likely to attempt this unless he or she had some experience with such things and/or also has the tools and time to do it mainly for maximum authenticity. The most likely type of person to indulge in this process is the owner of a weekend cruiser who has both the experience and the equipment to do the job with minimal fear of encountering any major problems.

Regardless of whether or not the work is done at-home, I've put together some observations and recommendations that should help ensure the end result is a better-performing and longer-lasting tranny.

The importance of keeping track of where various components belong as the transmission is being taken apart cannot be overstressed. Small parts can be a large problem when it comes time to put everything back together. There are many similar variations within the tranny itself, plus there is even greater variation from one transmission version to the next. I've tried to include some guiding information about a few of the more common differences in early Mustang transmissions. The majority of these variations are within the main case, except things like the input-shaft spline specification, which can vary depending on vehicle application.

The components of the manual transmission that do not reside inside the main case are similar in basic design, but they may vary according to power level, vehicle size, and other factors. Thus, you may have a tailshaft housing and a shaft that are different lengths. There could be different placements of the speedometer cable and/or shifter in some situations, in addition to

Manual Transmission Assembly CONTINUED

6 *The swap ring on the main shaft may be the one exception to the general rule of replacing all of the retaining clips with new parts. Replacements may not always be the correct thickness. If it's too thick, it will not fully seat in the groove, and if it's too thin, it will be too loose. The factory installed ring is the best choice if it was fitting properly when the transmission was taken apart. For easier removal, should that ever be necessary, it is better to install it with the taper facing outward rather than toward the gear. In any case, make sure it fully seats in the groove.*

7 *The finished main shaft/gear assembly with new synchro rings ready to be reinstalled. There should be a coating of assembly grease under and between all sliding surfaces on the shaft and the synchros/synchro rings. There doesn't need to be any grease under the sliding collars as these are oiled. Check to make sure the appropriate gears turn freely on the shaft and that the synchro rings turn freely relative to the gears. There will be some drag due to the grease, but there should be no stickiness or binding.*

REBUILDING TRANSMISSIONS

9 After pressing a new bearing onto the input shaft and verifying the retaining snap ring is fully seated, the roller bearings can be installed on the back side. Use assembly grease to hold the rollers in place and apply some sparingly and evenly on the surrounding area, which contacts the synchro ring.

8 Pressing the bearing off is the preferred way to remove it from the shaft. Use a sleeve to protect the shaft if the bearing is instead held in a vise while hitting the input shaft with a mallet. Under no circumstances should you strike the tip of the shaft. The mallet should only impact the sleeve that rests on the lower flange. Allowing the press to directly contact the shaft is acceptable, though using a sleeve even while pressing the bearing off/on would provide extra safety against deforming the tip.

10 Carefully remove seal on the underside of the input shaft bearing collar and then remove any residual gasket material with a wire brush/wheel or similar. After the collar has been cleaned up, the new seal can be pressed in using a seal installer or other flat surface such as the back of an appropriate-size socket. Make sure the seal is fully seated and is facing the correct way (closed end facing into the housing) before applying a light film of grease.

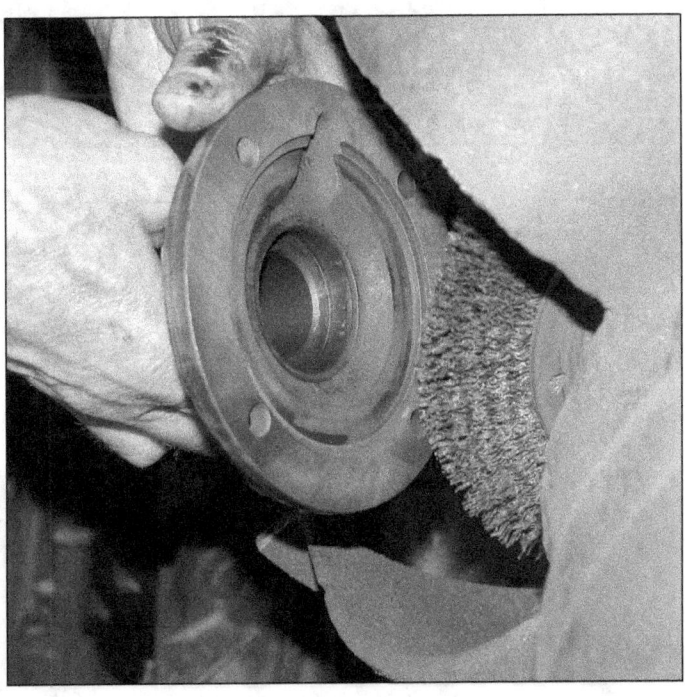

Manual Transmission Assembly CONTINUED

11 Be sure to verify the fit of the snap ring on the input shaft bearing to the inside of the collar. The snap ring must be fully seated to clear the collar and fit into the recess made for it on the underside. If this is not done, the snap ring could get caught under the collar and cause damage to the collar as it is being installed. The snap ring should sit right at the surface of the collar, basically even with it, and consequently, the thickness of the gasket allows the collar to properly compensate for the clearance.

12 Take extra care when removing the tailshaft housing seal to avoid scratching the sealing surface, which could lead to leaks. The best method is to lightly wedge a screwdriver or small chisel under the inside edge of the seal to lift it up enough so it can then be pried out. The point of the tool should be placed at the semicircular oil passage and the outer edge of the housing should be used for leverage. After the seal is out, remove the bushing. This must be driven out with the correct-size socket or tool. The new bushing is installed by lightly tapping it in with a seal installer or similar. It should be driven flush with the edge of the housing. There is no need to line up the groove with the oil passage. After the bushing is in the new seal can be installed with a thin coat of RTV on the outside and a bit of grease on the surface that touches the driveshaft.

13 All of the flat sealing surfaces of the housings, covers, and so forth should be lightly buffed with an abrasive wheel to remove any residual gasket material. They should then be wiped clean to remove any oil, grease, or other substance that might compromise the gasket seal. It's unlikely there would be any surface imperfections of these components; if there are, they can be ignored as long as they are not too deep. Minor scratches under the gasket can be filled in with a dab of RTV if they are only superficial. Any significantly deep rust or other damage must be repaired.

REBUILDING TRANSMISSIONS

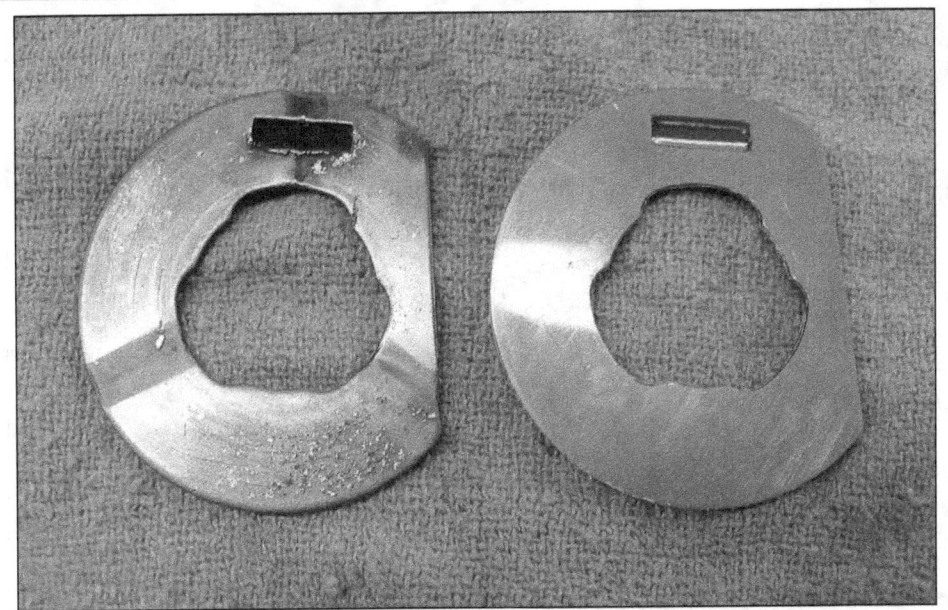

New thrust washers will be installed, but it is still useful to examine those being replaced. This washer came out of our transmission (on the left) and had a noticeable amount of metal particles on it. While it did not show much wear in terms of reduced thickness, these particles were a concern. We did not find any problems with any of the gears, shafts, or other internal components so we could only surmise this was residue either from the factory or from a previous rebuild. When the new thrust washer is installed, we will coat it liberally with grease and use the grease to hold it in place while we install the shaft. Note the different color, which indicates a change in the material specification versus factory spec.

14 As the components are reinstalled into the cleaned case, they should be lubricated with assembly grease, in most cases. After each assembly is installed, it should be rotated to spread the grease more evenly to ensure coverage at initial use but also to verify there is no stickiness or other issues that need to be immediately attended to. Shift forks should also be exercised for the same purpose; first squirt a small amount of oil on the shafts, splines, etc., for smoother operation.

the different-specification input shafts already mentioned. Since I cannot provide specific details for every possible iteration, I've provided some generic guidelines to follow regarding assembling the components mostly outside of the main case.

The final assembly process includes relatively simple, yet critical, procedures. These require few, if any, special tools or much expertise, but they do require attention to detail. Little things like the incorrect positioning of a gasket or an improperly installed snap ring can have serious consequences. Taking a little extra time to apply some sealant a bit more carefully and in places not called for in the manual can more effectively prevent fluid leaks. Manual transmissions, like this Toploader, are pretty stout and can take a lot of abuse if they're put together and maintained properly. They can still, however, fail prematurely if something as simple as a snap ring is not properly installed and a gear or other part is allowed to move around too much.

Manual Transmission Assembly CONTINUED

15 You can use a hose clamp to keep the gears and other components still when the shaft assembly is lowered back into the case. Do not overtighten the clamp as it could possibly scratch the shaft.

16 Follow the instructions in the service manual regarding the order for reinstalling various components. Be sure to grease the cavities in the housing where the shafts make contact. Similarly, squirt a small amount of oil on the exposed surfaces of the shafts and spread the oil evenly over the shafts to ensure the shift forks will move freely. Remember to remove the hose clamp after the shaft assembly is in place.

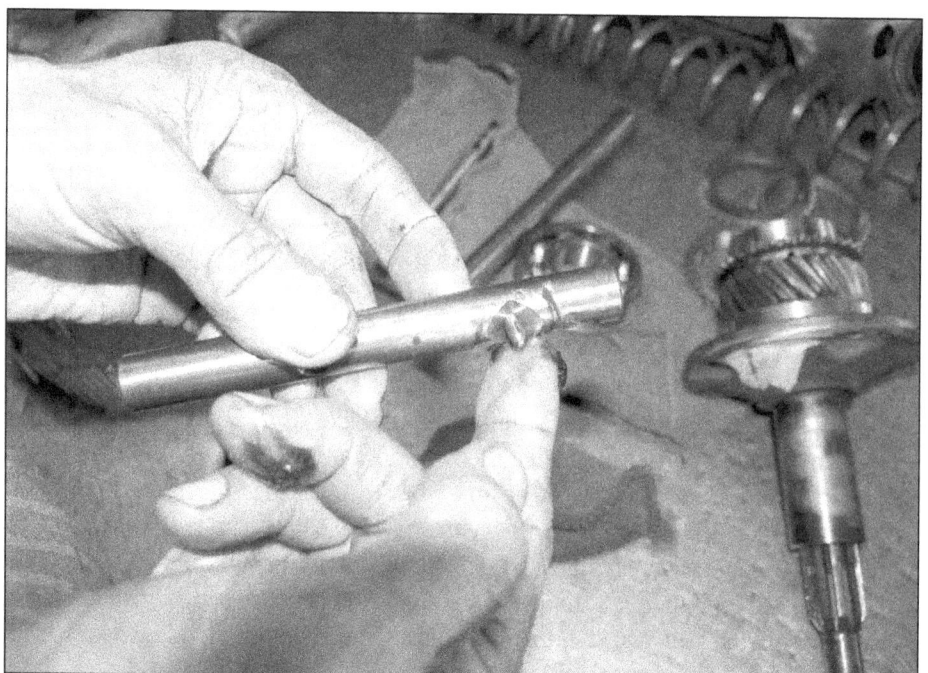

17 Be extremely careful with the many small parts like detent pins. It's often helpful to use a small amount of grease to hold these small items in place during reassembly. As was the case with taking these components apart, it may be necessary to specifically orient them when putting them back together. This is especially true with the detent pins and spring-loaded parts. One trick is to slide the part under the pin with the detent facing away from the pin and then rotate the shaft, so the detent is in the correct position when the shaft is fully installed. Remember to reverse locking pins if possible to ensure a more precise fit of the components.

18 You may have to drive the main shaft assembly into the case because of the tight tolerances of the new bearings and other components. Lightly tap around the inner race of the tailshaft bearing with a flat punch. Move around from one side to the other and shift over every other tap. Never strike the outer race. When the snap ring contacts the case, you are done. Turn the shaft to verify there's no binding/stickiness.

19 If you have to tap on the inner race of the bearing, lightly tap it all around with a punch (as shown) to make sure the snap ring is still fully seated. After this is done, turn the shaft again to verify it still turns freely.

Shift Linkage

Whether the shift linkage is for a manual or automatic transmission, the concerns are the same. Ensure there is no excessive wear of any of the components and verify all necessary adjustments have been done properly. If components are excessively worn, they generally need to be replaced unless it is possible to compensate for the wear via an adjustment. With an automatic tranny, you are pretty much limited to the adjustment between the shift lever and the shift rod and, in our case, the adjustment of the downshift control cable. Other automatic transmissions may have other possible options.

These adjustment procedures are provided in the service manual and not repeated here. Just remember to first verify the shift rod and shift lever do not have excess wear/play before you make any adjustment. Note the relative position of these parts prior to disassembly, to help with reassembly.

With a manual transmission, you have more shift rods/levers and thus need to use an alignment pin. The same principles apply for adjusting excess play at the shift levers or at the forward shift arms. However, there is now also the need to properly position the individual shift rods and levers relative to each other, in addition to being properly aligned with the forward shift arms/forks.

Manual Transmission Assembly CONTINUED

20 Reinstall the speedometer drive gear after it has been cleaned/inspected for damage. If the tire size, transmission, or rear axle ratio have not been changed, the same gear can be reused if it is in good shape. If any of the aforementioned components have been changed, then it may be necessary to get a new speedometer drive and/or driven gear to get the speedo to read correctly. The service manual has charts with the relevant color codes for these parts. Part numbers have likely changed over the years, so check the number of teeth on the gear and the color code to identify the right parts. The service manual provides a procedure for calculating what you need based on observed versus actual driving speed, so it is more practical to change the driven gear and leave this gear as is.

21 To further help prevent leaks, you should place a light film of RTV on the gasket or the metal sealing surfaces. These gasket surfaces should have previously been given the once over with a wire brush or wheel to remove any old gasket material. Do not overdo it with the RTV because the excess sealant will wind up in the transmission where it can do no good. Also dab a small amount around bolt holes that go through the case and around covered cap plugs. However, do not put any near the ends of shafts that rotate or the drain holes/passages. Do put some on the underside of the top cover but not on the side of the cover gasket that contacts the case to make for easier removal, if necessary. The tailshaft housing can then be put back on.

22 When installing the input shaft collar, the gasket should first be coated with RTV and placed over the snap ring, onto the housing. Be sure to align the hole in the gasket with the passage underneath the bearing. This allows oil to drain back into the main case. If this was blocked, it could increase the likelihood of a leak though the collar seal and cause other problems. Rub a light film of grease around the input shaft near where the seal will be.

REBUILDING TRANSMISSIONS

23 Before putting the cover back on, liberally squirt oil over the synchro rings, shift forks, shafts, bearings, and other moving parts that were not previously lubricated with grease. Turn the shafts while this is being done to ensure complete, even coverage. Try to get the oil on the parts instead of the case.

24 When the cover is put back on, be sure to put the two longer bolts in the holes specially designated for them. The smaller bolts go in the remaining holes. Do not overtighten the bolts because it will crush the gasket and/or warp the cover, thus increasing the likelihood of leaks. Note the cover vent hole.

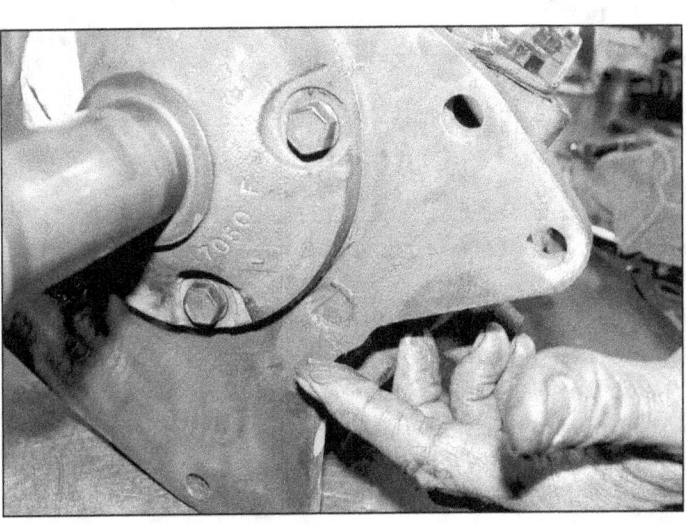

25 As a final preventative measure to guard against leaks, rub a small amount of RTV over any exposed cap plugs. Other than the shift linkage (which I address shortly), there is little else to do to this transmission before it goes back in, other than to plug the hole in the tailshaft housing for the speedo-driven gear/cable and then temporarily seal the input and tailshaft holes to prevent any dirt getting in. The mount also needs to go back on when it goes in the car, but we won't be using this transmission because our car was built as an automatic and we're going to keep it that way. If you reinstall a manual tranny in your car, do not put any gear oil in until the tranny is in the car with the driveshaft in place. Fill it per the factory manual instructions.

The shift levers are in line when the forward shift arms are properly set, the adjusting nuts are tightened, and the proper size pin is inserted by using a punch or similar tool.

Avoid excessive play between the shift rods and the shift arms on the tranny. If the upper holes in the arms (where the shift rods attach) become too large and/or the arms develop rounded corners in the lower slots (where the arms attach to the shift forks), the shift rod's motion will not fully transfer to the shift fork because there's too much play between the fork and the arm.

This can potentially cause missed shifts and/or dropping out of gear. If there is too much play, the arms and/or forks need to be replaced.

Weak retaining clips and/or excessive tolerances often prevent full engagement of the shift rods in the upper holes of the arms. New clips and a flat washer or two between the clip and the back of the shift arm may solve minor issues with excessive play.

The basic procedure is to make sure each shift arm/fork is in its neutral position; put in the alignment pin to line up the shift levers on the shifter; and then tighten each adjusting nut on each shift rod after you've made sure any excess play has been eliminated.

As for the shifters themselves, there is little to do other than clean them out/up and properly lube them before putting them back in. If their appearance is less than desired, you can replace the shift levers and/or handles with new parts. If the shifter mechanism is too loose, it's often more economical to simply replace the shifter than to fix it.

Those who must reuse the original shifter can rebuild it with new parts, but this is rarely the most cost-effective solution. (I discuss the cosmetic aspects of the shifter in Chapter 11.)

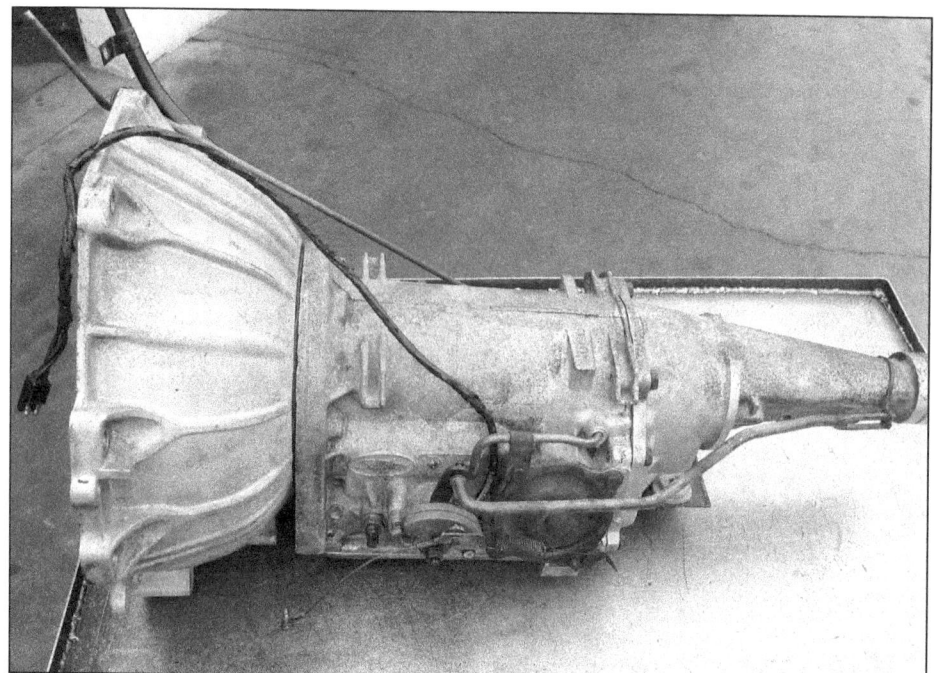

With an automatic transmission such as our C4, there are relatively few possible external adjustments. We are limited to positioning the shift lever relative to the slot in the shift rod (seen at right next to the tailshaft housing) and the downshift control cable (seen dangling from the neutral safety switch) that attaches to a throttle-actuated rod attached to the firewall.

The adjustment for shift levers on manual transmissions is more complicated than an automatic because of the extra levers involved. They must be properly positioned relative to the shift arms/forks in the tranny but also relative to each other. An alignment pin (in this case we just used a proper diameter punch) is inserted in the hole in the shifter housing to line up the shift levers. The shift arms on the tranny are then put in the neutral position (remember to resolve any possible issues with excessive play first) and, finally, the adjusting nuts for each shift rod are tightened as shown. The shifter itself should be clean and lubricated.

CHAPTER 7

DRIVETRAIN

For the purposes of this book, the drivetrain components include the driveshaft and the rear axle assembly. Since I am only addressing restoration of factory components, the concepts and procedures I cover are similar regardless of the specific parts used. Driveshafts vary in size, length, and the type of connection they have at each end, but the methods for refurbishing them are essentially common. Rear axle assemblies ("rears") also vary by size and length as well as by the specific type of housing (8-inch, 9-inch, etc.), but there are also internal differences such as gear ratio and type of differential, unique differences in seals and bearings, etc.

While I cannot show the specific procedure for every unique hardware variation, the fundamental procedures I do show are applicable to most drivetrain packages (with minor variation in some cases). You will need to look up specific information, such as torque specs and so forth anyway, so any unique requirements for a given application should become apparent as well. Many people choose to have their drivetrain parts professionally refurbished because of the type of equipment needed for many of the procedures. The following information will help ensure the proper work is done and that it gets done correctly.

The Driveshaft

Restoration of the driveshaft is one of the simpler tasks in any restoration project. This wouldn't be true if there were to be changes in hardware, such as an engine, tranny, and/or rear axle swap. But since we're sticking with the original factory parts, we are spared any such complications. The first thing to do after taking the driveshaft out of the car is to carefully inspect it. Check the U-joints for play/looseness. Inspect the sealing surface of the forward yoke that goes into the tranny to make sure it is smooth and free of any pitting, grooves, or other problems.

The factory-installed axle housing styles on first-generation Mustangs are 7¼-inch, 8-inch, and 9-inch. Our 1968 GT is equipped with the latter, presumably because of its GT status, and the fact it was a J-code/4V car. It actually has an 8¾-inch ring gear even though it is considered a member of the 9-inch family of rear axle assemblies. This is still a good axle for a high-performance application, if not so for racing.

The yoke of the driveshaft that gets inserted into the transmission must be smooth and free of any scratches, grooves, or pits, etc., in order to provide a good sealing surface. Minor imperfections can be removed with some fine emery cloth, but more major issues may require getting a new yoke.

HOW TO RESTORE YOUR MUSTANG 1964½–1973   109

CHAPTER 7

Inspect the driveshaft itself for any dents, scrapes, or sign of rust that goes beyond just the surface. A driveshaft is a pretty reliable part, but it still has to transmit all of the engine's power to the rear axle assembly. Factoring in the torque multiplication of the transmission ratios means there is a lot of stress on the driveshaft. Any kind of damage to the driveshaft could concentrate the stress and cause it to fail, so the threshold needs to be very low. The driveshaft should be smooth, solid, and free of any deformation. About the only other thing to look for is whether a balance weight might have come off. If that's the case, the driveshaft needs to be rebalanced after it's been cleaned up. Failure to do so results in unwanted vibration and possibly something worse.

If the driveshaft is otherwise in good shape, it simply needs to be cleaned and lightly wire brushed or sanded to remove any surface rust before it's given a light coat of spray-on paint, if desired. It's not necessary to paint it. But it improves the appearance and helps prevent any further rusting. Be sure to mask off the areas where the U-joints go since they must be free of any paint for proper fit.

The U-joints should be replaced in virtually any restoration project for no other reason than it is so easy and inexpensive to do. Realistically, the U-joints are the only part of the driveshaft system that wear and/or fail with any regularity because of lack of proper lubrication, driving through water, abuse (excess power, racing, etc.), or some combination thereof. Whatever may have been the problem, it doesn't matter at this point because the best thing to do is to just get new U-joints. About the only time you may want to keep the original U-joints (assuming they're in good enough condition) is if the car is a relatively rare survivor car and you want to keep everything as original as possible. Since such a car probably won't be driven very often and likely not driven hard, it may be reasonable to keep the original U-joints after they've been cleaned and lubed. But for most people, it's much better to replace them.

There are lots of options available for direct replacements and high-performance versions, but this is less important than making sure you get the right type/size for your application. A stronger, high-performance or heavy-duty U-joint won't hurt, but there's not much point in spending extra money on such parts if you don't plan to drive the car hard. It's much more important in the long run to make sure the U-joint is properly lubricated.

When installing new U-joints, make sure no parts (rollers and/or retaining clips, for example) are missing or out of place, and there is no binding or stickiness after it has been installed. U-joints generally come pre-lubricated, but you may want to use better grease, such as tacky synthetic marine grease. This grease is formulated to provide excellent overall performance and also stays in place better if it is submerged or otherwise exposed to water. You can put some in the bearing caps prior to installation and pump more in through the grease fitting if the U-joint has one. Be careful not to use too much; it will not only make a mess, but it could also potentially harm the grease seals, causing the U-joint to fail prematurely. Care must also be taken to not overtighten the U-joint strap nuts.

After the U-joints have been assembled onto the driveshaft and/or transmission yoke, check to make sure all required retaining clips are in place and that the U-joints rotate freely without any binding, stickiness, excessive end play, or other looseness. It's probably a good idea to wrap some tape around the bearing caps that mate to the yoke on the rear axle, so they don't pop off or otherwise get lost or damaged before the driveshaft is put back into the car.

In almost all cases, it is best to replace the U-joints while you have the driveshaft out. Simply remove the retaining clips from each side and use either a press or a hammer and appropriately sized sockets to push the U-joint bearing caps through the yoke one at a time. When installing the new U-joint, make sure it's properly lubricated and the retaining clips seat fully.

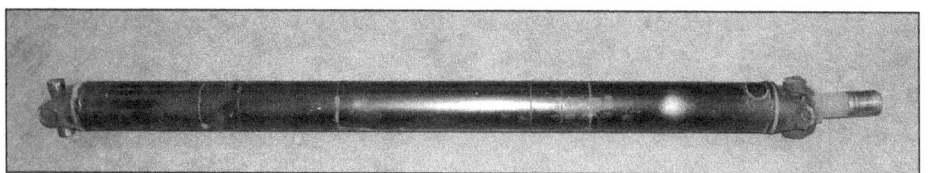

Inspect the main tube of the driveshaft for any dents, scrapes, rust, or other damage that might potentially lead to failure. Any minor scratches, such as those appearing as vertical lines here, can be sanded smooth as long as they are not too deep. Anything more than just a surface imperfection usually requires repair or replacement. Also check to make sure any balance weights that may have been used are present and properly secured. Rebalance the driveshaft if any weights are missing.

Rebuilding the Rear Axle Assembly

First-generation Mustangs came with one of three rear axle assemblies from the factory: 7¼-, 8-, or 9-inch. The axle size for a given car depended on a number of factors including engine size, trim level, and option choices. As a general guideline, the 7¼-inch axles were found in 6-cylinder cars, the 8-inch axle was found in most small-block V-8 cars, and the 9-inch was reserved for small- or big-block high-performance vehicles. There are exceptions to the rule, such as with our 1968 GT. It came with a 9-inch rear axle even though it is only a 302 0-ci V-8 because it is also a GT version with a 4-bbl carburetor, and thus is considered a high-performance vehicle. There's an easy way to identify the 9-inch rear end. If a socket won't fit on the rear end's two lower nuts, and an open end or box wrench must be used, then it's a 9-inch.

I cannot show how to rebuild every possible iteration or combination of axle assembly and vehicle; rather, I focus on rebuilding the 9-inch that came with our 1968 and include information about other versions as we go; the basic processes still apply.

After the rear axle is removed from the car, you must inspect it. If the rear axle has a valid factory ID tag, it tells you what you are dealing with. You can determine the gear ratio, type of differential (open or Traction-Lok), build date, and plant code from it. There are also other identifiers, such as the "base code," which signifies the particular axle model, plus other codes related to interchangeability.

A further visual inspection might reveal signs of leakage and other possible problems such as rust or damage to the housing. Leakage from seals, gaskets, or the vent tube usually show up as a dark area on the axle tubes. If it was a very gradual seepage of fluid, it could still appear relatively dry. More serious leaks are moist to the touch and are pretty obvious. There may also be leakage from other sources like wheel cylinders. Since you are rebuilding the rear and putting in all new seals and gaskets, etc., leakage is generally not a concern unless it's due to the sealing surfaces having been damaged in some way, such as by rusting, warping, or otherwise missing metal. Such problems need to be repaired.

Disassembly

A rear axle assembly is not especially complicated, but it requires specialized equipment due to the sheer force needed in some of the disassembly procedures. If you don't have some heavy-duty tools such as impact guns and 1/2-inch-drive sockets at your disposal, you should consider farming the job out to a shop that does, preferably one that specializes in axle work. You'll also need some decent upper-body strength and, ideally, some form of fixturing to hold the rear securely while you work on it. You can build a fixture inexpensively from wood or, if you're handy with a welder, steel plate and tubing. A large workbench also serves the purpose but it won't be quite as convenient for some of the tasks.

Refurbishing the Rear Axle Housing and Axles

After all of the major parts have been separated, they can be put in the parts cleaner to remove most of the grease and grime. We won't be reusing things like bearings and seals so we just left them on for now. The time needed in the tank varies based on the condition of the parts, but generally it shouldn't be too long if you have a decent parts washer. If you do leave any rubber or soft parts on (like our pinion snubber bumper) make sure the temperature isn't high enough to cause any damage.

The first order of business is making sure the axle housing is straight.

After we knew the axle housing was viable, we proceeded with the process of restoring it to virtually new condition by stripping it down to the bare metal.

Similar to what we did with the axle housing, we made sure the axles we intended to put in it are good to go as well, primarily regarding straightness.

Rebuilding the Center Section and Differential

The center section and differential are what gives the rear axle assembly its personality. The center section determines its strength and performance while the differential mostly delivers driveability and traction characteristics. The ring-and-pinion gear set, of course, affect all of these and also can be the source of the most common problem with rear axles: unwanted noise. I'll go through the process of making our original components better suited to our intended use as a weekend cruiser.

Our rear axle assembly showed signs of minor seepage from the axle seals as well as from the vent tube. We also suspect the wheel cylinders for the brakes contributed a bit. All leaks were likely due to the car having sat for such a long time without being driven. Seals get hard from sitting and the vent hose was broken, also from having lost flexibility due to age. The important thing is all of the metal was great; no warping, no rust, etc.

CHAPTER 7

Rear Axle Disassembly

1 The disassembly process begins with the removal of the axles. First, remove the nuts that hold the axle bearing retaining plates on. Then you can also remove the smaller parts, such as the vent hose fitting, plus the various brake lines and related brackets, etc. Be sure to keep these in a secure place as replacements are not always readily available and those that may be don't always look the same as the original Ford factory parts.

2 You need a slide hammer to remove the axles from this type of rear end because of the interference fit between the axle bearings and the housing and the parts' age. Other types of rear differentials use different retention methods and may not require this. Watch out for the loosened brake assembly.

3 With the bearing free of the housing, remove the axle and the brake assembly. Look for any irregularities (color, texture, smell, etc.) in the gear oil. Ours was especially dark because the car sat for so long. Inspect each tube end to make sure there are no signs of rust or pitting. A little scuffing from the beating is fine. The bearings have a press fit and should not move; there shouldn't be any signs that the bearing was spinning. If there is any damage to the bearing race area the tube end can be cut off and a new end can be installed. An axle shop should do this work.

4 Use a seal puller to remove each axle seal. Always use a new seal whenever the rear is worked on and/or the axles are removed. It's cheap insurance against leaks. This combination slide hammer and seal puller made the job extremely easy. Just turn the knob and slam! Then, once you have all of the nuts and washers off the center housing, it can be removed. It usually needs to be lifted on one side and then rocked back and forth to clear the studs. Be careful when using a screwdriver or other wedge to separate the center housing from the main housing because you must not scratch and/or dent the gasket sealing surface, which will cause a leak. A few hits with a soft mallet might help to dislodge the center section and gears from the housing.

5 After the axle housing is cleaner, check it for straightness. First, insert a precisely sized bar into the housing so that it bridges the center section openings where the axle's tubes attach. Second, slide stepped plugs onto the bar at each tube end to see if they fit properly within it. If the tube isn't straight, the plug won't go in.

DRIVETRAIN

6 Straightening the housing requires a specialized press and fixturing. Pressure is applied close to the center housing, one side at a time, until the axle housing is straightened. The accepted tolerance varies by the specific axle because of tube diameter and length, but it generally is only a few thousandths of an inch. Let a pro with the right equipment and the expertise/feel do this. After the housing has been properly straightened, the plug goes in fully.

7 After the housing has been straightened it can be fully cleaned in the "Steelabrator" machine. This process is similar to media blasting except that the material used consists of very fine steel balls and the part being processed is secured to a rotating fixture. The process is fairly quick and takes place in an enclosed fixture. After being subjected to the Steelabrator, the axle housing is about as pristine as you could want it to be. It will require some additional cleaning to remove residual media that remains inside the part, but it sure beats going at it with a wire wheel or even trying to media blast it outdoors.

8 To replace the axle bearings, they must be pressed off. You need to use a hydraulic press and retaining fixtures. The forces involved with this procedure are very high, so be extra careful. With the bearings off, inspect the axles to ensure there is no scoring/scratches, pits, or other type of damage in the area the bearings will again rest upon. Also make sure there's no groove where the seal was.

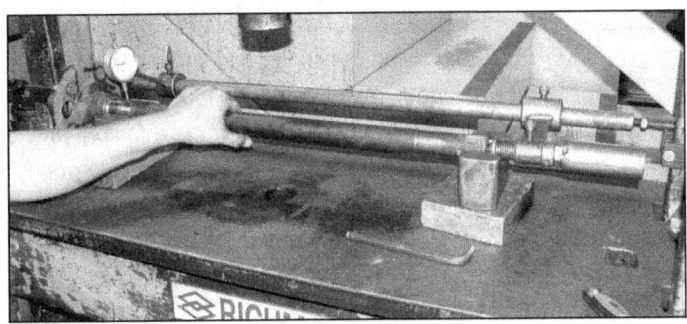

9 As with the axle housing, each axle is also checked for straightness although a different procedure is used. Each axle is checked for runout with a dial gauge after it has been secured in a special fixture. The axle is simply rotated and the maximum deflection on the dial is noted. A runout of ±.005 inch is normally desired. One of our axles was out of spec at .007 inch while the other was fine at .003 inch. Stock axles normally run .003 inch or so.

10 To straighten a bent axle, pressure is applied to the center of the axle after it has been rotated to the point with the largest error. This takes some experience and judgment to get right, but the guys at Currie Enterprises were able to get ours down to only .001 inch after just one try. A good thing to do when reusing axles is to take some ScotchBrite or emery cloth and lightly polish the area on each axle where the bearings go. It smoothes the surface and ensures a better fit with the bearing. The axles also get the Steelabrator treatment before they are reinstalled. This helps reveal flaws and to lesser extent, help stress relieve the surface of the axles. As long as the axles are straight and free of any such problems about the only thing that would prevent them from being reused (at least in an unmodified vehicle) would be damage to the splines. Either way, the center housing design makes the driver side axle shorter.

CHAPTER 7

Our car didn't have any obvious issues with the rear axle assembly, so it was reasonably quiet and smooth. We simply felt it was appropriate (it had been sitting for so long) to make sure it would provide seamless, reliable performance to match the rest of the restoration. We also wanted to upgrade it to a limited-slip differential to better exploit the higher-performance engine upgrades. As has been the theme so far, we stuck with mostly original Ford parts but chose them wisely to get the optimum balance of the factors for a weekend cruiser.

Differential Disassembly

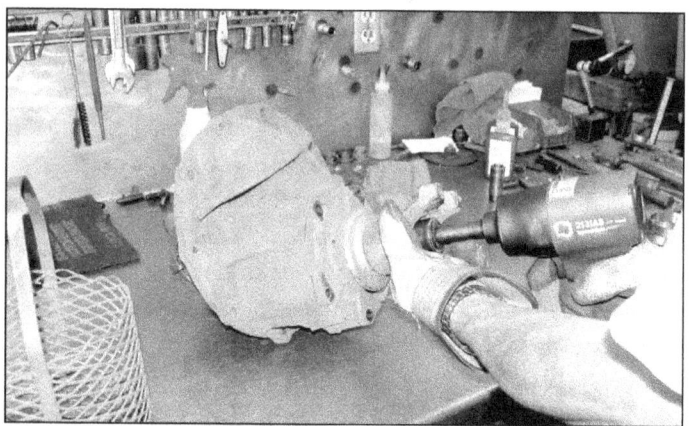

1 To start disassembling the center section, remove the bolts that hold on the pinion retainer housing and the pinion snubber. The pinion snubber on our car is a factory piece, which is relatively rare and hard to replace. This is also a good time to remove the pinion nut. While this is a fairly hard-to-find part, Currie Enterprises offers new ones with the correct flange and sealer already applied for most Mustang applications.

2 On the opposite side of the center section, remove the adjusting nut locking tabs and their bolts prior to removal of the main bearing caps. With the bearing cap bolts out, carefully remove the caps and the adjusting nuts. Then lift out the differential assembly with the attached ring gear.

3 To remove the ring gear from the differential, remove the bolts and then use a soft-faced mallet to knock the ring gear off. Strike different areas around the ring gear from the rear—don't keep striking it in the same place.

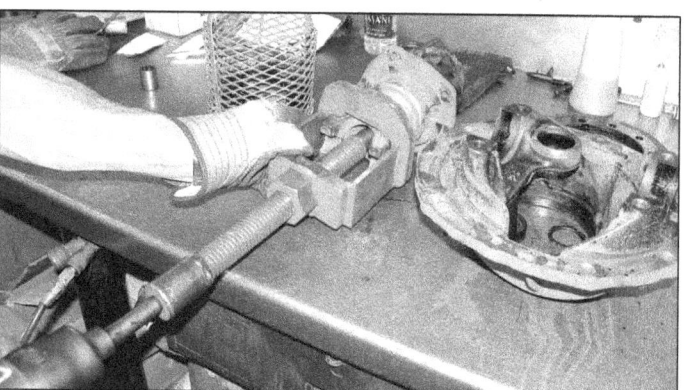

4 To remove the pinion gear and its bearing retainer, securely hold the center section and then place a large rod or punch at the center of the pinion gear at the pilot bearing. Tap it with a hammer to loosen it. There is a threaded hole in the center of the pinion gear that works fine for this. With the pinion and retainer housing free from the center housing, remove the flange from the pinion gear shaft using a puller-type tool. The pinion gear and bearings can then be separated from the pinion retainer.

DRIVETRAIN

Differential Disassembly CONTINUED

5 The outer bearing races can be pressed out of the pinion retainer. Replace these with new parts. There are two of them with one facing each way. They seat in machined pockets on either side of the central lip. These can be installed now because there will be no other work done to this part. Use a large enough soft metal tool to avoid damage while pressing them in.

6 The pinion retainer housing has an O-ring groove on the collar that sits inside the center housing. This is because variable thickness shims are used to ensure the proper preload of the pinion bearing stack. A regular gasket would not work because it would not be precise or durable enough. The shim can usually be reused as long as it provides the proper fit. The O-ring that seals the pinion retainer, however, should always be replaced.

7 Use the proper size of drift or the appropriate size of socket to remove the pilot bearing from the center section.

8 We decided to upgrade from the conventional/open differential to a limited-slip style. The limited slip provides better traction off the line, especially when using stock-size tires.

9 New tapered roller bearings must be carefully and fully pressed onto both sides of the new differential. A properly sized sleeve/tool, which only contacts the inner race of each bearing, must be used to avoid damaging the bearing.

Using a limited-slip differential rather than our original open unit is the only real deviation from a straight-up use of the rear axle assembly. This change doesn't really affect the overall restoration because the process of rebuilding the rest of the axle is essentially identical; the differential is pretty much a drop-in component.

The vehicle we're restoring does have one of the more-popular rear axle assemblies and the procedures I show for it illustrate the concept, if not the specific details. From the outset, I've made it clear you need to get the specific information for your exact car. This is especially true with the rear axle assembly because it requires strict attention to detail during assembly even though it is a relatively big, heavy component.

We were fortunate to be able to reuse our original ring-and-pinion gears. Factory gears, even used ones, often tend to have fewer problems than aftermarket gears, especially with noise. They may not always be as strong, but that's not a concern in our situation or for most projects. When rebuilding a rear axle, you need to decide if you want to change ratios, put in stronger components, and/or change the type of differential you're using (as in our case). We kept it simple and retained the original parts except the differential. Our emphasis was on restoring the car with a stock look and a few mild upgrades to improve overall performance and driveability. The following procedures relative to properly adjusting the gears and so forth are relevant to this type of situation and to more-aggressively upgraded restoration projects.

Differential Assembly

1 If the original ring and pinion gears are in good shape, they should be reused because they are typically a matched set from the factory. Here, we see the marking/dimple on the inner surface of the ring gear, so it can be properly aligned with the pinion gear during installation. We've highlighted it with yellow grease paint to make it easier to see as we drop in the differential. The ring gear bolts are different for a conventional differential than a limited-slip differential. The former uses the larger headed bolt while the latter uses the longer bolt and washer combination. These bolts do not interchange. Virtually every bolt in the rear axle assembly should also be assembled with the appropriate type and amount of thread locker applied.

2 First, the ring gear must be installed onto the differential. Thread-in the bolts and then use a star pattern while tightening them to gradually draw the ring gear onto the differential. Gradually tighten the bolts around the ring gear so it doesn't bind or stick as it draws onto the differential. It works best to slowly go from bolt to bolt and only make a turn or two at each point. When the ring gear is finally seated, use a torque wrench for the final tightening to the appropriate spec. It's best to do so in a couple of steps and to use the star pattern here as well. It takes longer, but pays off in less noise and wear.

3 Like the ring gear, the pinion gear also has a marking to help ensure proper alignment during installation. We mark this with some grease paint also.

4 After a new bearing has been pressed onto the pinion gear, the appropriate spacer must be placed next to the bearing before it is assembled with the other bearing and the pinion retainer housing. Unless there is damage or excessive wear, the spacer, like the shim that goes between the pinion retainer housing and the center section, should be reused. These components must have the correct dimensions and must be assembled properly for the pinion to be correctly positioned such that the appropriate amount of gear backlash can be obtained.

Differential Assembly CONTINUED

5 After the bearings and spacer have been properly assembled into the pinion retainer housing, a new seal can be installed as well. The seal only needs to be lightly oiled and gently tapped into place.

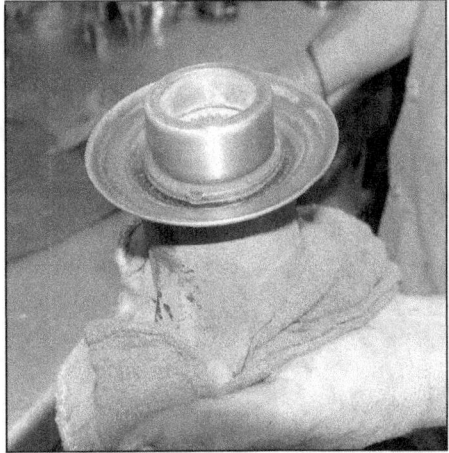

6 The sealing surface of the flange should be lightly buffed to remove any surface imperfections prior to pressing it onto the pinion gear. So long as there are no deep grooves or scratches, this part is almost always reusable. Even with minor wear and/or grooving, add-on sleeves can restore the flange sealing surface to the proper finish and dimensions. These are usually lightly pressed on and held with adhesive.

7 The flange and its integral deflector get pressed on over the new seal and bearings. The seal should easily ride over the surface of the flange due to the light lubrication we applied previously. With the flange completely seated on the pinion gear, install and torque down the pinion nut.

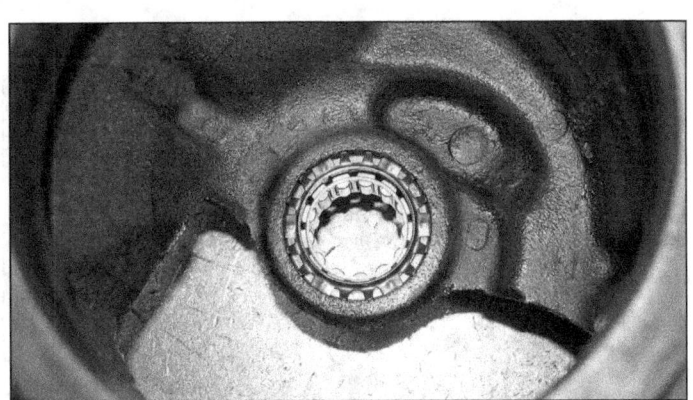

8 It's time to install a new pilot bearing. This is another example of where it makes no sense to reuse the old part, so put in a new one. Apply pressure to the outer race to ensure it is fully installed. After it's completely seated in the housing, install the spring clip/retainer.

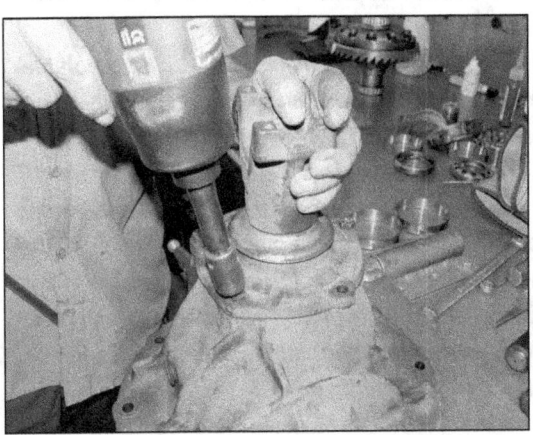

9 Temporarily assemble the pinion retainer assembly onto the center housing using only three of the five bolts. Apply some grease to the contact surface. This helps prevent the new O-ring on the pinion retainer housing from snagging or otherwise getting damaged when the housing is mated to the center section. Be sure to wipe off any excess that may get onto the surface where the shim goes. Start by first placing the original shim or an appropriate substitute on the housing and then carefully lower the assembly into the housing. Verify the gear backlash at this point.

Differential Assembly CONTINUED

10 Rotate the pinion gear, so that the index mark is facing where the ring gear goes. Assemble the outer bearing races onto the bearing cones and line up the yellow index mark on the ring gear with the one on the pinion. This ensures that the appropriate teeth stay lined up as you lower the ring gear onto the pinion. Place the adjusting nuts next to the bearing outer races.

11 All the components should look like this before the bearing caps go on. The index marks served their purpose regarding lining up the correct teeth on the gears, but they're barely visible now. The adjusting nuts must be snug against the bearing races and not tilted before putting the caps on.

12 Install the bearing cap bolts but don't fully tighten them. Make them just snug enough, so they don't move when you move the adjusting nuts or when you rotate the gears. The gears should be able to move smoothly.

13 Measure the gear backlash by setting up a dial indicator as shown. For used gears, you should see about .012 to .013 inch, with a maximum of .015 inch. New gears should be in the .010- to .012-inch range. These figures are for our particular setup. The Ford shop manual provides the data for other cars.

14 After determining that the gear backlash is within acceptable limits, it's time to check the meshing of the gears. Apply white grease or a lash checking compound to the ring gear and spin the gears to spread the compound between the gear teeth. Examine the pattern to ensure it has been evenly spread, thus indicating the gear teeth are meshing properly. Turn the adjustment nuts on each side of the differential to reposition it until you achieve the correct meshing pattern. You want the pattern to be even and centered on each gear tooth. The full checking procedure and related pattern charts can be found in the manual.

DRIVETRAIN

15 With the proper mesh set, install the locking tabs and their retaining nuts. You may need to rotate the nuts slightly so the tab will fit properly. This small amount of change won't affect the adjustment as long as you only move the nut to the nearest hole for each tab. In general, it is better to turn the nuts so they move toward the bearings, rather than away from them.

16 Carefully tighten the bearing cap bolts to the final torque specification for your particular application. It's best to do one cap at a time and do so in a couple of steps rather than trying to reach the final figure in one shot.

17 Next install the stock pinion snubber and the remaining pinion retaining housing bolts. Install the pinion snubber bolts and use thread locking compound. After they have been installed and torqued, remove the remaining two bolts that were previously installed. Apply the thread locker to them and then reinstall and torque them the same as the others.

18 A good tip is to remove the fill plug and re-insert it to make sure it hasn't seized up over the years. If it's hard to remove, use a suitable penetrating lubricant to help break it loose. A very small dab of anti-seize compound on the threads (and only the threads) can facilitate removing this plug later. The center section and associated parts can now be spray painted to prevent surface rusting. Be careful not to get too much spray on the surfaces where the U-joint bearings will rest because it could make their installation problematic. Be sure to keep paint off the gasket surface.

Reassembly

After all of the subassemblies were properly prepared, we began putting the rear axle assembly back together. We made sure the housing and axles were all straight and had no issues. We installed all new seals, bearings, etc., to ensure our rear axle gives us years of trouble-free service. We upgraded to a limited-slip differential using OEM Ford components for improved performance. Last, even though we decided to stick with the original gear set, we thoroughly checked and adjusted all of the various parameters and settings to ensure smooth, quiet operation in the car.

Other than the brakes (Chapter 8), we're mostly done at this point. The details for rebuilding a rear axle assembly for a first-generation Mustang vary by specific application but the general concepts are common. And you still need the Ford shop manual to get specific data for any given application. What I've shown should help identify the main topics of interest, whether you decide to try to rebuild the rear yourself or you send it out.

Axle Assembly

1 Clean the axle housing with a wire brush and wire wheels to remove all residue from the Steelabrator process. Pay special attention to the area behind the studs where the center section mounts. The folded-over lip in that area can easily retain the residue. Blow the housing out extensively with compressed air.

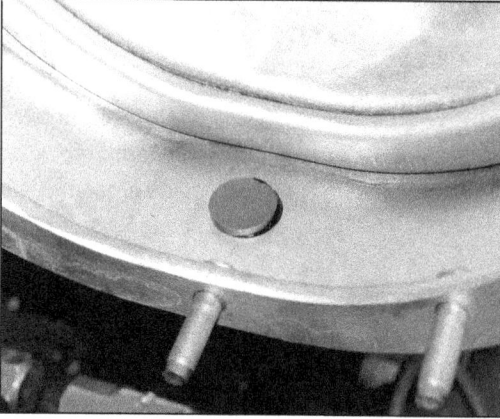

2 As an added measure of safety, install a reasonably strong permanent magnet to the bottom of the axle housing. The force of the magnet should be more than adequate to keep it in place, but using some suitable epoxy or RTV as well can't hurt. The magnet helps capture any stray residue from the Steelabrator and attracts most of the fine metal particles that are produced by normal wear.

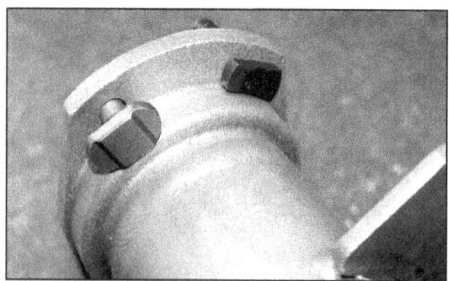

3 Inspect the tube ends to verify they are clean and install the correct bolts to retain the brake backing plate. Different factory retaining bolts and axle bearing sizes were used for different vehicles. Lower-performance and/or smaller cars got the smaller bearing (like our 1968 GT). These cars use the larger flanged bolt (left). This bolt wouldn't clear the larger bearing cup used on heavier and/or higher-performance vehicles, so they came with the smaller flange retaining (right). Both types were used on first-generation Mustangs.

4 New axle seals can be installed. Lubricate the seal at the sealing lip and on the outer diameter, so that it goes into the axle housing easily, and the axle goes into it more easily. Use of a proper installation tool such as shown is highly recommended to avoid seal damage that may result in leaks. Be sure to fully seat the seal.

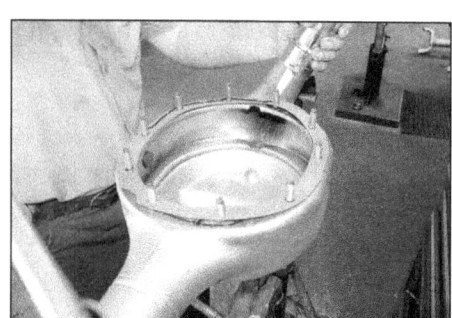

5 Put on the center section gasket. Run a fine bead of RTV sealer completely around the sealing surface of the housing. Make sure you fully surround each stud with bead of sealant. Place the gasket over the studs and lightly tap it down onto the sealant underneath, and then apply more RTV in a similar fashion to the top of the gasket.

DRIVETRAIN

Axle Assembly CONTINUED

6 Install the center section onto the housing. Reuse the factory copper washers beneath the nuts if possible. If they were too worn/damaged, aluminum versions are available. Torque the nuts to the correct spec. The two lower nuts have to be tightened by hand.

7 The refurbished brake backing plates can be installed next. Put the correct fiber gasket between the backing plate and the axle flange.

8 If the axle studs need to be replaced because of damage or age, this is the time to do it. Disc brake cars use slightly different studs than drum brake cars because discs require a small shoulder at the base of the stud so the threads don't contact the rotor. You need a shop press to remove and install the studs.

9 After installing the new retaining plates (for the brake backing plates), the axle bearings can be pressed on. Axle bearings should only be pressed onto an axle once because they shed some of their material as they are installed and bearings are cheaper and easier to replace than axles. On a used axle, you may need to use some thread locking compound (even under a new bearing) to make sure the fit is right.

10 Each axle can now be installed in its respective tube. As was the case with taking them out, a slide hammer or similar tool is needed to press fit the bearings to the axles. Be sure to fully seat the bearings. When driving the bearing on, the sound on impact changes when the bearings fully seat. The retaining plate nuts can then be installed and properly torqued down.

11 Install new brake drums, and you have a completely refurbished and enhanced rear axle assembly. Typically, the brake lines and other parts are installed and then the whole assembly is painted and prepared for installation into the car. Since we will be upgrading the brakes in Chapter 9, we leave the rear unpainted for welding on extra brackets and related items. If your plan were to install the axle in the car without such changes, it would be ready to go after painting it and putting on the brakes lines, vent hose, etc.

HOW TO RESTORE YOUR MUSTANG 1964½–1973

CHAPTER 8

BRAKES

The braking system is one of the most critical areas of vehicle performance regardless of the level of restoration. The car must have a properly operating brake system for safety and performance. The standard braking systems that came with early Mustangs were able to stop the cars, if only just adequately by today's standards. Few things can ruin the pleasure of driving an otherwise well-sorted-out car than a faulty or underperforming braking system. Despite numerous upgrades in both technology and materials since these cars were new, I do not cover the extensive upgrades to build a brake system for a typical restomod or pro-touring type of vehicle. I do introduce a few upgrades using Ford factory parts that greatly improve braking on a typical early Mustang, while also enhancing reliability/durability and maintaining the originality of these cars.

These modifications should be applicable and cost effective for daily-driver or weekend-cruiser projects. They provide overall performance superior to the stock setup, making more frequent use of the car possible. The steps for the front brakes can also be applicable to a show car, with the exception of the rear brakes because it involves too visual a change.

In this chapter, I mostly address the primary components of the braking system at the wheels. I briefly discuss other items, such as the master cylinder, power brake booster, and brake lines. Always consult the factory service manual for specific information on tightening torques, detailed assembly procedures, etc. I only provide some guidelines for what to watch for and how to best resolve any issues.

Usually, it is more cost effective to replace components than to rebuild them. With a show car, this may not be true if higher judge's scores for originality is a priority. The extra expense of machining and/or rebuilding are then more practical. Fortunately, many newer replacement parts can still be used for a show car because they are visually similar to the original parts. I point out some instances where this may be possible, and where only original parts will do.

For this project, we decided to upgrade one of the areas where great progress has been made in terms of improved technology: the rear brakes. The drum setup that originally came with our car was fine for the day, but we wanted better performance that matched our now higher contemporary expectations. Fortunately, Currie Enterprises offers a kit that adapts the much-improved Ford factory rear brake setup from a late model Thunderbird to the 9-inch axle in our 1968. It even allows us to still use the stock 14-inch rims so we can have much-improved performance with only the slightest hint of an upgrade for those willing to look close enough to tell. Here we see these brakes mounted to our rear axle just after welding on the tabs for the new brakes hoses.

Initial Inspection and Evaluation

Brakes wear as a normal consequence of use, so evaluating the braking system primarily involves trying to determine if there is excessive wear, damage, or leakage.

For disc brake systems, deep grooves in the surface of the rotor are evidence of excessive wear and/or damage. A normal rotor surface should be flat with only very fine surface imperfections that can barely be felt by running a fingernail across them. It should turn smoothly with no interruptions or sticking. Any significant grooving means the rotor has to be remachined (if there is enough material/thickness left) or be replaced. Also check for discolored and/or cracked rotor surfaces (a sign of overheating) and warping. The latter is not always visible but can often be felt by turning the rotor on the hub and experiencing intermittent sticking or drag, or a pulsating feel through the pedal. If any of these symptoms are observed, the choice is between remachining (turning) and replacement.

Inspect the seals around the pistons in each caliper for leaks. If there are none it is probably possible to simply clean and/or paint the caliper before reusing it. Always use a new hardware kit (clips, rubber parts, etc.). Check the rubber of the brake hoses for any excessive cracking or signs of leakage. Replace the hoses if there are any signs of leakage whatsoever. If the hoses are reused, it is a good idea to clean them and wipe them down with a silicone protectant.

Last, since the front wheel bearings and grease seals are replaced as a matter of course, it's only necessary to ensure there is no corrosion at either the bearing pocket in the rotor or on the steering knuckle where the bearing makes contact. If there is substantial rust on these parts, they must be replaced.

Drum brake systems are a bit more complicated to evaluate because they must be disassembled to a greater degree before they can be fully inspected. One of the first telltale signs of a problem is fluid on the backing plate. This is a sign that a wheel cylinder likely needs to be replaced. These are generally easy to find and are inexpensive, so this is no big deal.

The drum is often difficult to remove and is an important indicator of potential problems, such as a high degree of wear. As this wear occurs, a step that tends to grab the edge of the brake shoes is formed, and thus prevents the removal of the drum. Loosening the brake shoes via the adjuster wheel and a few evenly spaced, soft-faced mallet blows to the outside of the drum often helps remove it.

Even if the rotors on a disc system appear to be in fine condition, check the thickness of the brake pads for uniformity. Here are new pads on a four-piston caliper. The pads are uniformly thick from side to side, and about the same thickness, as you would expect with new pads. If the pads that were on the car were wearing unevenly, this could point to a problem with corrosion and/or broken or stuck hardware that needs to be corrected before the brakes are reinstalled. This is one of the reasons such hardware is usually replaced automatically; it solves such issues. As part of the cleaning process, remove any corrosion from parts that are reused; new replacement parts should not have any, or course. Besides changing pads much more easily/quickly, another advantage of a four-piston caliper over a single- or dual-piston design is that the extra pistons ensure the pads press evenly against the rotor and don't cock to one side or the other.

When inspecting the front brakes for the first time, look for any signs of leakage from either the calipers (discs) or the wheel cylinders (drums). If leakage is found, the affected parts need rebuilding (possibly, in the case of a show car only) or, more likely, replacement with new parts. Since most of the small hardware for either type of system will be replaced anyway, the next thing to check is the condition of the rotors or drums for any excessive wear, scoring, grooving, or other damage. In our case, the front brakes were in excellent shape, but we decided to use new replacement parts to benefit from improved design, materials, and technology. For a show-car restoration, you need to match the factory rotor design. Unlike most modern rotors (including the replacements we used), the factory rotors had a stepped design. That design is inherently heavier than the more integrated/modern approach and was a reason why we replaced them. For those building a show car, these original rotors would have been reused after a simple machining operation to ensure flatness and a proper surface finish.

CHAPTER 8

Inspect the inner passages of each rotor and remove any dirt or debris. Contaminants inside the caliper inhibit airflow and can cause an imbalance or a hot spot. Cracks or other damage generally mean replacement. Inspect the brake hoses for excessive cracks, wear, or other damage to the surface of the hose. Some superficial age cracks in the rubber are common, but any deeper cracks are not. In a restoration project, you usually replace the brake hoses unless they are in especially good condition. Ours were, so we decided to keep them and simply wipe them down with some silicone protectant later. The hose hardware (clips, copper gaskets, etc.) can often be reused but replace it for a bit of extra insurance. Those interested in improved brake performance, especially pedal response, can consider upgrading to brake hoses wrapped with steel braid. This minimizes hose ballooning and improves response and pedal feel. This isn't necessary for most daily drivers and would be unacceptable for an authentic show car. For weekend cruisers or where maximum braking performance is desired, this can be a very effective upgrade though it may be justifiable only with an aftermarket brake kit.

Inspecting the rear brakes is essentially similar to what must be done at the front. However, there may be differences related to the presence of rotating axles versus the simple, stationary spindles used at the front. A leaking rear axle seal, for example, is much more likely than is a leaking front grease seal. Friction materials contaminated by any such leakage should always be replaced. The presence of a parking brake system also has the potential to cause unique issues, though these are usually only a matter of the cable(s) not fully releasing the brake and are simple to resolve.

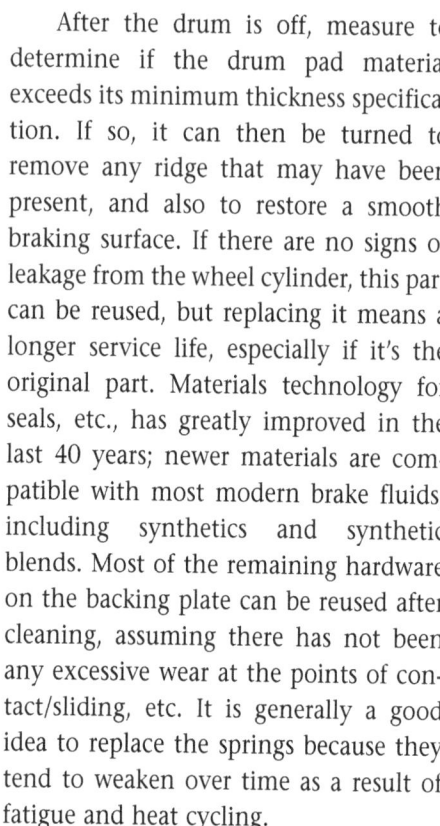

After the drum is off, measure to determine if the drum pad material exceeds its minimum thickness specification. If so, it can then be turned to remove any ridge that may have been present, and also to restore a smooth braking surface. If there are no signs of leakage from the wheel cylinder, this part can be reused, but replacing it means a longer service life, especially if it's the original part. Materials technology for seals, etc., has greatly improved in the last 40 years; newer materials are compatible with most modern brake fluids, including synthetics and synthetic blends. Most of the remaining hardware on the backing plate can be reused after cleaning, assuming there has not been any excessive wear at the points of contact/sliding, etc. It is generally a good idea to replace the springs because they tend to weaken over time as a result of fatigue and heat cycling.

New parts for most of the drum brake hardware, except for the pivot arm, the bridge, and the backing plate itself, are available if needed. Even the backing plates can be reconditioned and/or welded to return them to spec if they prove to be hard to find.

The rest of the braking system consists of the master cylinder, power brake booster/diaphragm (if so equipped), hydraulic lines, and pedal assembly. These items can usually be reused after a

At the rear of the car, also inspect the interconnection between the left and right brake lines, as well as how each line connects to the backing plate/wheel cylinder. The axle assembly is a pretty stout piece, so there usually aren't any problems. However, careless repair work and/or vehicle modifications can sometimes constrict or damage the lines. This is especially true where the lines pass by the U-bolts on each side. Look for any fluid leaks at the distribution block, which connects the axle lines with the flexible hose from the body. Don't be fooled by any gear oil that might have come out of the axle tube vent. Make certain any leaks are from brake lines before you try to tighten the brake line nuts. Use a flare nut wrench to prevent rounding of the edges of the nuts.

cleanup if there are no signs of leakage (fluid or vacuum) and the brakes were working properly.

The master cylinder can be rebuilt with new seals, etc., but, unless you rebuild it yourself, it's often less expensive to simply replace. With a show car, the original master cylinder should be retained but for a daily driver or a weekend cruiser, it is often more practical to simply replace the master cylinder rather than have it rebuilt. The power-brake booster can likewise be rebuilt, but it's also only practical for show-car authenticity.

The brake lines can almost always be reused unless they are damaged or corroded. For those who would like to make an upgrade from the factory galvanized mild-steel lines, it's often possible to get direct-fit lines made in stainless steel from companies such as Classic Tube of Lancaster, New York. These lines not only look better than the factory lines, but they also last almost indefinitely, even in cold climates where the roads are salted. This upgrade may not be suitable for show-car authenticity, but it clearly offers a significant and inexpensive benefit for most daily drivers and weekend cruisers.

For the pedal assembly, there is little to do other than possibly replace the rubber pads and maybe a bushing or two if any are worn. For almost all restorations, the pedal assembly is just cleaned, lubed, adjusted, and retained as is.

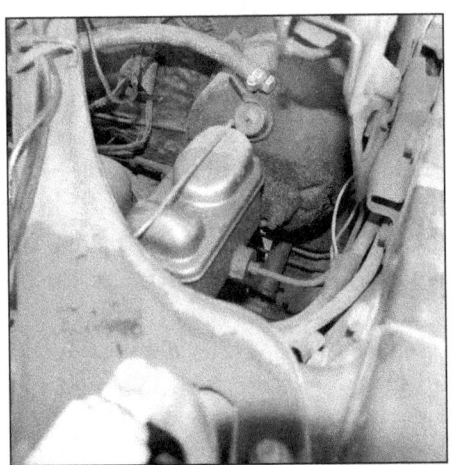

We had our power brake booster rebuilt because the car had been sitting for 20+ years and we were concerned the internal diaphragm might fail once we began using it again. The cost of a rebuild is usually less than buying a new unit plus you retain authenticity. Take care to bag and tag all of the small parts that go with the booster as these are not easy to find if you lose them. For the rest of the brake system a simple cleaning and lubrication of the pedal assembly is usually all that is required although there should also be a check performed to ensure there is no excessive free play or wear at contact points. Other than perhaps a readjustment of the brake light switch and/or the parking brake there is little else to look after.

Our master cylinder and vacuum booster did show signs of leakage, so we knew we would need to address the matter. We're not concerned with having perfectly matching/original parts on our weekend cruiser, so we decided to get new replacement parts for these. For a show-car restoration, a rebuild is often the preferred choice for authenticity. Besides being more cost effective (in most cases) as well as easier from a logistical standpoint, using new components ensures the best materials technology. Surprisingly, our switch to disc brakes at the rear didn't require a special master cylinder. The fluid volume of the calipers used in the Currie Enterprises conversion kit is similar to that of the wheel cylinders used in a drum brake setup. This may not always be the case; but, even if a different master cylinder must be used, there are plenty of suitable options. Most of these will directly bolt in with no need for change other than perhaps slightly relocating the brake lines.

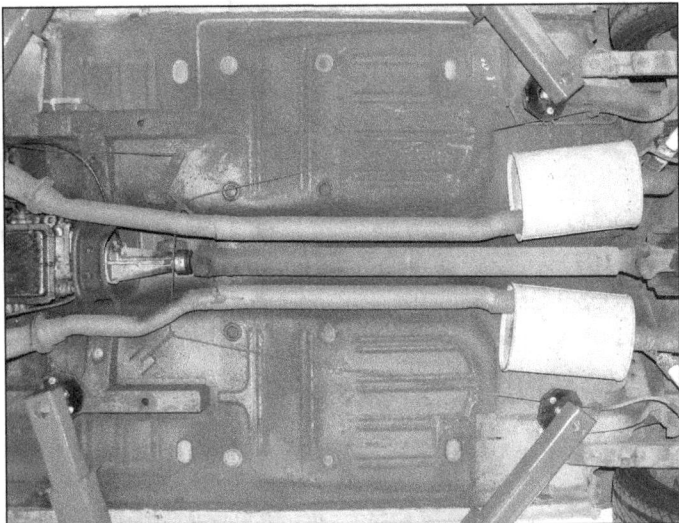

The main issues with the parking brake mechanism are whether or not the cables have been stretched too much through previous use or if they are starting to show signs of corrosion. In either event, they should be replaced with new cables. The pivot points of the short intermediate arm should be lubed after they've been cleaned. Also make proper adjustment to the cable collar to ensure correct parking brake function. Since we've upgraded our rear brakes to the more contemporary disc setup, we have to adapt the cable ends to match what's needed with the new parts.

CHAPTER 8

The parking-brake system is also generally just cleaned, lubed, adjusted, and reused as is. Worn or damaged components might require replacement.

Those original front brake parts, which were to be reused, were simply cleaned and painted as necessary for reinstallation. The dust shield gasket can usually be reused if it is carefully removed. If it is damaged, use a new one or make one suitable gasket material with the original as a template. Also check the surface of the spindle (where the wheel bearings make contact) for any surface imperfections or pitting. We ran our spindle through the media blaster to remove the old paint and dirt before painting. This also provided a smooth even surface that is better at holding the bearings in place than a surface that is too smooth.

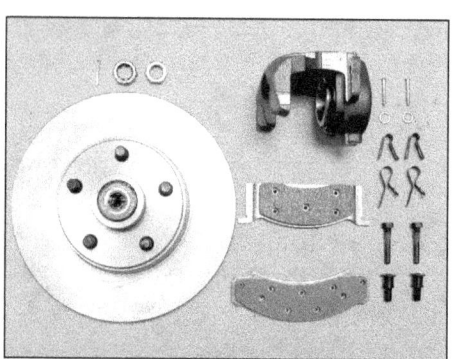

We could have reused our rotors and calipers, but we used new parts for the lighter weight and improved materials. The rotors we chose have been precision ground to ensure flatness and trueness from side to side. This is evident from the pattern on the rotor face. It pays to spend a bit more to get premium parts like these. These perform better and are more durable and reliable as well. We've already installed new high-quality bearings in the rotor. The new calipers also benefit from improved materials, especially the piston seals. Always install new caliper hardware with proper lubrication. We didn't intend to do any extensive high-performance driving, so we chose a high-quality ceramic composite pad material that would be suitable for most restoration jobs because they wear long and reduce dust.

The finished front-brake assembly looks great and should deliver both better performance and longevity than if we reused more of the original parts after reconditioning them. The rotor design is clearly different than that of the original parts, but we are not aiming for 100-percent authenticity. We've placed greater priority on performance, drivability, and cost effectiveness. This high-quality, direct-replacement-part approach is easier and results in a superior system to one using reconditioned original parts, generally for a lower total/overall cost. Our GT wheels would pretty much hide the calipers from view so we elected not to paint them or the rotor centers.

"Wear" can also include stretched braided-steel cables; they become too long to allow full engagement of the parking brake. If this cannot be resolved by adjustment, buy a replacement cable(s). We had to do this anyway because we converted the rear brakes from drums to discs, but this is common even when the factory parts are retained. These cables are usually easy to find and don't cost much, but there really is no need to replace them unless they've stretched or are otherwise not usable. As with the service brakes, the pedal (or handle) for the parking-brake system generally needs little attention other than cleaning, lubing, and possibly adjustment in most instances. Replacement parts are usually easy to find.

Front Brakes: Installation

Our car came with single-piston front disc brakes, which we felt sufficient for our intended use. These brakes are reasonably effective for typical street driving, but they were not suitable for high-performance driving (I address that later in this chapter). As noted earlier, it generally is more practical to replace the original factory parts than it is to rebuild them, unless you are building a show car. So we simply disassembled the front brakes, cleaned the parts we reused, and bought new replacement parts for the rest. Even though our rotors were in pretty good shape (they didn't even need to be cut), we decided to go with new ones for the smoother friction surfaces and the improved metallurgy in modern discs. Their design is slightly different than the factory parts. The new rotors also were slightly lighter than the originals; a minor performance benefit, in our particular case. We installed new bearings in the rotors and also new hardware for the calipers. All of these components were direct-replacement items, and thus go in exactly the same way as the original factory parts.

For brake pads, we selected a premium ceramic-based compound,

BRAKES

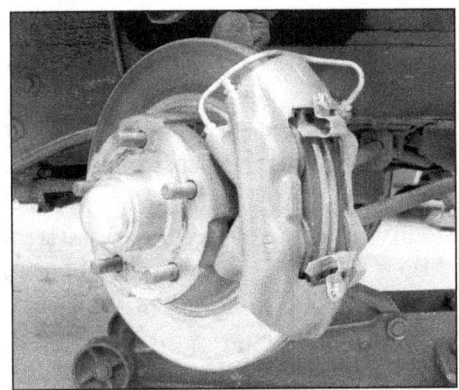

For even more braking performance (and a bit extra cost), use the factory four-piston setup to retain OEM look with improved performance over the single-piston design. For maximum braking performance, there are numerous aftermarket options. These can fit virtually any need for an even higher price, but at the expense of the factory appearance. We needed more than the original single-piston caliper, so we used an aftermarket upgrade. For a weekend-cruiser or high-performance driving, the four-piston or aftermarket choices are more attractive. The judged show car inevitably stays with the original system.

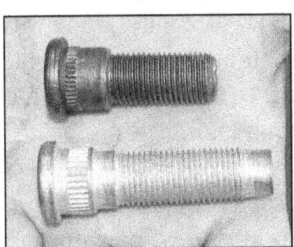

The conversion to discs also requires the installing new, longer wheel studs. These also must feature an unthreaded shoulder so the threads don't dig into the rotor. This isn't required with drum brakes because the drum is generally thinner in this area. The best time to install the new studs is before the rear axles are being assembled into the axle housing. It will be necessary to remove the axles in any event because the caliper mounting plate must go behind the axle flange, between it and the axle housing.

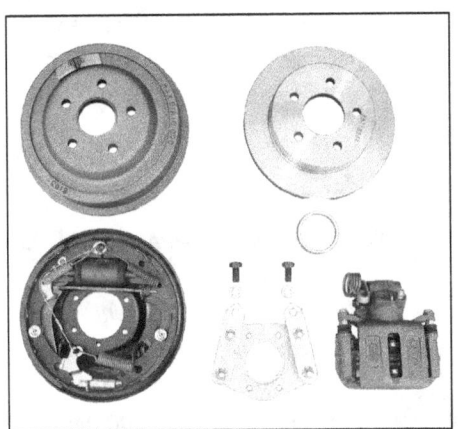

The Currie Enterprises rear-disc-brake conversion kit for our 9-inch rear axle uses all factory Ford parts from a later-model Thunderbird. The only new parts are the mounting bracket assembly and the hub centering ring. This system provides dramatically improved braking performance, is lighter and less complex, and fits inside a 15-inch wheel. Serviceability is also improved because the newer parts are easier to source and generally cost less. The only real adaptation required with this kit it the attachment of the parking brake cables and the fabrication of new brake lines on the axle. The same-style master cylinder can be used or reused.

which would not only perform better and last longer than the original factory compound, but should create significantly less brake dust. Make sure you adjust the wheel bearings correctly per the factory service manual. When using new direct-replacement parts instead of rebuilt or refurbished originals, there really is no difference beyond the benefits gained from the newer materials and technology. Just be sure to use good-quality grease on the bearings and keep it and any other contaminants off the friction surfaces. Also spray the rotors with brake cleaner and wipe them down with a lint-free cloth before you install the wheels and tires over them.

For those who may wish to upgrade front brakes to a higher level of performance, numerous aftermarket options are available, from mild to wild. (I do not cover the typical restomod options, other than to say the aftermarket offers very significant gains in braking performance.) Many are very reasonably priced yet still more expensive than the simple direct-replacement approach I've shown.

Another option for those who want substantially improved braking performance while retaining a more factory look is to install the factory four-piston front calipers that were optional on various models. These can be installed with minimal effort, although other components besides the calipers need to the changed as well. All of the needed parts are generally available from the various companies that specialize in Mustang restorations, and the total can often be less than the aftermarket alternatives. These don't match the performance of most of the aftermarket systems, but are a vast improvement over the factory single-piston caliper option or a front drum-brake system. They can also be used in many forms of mild high-performance driving while providing a factory-correct appearance that no aftermarket brake kit can. For ultimate braking performance, aftermarket kits are the only way to go. However, for a weekend cruiser where improved braking performance with a factory look is desired, this is a very viable alternative.

Rear Brakes: Conversion and Installation

While we were content to retain the factory brake setup in the front, we did not feel the rear drums that came with our car would handle the more-frequent driving schedule we had in mind. Drum brakes are less efficient in wet weather than discs and tend to be much more sensitive to adjustment. Discs are, by design, inherently more self-adjusting as they wear. You don't see many race cars with drum brakes. Discs are also far simpler and easy to service as well as lighter and more effective. There were many good reasons to convert our rear drum brake system to a disc brake system.

We wanted to retain a factory appearance, however, so our options became much more limited. There are numerous aftermarket options available for the rear brakes as well, and though our stock GT-style wheels hid the brakes well, we did not want to go this route, mainly for aesthetic reasons. We also really didn't need the ultimate in braking capability for this vehicle. We simply wanted to benefit from the advantages of a modern disc-brake system.

We found an alternative from Currie Enterprises in Anaheim, California. It offers a rear disc-brake conversion from a 1991–1993 Ford Thunderbird SC for 9-inch axle assemblies. This not only provides the factory look (albeit a newer factory look) we desired, but it also allows us to still use our original wheels and not have to worry about trying to find special parts when we need to service the brakes. Unlike many of the aftermarket brake upgrade kits, the Currie kit clears 14-inch wheels and does not require any axle modification beyond simply installing the unique mounting brackets for a given application. Other than adapting the parking-brake cables, this really is a cost-effective, true bolt-in system.

Compared to using the rear disc brakes from other, newer Ford vehicles (Lincoln Versailles, for example), these are not only more effective and much easier to find, but they also use a common pad that is available in various compounds to better suit your intended use. We went with a premium ceramic-based pad, as with the front brakes. If you don't want to change the original look of the car, this upgrade is clearly not for you. While it may not be necessary for a daily driver either, it clearly would be a benefit in that case and with a weekend cruiser such as ours.

The only other option for retaining a true early look and higher performance is to upgrade to some of the very rare factory rear-disc-brake setups. The parts for these are difficult to find (unlike the four-piston front caliper option) and very expensive. They also don't offer the performance and serviceability benefits of the Currie system either. Simply put, if you are going to upgrade the rear brakes of your early Mustang and don't need the highest performance or want the non-factory look of an aftermarket kit, you really can't do any better than the Currie solution. It provides better performance, reliability, and serviceability, along with the ability to still use most original factory wheels in a cost-effective and Ford-factory-appearing manner.

Because we upgraded our rear brakes, we also have to make some adaptations to the brake hoses, lines, and parking-brake cables. To finish, I show what needed to be done relative to our rear brake hoses and lines. On a vehicle where the brakes have been kept original these steps would not be necessary; just clean the lines and fittings prior to final assembly.

Disc Brake Conversion

1. After the studs have been pressed into the axle, install the correct-dimension centering ring around the hub to help center the rotor to the axle centerline. This is critical and prevents misalignment, which could create unwanted vibration and/or poor braking performance. Note how the centering ring has a small lip at the lower edge; this must be located next to the axle. The chamfered edge must be at top.

2. When assembled with the rotor, the centering ring locates the rotor concentrically with the axle centerline. It also can serve as a pilot for the wheel if it has the correct diameter hub bore. Conversely, the wheel hub bore must be large enough to clear the centering ring or else the wheel won't sit flat on the rotor hat—a potentially dangerous situation. This view also shows how the raised shoulders on the longer studs act to pilot the rotor hat in combination with the centering ring. The locating ring does the final centering while the studs merely help guide the rotor onto the ring. Since factory wheels from this era are "lug-centric," the presence of the raised center ring shouldn't be a factor. The lugs position the wheel and tire. However, if newer hub-centric wheels are to be used, then the dimensions of the centering ring and the wheel's hub bore must be properly matched.

Disc Brake Conversion CONTINUED

3 The caliper mounting plate must be installed over the axle, in the direction shown, before the axle bearing is pressed on. When pressing on the axle bearing, a film of thread locker should be spread over the bearing surface of the axle before the bearing is pressed onto it with a hydraulic press. Once the bearing has been pressed on, it cannot be reused because the inner bearing race has lost material as a result of the interference fit with the axle. After the bearing is pressed on, any such residue as well as any excess thread locker must be wiped off. A thin film of grease should be applied to the area where the axle housing seal contacts the axle to ensure it has proper lubrication when the axle is turned.

4 Ford used different-size axle bearings according to the vehicle application, which can be determined by the appearance of the axle housing ends. Our housing had the smaller size bearings, which is consistent with most Mustangs. Heavier and/or higher-performance cars usually came with the larger bearing housings, which would have a more pronounced step up from the axle tube to the bearing seat. Because the backing plate holes were in the same place, it required different size heads on the backing plate bolts. The larger-headed bolt (left) is the correct one to use with smaller bearing axle housings like ours. The smaller headed bolt (right) is correct for use with axles equipped with the larger bearings.

5 The former mounting plate bolts attach to the mounting plate as shown. Insert the correct socket through the hole in the axle flange, which is drilled specifically for this purpose, and torque these bolts down. No gasket is required between the mounting plate and the axle housing because the axle seals perform the needed sealing function. Do not over-tighten these bolts because it could warp the mounting bracket and misalign the caliper. At a minimum, this would cause uneven brake wear with the potential for even more severe problems. In some cases, the mounting bracket holes may need to be redrilled to rotate the calipers such that they clear the spring; this cannot be determined until all the parts are assembled.

6 When the caliper is installed on the mounting bracket, you can see how much space the package occupies. The rotors sit inward from the axle flange and toward the differential. This provides extra clearance to the wheel in the lateral direction. Note how the caliper mounting bracket and bolts neatly tuck behind the rotor to allow this. The low profile of the caliper is in part due to the type of parking brake mechanism, which moves most of the mechanism inward over the axle tube. This frees space within the wheel and provides the radial clearance to allow the use of 18-inch wheels. The caliper mounting bolts should always be coated with a high-strength thread locker to ensure they do not vibrate loose. Since only two mounting bolts are used and they are not especially large, this is especially critical. The correct bolts and locking washers are included in the Currie kit, but the use of a thread locker provides a bit of extra insurance for even more safety.

7 The Currie Enterprises disc-brake conversion kit includes new brake hoses, which are required for the new brakes. These hoses each feature a protective sleeve to prevent chafing or other potential damage. The hose attachment to the calipers is common, but a little creativity is required for the connection to the opposing rear brake and the incoming pressure line from the car. Before we can address that, however, we must first secure each hose to the housing by securing the loose end with a tab.

Disc Brake Conversion CONTINUED

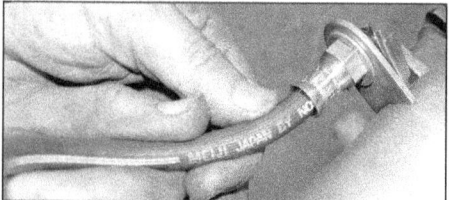

8 Position the mounting tab so that the hose is not stressed, yet it is still protected from road debris, exhaust heat, etc. The area where the original factory brake line was located is a good place to use, if possible. Here, we see the hose end reaches the factory line location, yet still has space for the incoming hard line, which comes from the vent tube area. The factory tab needs to be ground off.

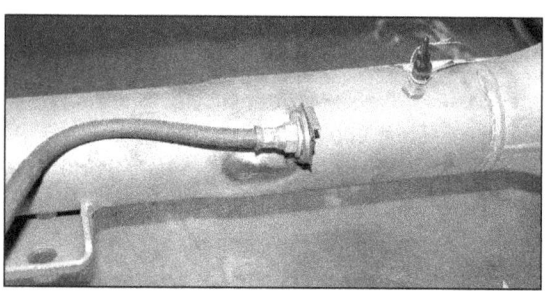

When installed, the new hose mounting tab is located the same basic area where the factory hard line was mounted. The new hose is protected and in an unstressed position. The axle tube vent is used to help secure the distribution block that ties the two rear brakes and the incoming pressure line together. Basically, we use Ford factory parts to retain the factory appearance while still gaining functionality for our upgrade.

The finished, painted rear axle assembly with the brakes installed shows the disc brake conversion setup. At this point, we need to determine if the calipers will interfere with the springs. Several factors, including the curvature of the springs and the position of the calipers themselves, determine this. If the calipers need to be repositioned, new holes need to be drilled in the mounting plate to rotate the calipers out of the way. This entails removing the calipers and axles and then pressing the bearings off of the axles, so the plates could be redrilled. New bearings are needed before the axles can be put back in. Fortunately, the likelihood of interference between the calipers and the springs is minimal. It remains possible, however, since it is virtually impossible to anticipate every possible combination of components and their relative positioning (static and dynamic) based on vehicle loading and operation.

After installing the axle into the car, we found that our new brake setup cleared the springs even though they were somewhat different than the original parts. Since there will be relatively little movement between the springs and the calipers we can be fairly confident there won't be problems under loaded and/or dynamic operating conditions. While we have not yet resolved the matter of adapting the parking brake cables to the new calipers, we're confident this can be accomplished in short order.

Fabricating custom hard lines for the rear brakes involved little more than using a standard tubing bender plus finding an extended vent tube and a suitable distribution block. The latter parts are pretty easy to source and they bolt right on. Bending of the tubes was a matter of just connecting the ports on the distribution block to the hose ends we had just mounted. For the shorter tube, we included extra bends so the ends of the line would aim directly at their targets. The longer line just followed the path of the original factory line except that it ended at our new hose end. The stock tabs on the housing were used to secure the longer hard line. We used a long-enough jumper hose to compensate for axle travel, and which also fit right into the stock mounting bracket on the body, to connect the pressure line to the new junction block secured by the vent tube.

CHAPTER 9

SUSPENSION

The suspensions on first-generation Mustangs were pretty good for their day. At a time when most vehicles were stuck with overly soft and vague setups that isolated drivers and passengers from most road features, Mustangs had sportier handling. Though relatively unrefined by modern standards, first-generation Mustangs actually could be made to handle rather well—just ask the Trans Am racers of the day. These suspensions were fairly simple, yet effective. They used a distinctive interpretation of a coil-spring, double-control-arm front suspension, combined with a fairly conventional leaf-spring rear suspension. Light vehicle weight and overall dimensions also helped performance.

Our intention was to not merely replace the standard suspension but to also introduce some refinement that more modern technology allows. Consistent with our restoration plan we remained true to the original designs wherever possible. For those wishing to restore a vehicle for show purposes, this is mandatory. Thus I briefly touch on repair and replacement of original components. To a large extent, this can also benefit those who have a daily driver.

While I do not get into extensive modifications such as coilover or multi-link suspensions, I do show a few

On initial inspection, our vehicle doesn't have any glaring issues that require special attention. There is the expected amount of normal wear and corrosion, yet no components are showing visible signs of failure. If you are considering reusing the ball joints, the control arm, strut rod bushings, etc., this is the time to fully check them to make sure they are reliable. The factory service manual provides the proper procedures for checking these components, which amounts to basically determining if there is excessive play/compliance due to wear. The forces involved in checking many of these components can be extreme, and thus breaker bars and so forth will likely be required. A good example of this is ball-joint inspection. This must be done with the proper loading to ensure a correct evaluation. It is common for service technicians to simply wedge a breaker bar between the control arm and the steering knuckle and then rock it to try to induce movement. This doesn't always yield a valid result if the vehicle is resting on the tires or even if the tires are hanging; it depends on the specific vehicle design and even the particular joint. Take care to ensure a valid result and avoid damaging the joints. The control arm bushings are a bit easier to evaluate because the length of the arm magnifies any excess movement. The trick is to apply enough load in the proper direction to see if there's excess movement. This is especially critical with the lower arms where the bushings are not as visible. The simple answer, of course, is to just replace all the bushings (except, possibly, for a survivor car) to ensure the best performance and reliability over time.

enhancements that can be made for those who want some enhanced function and don't require total authenticity. There are many more possible modifications, but I have chosen to only describe some which, for the most part, are relatively inconspicuous and simpler to implement. Your budget and your desire for authenticity will generally dictate which of these you use.

A reasonably experienced do-it-yourselfer can perform the majority of work needed on the suspension because much of it entails simple removal and replacement of components. However, welding the shock towers and subframe connectors to the chassis is a notable exception. This is generally left to professionals.

Retaining/rebuilding original parts for show cars is also best left to professionals. This typically requires a heftier budget, but such is the price of building a potential show winner. Those who are building daily drivers and/or weekend cruisers usually buy a suitable rebuilt part for less than what rebuilding the original part would cost. Always access the potential ("core") value of the original part before simply disposing it. One person's core may be another's "date code correct" part that is worth the expense of rebuilding. While this may not apply to all components, it can often help offset the cost of buying new parts.

In the following sections, I first show how to evaluate the condition of the existing components, and to then decide what the appropriate course of action should be. For building our weekend cruiser with enhanced functionality, I chose to use new parts rather than rebuild existing ones. I show some service-oriented procedures, though these are mainly for a functional upgrade rather than simply for repair and/or maintenance.

Here again, consult the factory service manual for the various torque specs and repair procedures for your application. While it is clearly possible to modify the suspension far more extensively than what is discussed here to achieve even greater upgrades in performance and/or durability, these are not within the scope of this book.

Inspection and Evaluation

For suspensions, there are two main concerns: bushings and wear. If the car was used in a colder climate, corrosion may also come into play. The simplicity of the suspensions used on early Mustangs pretty much limits the major concerns to deteriorated rubber bushings and worn metal components like adjusters. The former are generally the most noticeable because the rubber often can deteriorate to the point of collapse, thus affecting the vehicle's handling and/or causing clunking or other noises. The latter, are generally more subtle in their effect.

Tires may wear unevenly, and the steering wheel may pull to one side while driving, for example. So it's necessary to perform a thorough visual inspection of the front and rear suspensions while they are on the car. At least partially disassemble them in certain areas to make sure

The front strut rod bushings definitely perform critical functions yet are often improperly maintained. These are mainly rubber parts; they are very definitely affected by time and the elements, as well as wear. These bushings locate the lower control arms and thus directly affect the path of the vehicle. Too much play in either bushing, or even too much of a difference from side to side, can have a very negative effect on handling and, more often, on braking. A car that pulls sharply to one side under braking may not have any problems with the brakes themselves; rather the strut rod bushings may be causing the issue. These parts don't have a very large range of movement but they do still become loose. This looseness causes the car to lose directional stability, especially during braking when the rear bushings are in compression. At a minimum, these bushings should be inspected and adjusted during any restoration project. Considering their cost and accessibility, just replace them and install a new, properly adjusted set. Remember that any changes to these bushings will also require the wheel alignment to be readjusted because the location of the lower control arm will move with the adjustment/replacement of the bushings.

SUSPENSION

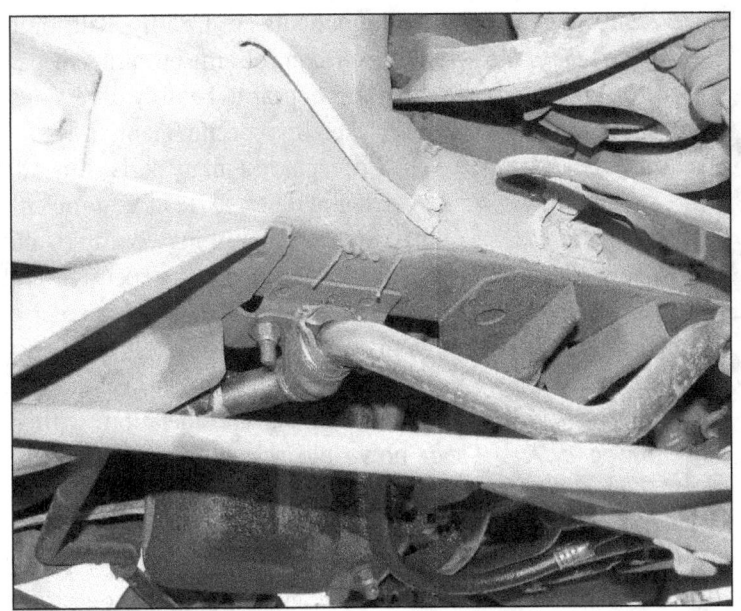

The anti-sway bar bushings and end-link bushings usually require attention. It is fairly common for the bushings to partially collapse and/or tear, often to the point of causing a clunking from metal-on-metal contact. The end-link bushing can also fail in such a manner though this is less likely. It is generally more noticeable, however, as degraded handling usually accompanies the inevitable noise. A more common scenario is that the bushings wear unevenly to the point that excess play is created. This negatively affects the vehicle's dynamic behavior, particularly during quick changes of direction. There may or may not be a noticeable increase in noise to go along with this handling change.

Our rear suspension was in pretty good shape to begin with. The car drove well and all of the original rubber bushings were in decent shape. The shocks had already been replaced at least once and showed no signs of leaking. If we were on a really tight budget with a daily driver, we could just do some cosmetic touching up and reuse the shocks and bushings, at least for a while longer. Clearly, this would not do for a show car unless it was a survivor car. For our weekend cruiser, however, we will replace and upgrade many parts for better performance. We replace them with parts that are similar to the factory parts but provide much better ride and handling. And these parts don't adversely affect collector value of the car. The U-bolts, the spring plates, and the rubber axle bumpers mounted in the frame are the only factory parts we keep.

The spring-eye bushings on our car were in good condition and didn't need to be replaced for daily-driver duty. And all of the mounting brackets, shackles, and fasteners were in good shape too. There was some surface rust but no serious corrosion. It is critical that the areas around where the springs mount to the car are free of any significant rust; this could cause big problems if the springs were to pull out. Another common issue is damage from improper jacking, which we luckily did not have. Problems such as these, which affect the structural integrity of the vehicle, must never be ignored and must be fully repaired before the car is restored and driven. Ideally, vehicles with such issues would be passed over in favor of using those in better condition as the basis for restoration.

HOW TO RESTORE YOUR MUSTANG 1964½–1973

CHAPTER 9

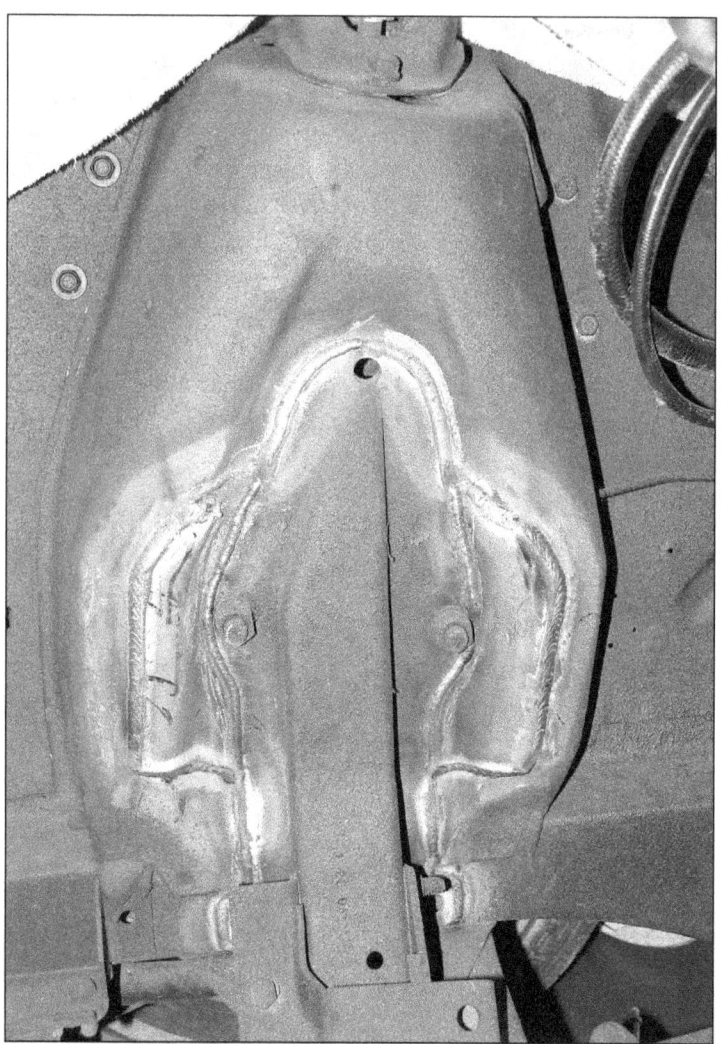

From the factory, the welding around the shock towers is, quite literally, spotty. This causes stress risers, which can lead to cracking and metal failure as the car ages. Aggressive driving and/or harsher climates can further compromise shock tower integrity. The simple remedy? Continuously weld the stampings that were only partially welded by the factory. This greatly enhances the structural integrity of the front of the vehicle, improves ride and handling, and prevents cracking. With the engine out of the vehicle, this is pretty easy to do; it probably should be left to a professional if you're not too proficient at welding. Proper preparation is a key. Any paint or undercoating must be completely removed to expose bare metal. Close any existing cracks and properly align the parts before further welding is done. Be sure to weld the inner and outer edges of each stamping and weld all accessible areas as shown. Make sure all other parts have been removed from the immediate area: the shock towers will get quite hot. The area, of course, also needs to be primed and repainted. The backside of the shock towers need to be re-primed and painted as well. We removed all of the burned paint and undercoating to get the best possible coverage. We also removed the accumulation of dirt that tends to build up on the flat horizontal surface beneath the control arm. After many years of dirt being thrown off from the tires, it is reasonable to expect this buildup to occur. However, drain holes in the corners of this area often get clogged so water and moist dirt remain in the area. This can lead to the steel rusting through, which is very undesirable in such a highly loaded area. We removed all of the dirt and opened the drain holes a bit to help prevent them from clogging in the future. This area sees much dirt and moisture, it is especially important to use a very robust primer before applying a paint and/or undercoating combination that will prevent any future rust issues.

the components are healthy. Ball joints and lower control arm bushings in particular can appear to be okay unless they are checked in a specific manner.

Also, replacing many parts while the car is being restored reduces problems and cost later on. Bushings, bearings, and the like are relatively inexpensive and usually pretty simple to install, so replacing them is a form of cheap insurance against unexpected failure. Give shock absorbers similar consideration. If there are no visible leaks or other damage and the damping action is acceptable, it may be possible to retain what you have, especially if they were recently replaced or are the original shocks (in the case of a survivor or show car). In most cases, however, there are significant ride quality and handling improvements if the shocks are upgraded.

In any case, the peace of mind gained from replacing an unqualified item with a new part of known quality is worth the relatively minor cost. And when a part is rebuilt to retain authenticity, using new consumable/wearable components generally does not detract points from scoring in a show setting. Suspension parts should only be reused when they are known to have been very recently replaced by known good components, recently rebuilt, or are being kept in original condition in a survivor car.

The rear suspension is considerably less difficult to evaluate than the front. You're basically limited to sizing up the bushings in the leaf-spring eyes and the condition of the fasteners like U-bolts and shackles. There is rarely a problem with or damage to the leaf springs themselves. They may need some cosmetic touch up, but if there is a problem with the springs being excessively corroded or having lost their shape, they are generally replaced. Only in a survivor or show car should the possibility of refurbishing and reusing deteriorated leaf springs

SUSPENSION

Many early Mustangs have various metal shields, such as this one, to protect fuel and/or brake lines as they cross over underbody surfaces. The idea was/is to protect the line from scraping the ground (or a speed bump, etc.) and then collapsing or leaking. You can imagine the problem if a fuel line got snagged on something and gasoline was sprayed onto a hot exhaust part. Those doing show-car restorations reinstall these parts anyway for the sake of authenticity, yet other restorers shouldn't ignore them. We decided to install subframe connectors and we won't be able to use this particular fuel line shield because it interferes with the subframe connector. However, this is not a problem because the subframe connector itself provides even better protection from anything that might be able to contact the fuel line.

Similar to the extra welding around the shock towers, the chassis areas must be stripped of paint and any other material and must not be overly rusted so the subframe connectors can be properly welded to the frame for maximum strength. Also, as with the shock towers, the attachment plates are welded completely around, rather than simply spot welded in just a few places. This ensures the best performance and durability of the subframe connectors, plus it eliminates gaps that could allow moisture to seep under the attachment plates. Finding the proper location of the connectors involves a bit of trial and error because they have a tendency to rock or move the opposite end when one end is pushed fully on. The best location (at both the front and the rear) is the point where the attachment plates have the greatest amount of engagement with the subframe stubs. The connectors should be relatively level and as snug to the floor of the car as possible. Don't be afraid to push up on the floorpan a bit to get a better fit. Any fuel or brake lines that must pass between the subframe connector and the body should be moved to an area that has greater clearance to avoid pinching the line(s). Our subframe connectors were manufactured by Global West Suspensions and are intended for a welded-in installation. These and other such products from other manufacturers can be simply bolted in as well, though this is not recommended. A bolted-in setup never matches the strength and effectiveness of a welded-in installation of the same part. Others who may not want to do any welding because of concerns over the potential impact on resale value need to consider that even welded in subframe connectors can be removed and the welds ground off to the point it would be difficult if not almost impossible to know they were ever there.

CHAPTER 9

This photo of a finished installation of the Global West Suspensions subframe connectors shows that they provide extensive stiffening to the vehicle structure and generally do not present ground clearance problems. Other components, usually the exhaust, often hang down lower and would contact the ground before the subframe connectors. Our 1968 fastback will not be used aggressively, so we only installed the subframe connectors alone, without the optional jacking rail kit. Weight gain in either case is negligible and is low and centered in the car.

Regardless of your type of restoration, one of the best things you can do to improve both vehicle handling and braking performance (and long-term durability) is upgrade the front strut bar bushings to a harder/higher durometer rubber than what came from the factory. You get the benefit just from installing new parts and ensuring the related adjustment is correct. You also realize a very noticeable improvement in overall vehicle dynamic behavior. The harder rubber prevents the strut rod from moving as much when a load is applied. This minimizes variations in suspension geometry that degrade performance and, in extreme cases, can cause the vehicle to swerve to one side or even completely out of control. The harder rubber may transmit a bit more noise and vibration into the interior, but it won't be very noticeable. Ride quality should also be minimally affected, if at all, due to the way the loads are transmitted to the strut rods. When you consider the minor cost premium of the harder bushings versus the stock replacements, it's an easy upgrade to make. Best of all, it looks just like the stock setup. A note of caution about using polyurethane bushings instead of rubber: While a little bit harder is better with the higher durometer rubber bushings, polyurethane can be too hard. The strut rods need to be able to pivot freely and the harder polyurethane bushings can restrict this movement. This can lead to the struts rods actually breaking, usually right where

SUSPENSION

even be considered. In our case, we went with an upgraded set of springs. In most cases all that likely is needed are new bushings, possibly shackles, and paint.

You also need to determine whether or not to upgrade the factory setup for improved performance. This isn't an option for a show car (authenticity); and, for a daily driver, the cost may not be justified if the benefits are not needed. For our weekend cruiser, however, this is beneficial and cost effective, even though we have elected to only pursue the subtle upgrades.

An example of where the factory design can use some improvement is shock towers in the front suspension. Cracks commonly develop in this area due to normal wear and tear. The more aggressively the car has been used and/or the more inclement weather it has been exposed to, the more likely this problem exists.

Similarly, the basic body structure of early Mustangs was not very rigid, especially by today's standards. Over time the body structure tends to increasingly flex under load, producing unwanted noise and reduced effectiveness of the suspension, brakes, and steering. For our vehicle we decided to implement a few modifications to minimize body flex. These include additional welding in the shock tower area, installing welded-in subframe connectors, plus the use of an adjustable Monte Carlo bar and an aftermarket export brace.

Front Suspension

The front suspension of our vehicle was in pretty good shape. If we were building a mild daily driver, we could have simply refurbished it with some new bushings and ball joints, for example. A show car would have received more attention, primarily from a cosmetic perspective with mostly the same parts being used. Since we are more concerned with function in our weekend cruiser, we used some modified components that are not required for a daily driver or desired for a true show car. The parts we chose are all relatively inconspicuous, as front suspension components tend to be, and generally resemble the factory parts. I show an overview of the installation for these parts and also describe the rationale for using them. Your decision to use these or similar modifications depends on your intended use of the vehicle, your priorities, and your budget.

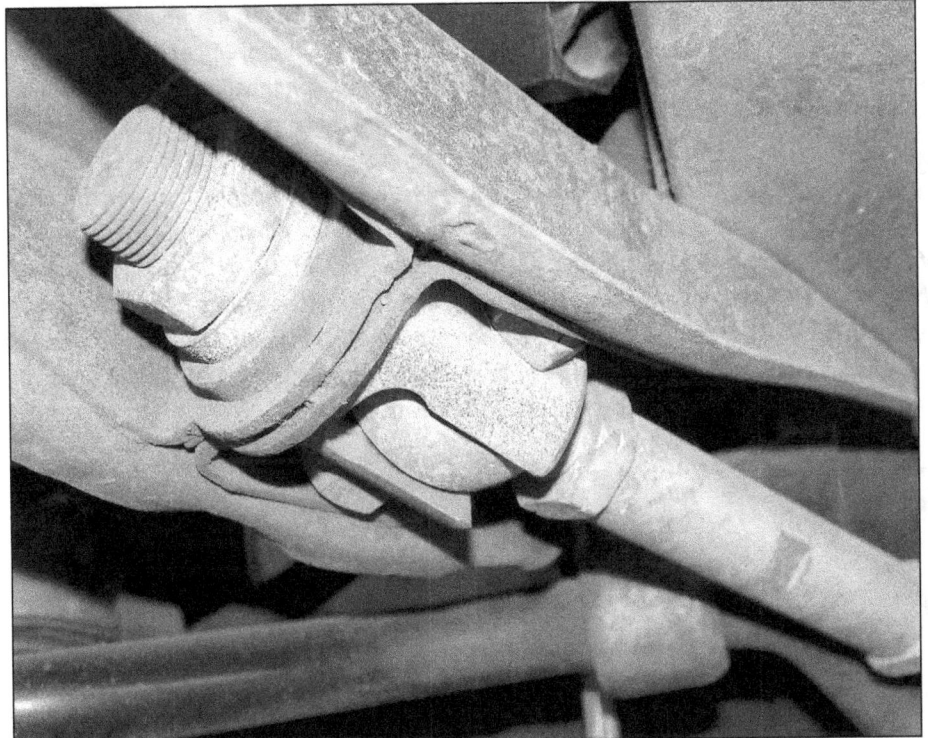

If you're not concerned about retaining a completely stock appearance and you don't mind a bit more noise and vibration while you drive, you can go even further than the harder rubber strut rod bushings. You can eliminate the rubber bushings altogether and replace them with a design that relies on precisely indexed rod ends instead. These rod ends have virtually no compliance so they virtually eliminate any unwanted movement of the strut rods. We chose a Global West Suspension design because it used a Teflon-lined rod end for reduced noise and vibration (though still a bit more than with rubber bushings) and because it also had an additional adjustment sleeve to help get the proper alignment settings. If you go with this type of design, you must ensure the rod end is properly aligned with the control arm and strut rod, otherwise you might risk binding or even bending/breakage. The parts from Global are designed to index to the pocket and can only be installed in the proper orientation. This type of setup is pretty much mandatory if you intend to do any vintage road racing with your early Mustang; it improves the overall handling performance and is also much more able to withstand the abuse compared to a setup that retains rubber bushings. There's a bit of tradeoff in vibration but the gains in handling, precision, and control under braking are well worth it if you don't mind the different look. Most people will never even know it's there since you have to get pretty low to the ground to even see these. These are worth considering for a higher-performance street car.

These aftermarket lower control arms from Global West Suspensions begin life as factory stampings but get a few clever upgrades to make them better. The first of these is that the opening on the lower side is closed off ("boxed") to greatly increase the strength of the arm. Special-cut plates are fully welded around each seam to completely close off most of the lower opening of the arm, so dirt and moisture cannot accumulate and cause rust. It's not really possible to close off the whole underside because access must be left for the anti-sway bar end link nuts. The other major improvement over the stock arms is the use of a flanged spherical bearing instead of a rubber bushing at the end that mounts to the body. This type of joint is far stronger and more stable than a rubber bushing; it also has less friction, which actually improves the ride a bit. It is much less prone to wear and pounding out, plus the flanges help prevent unwanted movement of the adjusting bolts that are used to set the wheel alignment. Using bearings instead of bushings improves ride, handling, and durability while being virtually impossible to detect, unless someone crawls under the car to look. If we were building a racer or a higher-performance street car, we may have chosen tubular arms instead. Because we won't be using the car that aggressively and we want to keep a stock look, this is the type of modification we want—one that greatly improves function with minimal change in style. This is a truly bolt-in upgrade that works very well indeed.

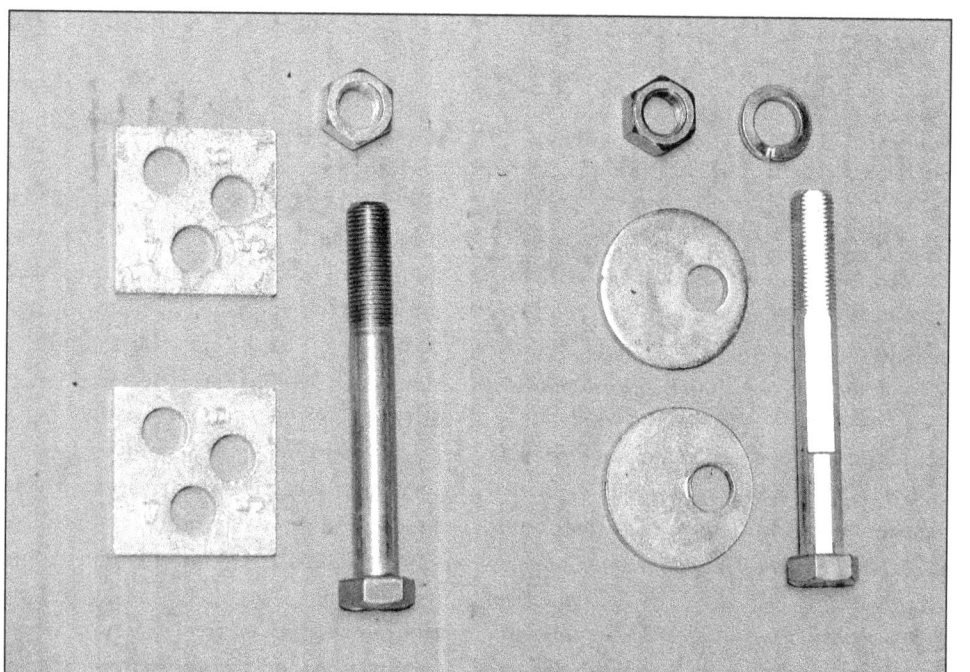

Another subtle improvement is the use of special "Lock Out" plates instead of the standard eccentric cams to adjust the position of the lower control arms. The factory eccentric plates have several inherent design weaknesses that can show up over time and/or with too much enthusiastic driving. The factory bolt has a flat side ground onto it that is meant to line up with a step in the offset hole in one of the corresponding plates. This basically indexes the plate to the bolt, so it cannot rotate on it; at least that's the concept. The hole in the other plate is round so it can go all the way to the head of the bolt, and it's free to rotate. The problem is that there is too much slop or tolerance between the flat on the plate and the bolt; they just fit too loosely from the start. Over time, the tolerance increases because of use and corrosion. It's mainly friction and the clamping force of the bolt that prevent the plates from slipping, so you need to have as little play between the bolt and the plates as is possible. If the bolts loosen because of wear or extreme loading, it's very likely the plates may move and throw the suspension out of alignment. A better approach is to use thicker plates with a series of offset holes, which are fixed in place by the same retaining flanges that locate the stock plates. The difference is that these new plates can't rotate and the holes in them are much closer to the size of the bolts that go through them. This greatly reduces any potential for movement after the whole assembly is tightened down. Rather than loosening the bolt to turn the plate you have to disassemble the whole system and pick a different set of holes in the plates to get the position of the lower control arm that you want.

SUSPENSION

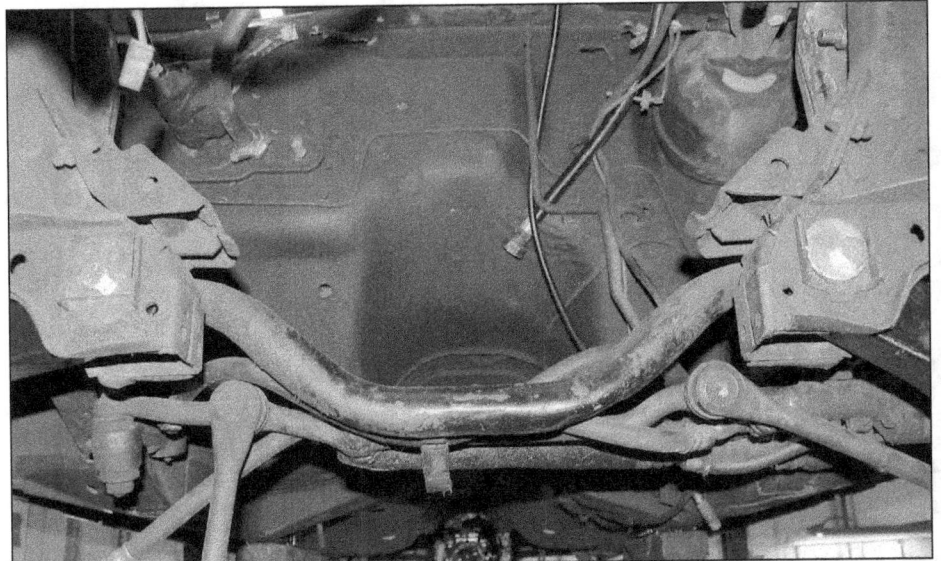

This side-by-side comparison of the stock eccentric-plate-style adjusters reveals the inherent advantages of the Lock Out plate. The Lock Out plates (left) fit the retaining flanges much more snugly and make much more contact along each side. The stock-style plates (right) only have point contact with the flanges and fit more loosely. These plates are also thinner, so it is more likely they can flex under load and thus lose their adjustment as they move. It is also more difficult to keep the stock plates from moving during the adjustment process because the rotation of the plates affects their adjustment. The Lock Out plates are relatively restrained in the horizontal direction and can only move vertically during installation. Choosing different combinations of holes results in movement in both directions, but the plates are locked into position when resting between the flanges. The Lock Out plates are clearly a superior design for any application but are really only needed in higher-performance and/or racing situations.

Lock Out plates are designed so each plate can be repositioned to yield a virtually infinite number of possible locations for the lower control arms. There are six possible combinations of holes in each plate (three per plate with front and back variations), plus the plates can be rotated. This provides more than sufficient adjustment range to find the setting you need. Each plate is marked with numbers for each hole to help ensure the two plates at each control arm are properly matched with each other. There's a trick in how the plates have to face each other, but it's explained in the instructions that come with them. It's a bit tedious, but you should only have to do it once because these won't wear or move like the stock components. If you're using lower control arms with flanged bearings, as we did, the plates shouldn't move or deteriorate over time because the plates and flanges clamp are firmly clamped together. While it may take more effort to set the alignment the first time, you can rest assured it will be far less likely to change over time.

For lower control arms, there are many options. Those building a daily driver or a show car generally just go with stock replacement parts, albeit most likely with different levels of quality and/or preparation. Those building a more performance-oriented vehicle with minimal concern over retaining the factory look probably go with aftermarket tubular arms if the budget permits it. We took a mid-road approach, which provides most of the benefits that switching to a tubular arm provides, yet does not sacrifice the stock appearance. As you see in the following photos, the change in appearance is relatively subtle, even though the improvement in performance is quite considerable, and noticeable. Installation is also not much different than stock.

The upper control arms are the parts most likely to simply be rebuilt, though they can still be enhanced somewhat. As long as the main stampings are in good shape (no major rust, corrosion, or cracks), they can be reused after some cleaning. A run through the media blaster and some good paint should be all that's needed to prepare them for reassembly.

The choice of components used during reassembly can be optimized a bit, as I show in the photos. Aftermarket tubular upper arms are also available for those who use their higher-performance and/or racing vehicles more aggressively.

CHAPTER 9

Upper Control Arm Rebuild

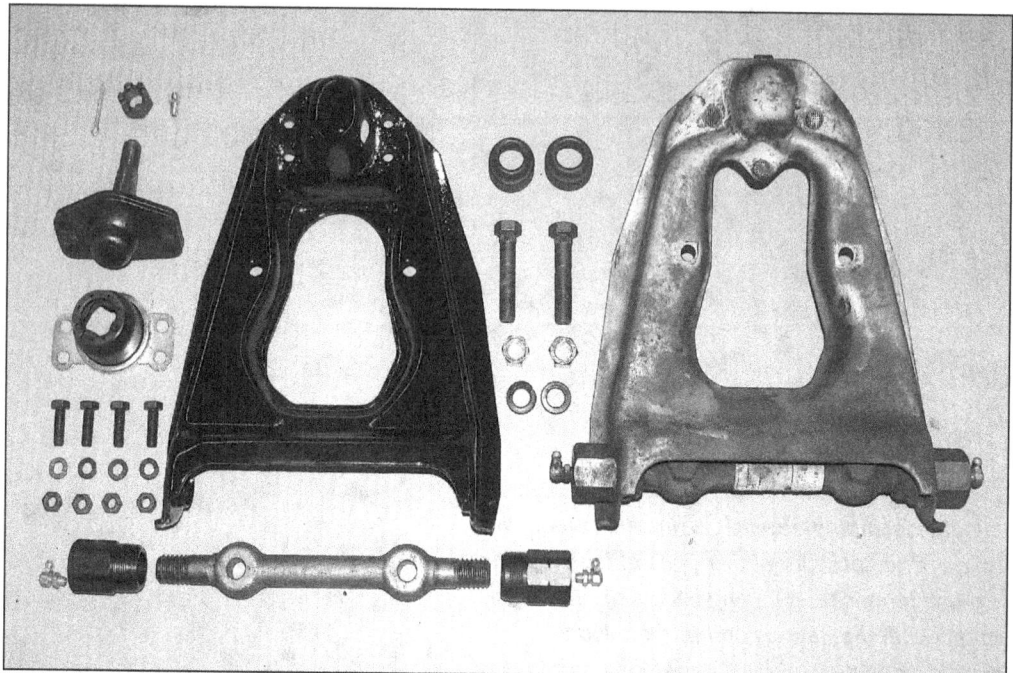

Rebuilding the upper control arms is not especially difficult, but it does involve some special procedures, which we will cover in the next few photos. All of the parts needed for a typical rebuild are shown here. Note that the control arms we used accept four-bolt ball joints (left). This design is a better choice than the three-hole design on the right because it is stronger and uses a more easily found ball joint. There's no real functional difference other than the greater load handling capacity. The shaft and nut assemblies can be reused if they are not worn or otherwise damaged. New ball joints should always be used along with new grease seals/boots and zerk fittings. We'll upgrade the spring perches, shocks, and springs, but first we need to make sure the platform they work from is both properly assembled and adjusted. There's not quite as much potential for improvement with the upper control arms as there is with the lowers, but attention to detail can still pay significant benefits.

1 When rebuilding upper control arms, make sure the threads on the arm itself and the retention nuts are in good shape. It's common for these to strip or wear to the point that new parts are required. These parts should be as clean and free of any surface irregularities as possible before you assemble them. If the nuts still don't turn freely in the arm, use some anti-seize compound or grease to make sure they do. The nuts will be fully tightened down to about 120 ft-lbs or so (check the factory manual) on the arms so you don't have to worry about the lubricant making them prone to loosening. Similarly, the grease that goes on the ends of the support shaft lubes the insides of the nuts, so you can be sure that some grease migrates to there anyway. Liberally grease the threads of the shaft and the ID of the seal prior to installing the rubber seals on the shaft. Also grease the interior of the retention nuts. Use relatively tacky grease that does not run out if it gets hot or wet. Be generous since both the type and amount of grease used will play a big role in reducing wear of the shaft/nut threads over time. The grease also helps make the control arm rotate more freely once everything is assembled, so also coat the face of the seal where it contacts the control arm. This will not only reduce "stiction" and improve the ride quality somewhat, but it will help reduce seal wear as well. There's no need to pack the inside of the nuts with grease. Just make sure there's enough to coat the threads fully and have a little left over for insurance.

SUSPENSION

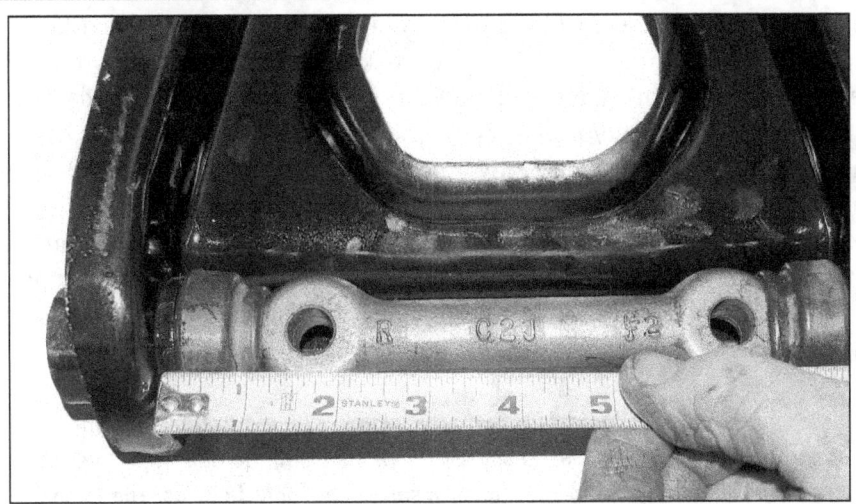

2 After all of the parts are assembled, it's crucial that you center the shaft in the control arm. Do this by measuring the distance from the inner surface of the control arm to the center of the mounting bolt hole on each side. You can also use one of the edges of each hole. Be consistent and make sure the point you use is the same distance from the control arm on each side. If there is a difference, just rotate the shaft in the correct direction to balance it out. Don't worry about how the seals look or if the letters on the shaft are showing. The critical requirement is that each hole is the same distance away from the inside of the arm so that the arm is centered.

3 Before installing the upper control arms on the vehicle, it is a very good idea to just rock the shafts back and forth to loosen them up a bit. This also helps properly seat the seals and make sure the grease is properly distributed. Do not rotate the shafts too far. If you do, they are no longer properly centered. Just rocking them back and forth through about a 120-degree arc should do it. You will likely need a fairly long (and strong) tool to get enough leverage to move the shafts, at least at first. Be sure to avoid damaging the shafts or their mounting holes. Any scratches, scrapes, or gouges could increase the chance of breakage under heavy loads. When the shafts can turn somewhat freely, still with some drag, you're done.

4 The mounting bolts should be pressed into the control arm shafts rather than trying to pull them in by tightening the nuts. Pressing them in with a hydraulic press or similar equipment ensures the bolts are fully seated; the serrations shown are completely engaging the shafts. It also helps avoid damage to the inner fender apron and/or to the bolt threads. With the bolts fully pressed into the arms, inspect and clean the threads with brake cleaner (or similar) if needed.

HOW TO RESTORE YOUR MUSTANG 1964½–1973

They generally won't be cost effective for a simple daily driver and clearly won't have the authentic look wanted for a show car. As with the lower arms, we were able to improve performance over stock with minimal difficulty, expense, or change in appearance.

Different vehicle applications have slightly different hardware combinations, but the procedures and components shown should work with all but the most unique combinations. In many cases, parts can be interchanged and care should be taken in deciding which to use. I point out a few of these issues as we proceed.

Rebuilding the control arms is the major task when restoring and/or enhancing the front suspension of your early Mustang. The remaining work mostly involves choosing the appropriate components to install for your application. As you see in the photos, we went with high-quality components that offer a significant performance advantage yet look similar to stock components. Some of these may not really be necessary in a daily driver or correct for a show car. We chose them to be consistent with our desire to make meaningful improvements where possible, consistent with our intended use of the car as a weekend cruiser.

For high-performance levels and/or those building racers, there are additional options like coil-over shocks and tubular anti-sway bars, for example. These can

The finished control arm assembly is ready to be installed into the vehicle with the exception of the spring perch. That is discussed shortly. When installing the ball joint, note that relatively little torque is often required, sometimes only 18 ft-lbs. The force of the spring and the weight from the vehicle basically push down on the ball joint in the upper control arm so the bolts serve more to locate it than to help bear this load. Be sure to install the grease boot, but wait until the control arms are in the car and are loaded before fully greasing the ball joints. This is due to how the internal structure of the ball joint changes under load. The best approach is to lightly grease the ball joints when they are installed on the control arms and then go back and fully grease them when the load from the spring/car weight is applied. Grease the shaft, however, before the arms are installed. This is due to the difference in sealing technique and also the lack of access to the zerk fittings after the arms are installed. Make sure you fully seat the zerk fittings into the retention nuts else you may have clearance problems with the shock towers. Fully grease each side until you see grease just starting to come out from under each seal. Use the same type of grease you used

Our choice of springs and shocks for the front suspension was fairly conventional, yet also quite an improvement. The valving of the Koni Classic shocks is optimized for applications like ours. They are designed for aggressive street driving and not competition, but they certainly can be used for mild track day events. Likewise, they are fine for daily use, though they are a bit stiffer than a regular replacement shock and they will cost more. They are extremely well made, high-quality, non-adjustable shocks that will surely prove durable in our situation. We chose slightly-higher-rate springs from Global West Suspensions. These also lowered the car in the front to match the lowering we would be doing in the rear. This mild lowering gives the car a more desirable stance and also helps to lower the center of gravity for better handling and braking. The higher spring rate will stiffen the ride a bit but the tradeoff is worth it in our situation. The combination of slightly higher rate lowering springs along with the improved shock valving should complement each other very well.

SUSPENSION

Spring perches are one area that is often overlooked on early Mustang suspensions. These parts can often be the source of unwanted noise and handling issues. Any restoration project should involve inspecting their rubber bushings, at minimum. If the bushings are in good shape, these can be reused in a daily driver or even in a show car, if desired. It's generally a better idea to replace them with new parts. The cost is low and the car is already apart. You can also upgrade to perches that use polyurethane (shown) instead of rubber bushings; we did, because the polyurethane minimizes unwanted compliance and can improve dynamic performance. There may be a very slight increase in noise and vibration, but we were willing to chance it. When using this material, be sure to use a part that has a provision for greasing the bushing because this minimizes the potential for any squeaking noises that can develop. A zerk fitting also helps improve durability because the grease reduces wear. It is best to grease the perches and rotate the shafts a few turns before installing them on the vehicle to make sure the grease is evenly distributed. Our perches were also plated to prevent rust and corrosion, a very nice feature. For the ultimate in functionality, some companies make spring perches that use bearings instead of bushings. These eliminate almost all compliance and reduce friction, though they also transmit more noise and vibration to the interior. They're also more expensive, but this may be of no consequence to those building a higher-performance street vehicle or race car.

undoubtedly provide additional benefits in a more aggressive driving situation, but they cost more and diminish the factory-looking appearance.

Rear Suspension

The basic leaf-spring-style rear suspension used on early Mustangs is simple, yet it has provided good performance and reliability for many years. There are, however, a few subtle changes that can be implemented to make it even better. I do not get into the full-blown restomod or racing upgrades where the leaf springs are removed in favor of other designs using trailing links, watts links, coilover shocks, and the like. I simply provide a few recommendations on how to enhance the stock rear suspension for a weekend cruiser or even a daily driver. A show car being built with maximum originality will not utilize most of these improvements. Although, in most cases, the tips provided for installation still apply because the process is generally the same.

Budget-minded restorers can reuse the stock springs if they are in good shape and want no further improvement. They can either use direct-replacement bushings and shackles or install upgraded items as budgets and personal priorities dictate.

The options we chose retain the basic factory design yet provide significant improvements in a relatively cost-effective manner. They do lower the car a bit, but we like the way it looks. Unless somebody is going to get down on the ground and look under the car, this lowered stance and possibly the color of the Koni shock absorbers are about the only obvious clues that we've deviated somewhat from using direct-replacement parts to get better performance.

The Del-A-Lum bushings must be pressed into the spring eyes because they have a very slight interference fit to prevent them from rotating in the spring. The bolt that goes through the bushing, however is free to rotate as needed, and the side/thrust washers made of Delrin also have negligible friction with the shackles when they are properly adjusted. This allows them to also rotate freely within the shackle, thus improving the response of the spring while also reducing both overall ride harshness and initial impact harshness when compared to either rubber or polyurethane bushings. Perhaps, most importantly, the far greater stiffness of these bushings also helps minimize axle hop because these bushings can never get into a resonance with the spring. To the extent the spring may wrap up during a hard launch, either the tire slips or the spring unwinds, but it is almost impossible for the pattern to keep repeating itself with virtually solid bushings like these. Therefore, axle hop is highly unlikely to occur, especially on street tires and even with race tires. We won't be getting anywhere near that type of test, so our main concern is the tradeoff between ride and handling which, as was stated, really isn't a tradeoff at all.

A slight increase in noise or vibration over the rubber or polyurethane is about the only downside to using these bushings. Our experience with other vehicles running, these bushings have proven this to be negligible, at worst. After all, we are talking about a vehicle with sporting intent, not a luxury car.

Virtually no car from this era could truly be said to have had very refined ride and handling by today's standards, and any concerns of a bit more noise and vibration quickly fade in comparison to the greatly improved handling, braking and durability, etc.

When installing the springs and perches, ensure the lower portion of the spring is properly indexed to the perch. Here you can see the end of the spring resting against a stop that's welded onto our aftermarket perches. The stock setup is a bit different, but it still requires the spring be rotated to the correct position. There is no insulator between the spring and the perch. Having one here would be of no value because there is one on the upper end of the spring, and the upper control arm bushings perform the same function at the opposite end of the noise path. Using one is undesirable, especially for a car that will be driven more aggressively, because it would add unwanted compliance to the suspension and negligible noise and vibration reduction. We left them out of our car; those building show cars should adhere to what the factory did, of course; the option remains open for daily drivers.

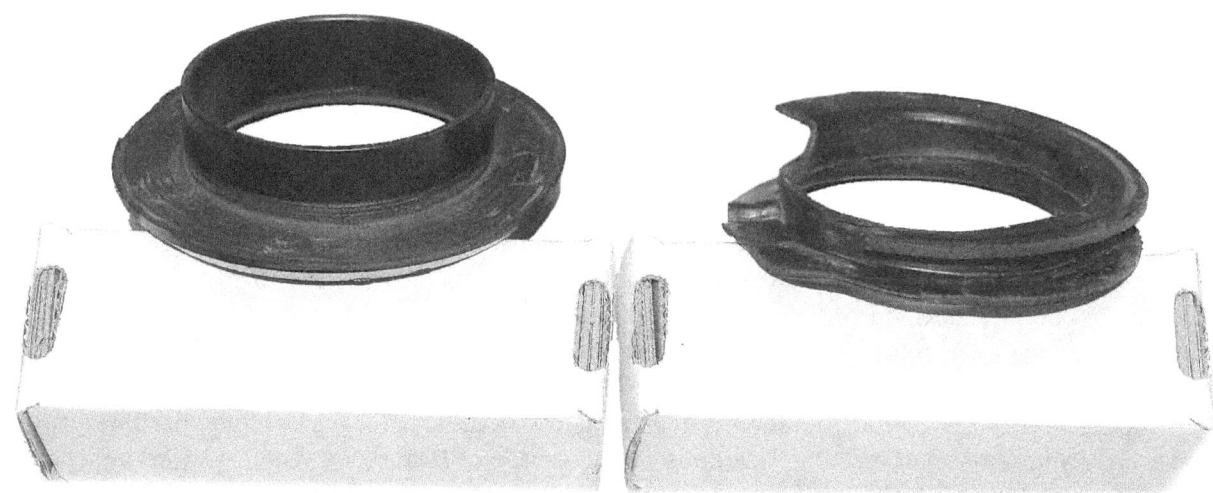

The factory upper spring isolators (on the right) are relatively thin and flimsy. The material used is also prone to getting brittle and cracking over time. Furthermore, they are designed to wrap around the coils of the spring and would not fit the thicker coils and flatter top coils of our Global West Suspension front springs very well anyway. We replaced these factory isolators with more robust polyurethane units. These fit better, lasts longer, and minimize unwanted compliance while still providing a reduction in noise and vibration. The inner sleeves also help keep the spring properly centered at all times.

SUSPENSION

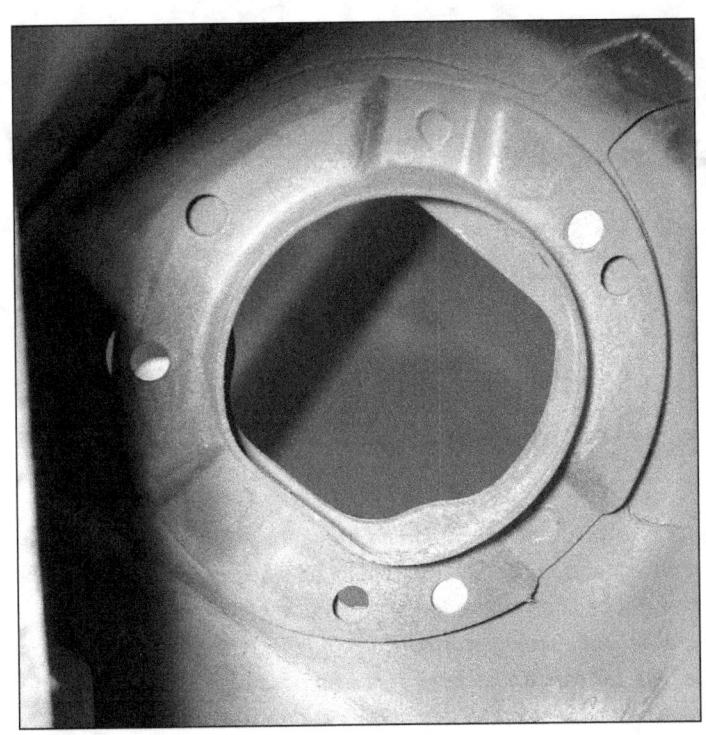

If you will be using stock or direct-replacement springs with factory-style upper isolators, make sure the spring and isolator are properly indexed to the underside of the shock tower. As you can see in this photo, there is a special shape on the spring seat to accept the factory-style spring and isolator. The combination of shapes on the seat and spring, along with the friction of the rubber isolator, prevent rotation with the factory components. The lower spring perch merely supports the spring, but you must still ensure it is indexed to properly transfer the load at both points where the bottom coil contacts the perch. Our setup indexes the spring at the spring perch instead, so it's necessary to line up the uppermost coil with the space in the spring seat. It wouldn't be possible in any case because our polyurethane spring isolator makes no provision for doing so. It does, however, pilot on the raised edge of the upper spring seat to ensure the spring remains centered.

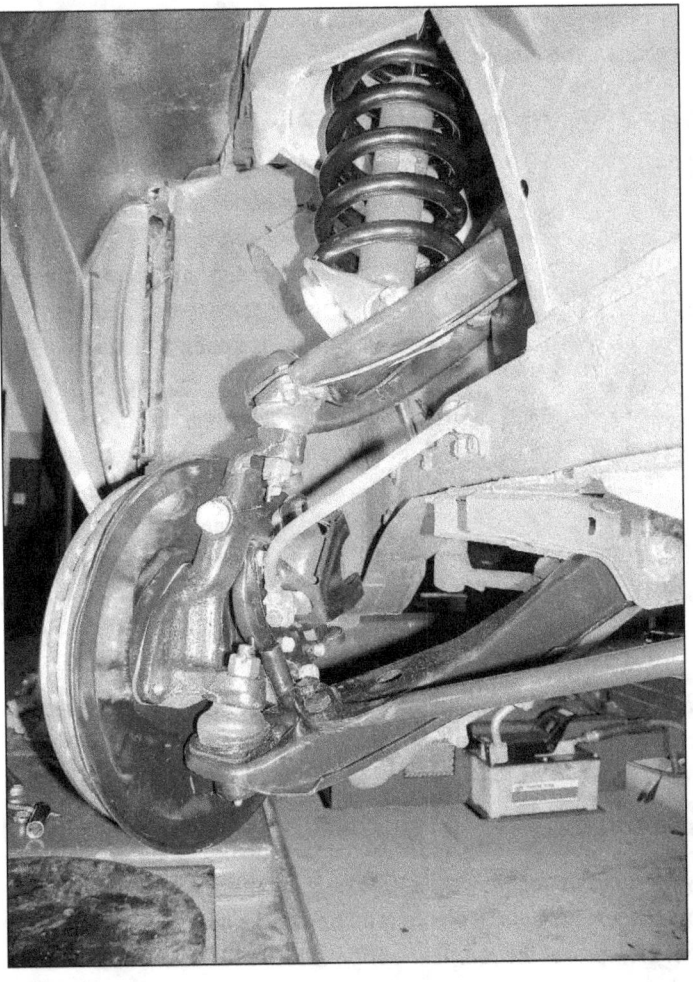

The front suspension is almost fully assembled. Note that you should never use an impact wrench to tighten the castle nuts for the ball joints. Doing so could seriously damage the ball joints. While it is acceptable to just snug the nuts using an impact gun or air ratchet, use a torque wrench for the final torque specification. Ensure all fasteners have been properly torqued and, where applicable, thread lockers or safety wiring have been used. Final joint greasing shouldn't be done until the car is resting on the wheels; when the front alignment is being set, it's time to grease the joints. We have not yet installed the front anti-sway bar and end links. The brake-line banjo fitting needs to be rotated to reduce the strain on it at full lock, but otherwise this is essentially what a finished stock-style suspension looks like. Obviously, it will be different for other vehicles, but the point is that we were able to install several significant upgrades while retaining the stock appearance. You can't see the boxing of the lower control arms or tell they have bearings instead of bushings unless you really look for these things. Likewise, the upper arms are factory pieces, but even the spring, spring perch, and shock differ mainly in color rather than design. These could be painted to be less obvious but it's unlikely those who use these components would. With few exceptions, these components install in a very similar manner to the factory components yet provide improved performance and durability without significantly departing from the original design. Those who want even higher-performance can install other, more extreme components.

CHAPTER 9

Rather than retain the factory setup, we installed a larger-diameter, direct-replacement anti-sway bar from Global West Suspensions to improve handling and reduce body roll. We felt this was fitting in light of the other suspension improvements we've made and the negligible effect this change would have on ride quality. In addition to the larger bar, the kit also includes new mounting brackets with firmer polyurethane bushing and new end links, also using polyurethane. These components allow significantly less deflection when turning, thus improving vehicle responses to steering inputs. These components go right back on where the factory parts come off. They only require some good grease inside the mounting bracket bushings to deliver enhanced performance with little, if any, perceivable loss in ride quality. These components should also be more durable, especially for cars driven hard. It is also possible to drill the mounting brackets and bushings to install a central zerk fitting to allow greasing the bushings in the car. We didn't feel this would be necessary because we used tacky, high-quality waterproof grease. And we don't mind dropping the bar to grease the bushings if we have to. There are, or course, much more exotic setups intended for vintage racers and higher-performance street vehicles, but these are not OEM or OEM-like and cost much more. Generally, they install in a similar way.

The final step to installing the front suspension is to secure the upper shock mount. We will be repainting the whole engine compartment to provide a more factory correct look and then paint the shock mounts to match. We have also installed the mounting brackets for the adjustable Global West Suspension Monte Carlo bar. Note, however, that the mounting brackets that come with this component are larger and stronger to better distribute the loads from one side of the vehicle to the other. The brackets are also secured by a total of four bolts, rather than the more common three-bolt setup, again to ensure strength and durability as well as reduced body movement under load. The overall integrity of the front section of the vehicle is improved significantly when the fully welded shock towers are combined with an improved export brace. This complements the improved stiffness of the center of the vehicle provided by the subframe connectors, plus the inherent stiffness of the rear leaf-spring system.

SUSPENSION

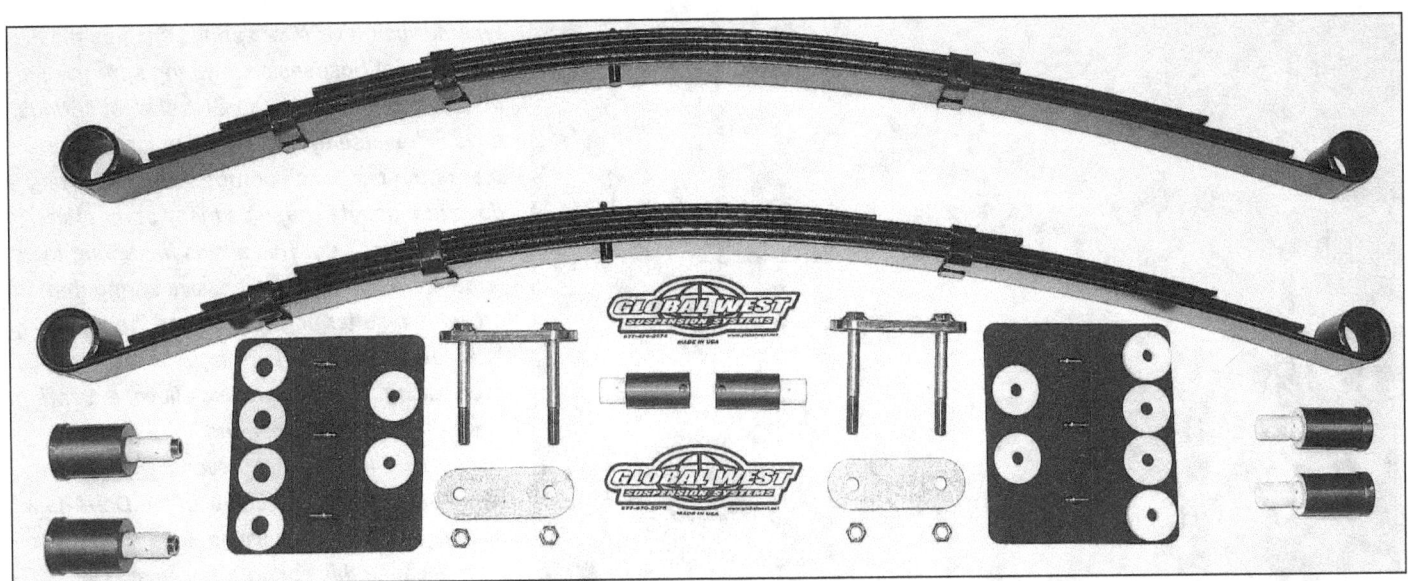

The components we've chosen are similar in design to direct factory replacements but have been improved in subtle ways to provide enhanced functionality. This rear spring kit from Global West Suspensions features higher-rate springs, which also lower the rear of the car by about 2 inches. It also includes upgraded shackles, hardware, and unique "Del-A-Lum" bushings instead of rubber or polyurethane bushings for the spring eyes. We also upgraded the shock absorbers and mildly reconditioned the spring plates and U-bolts. Note the construction of the Del-A-Lum bushings. These consist of a combination of metal and Delrin parts that allow for rotation of the spring eyes but prevent movement in other directions. This greatly improved the performance of the leaf springs because they are not able to twist or otherwise go out of alignment. Different thicknesses of side shims, also made out of Delrin, are used to properly position the springs and also to retain grease within the bushing while moisture and dirt are kept out. These bushings perform better than stock-type rubber or even polyurethane bushings, last much longer, and do not get noisy over time like the others can. The anodized color can make them a bit conspicuous if you look under the car, but this is a small price to pay for much improved performance.

It would make no sense to use the Del-A-Lum bushings in the spring eyes and then still use rubber or polyurethane in the frame rails. These special Del-A-Lum bushings go into the frame rails to resolve this matter. These are simply pre-greased and then pushed into place. Just as with their counterparts in the spring eyes, these bushings have side/thrust washers and provisions for grease fittings to allow adding more grease as is needed later on. Use tacky, waterproof grease as previously as other areas of the suspension. No steel inner sleeve is needed at either these rear frame rail bushings or in the bushings used at the rear spring eyes due to the action of the shackle that ties them together. The bushings in the front spring eyes, however, do utilize an inner steel sleeve for higher load capacity.

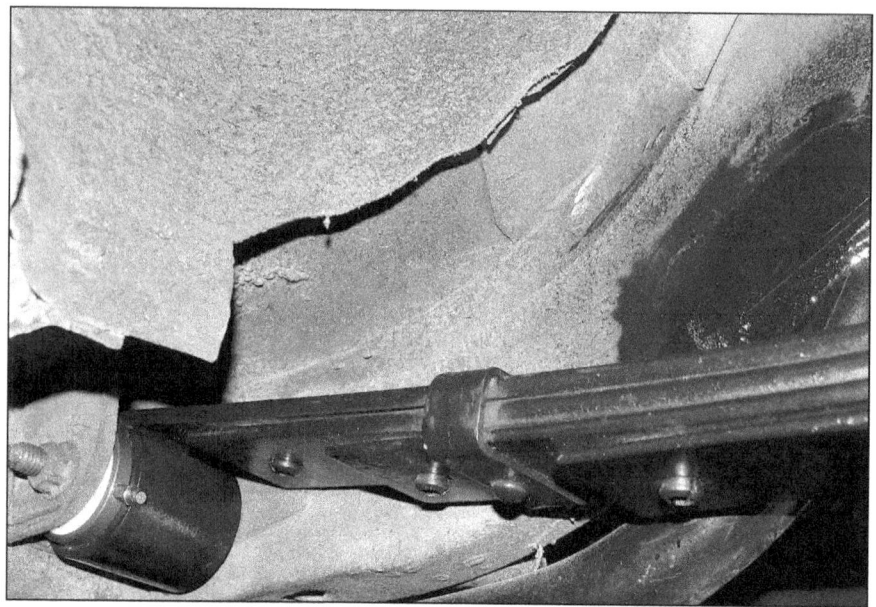

Whether using OEM or springs such as these Global West Suspension lowering springs, installation is similar. The Global West springs have a "reverse eye" design that lowers the rear of the car 1 inch or more. And the spring does not lose its shape as many other aftermarket springs do. This allows the spring to remain a rising rate/progressive spring that provides a softer ride yet still has the higher total rate needed for performance driving or even racing. This design also allows the spring leaves to remain thinner and lighter, thus saving weight while still preventing axle hop. When used in combination with the Del-A-Lum bushings, there is usually no need for traction bars because this spring/bushing system prevents axle hop. Higher cost, extra weight, and reduced ground clearance are penalties that would have been paid in most cases with such bars, but this system doesn't suffer those penalties. And, it retains a relatively stock look in the process. Other than having to do an occasional greasing, there is nothing different about using this setup. The benefits are: virtual elimination of axle hop and spring binding; better ride; greatly improved handling at minimal extra cost; and no obvious change in the overall look of the vehicle. If you're building a weekend cruiser and/or have high-performance or even racer goals, it provides the most cost-effective way to improve the rear suspension of your early Mustang and retain its overall design. While this may be more than is needed for a simple daily driver, it would be very beneficial in that situation too. The only thing Del-A-Lum bushings don't improve is authenticity.

The shackle kit provided with our spring kit is critical to its proper function. The design of the Del-A-Lum bushings and the progressive leaf springs place higher and lateral loads on the shackles than a setup with rubber or even polyurethane bushings, because no force is dissipated in bushing compression. The finish and flatness of the shackles also must be different to accommodate the side/thrust washers, so they are able to rotate freely yet with minimal clearance. This precise fit and matching of components ensure optimum performance and maximum longevity. The combination of these shackles with the Del-A-Lum bushings virtually eliminates any lateral movement of the springs and axle, and thus minimizes the potential for tire rub in addition to providing improved handling. The compliance found in rubber and polyurethane bushings is such that significant lateral movement is possible even when a Watts link is used. A panhard rod by its very design introduces some lateral movement as it swings through its arc. The system we have chosen allows virtually no lateral movement, so the springs, axle, wheels, and tires move in an almost perfectly vertical path perpendicular to the longitudinal axis of the car. This effectively increases the clearance between the tires and the body because their relative motion is much more stable and predictable. Therefore, we intend to slightly increase the section width of the tires we use on this car to take further advantage of this characteristic and provide additional handling and braking benefits.

SUSPENSION

When installing the rear axle onto the springs, make sure the axle properly indexes itself to the locating pins on the top of the springs. Some axle-pad designs have a recessed piloting hole (right). If the locating pins on the springs are not high enough, the pins won't go into these holes and the axle will be free to move on the spring—this is never good. The axle on the left will not have any problems because the pilot hole is flush with the mounting pad, and thus has to engage the locating pin on the springs and is positively held in place after the U-bolts are tightened. The solution to this problem, should it occur in your situation, is to use special inserts that effectively extend the piloting hole in the spring mounting pad so that they properly engage the locating pins. There is no need to weld these inserts to the pads because they are designed to fit the pockets in the axle mounting pads very closely. The tightened U-bolts cannot move off of the locating pins, and the axle mounting pads cannot move off of the inserts. In effect, the inserts expand the pins to fill the shape of the pockets in the axle pads, thus preventing movement. We were able to reuse the stock U-bolts and spring pads, so we media blasted them and painted them before we reinstalled them. There is very little to go wrong with these, but they still do need to be checked that they are properly indexed on the springs. In addition, there should be no rust or damage, etc., that could lead to subsequent failure. If you are not concerned with strictly original looks there are also spring plates that incorporate built-in tie-down loops to help secure a vehicle to a trailer. We don't plan on trailering our vehicle very much so we did not use them but they may be an appropriate option for certain types of show cars.

This finished rear suspension reveals a close-to-stock appearance, except the colors of certain components like the Koni Shocks and the Del-A-Lum bushings. Of course the rear brakes and brake lines are not authentic, either, so the differences in component color are minor by comparison. We willingly made these tradeoffs to realize the significantly enhanced functionality these components provide. The Koni shocks are a dramatic improvement over a stock replacement shock, just as those used in the front suspension were. Their valving is optimized for performance driving and their durability should be far better than standard shocks. They are not adjustable, but we don't need them to be. The benefits of the springs and bushings have already been covered with the exception of one final point: the use of the Global West Suspension springs and bushings we've chosen also eliminates the need for a rear anti-sway bar. This is primarily due to the virtually complete elimination of lateral compliance along with the rising-rate characteristic of the springs and the superior dampening of the Koni shocks. This saves a considerable amount of weight and cost. It also eliminates potential clearance issues with other components and the need to perform maintenance on the anti-sway bar bushings and end links. Using optimized bushing, spring, and shock designs eliminates the need for add-on components, such as traction bars and anti-sway bars. This reduces cost, complexity, and weight while also providing improved durability. These optimized components install just like the factory components with very minor exceptions and they look very similar to them as well. They may not be desirable for a show car where authenticity is a priority, or a daily driver, where budget is a greater priority than performance, but they're sure a great way to go for the performance-oriented weekend cruiser we are building.

CHAPTER 10

ELECTRICAL

Electrical systems of first-generation Mustangs are relatively simple, especially when compared to modern vehicles with electronic fuel injection. While tracking down an electrical problem can be tedious, repair and restoration should not prove too difficult, in most cases. Even for vehicles that require extensive repair, just about every replacement component is available either new or used. Also, complete replacement wiring harnesses are available. In some cases these even incorporate new technologies and/or features that actually make them better than OEM.

Since I cannot cover every electrical system for every variation of early Mustang, I instead discuss some basic guidelines that can apply to all vehicles in terms of helping to avoid and/or repair problems. The factory service manual and/or an experienced technician are often essential for specific repairs. However, I also provide some insight into some of the more common maladies that affect these cars. I sought the advice of veteran techs from well-known and respected Mustang specialty shops so I could share some of what they've learned over the years. I also included a few common upgrades that can be done to make your ride more drivable while still retaining a mostly factory appearance. I continue to emphasize weekend-cruiser and daily-driver projects here, but most of what I cover can also be applied to most show-car projects.

The Basics: Grounds, Connections and Shorts

The passage of time affects any vehicle. How much (as well as how) the car was used and maintained plus the environment it was used in are the primary factors in how much wear and tear any vehicle has. While we can't undo what was done, we can certainly compensate for it as the need arises. Since I generally discourage purchasing a vehicle that's in

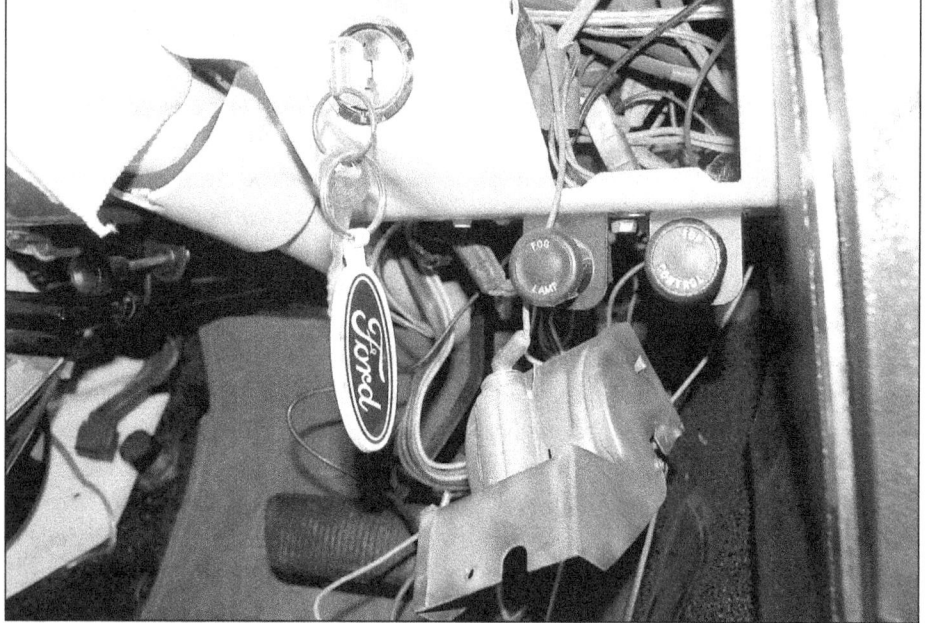

Over time, the elements, attempted modifications, or just normal wear and tear can cause factory wiring harness malfunctions. Here we see how the wiring behind the dash panel has become somewhat crowded due modifications. When add-on fog lights, which are intended to look like they were put on at the factory, are installed; they can add a lot of difficulty and expense to a project. It is far easier, though clearly not as authentic-looking, to instead splice them in underhood and use a remote switch.

ELECTRICAL

Underhood electrical components are particularly more prone to fail if they aren't properly maintained. Here, we see the foam gasket that seals the blower motor to the firewall is in excellent shape, as are the various electrical connectors and even the nearby ground wire. Ideally, the wires would not be routed such that they are in contact with the dipstick tube (or at least should be behind it so they'd hang lower, away from the cap). The wires should also be tied farther from the exhaust.

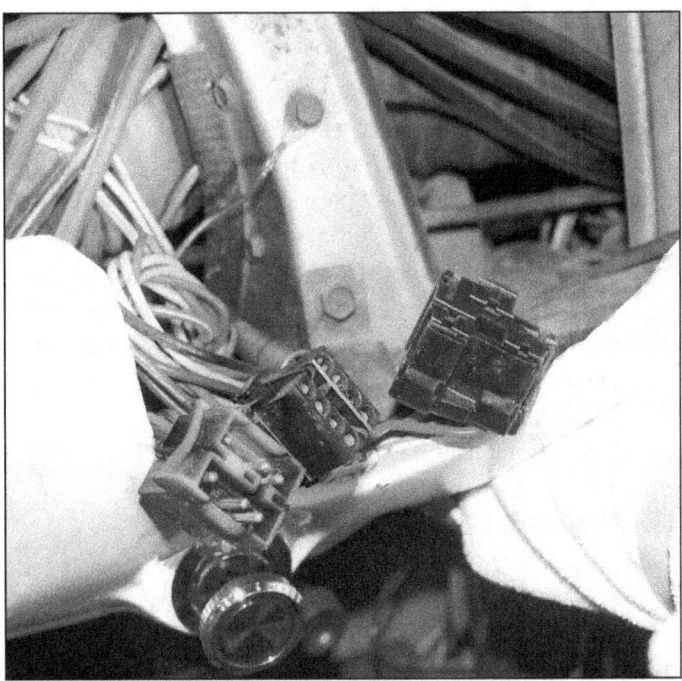

Electrical connectors such as these can often be the cause of open or intermittent circuits. If practical, open and inspect all such connectors to ensure the contacts are clean and corrosion free. Using various electrical greases and sprays can also help keep them that way.

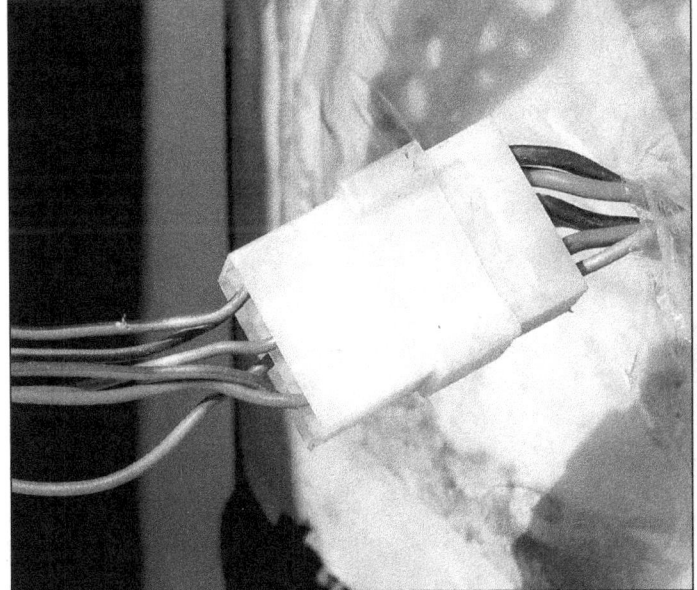

Simple electrical connectors are fine for areas that are not exposed to the elements. After cleaning, any connectors that are exposed to dirt and/or moisture should have their own internal seals, electrical grease, or an equivalent sealant applied to help keep dirt and moisture away from the metal contacts. They are not usually visible, and are acceptable for a show car.

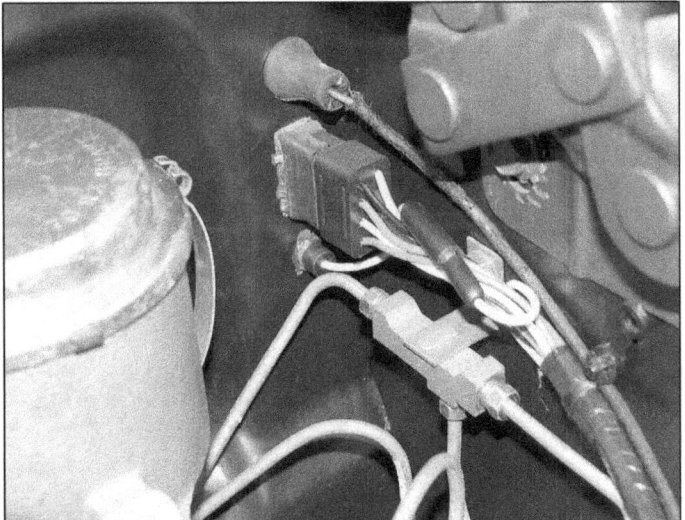

These connections show the approach the factory took to keep dirt and the elements away from some underhood electrical connections. The rubber grommets and/or plastic connectors that go through the firewall can deteriorate over time and should be replaced if they are cracked or otherwise damaged. Otherwise, the wire bundle is nicely wrapped with electrical tape and is also properly secured to the inner fender panel with a plastic clip/loop.

HOW TO RESTORE YOUR MUSTANG 1964½–1973

really bad shape, I don't need to list the types of things that are usually only found in such basket cases. Instead, I stick to the more common types of problems that most people might run into in a decent vehicle, whether it's been stored for years or regularly used.

Faulty grounds are perhaps the most common category of electrical problem. This can mean anything from a missing or disconnected wire to a problem caused by rust or corrosion where the ground is connected. Obviously, if a wire is missing or disconnected, it needs to be fixed, assuming there is no other underlying issue that needs to be corrected first, such as a short circuit. A wiring diagram tells you what grounds need to be present and where they need to be.

Wherever ground wires are connected, good metal-to-metal, rust-free contact is crucial. Use a wire brush, steel wool, sandpaper, or other suitable abrasive to remove any contamination from where the ground wire meets the body or component. Make sure the fastener is tight and doesn't strip out when turned, thus creating a loose and intermittent connection. It's often helpful to add extra ground wires, especially when an upgraded audio system or other electrical upgrades such as gauges, ignition, or lighting are added (I cover some of these upgrades later in this chapter).

Because all Mustangs are unibody construction, there is no need to electrically connect the body to the frame; they are already a single unit. However, it is still a good idea to run a relatively thick ground strap from the engine to the body, and another from the inner support of the instrument panel to the same point on the body. This helps ensure there is a good ground for the ignition, gauges, and switches. It can also improve the performance of the radio and lights, in some cases.

The next consideration is the condition of the many electrical connections on the car. As with the grounds, any connection should be tight and free of rust or corrosion. It should be appropriately cleaned and/or tightened. For direct, visible connections this is usually fairly obvious. The bigger problems come from hidden connections in plastic or rubber housings or in the wiring harnesses. Even though older cars have far fewer wires than new ones, there are still hidden connections that can sometimes cause a problem.

Similarly, harnesses can sometimes get pulled from their clips or otherwise be stretched so connections become open or intermittent without being obvious. Water or other liquids can get into connectors and corrode the internal terminals until resistance increases to the point where the circuit becomes open or

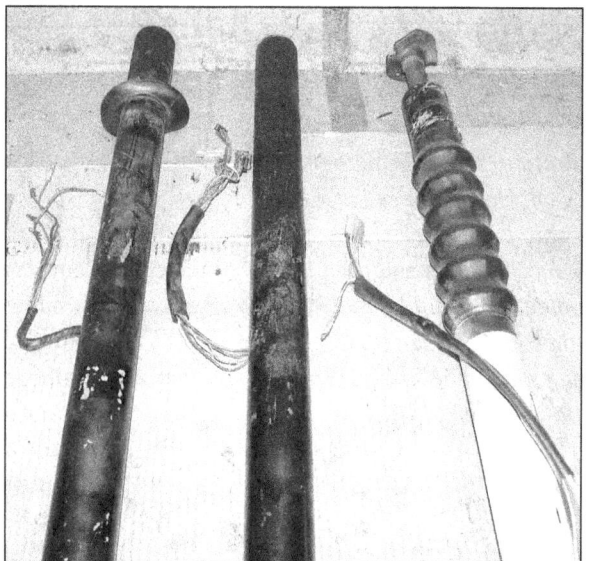

These steering columns provide an example of how common components vary between models. The 1964½ Mustang column (left) shows how these models used individual wires that were wrapped with electrical tape. The 1965 to 1967 column (center) shows how multiple electrical connectors replace the individual wires while a protective sheath replaces the tape. The 1968+ column (right) is the collapsible variety, but it also has a single, flatter electrical connector instead of the multiple connectors.

This view of the top of each column shows some other differences. Two of the steering columns have dual contacts while the plastic turn signal switch assembly on the 1964½ column (left) has a single horn contact. It can also be replaced when worn (shown on the plastic cap in the foreground) The 1968+ column also features tilt capability and an emergency flasher switch the earlier columns lack. The wires exit higher up as well.

ELECTRICAL

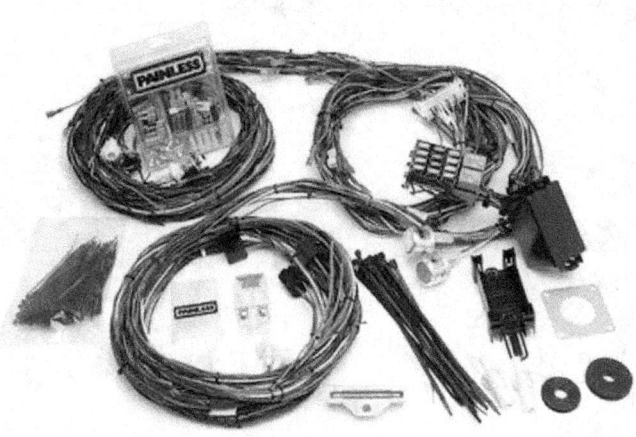

High-quality reproduction harnesses are available for vehicles where one or more of the factory harnesses are so severely damaged that they're not worth repairing. These can either be of the exact-replica/factory-correct type or they can be fully functional direct-fit upgrades that use newer, improved materials. The latter can also add extra circuits and/or features to support other potential upgrades. The appearance of these harnesses may not match that of the original factory harness as closely, but they make upgrades easier.

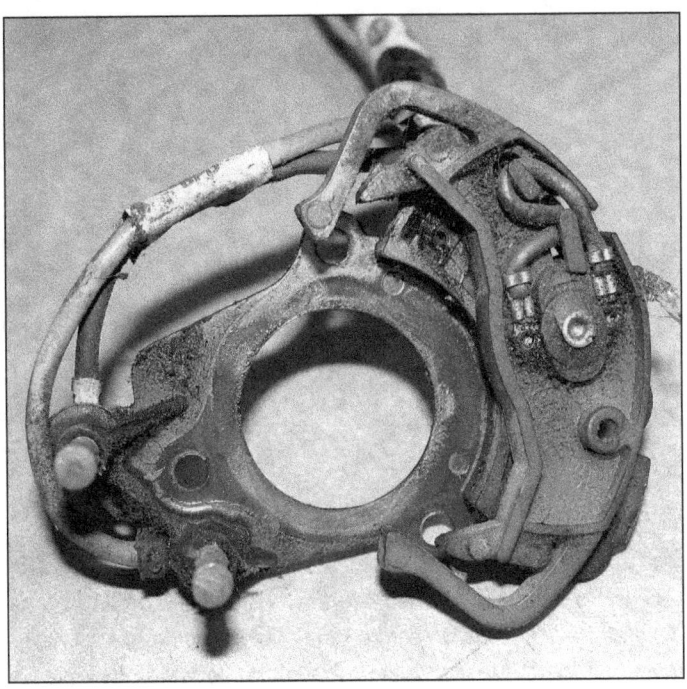

The turn signal switch assembly is a common source of trouble because the plastic pegs, which get moved as the steering wheel turns, often break off. The only option in such cases is to remove the switch and replace it. If the original switch is to be reused, it should first be cleaned and properly lubed.

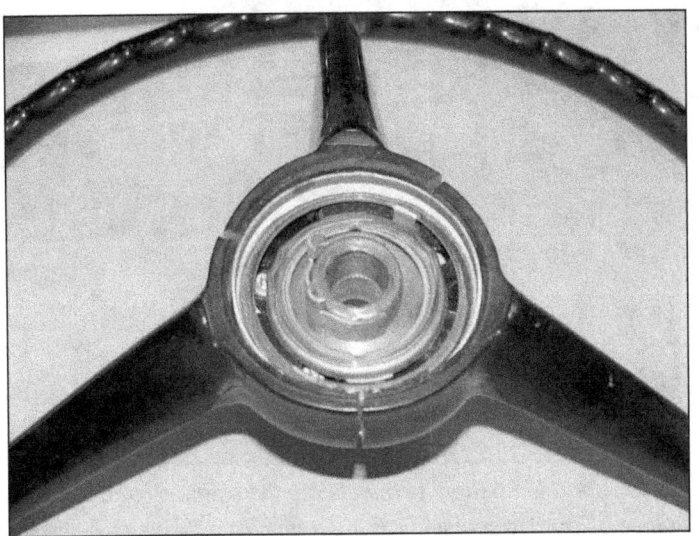

A somewhat odd yet also common problem is cracking of the steering wheel. How is this related to electrical issues? When the wheel cracks it can cause the horn contacts to short internally, thus causing the horn to stay on constantly. Until the steering wheel can be replaced (usually the only viable option) the electrical connectors can be pulled from the horn(s) and be secured out of the way to silence the horn(s) until repairs are made. A cracked wheel can also cause turn signal malfunction.

The fuse block can be a common problem in some early Mustangs. The reason is mainly its location within the car rather than complex circuitry. This block from a 1964½ to 1966 car exhibits the corroded terminals often found in these applications due to water leaking from the cowl area on the block. Later cars don't have this issue since the block was moved to a location above the throttle pedal, where there was almost no chance of contact with water. The terminals can usually be cleaned with a wire brush. Weak/broken terminals require replacing the block. Luckily, there are relatively few circuits to rewire.

CHAPTER 10

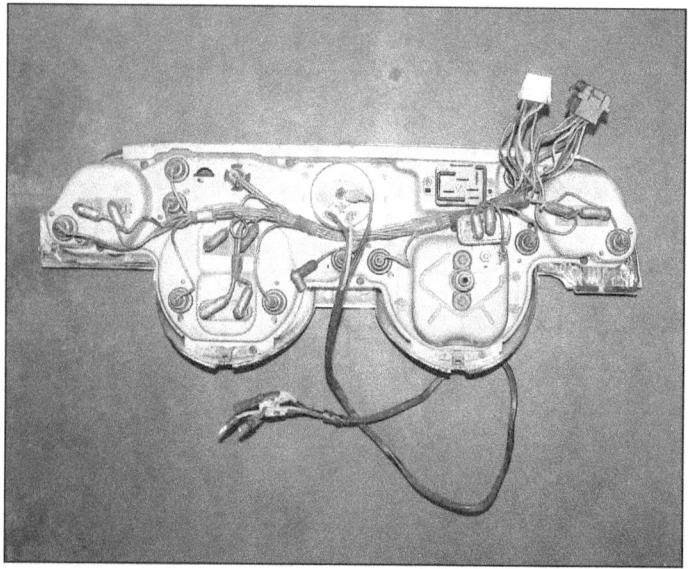

Access to the bulbs for the instrument cluster can be difficult when a Rally Pack is present on the steering column; it has to come off to get the instrument cluster out. With the cluster out, changing the bulbs is a snap. The wiring harness should also be checked (as should the plastic connectors) for any defects/problems that need to be fixed. Note the added-on aftermarket gauge in the center of the cluster.

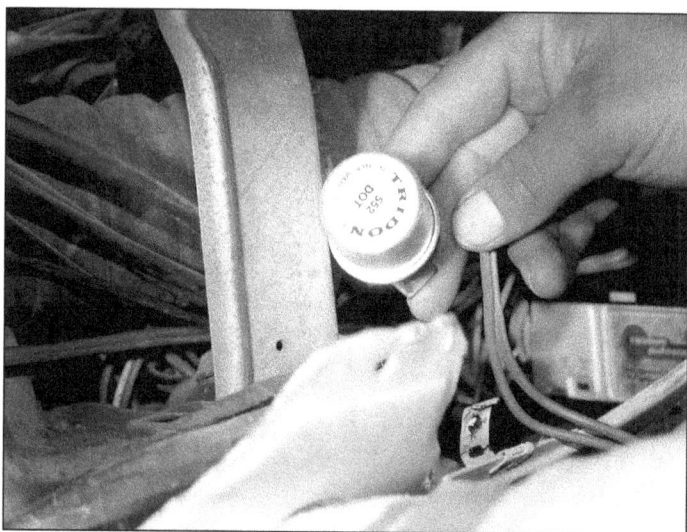

The turn signal flasher is somewhat prone to failure. Replacement is a matter of removing the very inexpensive part and replacing it with a new one found at just about any auto parts store. The flasher on 1967–1968 cars is especially difficult to reach since it is located directly behind the instrument cluster. The cluster must come out to reach it. Other models usually provide access from under the dash without the need to remove any other components.

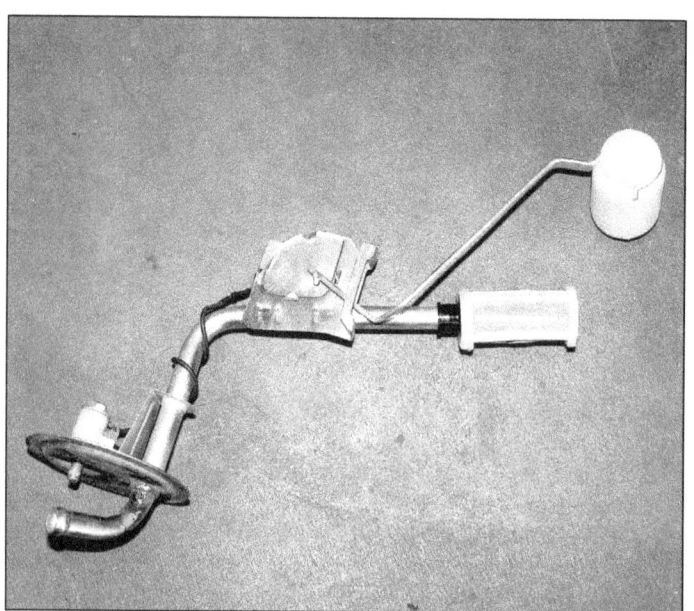

The fuel tank sending unit is often to blame when the fuel gauge doesn't work. The gauge is usually fine; the problem is that the float usually fills with fuel, and thus no longer moves to provide a proper electrical signal. The OEM-style brass floats are inferior to the plastic ones used in most reproduction parts. Unlike older mixtures, modern fuels have sufficiently high levels of ethanol in them to cause the brass floats to corrode.

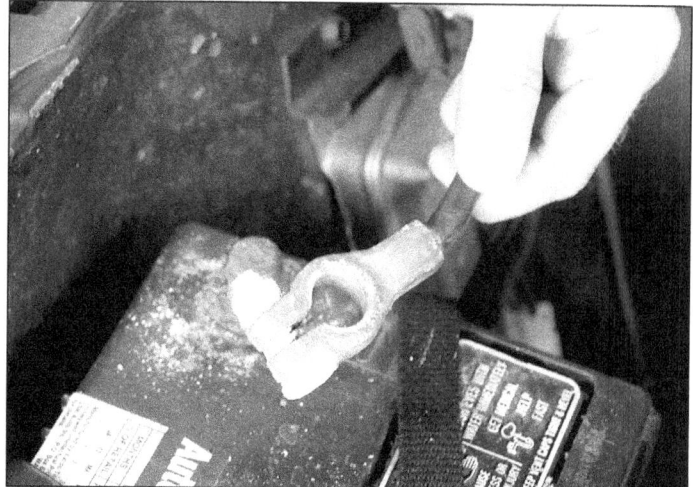

By far, corroded battery terminals are the single most common cause of starting problems. If the terminals on your project are corroded, use a terminal cleaner to clean the terminal and the battery cable. If the cable is severely corroded, get a new, correct-length cable with the correct gauge conductor. Watch out for cables that look thick but have a thinner wire core. If you must use an older-style vented battery for the sake of authenticity, then put anti-corrosion rings under each battery cable end. The better choice is to use a modern, sealed battery of sufficient capacity.

ELECTRICAL

The starter relay often fails but is an easy and inexpensive part to replace. But before replacing the relay, be sure to check the push-on terminals for internal corrosion and/or looseness. This can cause unreliable starting, which can appear as if the relay is faulty when the problem is just a poor connection. Clean the contacts in the push-on terminals and, if necessary, pinch them slightly so they make better contact. And if the car starts normally when the relay is jumped with a remote start switch (or a properly placed screwdriver) the problem may be the start switch or the wiring and/or connections between it and the starter relay.

intermittent. The only way to resolve these issues is to carefully inspect the whole harness and look for any external signs of damage, leakage, or separation. Pull connectors apart to make sure the terminals are clean, and to the extent practical and/or necessary, test the continuity of individual wires/circuits with a test light or a digital volt/ohm meter.

There are no short cuts here. If the harness and/or connectors have a problem, you must carefully and methodically track it down. After you've fixed a current problem, take steps to prevent them from reoccurring. Make sure the harness is properly wrapped with tape or another suitable form of insulation, and that the connections are clean and tight. Use electrical grease or other suitable sealants to prevent new corrosion.

Except for shorts caused by component failure, most short circuits are the result of wear and/or failure of the

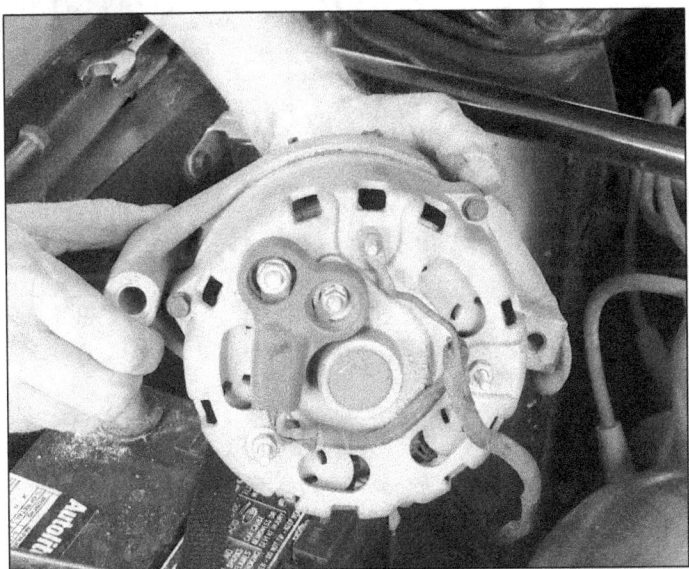

The alternator harness terminals frequently become corroded to the point the alternator does not work properly. Clean the terminals with a wire brush to restore proper function, in most cases. If the terminals are too weak, replace them. The harness should be properly taped and there should be no signs of worn tape or wire insulation. If the alternator makes any significant noise when the engine is running, it probably needs to be replaced.

One very effective way to prevent some common charging system problems is to upgrade the alternator to a single wire type with an internal voltage regulator. This eliminates numerous connections that can corrode or otherwise cause problems. These newer alternators also have much higher idle and peak output, so high-powered audio systems, electric cooling fans, and higher-output headlamps don't discharge the battery as often. They also generally run cooler and last longer.

insulation around the wires. This is often a result of the wire's insulation cracking as it ages, so the conductor inside can then ground out somehow. Shorts can also often be the result of the wire rubbing against something such as a sharp edge until the insulation wears out. This is especially common where a wire goes through a metal panel or has been tied down too tightly and rubs. The repairs for both conditions are simple, if sometimes tedious.

The individual wires simply get replaced, ideally with wire of the same gauge and color(s), using the same type of termination. When whole sections of a harness need to be replaced, it's often better to just get a replacement harness instead of trying to fix each wire individually. Well-known companies, such as Painless Performance, offer complete replacement harnesses that feature all the correct factory connectors. Some harnesses have additional features to accommodate various modifications and upgrades. However, for the wires and/or harness that are repaired, you must also make sure you used the proper grommets, wire guides, and other items, so the wires/harness are properly located and kept away from moving parts, excessive heat, and moisture. If you use zip-ties to secure the wires and/or harnesses at various points, make sure these are not too tight and cause wear or cause the wire(s)/harness to press against something that will cause wear.

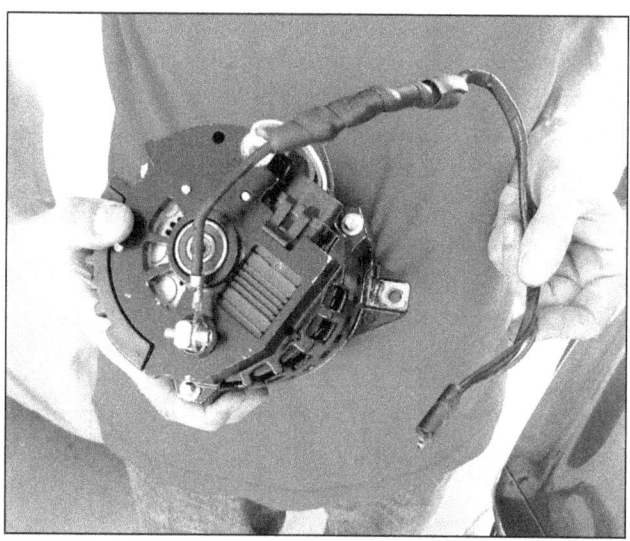

Adapting the factory wiring harness is usually just a matter of splicing some wire into the harness provided with the new alternator. Basically, the wires that would have gone to the external factory voltage regulator (no longer used) are re-routed to the side connector of the new alternator. These alternators bolt right in and only require relatively minor wiring modifications such as these to work just fine. Some, such as this one, even allow you to manually adjust the control/output voltage to suit unique needs.

Breaker point ignition systems were fine for their time, but technology has improved since first-generation Mustangs were new. Breaker points are inherently inferior because they wear out relatively quickly, reduce max coil voltage, and can become unstable at higher RPM. They are cheap but long obsolete and getting harder to source and also require periodic adjustments to perform optimally.

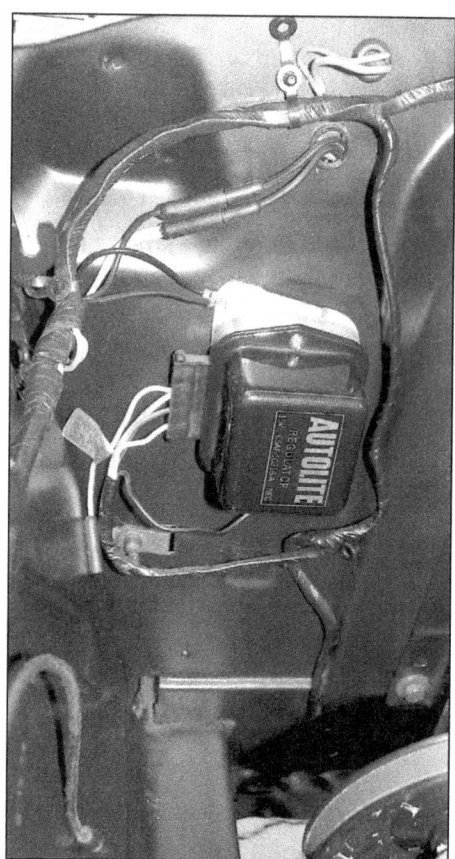

On cars with an external voltage regulator, it is critical the regulator is properly grounded and the connector terminals corrosion free. These problems can also prevent the battery from properly charging even though the alternator may be fine. Being an electrotechnical part, external regulators are more prone to have problems than internal units. They're also getting harder to find in parts stores, especially if you need a less common type.

ELECTRICAL

A far better way to trigger the ignition is with electronic modules, such as this Pertronix Ignitor II unit. It fits inside the distributor so it is invisible except for the two external wires instead of only one. This is a good tradeoff for far better accuracy, higher spark energy, and eliminating constant wear and adjustment. It's not original equipment, but far superior for cars that get driven.

If the coil case is damaged or leaking, replace it. If you use a breakerless ignition upgrade, also upgrade the coil to a low-resistance unit to get max performance from the new ignition. This coil is only 0.6 ohm. This figure would be far too low if points were still being used because this would cause them to arc and burn up prematurely. Higher-output coils are an effective upgrade as long as other parts of the system are compatible.

Some Common Trouble Areas

There are far too many variations among the different models of early Mustangs to cover each one in detail, but I can provide some insight into problems that seem to have plagued multiple versions. There can be some significant hardware changes in a relatively short period of time, and I show how these affect the repair process.

The source of more common problems has more to do with the location of the components in the car and less to do with the design of the components. Therefore, exposure to the elements, chemicals, and excessive temperatures can cause the failure of many electrical components. Such is the case in the few examples I illustrate.

Starting System

The starting system generally suffers from few problems if it is properly maintained. Other than for the battery, there should really be no need to replace any of the major components on a regular basis. If anything needs to be replaced, however, the parts are often available at local parts stores for relatively modest prices. Those needing exact authenticity for a show car should go elsewhere and may pay more. Whatever the type of project, the key to a trouble-free starting system is regular maintenance.

Charging System

As with the starting system, there is seldom need to replace the components in the charging system if it is properly maintained. The most common problem other than failure of the alternator or regulator is poor grounds and/or connections. These can cause improper charging and inaccurate gauge readings. These should be repaired, as previously described. A more recent issue is the lack of output of the factory alternator when modern equipment such as upgraded audio systems and electric cooling fans are added. I show how this can be easily addressed with only a slight change in the underhood appearance of the vehicle, if total authenticity is not necessary.

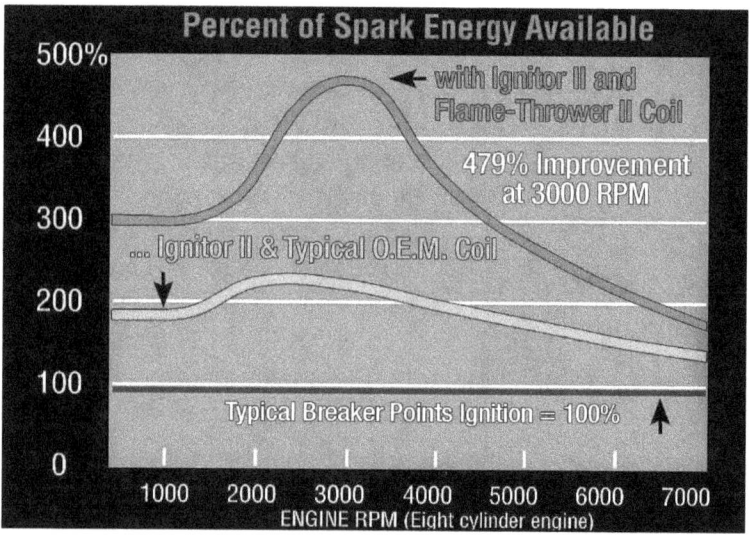

This graph shows the improvement in available spark energy of the Pertronix ignition versus breaker points. The benefit of doing this alone is considerable, especially at lower RPM. When combined with a more optimally matched, high-output coil, the results are even more impressive. More spark energy usually means better starting, faster acceleration, and improved overall performance including higher mpg.

A very common upgrade for early Mustangs is to convert the standard sealed beam headlamps to more modern H4 lamps. These Hella units give the higher light output inherent in the H4 technology and have a more sophisticated lens design that gives a sharper light pattern.

Ignition System

The ignition system of these vehicles is not so much prone to failure as much as it is prone to wear. Rarely does an ignition-system component completely fail. Rather, the performance gradually deteriorates to the point where the vehicle no longer runs acceptably. The primary reasons for this phenomenon are the ignition breaker points and the spark plug wires. While most people are aware of the need to periodically change the spark plug wires, distributor cap, and rotor, they neglect the need to maintain these even-more-critical parts. I show how to eliminate the need for any maintenance other than a periodic inspection for the ignition-triggering system and the spark plug wires. I also comment on choosing the cap, rotor, and spark plugs.

After breaker points, factory spark plug wires are another source of frequent problems, especially for higher mileage vehicles. Over time, the internal resistance of most factory wires increases and reduces the spark energy available at the spark plug. This hurts performance and can even get to the point where misfires occur. The solution is to measure the resistance per foot of each plug wire and ensure it is within specification. If not,

When installing higher-output H4 headlamps, it may be necessary to install a headlamp relay kit to get the highest output and avoid any problems with the stock wiring being unable to handle the extra current of the new lights.

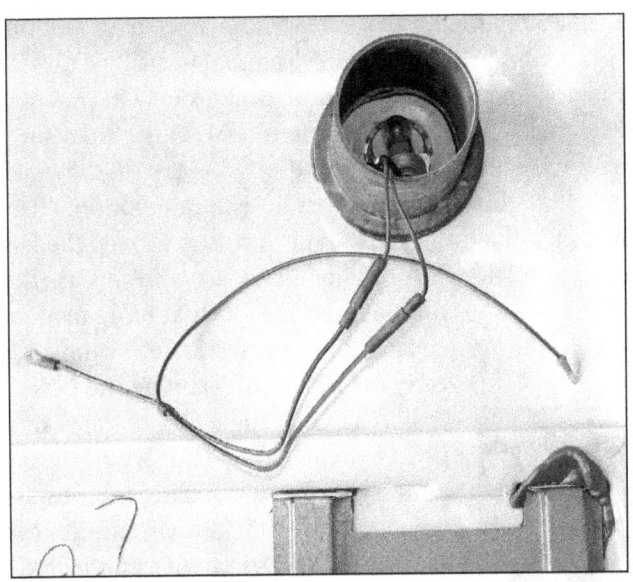

Internal lights, such as this one on one of the rear seat trim panels, have bulbs that are easy to change. These can often be replaced with LED bulbs that cost more but are brighter and likely won't need replacing.

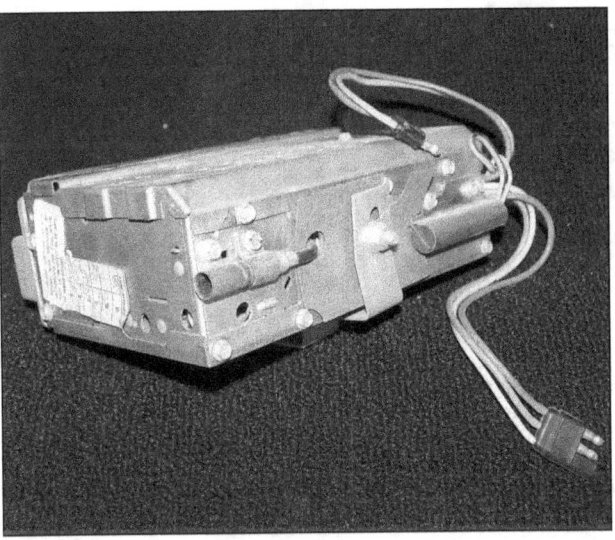

Our stock AM/FM radio was a very rare option, which, thankfully, was in great shape other than missing a pushbutton. Had we needed any repairs we would have surely left these to a professional. Unless your car has a rare/valuable setup, such as this, you can usually benefit from an aftermarket unit.

This Custom Autosound radio looks just like the original 1964½ to 1966 Mustang radio, yet it provides significantly upgraded capabilities— more power, a front/rear fader, and four speaker pre-outputs. It delivers vastly improved sound, can control a 10-disc CD changer, and has an auxiliary input to allow connection of and iPod or similar external devices.

replace the wire(s). Even if the factory wires are okay, it's still best to replace them with high-performance wires that use a spiral-wound metal conductor. These provide far greater energy to the spark plugs while also being more reliable and still preventing ignition noise from being heard on the radio. High-performance spiral-wound spark plug wires are available in custom-fitted kits that are cut to the correct lengths for specific vehicles; they also look just like the factory wires in terms of color, diameter, and boot style. We used wires from Pertronix, which were a direct fit for our 302 "J code" V-8. They had much lower resistance than our factory wires and look great.

Lighting Systems

The various lighting subsystems on the car are some of the simplest and yet most critical systems from a safety perspective. Failures of various switches are common, but these are simple (if often tedious) and relatively inexpensive to replace. Bulb replacement is a common and affordable exercise and accessing the bulb typically determines difficulty. This may not always be the case, however. When water seeps through the gasket behind the plastic lens in the tail lamps, the bulb socket may become so corroded and/or loose due to contact with water that it needs to be replaced. New housings are easy, if not always inexpensive to come by. The key is to use a new rubber gasket under the lens and to make sure it is properly seated to prevent the problem from reoccurring. Poor light output from any of the external lights is often due to poor grounds and/or other connections. Up to 1968 models, for example, the parking lights and turn signals share a ground wire. If the wiring is not connected properly the parking lights are overly bright while the turn signals are too dim. The connectors for the external lights in particular are prone to corrosion and should be checked/cleaned regularly. I show how you can greatly improve the output of the stock headlights for relatively modest cost and effort.

Audio System

As hard as it may be to believe, when most early Mustangs were sold they came with little more than a simple AM radio and a single, dash-mounted speaker. Very few people chose the more elaborate optional audio systems. In fact, the factory AM/FM radio in the 1968 fastback we used for much of this book was one of the main things that made the car a rare "1 of 1" vehicle according to its Marti Report.

Our radio only needed minor repairs (replace a missing push button) and a mild cleanup. But had we needed to repair it, we would surely have sent it out to a professional. Other than for a show car and/or in a case like ours in which the radio is a rare option, there really isn't much reason to keep the factory radio these days. Far superior options are available that bring modern capabilities and technologies to your early car while still retaining the factory look. The same applies for the speakers. If you decide to upgrade your factory radio, you may also want to consider upgrades to the antenna and the speaker wiring so you'll get the most from your new unit.

Miscellaneous Accessories and Possible Upgrades

Various other electrical systems on these cars can also be prone to specific types of failures. The floor-mounted windshield-washer pump on 1968 Mustangs, for example, has a foot-operated bellows pump that sprays the fluid onto the windshield, yet it also has an internal switch that turns the wipers on while you're pumping—not a common design. If this needs to be repaired, the shop manual is your best guide, but this is one area with reliability issues. A cracked steering wheel can affect horn function, but this relatively simple system is otherwise fairly reliable. Power windows and door locks can have problems with their switches and actuators/motors, especially in harsher and wetter climates.

I've included some detils on various options to add these and other capabilities to your car if it didn't come with them. Finally, I've also shown a few other possible upgrades for improving overall performance and usability at a reasonable cost while also keeping the external appearance of the car close to stock.

Custom Autosound also offers radios with more features and power if you don't mind a slightly less-factory look. This one also includes LCD display for song titles/station numbers, full electronic tuning, control of a power antenna, a digital clock, and 16 memory presets.

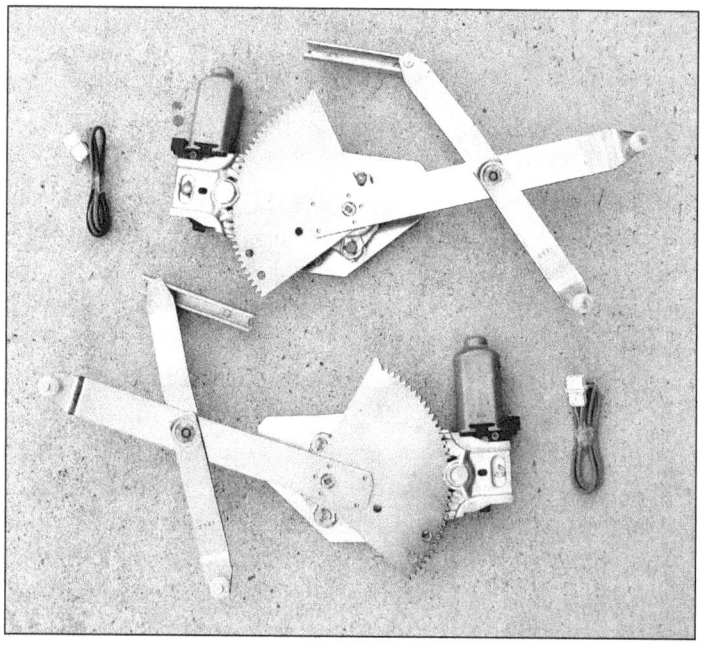

Several kits, such as this one, are available to upgrade original Mustangs from manual windows and locks to powered systems that duplicate the function of the factory parts.

ELECTRICAL

Another alternative is a kit such as this. It retains the factory manual window lift mechanism, and a powered hub is connected to the stock window crank lever. This system is a bit lighter and easier to install (no need to remove the factory regulators), but it is not quite as powerful as the factory-type kits. Lift time/speed can be less with larger windows.

An aftermarket distributor can be a viable option when an authentic look is not a priority. These upgraded distributors already include an electronic triggering system and provide more stable timing due to tighter tolerances. They are also more accurate and durable at higher RPM and can also provide more flexibility in modifying the timing/advance curve. Another upgrade, ignition amplifiers, can improve overall performance, starting, and even fuel economy. The spark plug wires would also need to be upgraded to handle such a unit's higher voltage and to get the most benefit.

An electric cooling fan is one of the best upgrades for an early Mustang. Electric fans free up power from the engine by eliminating the drag of the stock fan. They also can provide greatly improved cooling at low speeds or RPM, especially on 1964½ to 1966 cars with smaller radiators. Electric fans can also be set to come on at a specific temperature or when the air conditioning is on.

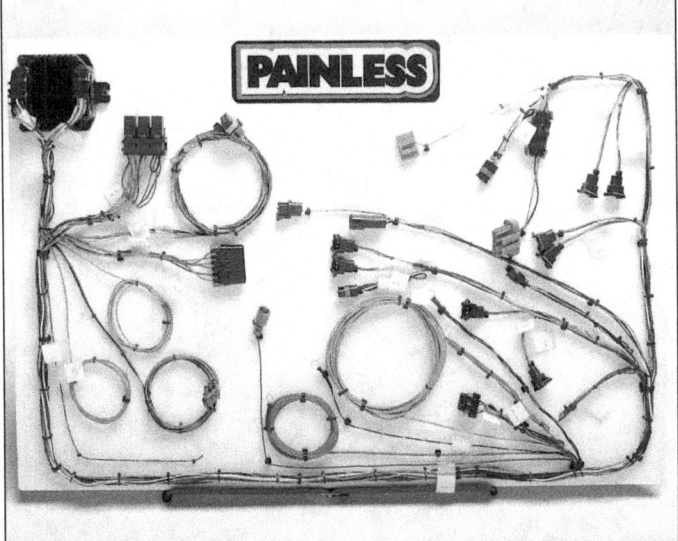

It's is now far easier to convert a carbureted early Mustang to electronic fuel injection (EFI). Conversion harnesses are readily available to improve performance, reliability, and fuel economy. Products are available which use either their own computer or 5.0L Ford OEM computer.

HOW TO RESTORE YOUR MUSTANG 1964½–1973

CHAPTER 11

INTERIOR

The interior of a vehicle is one of the most important areas of restoration for no other reason than it is the area you see the most when you drive your car. If you drive it frequently, you surely don't want to be looking at an interior whose better days are long past. After a few decades, it's not unheard of for dash pads to crack and seat covers to split, for example. Interiors see a fair amount of wear and tear, plus certain parts get some abuse from the elements, the sun in particular. The good news is that restoring the interior is usually pretty straightforward, and the vast majority of the parts are readily available.

Most of the reproduction parts are pretty true to the OEM components, even at the lower price levels. There still are differences, but they're not as drastic as with some other parts of the car. This is probably due to the heavy use of vinyl, which is relatively inexpensive to manufacture. The most significant cost involved in interior restoration is often labor charges. If you've got the skill and access to tools, you can restore an entire interior at relatively moderate cost.

The decision to do it yourself really comes down to your skill/experience and the scope of the project. Refurbishing the interior panels, replacing door panels, and installing new dash pads are things most people can handle. Putting in new carpet is also relatively simple, but I'll show you what makes the job come out nicer.

When you start getting into things such as installing a new headliner or reupholstering the seats, it becomes more complicated. Tasks such as these require a significantly higher level of knowledge as well as a certain feel to have the best result. Unless you have some experience with this type of work, you may want to let the professionals do it for you unless budget is a real concern. And some interiors are easier on certain models than others. I've seen some cars where it was really difficult to get the headliner to look good with no wrinkles or blemishes.

While I cannot go into detail on every aspect of interior restoration, I cover the most important procedures. *Muscle Car Interior Restoration* by Daniel Strohl covers all facets of interior in exceptional depth and detail. There aren't that many special tools required to do this type of work, and you don't need a paint booth, but the pros know the tricks to make it look best. And they do have some special equipment that makes the job go a lot faster while keeping the quality high.

Our 1968 fastback was in reasonably good shape. Still, components such as the armrest, carpet, and seat covers were in pretty bad shape, but they were easy to take care of. We will take care of the carpet and seat covers but can skip the arm rests since they and the sill plates simply bolt-on. We'll just get new replacements.

I can't show every part of the interior, but I've picked some of the more important areas. The type of restoration also dictates how far you go and what you do. A daily driver or a weekend cruiser can look almost as good as a show car for a relatively moderate sum. A show car requires the highest quality parts and materials that most closely match the OEM. The extra attention to detail and care a show car requires comprises the bulk of the extra cost you inevitably incur in such a case. Still, for all but the most discriminating judges and owners, there can be surprisingly little difference in appearance among the different levels of restoration. Unless you need to find real OEM/NOS parts or have to take it to the top level in every respect, you can probably do a fair amount of work yourself and leave little to the professionals. As you can see, we didn't have to replace everything.

Initial Inspection and Evaluation

Interior inspection is pretty simple. You'll generally know if you need to replace or repair something just by looking at it. The real question becomes: What is the best method to resolve each issue? Torn seat covers or a torn headliner must be replaced; ditto for the carpet and the door panels. The interior trim panels, however, and even the dash pad can generally be refurbished. It's almost always easier to install a new dash pad rather than restore an old one. If the car will be judged on authenticity, however, it may be necessary to repair the original dash pad to get the most credit. Surprisingly, a relatively poor dash pad can often be repaired to look as good as new.

First, I go over our interior to illustrate some of the choices that may have to be made and then show some of the things we did to restore it.

We were very lucky to have a headliner that was in such great shape, so there was nothing except clean it. Since we knew there was no roof damage, we just left it alone. Replacing a headliner is pretty straightforward and good reproductions are readily available. There's clearly some finesse/technique involved, but it doesn't require a pro.

Our dash pad was in great shape, so we just gave it a mild cleaning and then applied a coat of matte finish protectant. In most cases a damaged dash pad is replaced. It's inexpensive and there are plenty of good reproductions available. If good is not good enough and/or you need to reuse the OEM dash pad, it can be repaired professionally, usually for a fairly high cost. This may be a necessary choice for a show car that will be judged, but it rarely makes sense for a car that will be driven often and/or when the budget is lower.

The main surfaces of the dashboard and instrument panel rarely require much repair if the car has been maintained. Painted surfaces can be repainted and the woodgrain or "camera case" coverings can also be removed and replaced without much difficulty. However, the plastic "chrome" finish is difficult and costly to refinish. If it is very deteriorated or scratched/damaged, this usually requires replacement. It is possible for these parts to be stripped and a new finish applied, but it's very costly and environmental regulations make finding a shop that does it is increasingly difficult.

CHAPTER 11

Replacing the clear lenses over the gauges is a common task during a restoration. These can become scratched, cloudy, or otherwise damaged over time. Remove the instrument panel to gain access to them. The difficulty varies by vehicle but it can be more difficult when there is a Rally Pac on the steering column. Be extra cautious about not pulling too hard on any of the wires.

The interior trim panels in our car were in decent shape, for the most part. There were some scratches that would need to be sanded out but no major cracks or pieces broken off. Spot putty and/or sandable primer disguises most minor blemishes. We reused all of these trim pieces by simply sanding, priming, and then painting them. Replacements are available but they generally don't match the originals perfectly; either replace them as a set or reuse the originals. In some cases they can be mixed, but not usually when the panels are directly next to each other. For example, you might be able to replace only the panels above the steel molding, but you would likely need to replace all of them as a set to get the best appearance. The chrome on the vents and the circular light fixtures was only mildly pitted and thus a good candidate for the steel wool treatment and some touch-up paint.

Another common restoration issue is replacing various interior knobs, buttons, and switches, etc., that have been lost or damaged. Here we see the radio is missing one a button and the knobs can use a bit of a freshening. Replacements are available for most missing parts and little more than a good cleaning is usually required for those parts that are acceptable. Here, again, we have the issue of a less-than-perfect "chrome" finish on the trim piece that surrounds the radio. Real chrome can usually be rubbed out with 0000-grade steel wool and polish to restore a good finish. More severely pitted chrome or plastic parts with a chrome-like finish generally need to be replaced.

Carpet Replacement

Putting in a new carpet involves more than just taking out the old one and installing new pieces in its place. Either way, you need to remove the seats, console, and other items. However, if you want the end result to look good, what you put back in and how you do it involves much more than just installing the new pieces.

First you need to make sure your floorpans are in good shape. No point in putting a nice new carpet on top of rusted areas that might give way. (If you need to do any metal repair, refer to Chapter 3.) The next decision involves whether or not to put down any sound-deadening material or any kind of matting under the carpet. The former is relatively thin and thus has a minimal effect on the installation. Usually the material is sticky on one side and has foil on the other. Sheets of the stuff are cut to fit and rolled into place with the foil side facing the interior of the car. These do add some weight, but they can make a real difference in the interior noise level. You probably want to do this if you are spending some big bucks on a killer sound system. If you're going to be running a relatively loud exhaust,

INTERIOR

Installing Carpet

1 Removing the original carpet revealed solid floors to work with, a blessing we expected based on the condition of the car when we got it. We will not use any sound deadening or matting in our car but, if you're going to use the material, you need to install it at this stage. First clean the floors and seal any rust spots before rolling on the sound-deadening material. If you use additional matting, place it on top of the sound-deadening material. Normally the sound deadening alone is sufficient for both noise abatement and heat insulation. More matting adds more weight and makes proper fitting of the carpet more difficult but it may be suitable for certain situations/tastes.

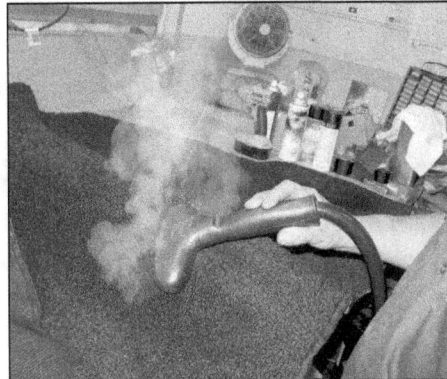

2 Mustang Country showed us that steaming the carpet makes it much easier to fit it to the vehicle. Do this with a simple carpet steamer and a suitable model that approximates the shape of the transmission tunnel. This helps make the carpet less stiff to work with and also helps keep it from moving around so much while you are working on it. Steam can also be used after the carpet has been put in the car to help it better conform to irregular shapes.

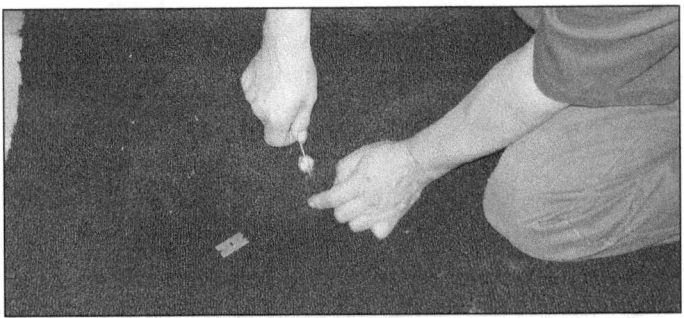

4 Another trick is to anchor down the middle of the carpet first and then work your way out to each edge. Here we see the holes for the inner seat belt bolts being cut. Use an awl or similar sharp object to locate the bolt hole and then a razor blade or X-acto knife to cut away the carpet and backing from the area. Make sure you leave a neat, clean hole.

3 The rear section of the carpet is generally installed first. Be sure to center it as best you can and leave sufficient material to overlap the sills and the rear seat ledge. It is less critical to bring the front edge up to the edge of the seat pedestals because the front carpet section covers these areas anyway. Use steam to help make the carpet conform to the floor's shape.

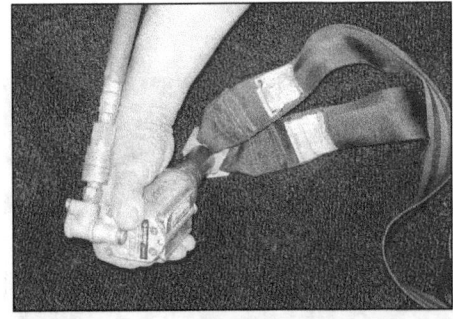

5 The inner seat belts are installed on each side of the transmission tunnel. Smooth out the carpet and make sure it is properly positioned before you install the bolts. The bolts have a shoulder for the belt buckles to rest on so they both can still rotate after the bolts are tightened. This car had a factory shoulder belt setup, thus the dual belts per side.

Installing Carpet CONTINUED

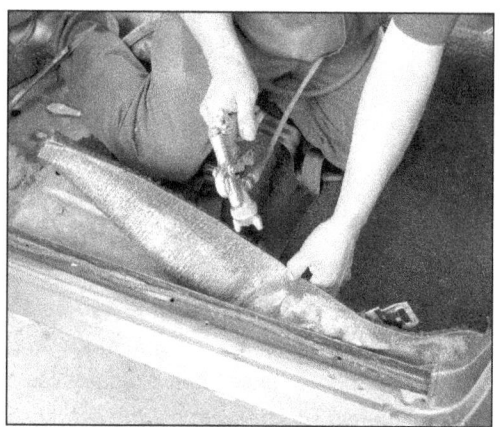

6 After steaming the carpet so it conforms to the shape of the floorpan, spray adhesive (3M Interior Trim Adhesive or similar) on the back of the carpet at the rocker/sill area before you place it. This helps prevent it from moving around during installation and in use. Don't spray too much; it could seep through the backing onto the carpet.

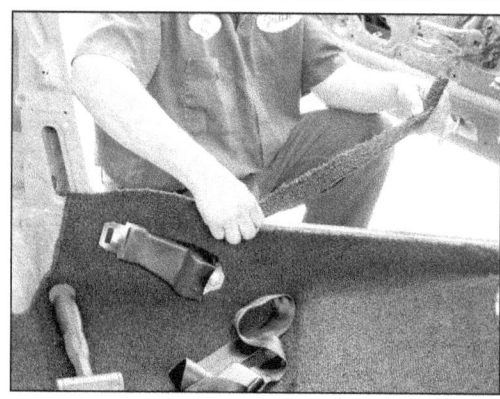

7 After installing the seat belt and retractor (again, the bolts must allow rotation after being tightened) cut off the excess carpet. The edge of the carpet should slightly overlap the metal flange on the sill to prevent gaps after the sill plates are installed. Remember, mold the carpet to the shape of the floorpan before cutting; let the adhesive work for you.

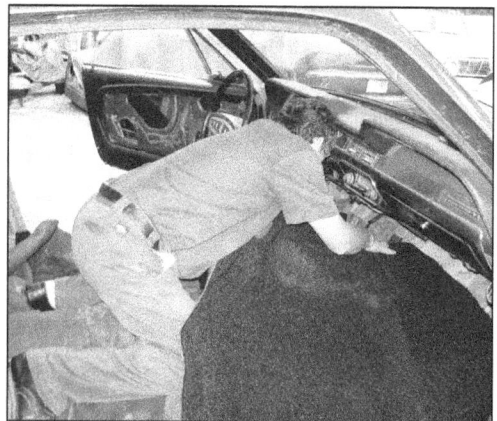

8 The front section of the carpet is installed after the rear section has been glued down and cut. The length of the front section must usually be cut according to the position of the edge of the rear carpet section and floorpan. However, you need to ensure the carpet goes far enough up the transmission tunnel and foot wells. It usually helps to place the rear edge first and then roll back the front edge. The front edge can then be unrolled as needed and marked for cutting. Treat the sides as before.

9 There are no seat belt bolts to hold the front section of the carpet in place, so use sheetmetal screws to hold it down. Locate these screws on each side of the transmission tunnel at the rear edge of the carpet, as shown. Adhesive can hold down the front edge of the carpet, so screws are not needed there. Punch a starter hole and then use a sheetmetal or self-tapping screw to keep the carpet in place. Check the back side of the panel so there are no fluid lines or wires where the screws will go. It may also be advisable, especially in harsher/wetter climates, to use waterproof sealant on the screws/holes.

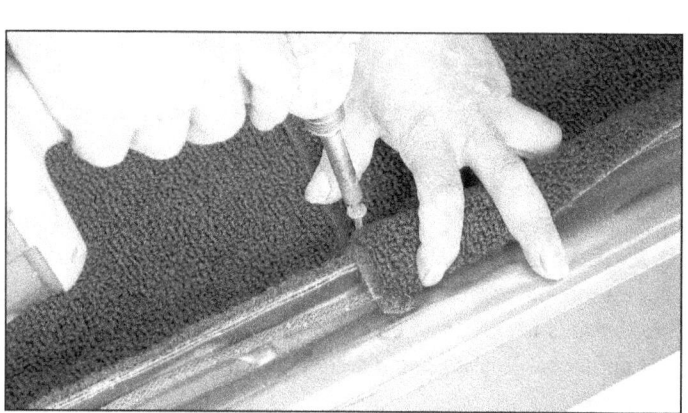

10 Install another pair of screws at the rear edge of the carpet near the rocker panel/sill on each side. The same precautions and procedures apply. Pull and smooth the carpet to eliminate any slack or unevenness. It is more critical to make sure the screws hold the carpet tight than it is to worry about the carpet molding to the step in front of the seat platform; that can be addressed later with steam and some force. Make sure enough carpet overlaps the sill to ensure coverage.

there is little point. We didn't have a loud exhaust and wanted to save both weight and cost, so we did without any kind of sound deadening or cushioning material under our new carpet. We went with a higher-quality carpet set and had it installed at Mustang Country, so I could show some of the tricks an experienced, professional installer uses to make the carpet look its best.

The fold-down rear seats found in many early Mustangs also were carpeted from the factory, and these should have their carpet replaced if the floor carpet is replaced, to ensure a proper match.

Rear Seat Carpet Replacement

1 *When the carpet is replaced on cars with a fold-down rear seat, it is usually necessary to also change the carpeting on the seat to better match the floor. This begins by removing and disassembling the seat panels. The chrome moldings can usually be rubbed with 0000-grade steel wool to remove most mild to moderate pitting or other surface roughness. More extensive damage requires replacement or re-plating. When removing the chrome, take care to remember where it went and to avoid stripping out the threads for the screws. All hardware comes off.*

2 *The process continues with a ScotchBrite-type pad to remove the residue of any adhesive that was used to hold the carpet on. You don't need to remove every last bit as much as you just need to knock down any high points; make it smooth and clean.*

3 *Lay the new carpet over the panels, so you can get an idea of how to trim the various pieces. Most kits come with considerably oversized pieces, so you have plenty of material to work with. It usually helps to line up the best/straightest carpet edge with an edge of the panel.*

4 *Spray adhesive on the carpet and the panel, but don't overdo it and soak through the carpet. It is usually better to spray a section of the carpet and then lay it down than it is to fully spray both pieces and then try to match them up. The adhesive dries quickly so spray a bit, roll and smooth the carpet, and then spray more.*

Rear Seat Carpet Replacement CONTINUED

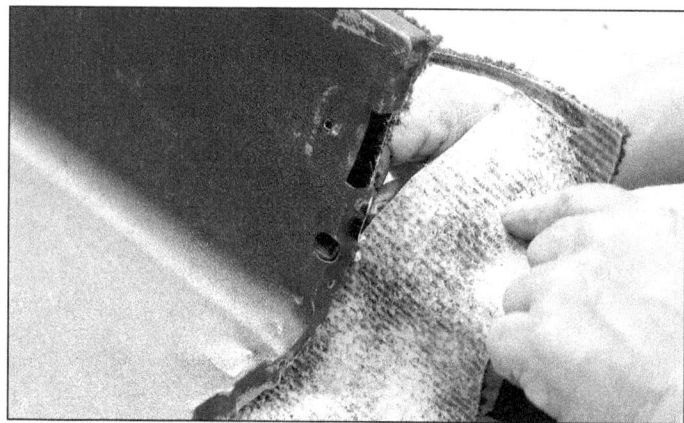

5 After the carpet has been applied over the whole panel and has been checked for both straightness and smoothness, trim it with a razor blade or razor knife. Don't leave any material past the edges because the chrome molding pieces will fully cover the ends. Be sure to cut the carpet away from any functional holes.

6 Some molding pieces need to be slipped under or into others to fit properly. Loosely assemble all of the pieces for a panel, attain proper fit, and then fully tighten the screws. Tighten the screws by hand to prevent stripping.

7 The proper alignment of the various mounting points as well as the locking hardware determines the proper functioning of the fold-down seat. A common problem is these latching plates are not positioned properly or are loose, causing the seat back to not latch properly. Make sure the screws are tight and the latch is flush and flat.

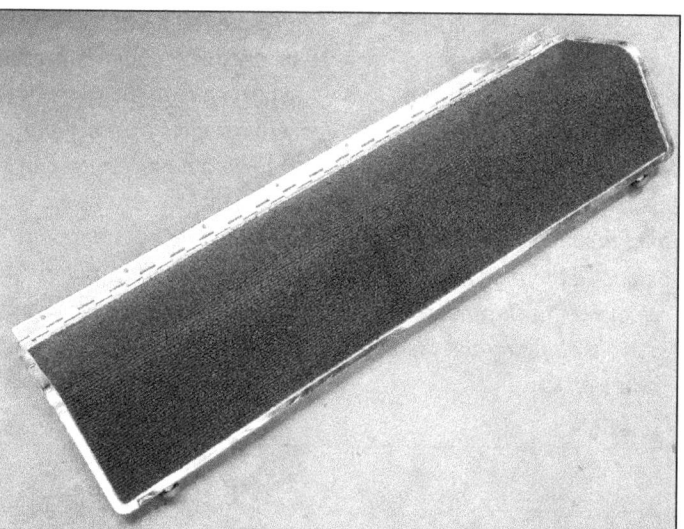

8 The finished panels should have a smooth, tight look. The carpet should be fully glued down and the chrome moldings should all be tight and straight. It is especially important to make sure all of the screws are used at the hinge because leaving even one or two out can result in the others being stripped out over time. Stripped holes can be filled, re-drilled, and threaded, but it is not a very good fix even though the metal hides it.

Interior Trim Panel Refurbishment

The panels that comprise the interior of most first-generation Mustangs can almost always be repaired or refurbished to at least an acceptable level. While there may be issues, such as pitted chrome, that can't be completely eliminated in all cases, enough can often be done to make the result pleasing to all but perhaps the show-car owner. (The restoration details are covered in the following procedure as well as in Chapter 2.) Even then, the desire to retain the authentic OEM part may overrule the desire to have a completely flawless appearance.

INTERIOR

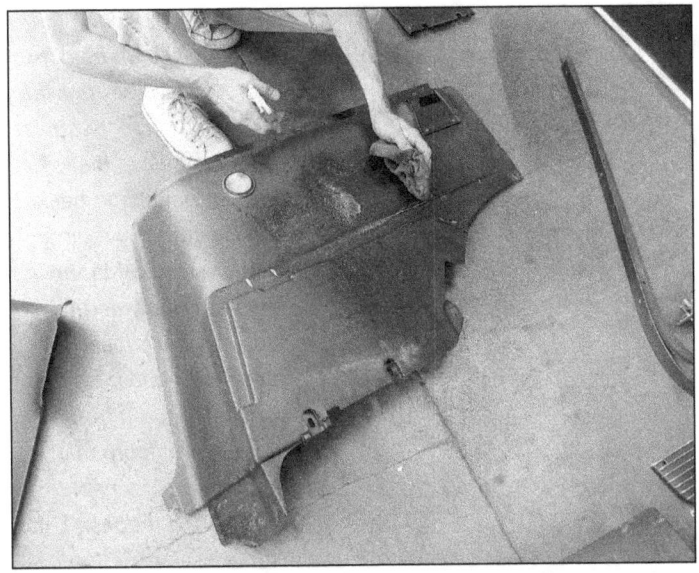

If there are no scratches or other damage on the interior trim panels, they can be cleaned and repainted, if necessary. If you paint one panel you will likely end up painting them all to get the proper color match. Note that there is a section on some panels where a small piece of carpet is attached. The preparation for these sections is similar to the fold-down seat, minus the metal trim pieces.

You can usually remove scratches and other damage in smooth, non-textured panels by sanding them out, priming, and repainting the panel. Deeper scratches may require using spot putty or even body filler, but most minor imperfections can be hidden with a few coats of high build, sandable primer and paint. Panels that have a distinct pattern or texture to them can be repaired, but this is best left to professionals. Replacement panels are usually a more cost-effective solution. Heavy damage can be repaired with fiberglass mats and similar techniques, but this is usually only reserved for when replacement panels are unavailable and/or you wish to retain the original panels for the sake of authenticity.

Fine (0000-grade) steel wool can be very effective in removing mild to moderate pitting and surface imperfections from chrome. Here a chrome vent section of one of the interior panels is reconditioned. Steel wool was used to remove most of the surface roughness. The black painted area between the chrome bars can be easily restored. We simply spray over the chrome and then wipe the paint off of the chrome. Use a cloth if it is still wet or the steel wool if it has already dried. Wrap either around a flat bar or a piece of wood first to help promote contact with the top edge only.

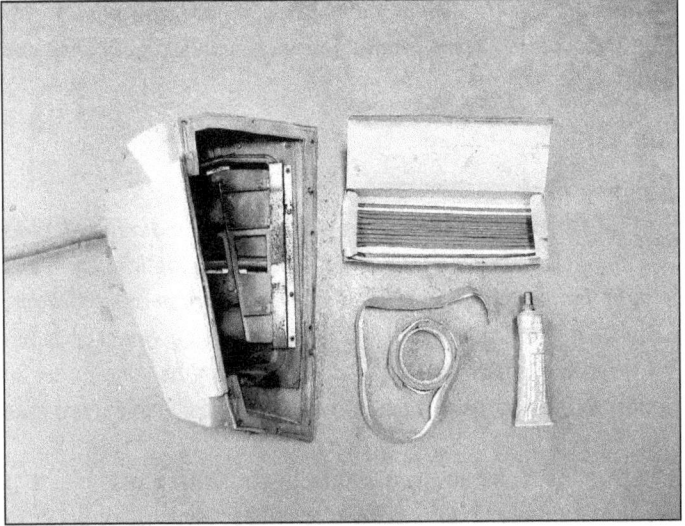

The gaskets on the vent units should generally be replaced whenever the vents are removed. The rubber hardens over time, and these don't seal that well in the first place. Use RTV to seal the gasket to the vent assembly and then either foam backed tape or sealing strips between the gasket and the car body. The original gaskets can be reused if they are in good shape, but either way, these other materials should also be used. Tighten the retaining nuts evenly and not too tightly with the factory offset spacers under all of them.

CHAPTER 11

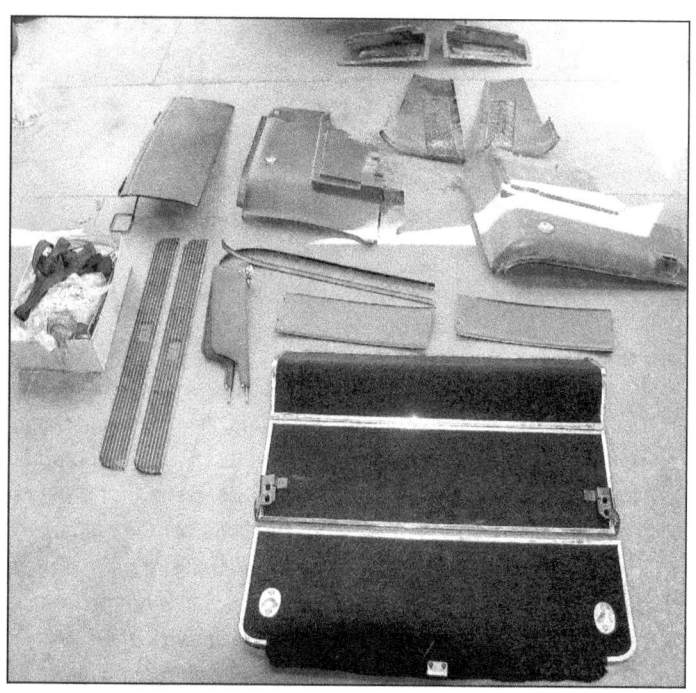

These interior parts have been refinished and are ready for installation. We also had refinished the seats and the floor carpets but didn't do the headliner or dash pad. All of the chrome looked great after rubbing it with the steel wool, while the metal and composite panels looked like new after being sanded and painted. All of the installation hardware was previously marked and bagged to make reinstallation considerably easier.

Installing the vent assemblies can be done either before or after the carpet is put in, but must be done before the interior panels go back on. Be sure to properly seal the gasket to the vent assembly and to the body as described. The drain hose must also be properly routed to the hole in the floorpan. It should fit reasonably tight, but if it doesn't, use some sealer (RTV or similar) where the hose meets the floorpan. Use some silicone spray and/or some spray-on white grease on the vent mechanism if it sticks when you try to move it.

Check to make sure the ground wires and other electrical connections for the interior lights found on the trim panels are tight and corrosion free. If not, use a wire brush or steel wool to remove any oxidation and then make sure the connection is tight when you reassemble it. If any of the metal backing plates are loose on the trim panels use the proper adhesive to secure them.

The hard panels can generally be repaired, using body filler for mild scratches or fiberglass for more severe damage. Minor scratches generally disappear under a few coats of sandable primer. Replacement parts, either new reproductions or used/NOS OEM parts are also an option, but this is generally more costly. Oxidized or pitted chrome usually responds quite well to rubbing with fine (0000-grade) steel wool. There may also be a need to repair gaskets, wiring, or other unique features on some panels/parts. Normally, little more than general cleaning, sanding, priming, and/or painting is required.

Rear Fold-Down-Seat Installation

The installation of the fold-down rear seat is a relatively simple procedure, but it is often done incorrectly. This results in misalignment that not only can look odd, but it also can cause problems with rubbing on adjacent panels, loose fit, and/or falling seat backs. The most common causes of these issues are failure to use the required shims, using improper retaining bolts, and/or the failure to install all of the necessary fasteners. In the photos, I show some of the common things to look for to avoid trouble.

The cover plates for the fold-down seat latching mechanism were also touched up with the same paint used on the panels. The screws that hold these on frequently strip out the threads in the panel even when tightened relatively lightly. A nut and bolt setup can be used instead, but this doesn't look very good. A better option is to glue a small mat of fiberglass behind the panel and then drill it so the screw can make new threads, or use epoxy on the threaded portion of a metal panel clip that has been cut down.

In order to properly install the fold-down seat, you need to use of the correct wide flange bolts and number of mounting shims, both of which are shown here. These help properly locate the mounting tabs of the seat assembly and prevent them from loosening over time. The shims are cut out on one side so they can be slid in under the seat's tabs while the bolts are still installed. This allows the best possible alignment.

Properly installed, the fold-down rear seat back is relatively level with the contoured edge of the side trim panel. Proper alignment is desirable from aesthetic and functional standpoints. The seat panels must be straight, centered, and as level as possible for the seat to fold correctly without hitting the side panels. The height established by the shims also affects the alignment of the rear-most panel (not yet installed). The required fastener clip is not shown in the rear attachment tab but it just pushes on.

With the rear panel is installed, make the holes in the carpet and install the proper fasteners. Here we use a longer pilot fastener to help line the panel up before we carefully install the correct ones (they strip easily). Since this panel does not move with the others, it can be placed with a bit more flexibility for the best appearance.

Inner Door Panel Replacement

Inner door panels are relatively inexpensive and easy to replace. There are, of course, differences in quality among manufacturers, but the better known brands tend to be roughly equivalent and very close to the OEM parts in appearance. If your car's original door panels are in good condition with minimal to no damage, you should reuse them. If there is no undesirable wear at the armrest area or at the bottom near the door sills (the most common wear spots), these can be reinstalled after cleaning. Exceptions are rips/tears on the front or damaged clips that anchor on the fiberboard. These usually become a problem only when the door panels are removed too often and/or when a lower-quality product is used.

If you think the door panels may have to be removed frequently, you can buy panels that use plastic instead of fiberboard; they're less prone to damage in the clip attachment areas. Opinions differ on how well such parts replicate the originals, but this may only be a concern to those desiring maximum authenticity. For daily drivers and weekend cruisers, this approach can also minimize the warping and/or waviness in the panels that sometimes occurs.

Inner door panel removal often requires some insight and tools to the remove door handles and/or window crank handles. Considerable skill and care are needed when undoing the many clips that hold the panels on. To highlight this, I show a few of the things we addressed when replacing the door panels on our car.

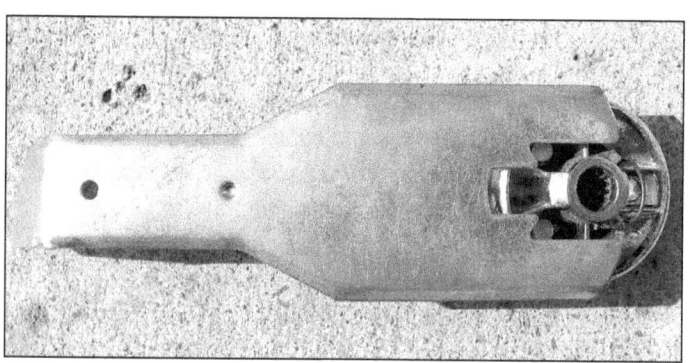

Removing the door handles and window crank handles often requires a special tool such as this one. It slips under the handle and engages the tips of the spring clip that holds the handle on. It spreads the clip apart as you push the tool forward, allowing you to remove it and the handle. Finesse matters more than force when using such tools.

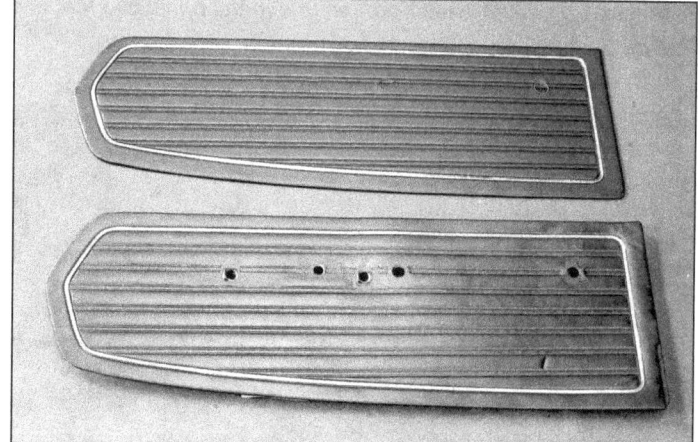

Inner door panels are another area where very good reproductions are available for most early Mustangs regardless of color or trim level. Our original panels were good enough to reuse, but the reproductions were relatively inexpensive. They proved to be the easiest way to eliminate the few flaws that were on the OEM pieces. We would use the originals as a template for the holes that needed to be punched.

We chose new speakers for the doors; the old speakers could fail because they had sat for so long. The newer speakers also benefit from improved materials technology and a coaxial design that will provide better sound. They bolt/hook right up.

Door Panel Installation

1. Another example of improved materials technology are reproduction watershields designed specifically for specific applications. Not only are these items cut to fit precisely over the required area of the door, but they also are made from a much more durable material than the originals. They may not look exactly the same but they won't be visible anyway so that's no problem. Before installing the new watershields, we applied the correct adhesive/sealer using a caulking gun, as shown. The old material does not necessarily have to be completely removed, but eliminate any high points or rough spots before the new stuff goes on. Use enough material to get a good seal without it spreading too much.

2. The watershields typically come pre-punched for at least the retaining clips, but you may have to punch holes for the other items like the door and window handles because these may vary with car factory options. We used a standard "cardboard" style door panel. There are also plastic versions, which are supposed to be more durable and less susceptible to damaged clip holes. We also used some improved part-plastic clips along the lower edge of the panels to reduce the chance of pulling out or not lining up.

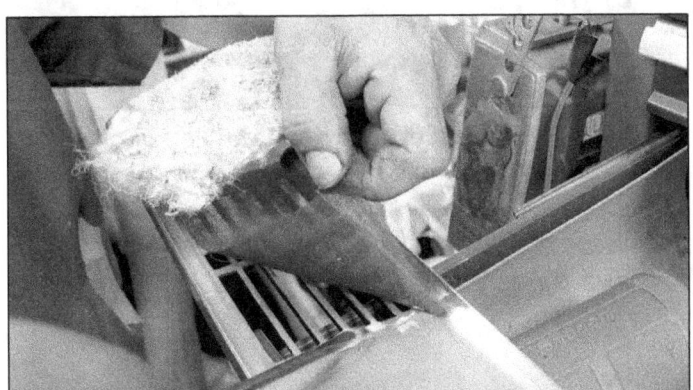

3. The metal strip pieces for the lower edge of the doors needed a little attention. We used steel wool and paint to refinish the front side. The speaker openings needed some new fabric to hide the speakers. This is a special fabric that does not overly muffle or distort the sound. It simply is cut to size and then is held in place with adhesive. Here we see how the adhesive can be spread more carefully and sparingly with a flat blade screwdriver tip.

4. As for the lower metal trim piece on the door, we can see how much better it looks. The door was painted in the correct finish while the new inner panel sits flat and looks just like the original. The new armrest is clearly a vast improvement over what we had. Finally, some steel wool and chrome polish really made the bright work look better too.

HOW TO RESTORE YOUR MUSTANG 1964½–1973

Miscellaneous Interior Refurbishment

The remaining interior areas usually require replacing parts rather than reconditioning or refurbishing. Dash pads, pedal pads, and other parts are readily available and easy to replace. The same goes for new, clear lenses for gauges as well as the gauges themselves. Again, used OEM or NOS may be what's needed for a show car, but very high-quality reproductions are available for other projects.

One of the hardest decisions often encountered is whether or not to buy a new instrument cluster if the plastic chrome-looking, woodgrain, or "camera case" finishes are worn, peeling off, or damaged. These can sometimes be refurbished, but replacement is often the only option. Cost can be prohibitive, so these trim issues are often not addressed. Fortunately, these issues are less common in less extreme climates and they are not always very obvious.

A cracked dash pad, a damaged/cracked steering wheel, or very worn pedals, however, are much more obvious and (thankfully) are also less costly to

The lenses on our gauges were cloudy and a bit scratched up and the finish on the center piece had also come off, so we replaced them. We had the trip odometer, so we needed to get correct lenses that made provisions for the adjustment knob that passes through it. Always verify a part is the right one for your car before you install it, otherwise you may not be able to exchange it for the correct item. We would need to remove the entire instrument cluster to change the lenses.

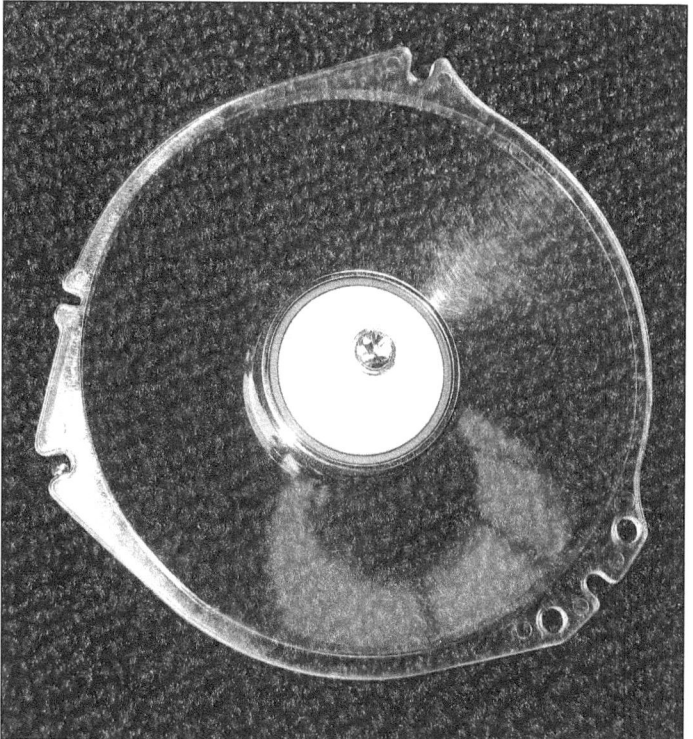

The new lenses are crystal clear in comparison to the ones that were on the car. Decades of dust, dirt, and daylight deteriorate plastic. The new lenses should hold up better due to better technology, plus they also fit at least as well due to tighter manufacturing tolerances.

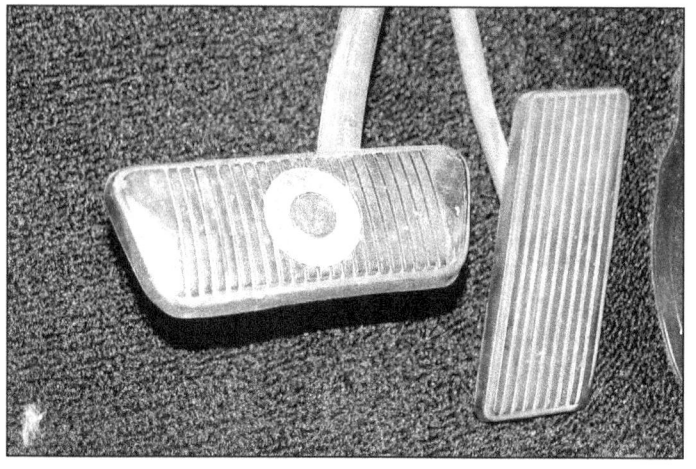

The throttle and brake pedal assemblies generally require little more attention than the replacing the rubber pads and maybe some touch-up painting of the visible metal parts. If the rubber is good enough, just clean and then protect it with a designated product. Don't use anything that's too slippery on these rubber pedal pads; it could cause a safety problem if your foot slips off the pedal too easily.

INTERIOR

remedy. The dash pad and dashboard/instrument panel surfaces (as well as those of the steering column and steering wheel) on our car were all in very good condition and did not require anything more than a cleaning.

We needed to replace the clear lenses in some of the gauges and had to send out the radio for refurbishment, cleaning, and replacement of a missing button, but we were spared having to do any major parts replacement or reconditioning. If these components required a higher level of restoration, we would have bought quality reproduction products where possible and would have repainted whatever we could that required it. We did touch up some of the chrome (real, not plastic) knobs with steel wool. And we repainted some of the visible metal (brake and throttle pedals, for example) that needed it, but the extra cost didn't justify doing more in our case.

Seat Reupholstery

Installing new seat covers is a lot harder than you might think, especially if you want to do it right. There are many little procedures required to get the new covers to fit properly and look right. A professional often produces a better result, but I show some of the main aspects to consider if you try to tackle this job yourself.

Although I only show a front seat as an example, the same basic steps apply to most seat types and variations. The key is to be very attentive as you take the original seat apart so you see where everything goes and how the cover is supported and positioned. Taking the old cover off will be a whole lot easier than putting the new one on, especially if the foam bun pad is not in good shape and a new one is needed. Installing even the highest quality covers requires considerable pulling, pushing, and stretching to get the correct fit/look.

I show some of the tips an experienced installer uses to get the best result. I also show some of the things to watch out for, plus a few precautions to take when putting the seat back together, to ensure many years of trouble-free use.

Disassembly and Detailed Inspection of Original Seats

When removing the original seat covers, take extra care to bag and tag the many clips, washers, rods, and other small parts that will be reused with the new covers. As the seats are disassembled, the location and orientation of each part should be carefully noted for subsequent reassembly. Many of these small parts are no longer readily available.

Front Seat Refurbishment

The original passenger seat looked pretty good; we could have kept the original seat cover if we'd wanted to. The driver's seat, however, had several tears in it. You pretty much have to change all of the seat covers so the materials match and the interior looks clean. Even with high-quality reproductions that closely match the OEM fabric, you still have to deal with the difference between what new fabric looks like versus faded/worn fabric. No manufacturer can accurately compensate for aging.

1 After removing all of the various levers, plastic covers, and retaining clips, separate the top seat back from the lower seat cushion. Use a strategically placed pry bar, as shown. Bench and rear seats will require another approach. I only show the generic process for removing and installing seat covers. We used the upper and lower sections of a 1968 front bucket seat. The basic procedure is common for most early-Mustang seats, though there will naturally be some differences for each different model.

Front Seat Refurbishment CONTINUED

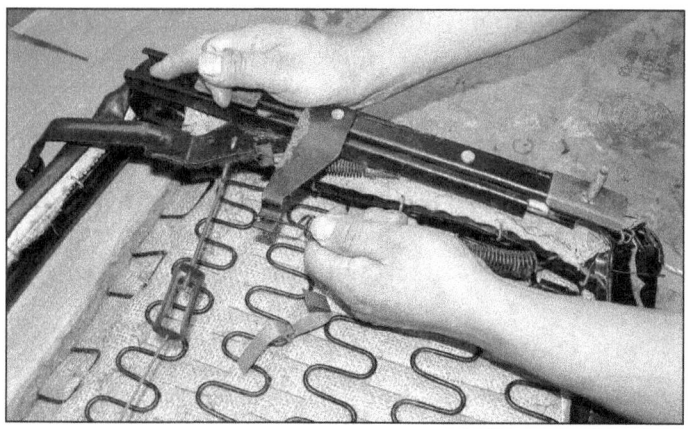

2 First we started with the lower cushion and then removed the various springs and other related parts underneath it. This is also a good time to remove the two circular bumpers on the rear of the lower cushion.

3 You can easily remove the seat tracks by taking out the two mounting bolts on each track. You'll need to slide the tracks as needed to gain access to the bolts. Be sure to note the use of any spacers, washers, etc., that may have been used to raise and/or tilt the seat. Keep these together and labeled.

4 To remove the original seat cover, you need to remove the outermost retaining rings on each side. These go around the seat frame and a wire rod that's in a sleeve on the seat cover. There's one per side. These are simply twisted until they are spread apart enough to come off.

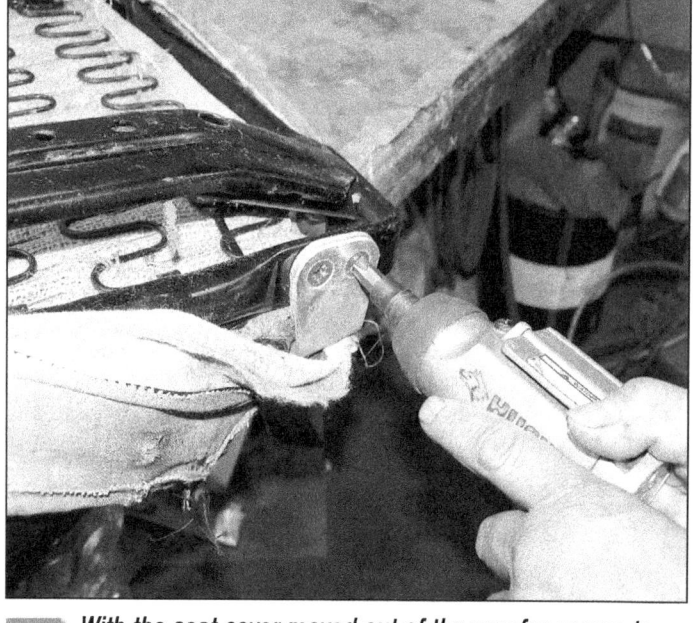

5 With the seat cover moved out of the way for access to the fasteners, remove these brackets after noting their position. You'll need to apply a reasonable amount of pressure to prevent the bit from skipping and/or stripping the fastener. Set these aside as they'll be reused.

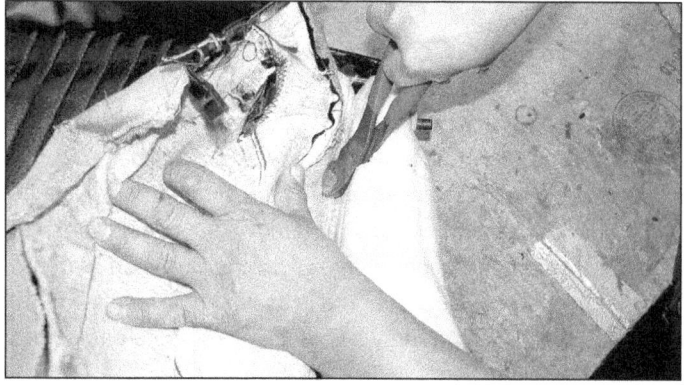

6 Next, remove the smaller rings on the inner surface of the seat. These go around another wire rod in the seat cover (longer, but also in a sleeve), through foam and around the seat frame. These are much easier to take out than to put in. Note how they look as you take them out.

INTERIOR

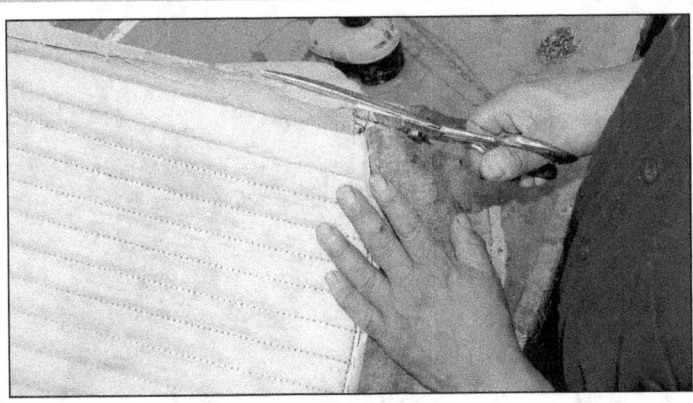

7 After the cover has finally been taken off of the lower cushion, you need take out the three wire rods in the cover. There is a fairly long, U-shaped one in the center of the cushion (on the top side), and two shorter, straight-yet-wavy pieces that are in the sleeves on the underside of the seat.

8 Inspect the seat "bun" (foam) for any damage, such as crumbling, tears, etc. If it looks good, as this one does, it can and should be reused. The original buns will generally give the best fit if they are in good shape. Some reproduction buns are not very close to the original's size, density, and feel. The buns for 1968 cars like ours tend to be higher than other years for some reason, so the repros can be off even more.

9 Carefully inspect the metal seat frames for any excessive rust or broken welds. The high-stress areas, like that shown, are common sites for failure. If the frame is broken, it can usually be welded to be as good as new as long as there isn't too much metal lost to rust. If there is a lot of rust and broken springs, replace the frame.

10 The original burlap had metal reinforcing bars in it as shown here. The edges of the burlap on three sides were also covered with a felt-like material as you can see. These materials are no longer readily available in most cases and they don't perform as well as what we used. If, however, you need to retain maximum authenticity, you should save the original materials or find suitable replacements. In our case we only need to keep the paper-wrapped curved wire for later reuse. Make a note of how the wire is secured to the frame (how many rings, etc.).

11 The seat can be reconditioned after the seat frame has been stripped of all other items and has been repaired and/or verified as being sound. Basically, remove any rust with a wire brush and then spray paint the frame to make it look better and prevent future rust.

Front Seat Refurbishment CONTINUED

12 The process for the upper seat back is essentially the same as for the lower with a few minor differences. First, remove the back cover from the seat back by prying it off as shown to gain access to the inside. Just go around the seat back and pry at the location of the retaining clips.

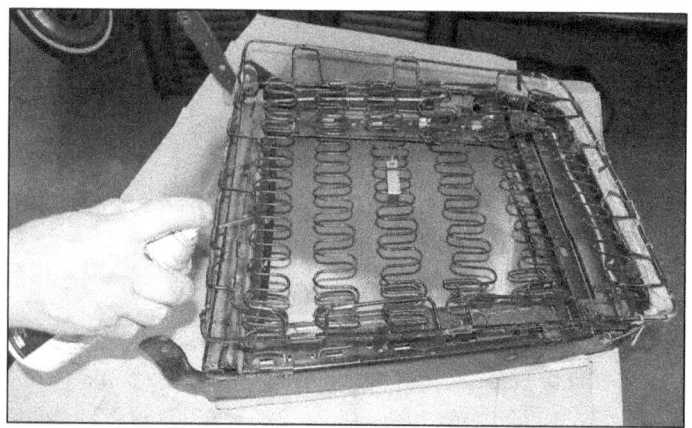

13 The upper seat back is a bit easier to do than the lower seat cushion because it doesn't use the system of rods in sleeves on the back side of the frame. The retaining rings alone hold the cover in place; the U-shaped wire in a sleeve is still used on the front side. Remove the old rings and note how many were used and where they were located. Note the folds also.

14 The metal frame should at least be painted whether or not repairs are needed. Take extra time/care to make sure the paint doesn't get into the release mechanism or into any other unwanted areas, but a little overspray won't hurt. Make sure the foam pads are properly adhering to the frame; apply some adhesive if they are not.

Assembly of Lower Seat Frame and Cushion

Generally, it's advisable to use new burlap because this is one of the things that tend to deteriorate over time. When maximum authenticity is desired, however, the old burlap may be reused if it is in good enough shape. The original burlap has metal support rods, which plain burlap cloth lacks. Notice that additional batting was glued in place in the photos. This is not like the original, but it helps to give the finished seat a better shape.

Installation of New Lower Seat Cover

There is much more to installing the new seat cover than simply stretching it into place. As you see, we used additional foam, a heat gun, and lots of elbow grease to make sure the hog rings were tight and properly placed. I've also shown a few tips relative to finding/cutting holes and so forth.

Assembly of Upper Seat Frame and Cushion

The seat back required using two different types of additional foam as well as cutting holes for the seat-back retention clips. The extra foam helps minimize sags and wrinkles, and ensures a more proper shape.

Final Assembly of Seat

Final assembly involves not only putting all the parts back together but also protecting them beforehand. Applying paint prevents rust and improves appearance. The tracks and other moving parts must also be lubricated.

INTERIOR

15 Cut new burlap for the lower seat frame and begin installing it using the paper-covered, curved wire as your guide. Try to duplicate the location and number of rings used based on what you saw when you took it out. Make sure you press down hard enough for the rings to grab the metal frame. You need special pliers for doing this, plus a little practice to get it right.

16 After the burlap has been secured at the front frame and sides spray some adhesive around the round bar at the back. Then gently stretch the burlap and roll it around the bar while pressing down, so the adhesive holds it in place. Trim any excess burlap and let the adhesive dry for a few minutes.

17 To prevent the rings from being visible and making the seat bumpy and uncomfortable, they must be covered with padding. The factory used a thin felt-like material that didn't work as well as the thicker material we used. This material is made from fabric scraps and is very inexpensive but still soft and easy to work with. Simply cut it into strips long enough to wrap around the seat frame and wide enough to overlap both sides by an inch or so. Spray the padding and the burlap with adhesive before pressing it on and molding it to match the frame contours.

18 The finished seat frame should look like this prior to being assembled with the seat bun. Note the padding extends all the way around the frame, all the way to the rear where the seat back will pivot. There is no need to cover the inner rings; the thickness of the bun will be enough to do so.

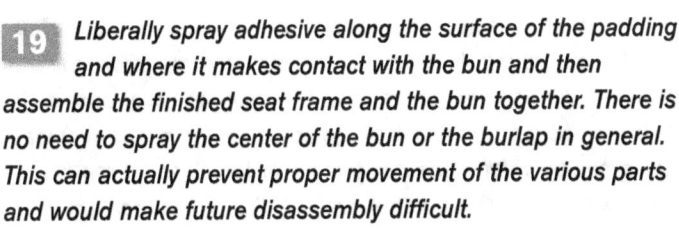

19 Liberally spray adhesive along the surface of the padding and where it makes contact with the bun and then assemble the finished seat frame and the bun together. There is no need to spray the center of the bun or the burlap in general. This can actually prevent proper movement of the various parts and would make future disassembly difficult.

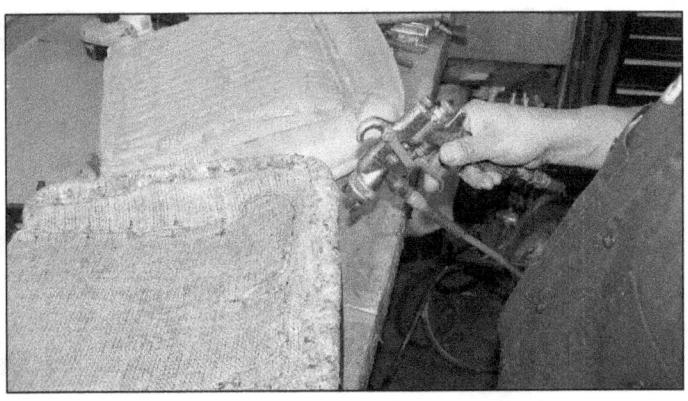

Front Seat Refurbishment CONTINUED

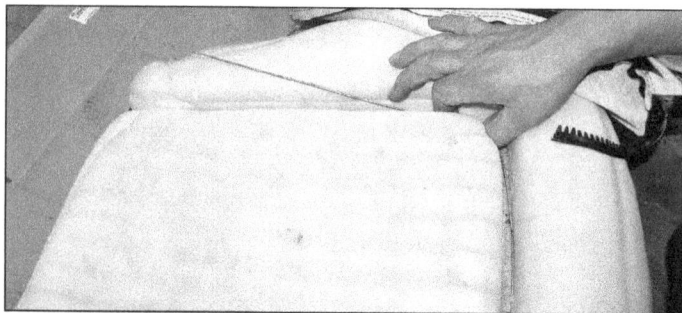

20 After the bun and frame have been assembled together, allow time for the adhesive to dry. Then take the U-shaped wire rod you saved from the original seat cover and place it in the groove in the bun. Use the bun as a guide to bend the rod back to the proper shape before inserting it into the designated sleeve in the new seat cover. Feeding the rod into the sleeve takes a fair amount of patience but it eventually goes in.

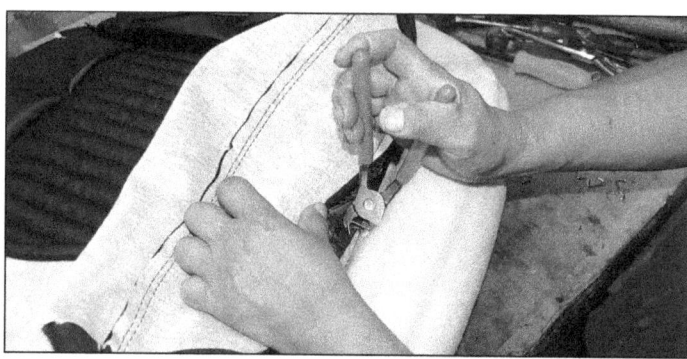

21 Place the cover with the rod in it over the bun and begin installing the rings in the groove. Make sure the ring grabs both the wire rod and the underlying metal of the seat frame. It's necessary to compress the foam to reach the seat frame. Put the rings where you found them when you took the old cover off. Too many rings are better than not enough.

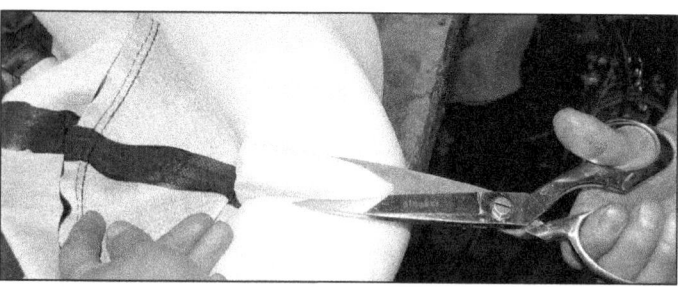

22 To help make the seat a bit more comfortable and look better, it is a good idea to add a thin layer of extra foam along the top edge of the lower seat cushion. As with the padding used on the frame, cut a strip to size—long enough to wrap around the seat and wide enough to cover the outer cushion. Then spray the bun and the foam with adhesive before pressing the foam on the bun and molding it to shape. Excess foam can be squeezed together at the corners and trimmed as shown to remain even.

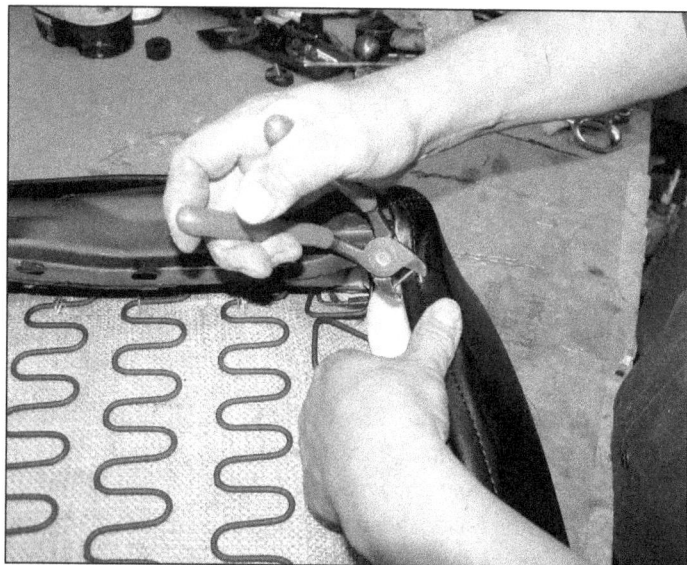

23 The first part of the new cover to be secured to the frame is the front edge. Place the cover (with the wire rods installed in the special sleeves) over the foam/bun after the adhesive has had a bit of time to dry. Then clamp the rings on at the proper locations so they grip the seat frame and the wire rods in the sleeves.

24 Stretch the new seat cover over the rest of the foam/bun and around the sides. This may take some effort and patience. A heat gun can be used to soften the cover enough to help pull it over the foam/bun easily. Be careful not to overheat any areas by holding the gun too still or too close for too long. The idea is to stretch and remove wrinkles, not to melt anything.

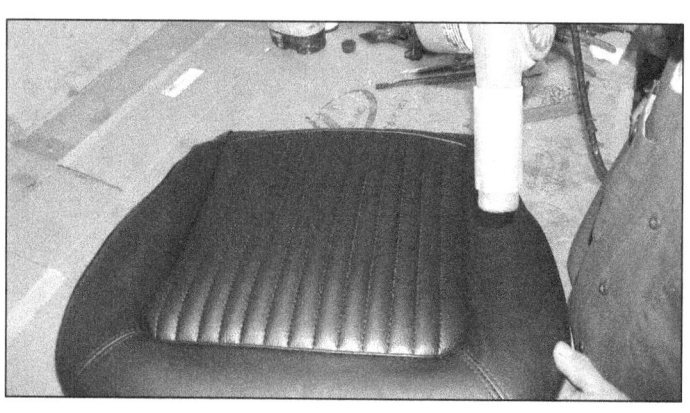

INTERIOR

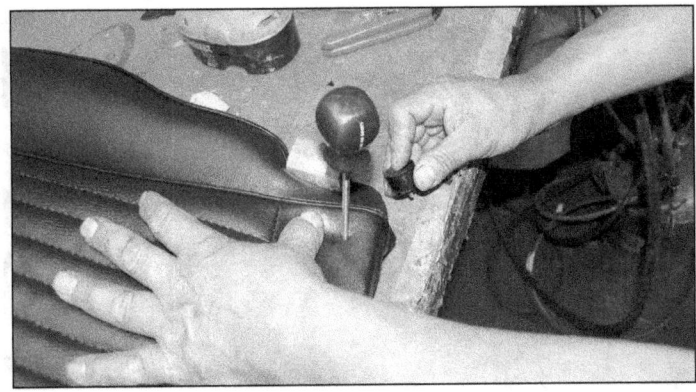

25 To locate the holes for the installation of the circular bumpers, use an awl to poke a hole in the seat cover after dragging the point to find the right spot. Then use a razor blade or knife to make the hole large enough to clear the mounting bolts. As you can see, we've already installed the side brackets.

26 The hinge pin must be exposed, so cut the seat lower cover enough to allow it to poke through. Trim away all excess material such that the cover is even around the pin. A washer slides over the pin and sits on the cover to protect it from wear when the seat back/hinge is moved.

27 The painted seat back/frame is assembled in much the same manner as the lower seat with a few differences, which are shown in the next few photos. The foam collar that surrounds shaft for the seat back release lever is held in place with a small amount of spray adhesive. The mechanism for the seat back release should also be lubricated with a small amount of spray-on lithium grease at the pressure points of movement.

28 The seat back has a main bun like the lower seat frame and an upper foam piece on the back. After spraying adhesive on the bun and the frame, place the bun on the steel frame. Take care to ensure the foam is properly placed and the adhesive has had enough time to dry before proceeding.

29 As with the lower seat cushion, add a thin layer of additional foam to provide extra comfort and a better look. Cut a strip to size and apply it with spray-on adhesive along with mild pressure to mold it into its final shape. The extra foam should wrap completely around the upper bun and overlap slightly onto the rear foam cap such that it helps hide the parting line.

Front Seat Refurbishment CONTINUED

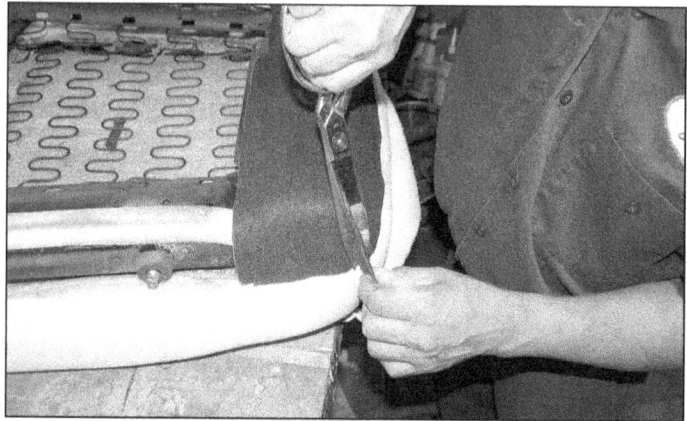

30 Glue a piece of thinner foam to the rear foam cap, so the other extra foam is less obvious. Cut this piece to size and trim it in the same manner as the extra foam on the lower seat cushion. Give the adhesive time to dry here as well.

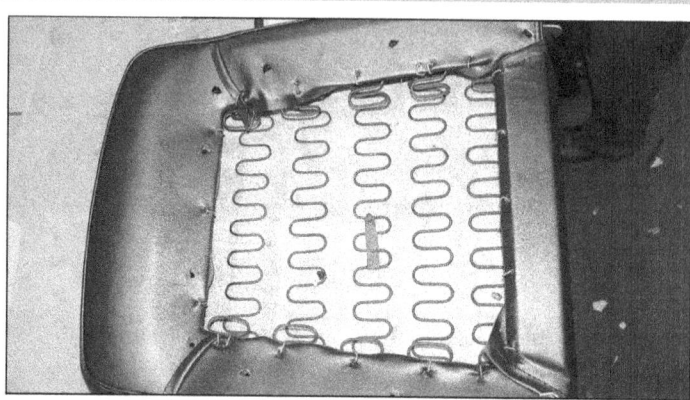

31 Pull the cover over the upper seat frame bun/foam; carefully use a heat gun to help if necessary. Install the rings in the original locations and verify the seams are overlapped as necessary. Then use the awl to find where to cut the holes for the seat back cover clips and cut the holes.

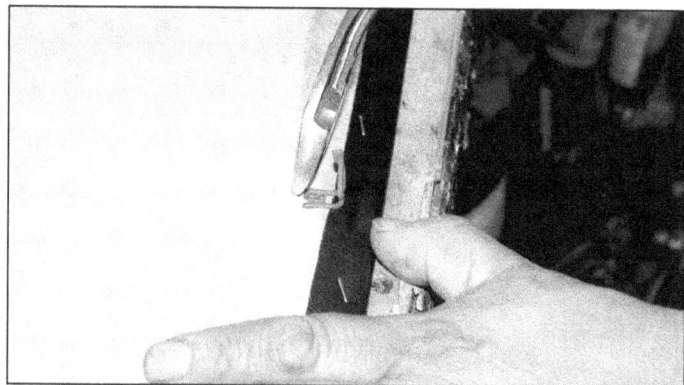

32 Install the new clips into the new seat back. Make sure the clips are pushed far enough forward and grab the cover tightly. The clips can be closed or spread as needed to get the right amount of grip—too tight, however, damages the cover. Special clips with plastic discs are also available. These spread the load and minimize damage to the cover.

33 Line the clips up with their respective holes and simply press the new rear cover onto the seat back. All that should be needed is a gentle push over each clip. The replacement seat cover and rear panel match perfectly with each other and integrate well with the original factory items.

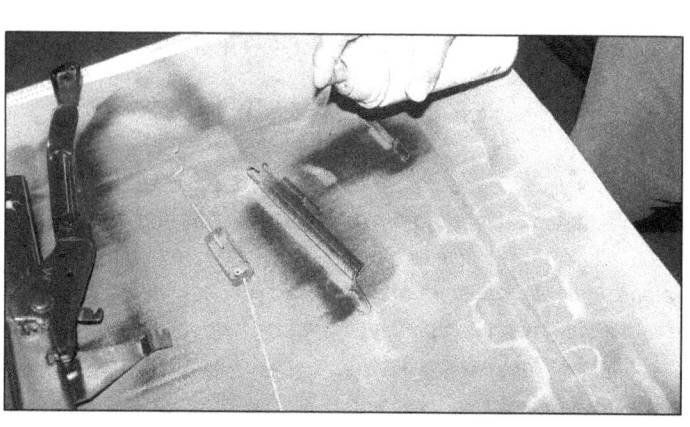

34 The miscellaneous hardware from under the seat needs to be freshened up (repainted) a bit. Do it before reassembly, but make sure the paint dries well enough to handle the parts. Simply remove any rust with a wire brush and then paint.

INTERIOR

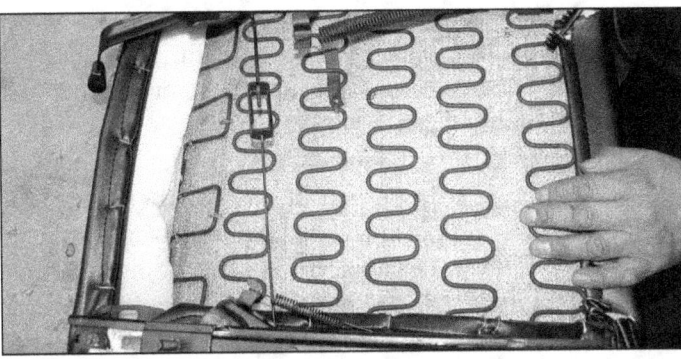

35 The tracks can be reassembled onto the seat bottom after holes have been cut for the mounting bolts. The tracks need to be moved from one side to the other to gain access to each bolt. When the tracks are back on, lubricate them with some white grease at the contact points.

36 After the paint on the miscellaneous hardware has dried, reassemble these items onto the bottom of the seat. Use each of the various mechanisms several times to ensure they're working properly. Also, spread the grease over the full sliding surface of each track. Check for loose rings. Then return the seat-back assembly onto the lower seat frame in basically the reverse order in which it came off. Place the hinge arm over the support pin and washer with the clip and cover following.

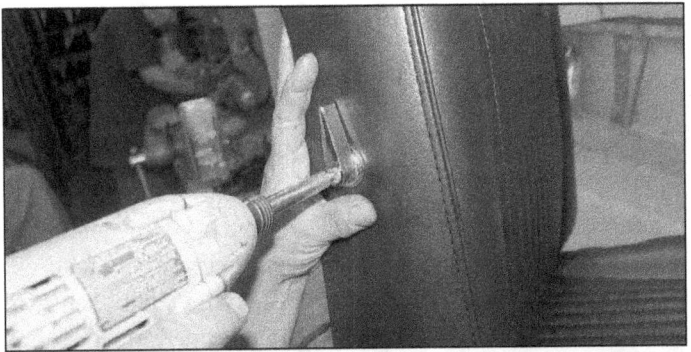

37 Reinstall the seatback release lever and any other items removed from the upper seat back to their original locations. Verify their proper function. The seat back should easily tilt forward without the cushions rubbing too much on the hinges. Verify the seat cover does not stretch with movement.

The finished seat looks just like the original did, only better. The pattern and texture of the seat cover is virtually indistinguishable from the original. The extra foam padding gives the seat a smooth, wrinkle-free look that also is a bit more plush and comfortable than the originals were. Each different seat type requires somewhat different procedures and processes, but the basic elements remain the same: the seat must be disassembled; the parts that need it must be reconditioned or replaced; and the new seat covers must be installed. Regardless of the type of restoration project you choose to undertake, these remain common.

CHAPTER 12

OTHER MECHANICALS

In this chapter, I address a few areas for improving performance while still, for the most part, retaining a stock look for the original components. I cannot discuss every remaining area on the vehicle or delve into areas that are more service or repair oriented; these are well covered in the factory service manuals and similar materials. The remaining topics I address in greater detail are fuel system, exhaust system, cooling system, and air conditioning (underhood area only) system. (I don't cover radical modifications because those are outside the scope of this book.)

A final matter to also address is wheel and tire choice. For a daily-driver project, cost and durability are a higher priority, while performance and appearance are often more important for a weekend cruiser. Show cars require the most authentic look.

Because the choice of wheels and tires also can be a very subjective matter, I simply state that the original steel wheels are easily refurbished/repainted—with factory-matching coatings from The Eastwood Company and others if maximum authenticity is a priority. There are also aftermarket aluminum wheels available in an almost infinite number of styles, including some that mimic the original factory wheel styles. These are available in factory sizes and in larger diameters and/or widths, which have the correct backspacings for use on first-generation Mustangs.

Similarly, tires that duplicate the original factory offerings on the outside while providing updated technology (including radial construction) on the inside are available in original and larger sizes. Clearly, a significant improvement in ride and handling can be realized with a change in wheels and tires. It's fairly common, for example, to upgrade to a lighter aluminum wheel that resembles the factory style yet is a larger diameter and width, thus allowing more flexibility in choice while still providing a factory appearance.

Fuel System

There aren't too many things you can change in the fuel system beyond the fuel tank, fuel pump, carburetor, and air cleaner. The decision to change the fuel tank is based either on need (if the original is damaged) or the desire for greater safety (an upgrade to a fuel cell). But replacing the other components can also add potential for performance gain.

Exhaust System

If maximum authenticity is the desired goal, the solution is to simply

Most anyone would be happy to have an engine compartment that looks as good as this Mustang, which was restored at Mustang Country. This vehicle emphasized authenticity a bit more than our car did, yet it still has a few minor modifications such as the non-OEM carb.

If your original fuel tank is in decent condition, you can simply clean it and then refinish it with a suitable coating, such as Eastwood's Tank Tone (see sample can on tank) to maintain an OEM appearance. (For tanks with more than surface rust damage, follow the procedures described in Chapter 3 to repair the damage before painting.) Fuel tanks that are too heavily damaged are best replaced with a high-quality replacement such as the one shown here. This tank has not yet been coated with Tank Tone, though it came painted to prevent rust.

Those concerned about safety might want to consider installing a fuel cell instead of a regular fuel tank. Early Mustangs are vulnerable to fuel entering the passenger compartment in a severe rear-end collision because the OEM tank is in the trunk and not isolated by another panel. A fuel cell minimizes fuel slosh under heavy braking or turning greatly reduces the chance of fuel spilling into the passenger compartment in a crash. Fuel cells are not terribly expensive, and there are specific, drop-in models made for most early Mustangs.

A standard mechanical fuel pump is usually more than sufficient for a carbureted car that will be driven lightly. If the fuel pump isn't working properly, replace it. If more flow is needed for a higher-output engine, there are higher flow mechanical units and electric pumps available. The latter are usually mounted below the fuel tank at the rear of the car. Some electric pumps are meant for racing use only and shouldn't be used on most street-driven vehicles. For cars that will be driven often and/or in inclement weather, an electric pump is ideal for such work.

Carburetor choice has a significant impact on the performance and drivability of the car. If you want to remain authentic, then either rebuild the stock carb or buy a direct replacement from a company such as Pony Carburetors, which specializes in early-Mustang applications. In many cases, a non-standard Autolite carb can provide better performance while still retaining a factory look. This Autolite 4100 series carb wasn't the stock carb for the 1968 GT, but it should provide better performance with the modifications we've made. Note the inline fuel filter to prevent dirt from entering the carb. Always use some form of inline filter between the pump and the carb. There are also many aftermarket performance carbs that may be a better choice with a more modified engine, but they do not usually retain the factory look.

If your engine has been modified, a high-performance open-element-style air cleaner, like the one shown here, provides increased airflow and hence performance. These came standard on many factory high-performance models. While not as good a solution as a sealed ram-air/cold-air system, they are much less restrictive than a regular snorkel style air cleaner housing—plus they look a whole lot better. In some cases, you can also use a taller filter element to reduce flow restriction, at least until hood clearance becomes an issue.

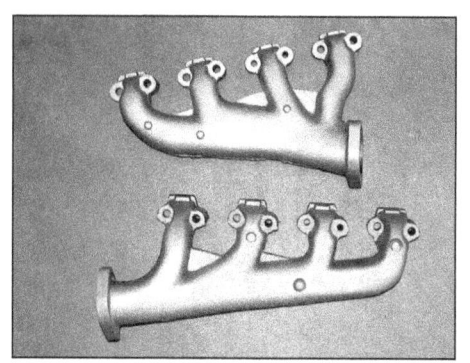

These factory high-performance, Classic Auto Supply K-code exhaust manifolds are significantly less restrictive than the standard log-type manifolds, yet they are also much more durable than headers. Headers usually make more power, but they are also noisier and pose problems with fit and appearance if you want to keep a stock look. You also need to make downstream changes. These manifolds would be fine for the power level we were at, plus they looked OEM and kept the noise level down. We coated them with Eastwood's Factory Gray High Temp Coating Spray to retain their cast-iron color and prevent rust.

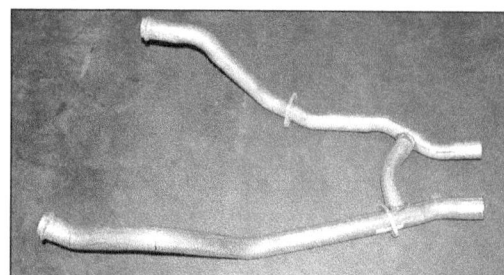

Using the K-code exhaust manifolds required a little change in the H-pipe because the exit of these manifolds is not in the same place as on the standard manifolds. Luckily National Parts Depot (NPD) had just the part we needed in stock. The 1967 289 K-code option used this pipe, which would work just fine on our 1968 (same body style) with a 302 (same external engine dimensions). The NPD piece is an exact duplicate of the factory part, right down to the flanges and type of exhaust seals ("donuts") used. With a higher-performance application, you may want to use larger-diameter tubing that's been custom mandrel bent to provide even less restriction.

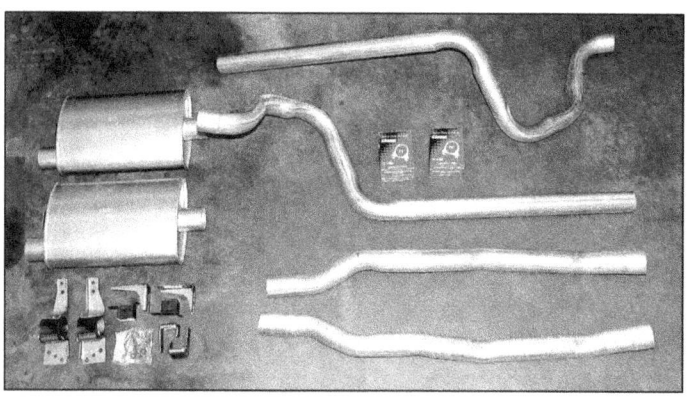

NPD also offers a complete exhaust kit for our 1968 Fastback, as it does for virtually all early Mustangs. The kit included precision bent tubes that are a direct fit along with the correct type of mufflers and factory-style hangers and hardware. We chose slightly different quad-style exhaust tips (shown), which resemble a style offered by the factory. While this system is perfect for moderate performance levels, a larger-diameter system with mandrel bends and less-restrictive mufflers would likely be a better choice for a higher-output engine where noise is less of a concern.

One trick to consider on cars that have GT-style exhaust trumpets is to have hidden exhaust outlets behind the rear valence panel instead of keeping the OEM trumpets functional. The OEM trumpets look great, but they tend to get dirty from the exhaust very quickly. They also restrict exhaust flow, a compromise we didn't want to make. Using dummy trumpets to keep that particular look, while having the real exhaust outlets hidden, keeps the trumpets clean and also improves performance.

This view shows what a typical true dual exhaust system looks like when it is installed on the vehicle. This particular car was a convertible and had the extra underbody bracing for the pipes to clear. The H-pipe was also a more traditional design than our K-code version, plus the mufflers are aftermarket units, which have a more aggressive tone than our stock replacement-style parts. This system has welded joints instead of using clamps to minimize the potential for exhaust leaks or the parts coming apart.

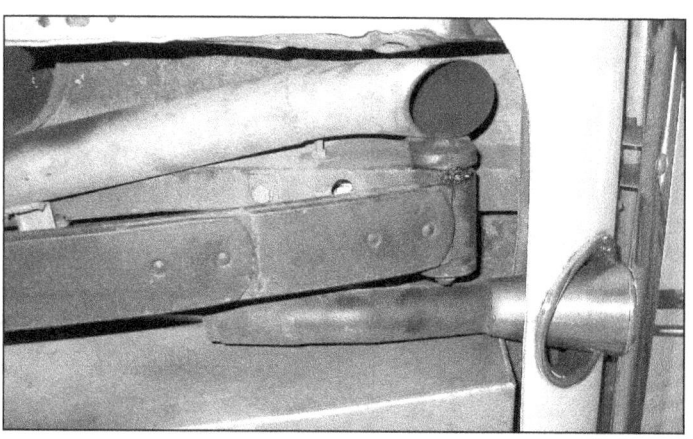

reuse the parts that were on the car or replace them. Direct-replacement components or kits that are readily available for most first-generation Mustang models. In our case, we wanted to do a bit better because we had upgraded the engine to achieve higher performance. These engine modifications would be pointless unless we used a freer-flowing exhaust system that's commensurate with our resulting airflow increase. We did not want to use headers, both for durability and aesthetic reasons, so we decided to use the higher-flow cast-iron exhaust manifolds that were standard equipment on high-performance K-code models of the 289-ci engine. The factory rated these at a similar power level to what we believe our engine would produce and thus we felt the use of these freer-flowing exhaust manifolds would be best for the goals we had in mind.

We would surely have opted for headers had we wanted to achieve a higher level of power/performance and not been as concerned with keeping a factory appearance. Many different types of headers are available for those who choose that option. Our choice did require a bit of luck since the 289 K-code engine was no longer offered in 1968 Mustangs. Fortunately, it was still available in the similar 1967 body style, which allowed us to piece together a system that would work. In the photos, I show the components we decided on and further explain their features and rationale. I also touch on a couple of other performance tips you might want to consider implementing in your restoration.

Cooling System

First-generation Mustangs, particularly the 1964½ to 1966 models, were not known for having great cooling systems. Part of this was due to packaging; the earliest cars didn't have room for a larger radiator and/or cooling fan. In part, the radiator's materials and technology was not expected to last for the eventual life span of these vehicles. When the first Mustangs were designed in the early 1960s, few thought so many would still be in use so many decades later. Time, wear, metal fatigue, internal deposits, and so on simply reduces the effectiveness of the original cooling system.

The upgrades we chose to implement on our car negate any loss of cooling-system efficiency that may have occurred over time, provide increased cooling capacity under all conditions, and reduce parasitic drag on the engine. I describe each upgrade and the benefits that were realized. These modifications can be implemented one at a time or together, as the situation allows. An electric fan, however, should also be accompanied by an upgrade to a higher-output alternator and/or a higher-reserve-capacity battery.

Steering System

Power is nothing without control. We improved the performance of our engine, transmission, suspension, and brakes, so the steering got our attention as well. Had we not wanted to retain the factory look of the car, we likely

To improve the cooling of our moderately modified, higher-output engine, we upgraded to an aluminum radiator that we got from Mustangs Plus. Not only is this radiator much lighter than the original part, but it also cools better due to more surface area and improved fin technology. The direct bolt-in component has all the correct fittings and dimensions. The radiator comes in bare aluminum form, so we coated it with Eastwood's Radiator Black to make it look more like a factory radiator. This special coating duplicated the factory appearance and also ensured proper heat transfer. Using regular spray paint can actually make the radiator less effective because the thicker paint acts like an insulator, which somewhat offsets the benefit of the better radiator. Besides, the stuff looks really good and lasts.

We also upgraded the water pump to further improve cooling. Our car will be located in southern California, where the temperatures can regularly stay over 100 degrees, so we made sure we'd have plenty of cooling capacity. This Edelbrock water pump provides higher flow due to improved impeller design, plus it helps ensure more balanced flow between cylinder banks. The pump components (seals, bearings, etc.) are also heavy-duty parts, which should provide better durability and less potential for leakage. These and similar water pumps are available for most Mustang applications.

CHAPTER 12

A common upgrade for performance is to use a flex fan that flattens out at higher RPM, thus freeing up some engine power. An extended spacer is also usually necessary to get the fan closer to the radiator face, thus improving flow through the radiator core. Flex fans often do not work well at slower speeds, however, and could become a problem in stop-and-go traffic in a hotter climate. A stock fixed blade fan costs a little power but it works better in such conditions. The dual V-belt drive is simple but not the best choice when experiencing higher engine speeds or belt loads.

Using an electric cooling fan is a way to improve cooling under all conditions while freeing up the most power. Electric fans can be turned on at any time based on either a thermostatic setting, actuating an accessory such as the air conditioning, or any number of other options. This ensures the best possible cooling regardless of engine or vehicle speed. It also removes any direct parasitic drag from the engine, thus improving performance. While an electric cooling fan does not retain the stock underhood appearance as much as a fixed blade or flex fan, we felt the significant improvement in cooling under all conditions was worth it. This car also has a serpentine drive belt, which offers numerous improvements over V-belt drives. Serpentine drives are used on modern production vehicles due to their efficiency, stability, and durability.

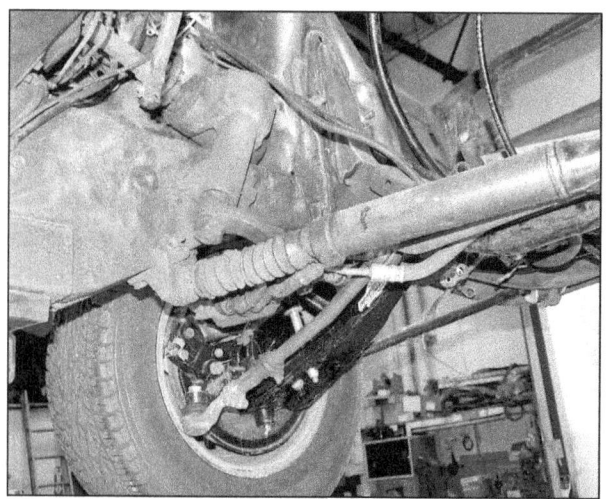

The original steering system on early Mustangs does not provide the best feel or response, but it can be made to work pretty well with a few fixes. The steering box can be rebuilt, to tighten it up and eliminate excessive play. Newly rebuilt boxes with standard and quicker ratios are also available. Replacing the cloth and rubber steering coupler on the steering shaft typically revitalizes performance. As these couplings age they allow more steering wheel free play and eventually need replacement anyway. The hydraulic power assist ram/cylinder can be rebuilt, although it is often just as easy to buy a new or remanufactured unit. The valve at the end of the cylinder can usually be cleaned up and reused, but there are rebuild or replacement options for this as well. Hoses are generally reused unless they are cracked or otherwise damaged. The bushings and the protective sleeve at the end of the hydraulic cylinder must always be replaced. These are inexpensive and tend to degrade often.

would have replaced the original steering system with a rack-and-pinion conversion. While somewhat expensive, the improvement in steering feel and performance from such a system is far superior to rebuilding the original setup. If we were going to be using our car on the track or had gone much farther in terms of suspension and brake modifications, such a system might have been appropriate.

We did not go that far and we wanted to keep the original look, so we simply went through the stock components and replaced them where necessary. There are many different steering-system designs on early Mustangs, and our 1968 GT is representative of a typical power-assisted setup. The external ram/cylinder design is not the best for driver feel, but it can be made to function well with the correct parts and adjustments. I briefly discuss some of the major undercar components and give a few tips on them, which apply to manual steering systems as well. Regular, proper lubrication is a must in any case.

Other than the steering box, the idler arm probably has the greatest influence over the feel of the steering because it is the part that keeps the rest of the steering links stable and properly located. If there is excess wear in the idler arm, it will be magnified throughout the rest of the system. These are easily obtained and replaced, but regular and proper lubrication can usually prevent the need for a new one any time soon, in most cases. The other steering links can be reused as long as they do not exhibit excessive wear/play. Minimal play is crucial to setting/maintaining wheel alignment.

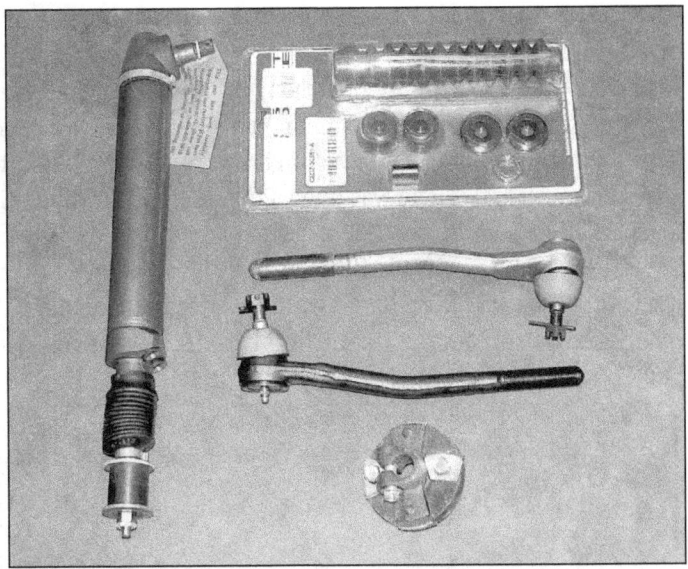

We replaced some of the steering system components in this photo. The hydraulic cylinder (left) came with new bushings and a new sleeve, but we wanted to show these parts are available as a separate kit (top) as well. The inner tie rod ends shown are an improved design that are stronger and more durable than the original parts. They also have grease fittings and improved-material grease seals to further extend their service life. The steering coupler (bottom) also is an improved design.

Air-Conditioning System

The air-conditioning system offered on first-generation Mustangs was as good as any, in its day. However, several things have occurred to make such systems less appreciated. First and foremost of these external forces is the ban on the R12 Freon refrigerant these systems were designed for. While it is still possible to buy R12 that has been recycled, this is becoming an ever-more-scarce and expensive resource. Fewer shops are willing to work with it due to very stringent recycling laws and the need to maintain special equipment. Also, fewer technicians are trained to work with it. At some point most people will not have an R12-based air-conditioning (A/C) system in their car(s). For this and other reasons, we decided to switch to a more modern compressor that was designed to use the newer R134a refrigerant. Other

The original air conditioning systems on early Mustangs were designed to use R12 (Freon) refrigerant, which has since been outlawed from production. R12 is getting increasing expensive and difficult to find. The heavy factory compressor can be rebuilt if necessary, but it is not really ideal for use with the newer R134a refrigerant, even with higher-efficiency components used elsewhere in the system. We decided to upgrade to a modern Sanden compressor and use R134a refrigerant instead of sticking with the original components. For us, the overall improvement in cooling performance and lower weight, plus the greater availability and lower cost of the newer refrigerant, outweighed the change in underhood appearance.

changes are necessary as well, which I touch on briefly.

We were able to limit our changes mostly to the underhood components and keep the appearance of the interior essentially original. There was quite a bit of specialized work involved to make our hybrid (new underhood, old in car) system work. That fact, combined with the many state laws that prohibit intentional release of any refrigerant into the air, makes having a professional shop do the installation a very attractive (though more costly) alternative.

The other alternative is to buy a complete direct-fit, OEM-style system that was designed specifically for a first-generation Mustang and either install it yourself or have it professionally done. Such systems yield the best performance, but they also cost more and involve more tear up of the vehicle. Some can be relatively discrete in appearance while others are more obvious. If you have one of the early "knee-knocker" factory systems, there are aftermarket units that even mimic the look of the factory system. In any case, it is best to switch to an R134a-based system if strict authenticity is not a priority.

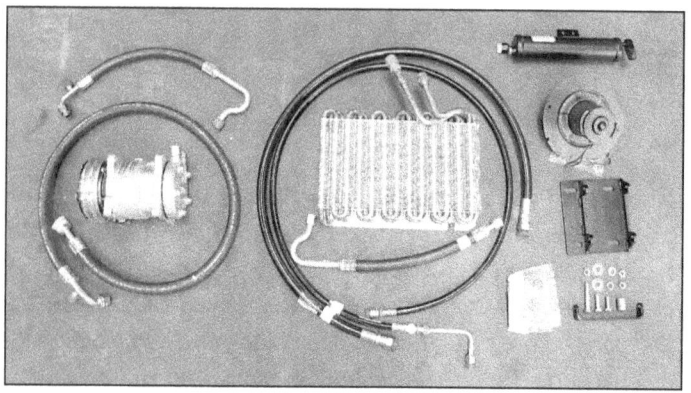

When converting from R12 to R134a, you will need new hoses, a higher-efficiency drier, a higher-efficiency evaporator, and a better blower motor as well as the Sanden compressor. The new refrigerant changes the way the system operates, and thus requires these modified parts to get cooling performance that equals or exceeds the original R12 system. Due to stringent laws regarding the release of A/C refrigerant, it is often best to let professional shops with the proper equipment handle most A/C work.

The original condenser on our car was destroyed from sitting for so long; the fins were literally falling out from between the tubes. This high-efficiency replacement unit replaces the original and is also designed specifically to be used with the newer R134a refrigerant without a loss in cooling system performance. This component, as were all of the other components including the Sanden compressor, were designed to bolt right in to our car without the need for any major modifications.

Using the newer Sanden compressor is made simpler due to vehicle-specific mounting kits and the choice of either serpentine or V-belt drive. In the application shown here, a late model 5.0L engine replaced the 289-2V the car originally came with, yet it was still possible to mount the new compressor and also retain power steering and an electric fan as well. There is even a wire running from the A/C compressor clutch wire to the electric fan to automatically turn on the fan whenever the A/C is running. This helps prevent overheating and improves the efficiency of the A/C by sending air flowing over the front-mounted condenser.

CONCLUSION

In this book, I've provided much information about how to complete a restoration project that allows you to retain the original look of your first-generation Mustang, while also making it more usable and enjoyable to drive on a regular basis. Those who want maximum authenticity and minimal change from the factory configuration can still find numerous tips and guidelines to make their vehicle perform better and last longer with less trouble, even while maintaining its originality. Those with a daily driver may not always have the budget or the inclination to implement all of what I've shown, at least not all at once, but they still benefit from seeing what can be done. They can often implement the principle if not the specific recommendation or component. Alternatively, they can potentially implement some concepts and/or specific components immediately and the rest at a later date. In either scenario, the end result is a better driver.

The builder of the weekend cruiser gets the most benefit by being able to apply the most of what was recommended, usually in the shortest time. The balance between functionality and retaining the original appearance is the key to deciding how far to go for such projects. I chose to place a fairly high priority on keeping the external appearance of our car close to the way it came from the factory. If you look at the car with the hood closed, there are few signs of the modifications we've made to the interior and the exterior. Many may choose to go even further with what can be done under the skin.

We didn't convert to fuel injection, install an overdrive transmission, or totally replace other systems with more modern componentry. We could have done so and still kept the outward appearance of our car relatively original. Instead, we decided to not go so far because we have a relatively rare combination of original parts ("1 of 1," per Marti) and our vehicle was in extremely good shape when we got it. The problem with extensive modifications is that you usually have to go back to the original configuration of the vehicle to get the most for it, if and when you sell it. If the vehicle is not a particularly rare car, further modifications are less of a concern.

For whichever Mustang and type of project you've chosen, the key is to take it to the level you want and enjoy it, preferably by driving it—often. I hope I've helped to show you how.

If you want to take functionality further and are not concerned about retaining a factory look underhood, you can do something like this. Here, a 5.0L engine out of a 1992 Mustang was swapped into a 1965 Fastback along with a T5 overdrive transmission. Numerous other mods/upgrades include: an aluminum radiator, electric cooling fan, a high-output alternator, a direct-fit R134a-based A/C system, a ram air system, and nitrous oxide. With the hood closed the car still looks relatively stock. With it open, it's obvious authenticity was not a priority. Which way you go and how far you go is up to you. Early Mustangs provide numerous options.

Source Guide

Auto Krafters, Inc.
P.O. Box 1100
New Market, VA 22844
540-740-8000
www.autokrafters.com

Big 4 Transmissions
7121 Somerset Blvd.
Paramount, CA 90723
562-633-4253

California Mustang
19400 San Jose Ave.
City of Industry, CA 91748
800-775-0101
www.cal-mustang.com

California Pony Cars, Inc.
1906 Quaker Ridge Pl.
Ontario, CA 91761
909-923-2357
www.calponycars.com

CJ Pony Parts
7461 Allentown Blvd.
Harrisburg, PA 17112
717-657-9252
www.cjponyparts.com

Classic Auto Supply
8719 Passons Blvd.
Pico Rivera, CA 90660
562-949-8976
www.classicautosupply.net

Classic Mustang
24 Robert Porter Rd., Unit A
Southington, CT 06489
860-276-9704
www.classic-mustang.com

Classic Tube
80 Rotech Dr.
Lancaster, NY 14086
716-759-1800
www.classictube.com

Comp Cams
3406 Demcrat Rd.
Memphis, TN 38118-1541
www.compcams.com

Currie Enterprises
1480 N. Tustin Ave.
Anaheim, CA 92807
714-528-6957
www.currieenterprises.com

Dallas Mustang
10720 Sandhill Rd.
Dallas, TX 75238
www.dallasmustang.com

Daniel Carpenter Mustang Reproductions
4310 Concord Pkwy. S.
Concord, NC 28027
704-786-0990
www.dcmustang.com

Distinctive Industries Specialty Division
2930 S. Vail Ave.
Commerce, CA 90040
800-421-9777
www.distinctiveindustries.com

Dynacorn International, Inc.
1400 Pacific Ave.
Oxnard, CA 93033
805-486-2612
www.dynacorn.com

East Coast Bolts
540-905-4812
www.eastcoastbolts.net

Eastwood Company
263 Shoemaker Rd.
Pottstown, PA 19464
800-343-9353
www.eastwoodco.com

Gateway Classic Mustang
10461 N. Service Rd.
Bourbon, MO 65441
www.gatewayclassicmustang.com

Global West Suspension
655 S. Lincoln
San Bernadino, CA 92408
www.globalwest.net

Julian's Collision Center
6926 Lankersheim Blvd.
North Hollywood, CA 91605
818-765-8500

K.A.R. Auto Group, Inc.
1166 Cleveland Ave.
Columbus, OH 43201-2924
614-294-4433
www.karmustang.com

KONI North America
1961 International Way
Hebron, KY 41048
859-586-4100
www.koni-na.com

Marti Auto Works
12007 W. Peoria Ave.
El Mirage, AZ 85335
623-935-2558
www.martiauto.com

Mansfield Restoration Parts LLC
498 Stearns Ave.
Mansfield, MA 02048
508-339-5409
www.mansfieldmustang.com

Mustangs & More
2065 Sperry Ave., No. C
Ventura, CA 93003
805-642-0887
www.mustangs-more.com

Mustang Country International, Ltd.
14833 Lakewood Blvd.
Paramount, CA 90723
562-633-2393
www.mustangcountryintl.com

Mustang Depot
2510 E. Sunset Rd., Suite 7
Las Vegas, NV 89120
702-262-0011
www.mustangdepot.com

Mustangs Plus
2353 N. Wilson Way
Stockton, CA 95205
209-944-7145
www.mustangsplus.com

Mustangs Unlimited
2505 Newpoint Pkwy.
Lawrenceville, GA 30043
888-398-9898
www.mustangsunlimited.com

National Parts Depot
900 S.W. 38th Ave.
Ocala, FL 34474
800-874-7595
www.npdlink.com

Orange Engine Rebuilders
1911 E. Ball Rd.
Anaheim, CA 92805
714-635-4030

The Paddock, Inc.
P.O. Box 30
Knightstown, IN 46148
800-428-4319
www.paddockparts.com

Painless Performance
2501 Ludelle St.
Ft. Worth, TX 76105
817-244-6212
www.painlessperformance.com

Pertronix Performance Products
440 E. Arrow Highway
San Dimas, CA 91773
909-599-5955
www.pertronix.com

Pony Carburetors
112 Westgate St.
Las Cruces, NM 88005
888-280-4630
www.ponycarburetors.com

Reenmachine
1090 E. Front St., Unit B
Ventura, CA 93001
805-648-7336
www.reenmachine.com

The Restomod Shop
2461 N. Wilson Way
Stockton, CA 95205
209-942-3013
www.therestomodshop.com

SEMO Classic Mustang, Inc.
171 State Highway Z, P.O. Box 78
Gordonville, MO 63752
573-243-7664
www.semomustang.com

Scott Drake Enterprises, Inc.
130 Cassia Way
Henderson, NV 89014
702-853-2068
www.scottdrake.net

Ssnake-Oyl
114 North Glenwood
Tyler, TX 75702
800-284-7777
www.ssnake-oyl.com

TMI Products Inc.
1493 Bentley Dr.
Corona, CA 92879
800-624-7960
www.tmiproducts.com

Tony D. Branda Shelby & Mustang Parts
1434 E. Pleasant Valley Blvd.
Altoona, PA 16602
814-942-1869
www.cobranda.com

Virginia Classic Mustang
195 W. Lee St., P.O. Box 487
Broadway, VA 22815
540-896-2695
www.virginiaclassicmustang.com

Year One
1001 Cherry Dr., Suite 1
Braselton, GA 30517
706-685-2140
www.yearone.com

www.ingramcontent.com/pod-product-compliance
Lightning Source LLC
Chambersburg PA
CBHW081444070526
44586CB00019B/2229